Psychoanalytic Conversations with States of Spirit Possession

PSYCHOANALYTIC STUDIES:

Clinical, Social, and Cultural Contexts

Series Editor

Michael O'Loughlin, Adelphi University

Mission Statement

Psychoanalytic Studies seeks psychoanalytically informed works addressing the implications of the location of the individual in clinical, social, cultural, historical, and ideological contexts. Innovative theoretical and clinical works within psychoanalytic theory and in fields such as anthropology, education, and history are welcome. Projects addressing conflict, migrations, difference, ideology, subjectivity, memory, psychiatric suffering, physical and symbolic violence, power, and the future of psychoanalysis itself are welcome, as are works illustrating critical and activist applications of clinical work.

See https://rowman.com/Action/SERIES/LEX/LEXPS **for a list of advisory board members.**

Recent Titles in the Series

Psychoanalytic Conversations With States of Spirit Possession: Beauty in Brokenness by Shalini Masih

Psychic Mimesis From Bible and Homer to the Present: Inner Life Over Time by Nathan Moses Szajnberg

The Healing of Trauma during Pregnancy, Birth, and the First Years of Life: From Dreaming to Being by Norma Tracey

The Borderline Culture: Intensity, Jouissance, and Death by Željka Matijašević

In Search of Return: Mourning the Disappearances in Kashmir by Shifa Haq

Trauma and Repair: Confronting Segregation and Violence in America by Annie Stopford

Psychoanalysis as a Subversive Phenomenon: Social Change, Virtue Ethics, and Analytic Theory by Amber M. Trotter

A People's History of Psychoanalysis: From Freud to Liberation Psychology by Daniel José Gaztambide

Rethinking the Relation between Women and Psychoanalysis: Loss, Mourning, and the Feminine edited by Hada Soria Escalante

Lives Interrupted: Psychiatric Narratives of Struggle and Resilience edited by Michael O'Loughlin, Secil Arac-Orhun, and Montana Queler

Women and the Psychosocial Construction of Madness edited by Marie Brown and Marilyn Charles

Revisioning War Trauma in Cinema: Uncoming Communities, by Jessica Datema and Manya Steinkoler

Women & Psychosis: Multidisciplinary Perspectives, edited by Marie Brown and Marilyn Charles

Psychoanalytic Conversations with States of Spirit Possession

Beauty in Brokenness

Shalini Masih

LEXINGTON BOOKS
Lanham • Boulder • New York • London

Published by Lexington Books
An imprint of The Rowman & Littlefield Publishing Group, Inc.
4501 Forbes Boulevard, Suite 200, Lanham, Maryland 20706
www.rowman.com

86-90 Paul Street, London EC2A 4NE

British Library Cataloguing in Publication Information Available

Library of Congress Cataloging-in-Publication Data

ISBN 9781666902112 (cloth) | ISBN 9781666902136 (paperback) | ISBN 9781666902129 (epub)

To Skylar, for loving me and teaching me to love despite all odds.
To Lawrance, for doing exactly that . . . because of all odds.

Contents

Foreword

Marilyn Charles

Psychoanalysis had its origins in late-nineteenth-century Vienna, at a time when what was displaced and dispossessed in women was written into history as hysterical symptoms, needing exorcism through interpretation. In contrast, Shalini Masih offers us another rendering of what becomes displaced and dispossessed in human experience, one embedded in her own culture of origin. Cultural values affect how human qualities are perceived; context is everything. In our quests for knowledge and relief from suffering, too often omitted are the truths from our more fully embodied sensibilities that must be integrated with rational knowledge to honor the complexity of human being and meaning.

In her extraordinary book *Psychoanalytic Conversations with States of Spirit Possession: Beauty in Brokenness*, Shalini honors this complexity. She looks at spirit possession, not through the lens of psychopathology, but rather through the lens of the culture in which this phenomenon can be respected for the ways in which it speaks to particular dilemmas in human experience. She takes as her starting point the fact of disruptions that can be frightening and alienating. In such moments, the very possibility of meaning-making can make the difference between further disruption—and marginalization—or repair.

By inviting us into a culture in which spiritual possession is taken seriously, as a challenge in its own right, with communicative value and potential intra- and interpersonal resolutions, Shalini invites us to set aside the blinders of Western culture—and psychoanalysis—which have tended to oppose religious and spiritual vertices. Such a position has resulted in a tendency to pathologize extreme states, thereby making it even more difficult to parse the messages offered. We know that qualities deemed problematic through the language of medical meanings lens may be prized by cultures that consider them *extra*ordinary (Charles, 2021; Johnson, 1981). For example, the experience of "oneness" can be found in both mystical and psychotic experience (Heriot-Maitland, 2008), an immersion into a primary unity that also typifies the aesthetic moment (Milner, 1987). The profound openness to experience and capacity for absorption, integral to creative engagement, can be capsized by fear and misunderstanding, inviting us to mistake messages that might otherwise invite growth.

Considering commonalities and distinctions between the qualities of experiences deemed psychotic or mystical helps mark how culture can either contain the person undergoing an extreme state or alienate them in ways that drive them mad. Notably, the limits in understanding of those making such decisions can alienate us all from qualities that have deep and profound social and human value and, therefore, from ourselves and from one another. Our fear of the unknown can lead us to founder the developmental efforts and creative capacities of those very seekers who might otherwise open possibilities for us all. And yet, as psychoanalysis has taught us, the voices and images that come to us in dreams, reverie, and also in extreme states such as spirit possession have a potency all their own, rooted in our histories and pre-histories. Respect is required to parse these meanings.

In contrast to the scientific vertex, in which drives—and therefore meanings, themselves—became sexualized and biologized, Bion (1977) marks that there are other vertices through which to explore human experience, notably the religious and the aesthetic. These latter two, as Shalini shows us, can be intricately intertwined. Mancia (1989) offers what he terms a *theological* reading of dream images, which is also an aesthetic one, in which the internal objects acquire a "sacred meaning," becoming "gods and demons" of their mental universe (p. 328). From this framework, the language of dreams and visions is a poetic language (Meltzer, 1984) an embodied relationship with the aesthetic underbelly of meaning as it has been experienced.

The Freudian perspective, in moving away from psyche's roots as soul, has been part of a broader turn in Western thought away from the potency of the image toward a more abstract conceptualization that loses its power and its possibilities, as "images have become allegories rather than presences" (Hillman, 2005, p. 69). The allegory de-potentiates the image, whereas, from a Jungian perspective, images are the language, not only of the unconscious, but also of the soul, an immediacy mirrored in the stories we are offered in this extraordinary volume, in which the haunting is profoundly personalized and embodied, and the struggle, at core, would seem to be precisely over one's soul.

Inviting us to enter this territory, Shalini brings the experiences of those she encountered in her investigation to life. Through her evocative language, the reader is invited into an encounter with a Real that takes us beyond the traditional bounds of western culture. Much as can happen through psychoanalysis, her vividness of detail affords the reader a vicarious experience that can be transformative, to the extent that we allow ourselves to be immersed in it. In these encounters, our consciousness is expanded into a realm that takes seriously the power of the image. According to Hillman, "All consciousness depends upon fantasy images. All we know about the world, about the mind, the body, about anything whatsoever, *including the spirit* and the nature of the divine, comes through images and is organized by fantasies into one pattern or another" (p. 70). Recognizing symptoms as attempts at communication, rather than merely being reactive to them, helps in the transformation from concrete experiences to meaning and then to words. Making meaning from embodied experience potentiates our creativity and enriches our lives (da Rocha Barros, 2000).

In contrast to a psychoanalysis so heavily saturated by secondary process, Shalini invites us to rest more fully in what Bion (1977) calls the *aesthetic vertex*, the embodied underbelly of experience that grounds all meanings. Notably, he warned against our tendency to obscure our vision by investing too heavily in the theoretical constructions that can blind us to what might otherwise be visible beyond the glare of our "illuminations" (Bion, 1990).

Recent interest in symbolization and how it develops has added to our understanding of ways in which meanings accumulate that are difficult to parse, often because their origins are unknown and therefore enigmatic. Complicating the perplexity, Laplanche (1995) tells us, are the *enigmatic signifiers* that are received by the child but cannot be parsed because the child's sensibilities have not yet sufficiently developed. In addition, the adult, too, has an unconscious such that portions of the communicated message will be unknown to them as well. In this way, unformulated messages are carried across the generations, requiring the ability to look back and make sense of unintegrated meanings in relation to the cultural vertices within which the family system was embedded. To the extent that the rational overshadows the aesthetic, embodied, symbolic messages from the unconscious, this process of integration becomes waylaid.

Even underneath this level, we find Aulagnier's (2001) descriptions of the earliest infantile experiences of flesh upon flesh, infused by the caretaker's pleasure or displeasure, that form a template, a pictogram, on which all meanings become patterned. Aulagnier's theorizing meets that of Mancia (1989) in pointing to the primacy of our earliest experiences, making it important to recognize ways in which the particular assemblage of "signs and bodily inscriptions . . . can lend themselves to this function of temporal and relational reference points" (Aulagnier, p. 96), providing a conceptual map through which to make sense of the signals (Charles, 2010). Because these signs are particular to that person's life story and embodied experience, there is a profound element that "transcends them and which enters the realm of the sacred" (Mancia, p. 347). Focusing on the level before and beyond formulated meanings help us to integrate into our formulations what da Rocha Barros (2000) has termed the *absent meanings* that are known through their impact even though they may never become directly accessible to conscious thought.

Shalini brings us directly into this territory of absent meanings. This volume well represents her intention to "illuminate the 'beauty in brokenness,'" by vivifying some of the enigmatic messages involved in spirit possession that can only be understood through respectful engagement with the person's story as it is nested within the culture of origin. Such deep engagement brings us closer to the aesthetic dimension of our very early experiences, in which the basic mechanisms of what Leikert (2017) terms *kinaesthetic semantics*—rhythms of repetition and deviation—structure meanings. We cannot do justice to a person's story without respect for the aesthetic underpinnings, Milner's (1987) primary rhythms of experience, Kristeva's (1986) *chora*, the melodies that undergird all meanings; and also the spiritual, poetic underpinnings, Bachelard's (1964) *poetic space*; Lyotard's (1985) *being in motion*, or de Certeau's (1992) *mystical moments*, without which human being becomes meaningless.

Marginalization tends to be experienced as a mark of personal deficit rather than a social problem. Countering that tendency, psychoanalysis helps to contextual character by viewing symptoms in relation to the story being told. This stance is crucial with extreme states, where the possibility of holding meaning is critical. Lacan (1997) speaks of psychosis as a position rather than a disorder, a marginalized position in which speech becomes distorted and it is difficult to hold meanings between people. Clinical experience speaks to the validity of this perspective; that people are driven mad when sense cannot be made from their experience, and that psychotic symptoms tell a story that cannot otherwise be told. Context is everything, and context is various, as Shalini reminds us.

When there are meanings that cannot be parsed within the family system, symptoms mark the forbidden meanings in disguised form. In families where the sequalae of trauma is carried across the generations, inconsistent parenting leaves children both vulnerable and dependent, inviting a "madness" that is socially constructed, driven by the desire to avoid facing difficult truths. When meanings cannot be parsed, it is difficult to make sense from embodied experience, alienating us not only from others, but also, more terribly, from ourselves. This volume does a great service in attempting to fill the gap left by the female voice in psychoanalysis, that has too often gone missing.

Despite valiant efforts, the woman's voice, while present, remains, I believe, under-integrated.

In that spirit, I would like to end with a quote from Hélène Cixous, from 1976, on what remains secret in women. She says: "her shameful sickness is that she resists death, that she makes trouble" (p. 876). I think we have not made nearly enough trouble, and everyone suffers from that lack. The trauma of repression in women is the backdrop in Western culture, where we see that the *most* destructive force waylaying development comes from failures in mourning that leave parents unreliably attentive to the needs of the child, the type of small-t trauma that impedes growth. In that context, Shalini Masih's volume, *Psychoanalytic Conversations with States of Spirit Possession: Beauty in Brokenness,* is a welcome voice in the wilderness, reminding us of the richness and variousness of human spirit and experience, and of the importance of integrating knowledge gleaned through primal and primary process, along with the voice of reason.

References

Aulagnier, P. (2001). *The Violence of Interpretation: From Pictogram to Statement*, A. Sheridan (Trans.). East Sussex: Brunner-Routledge.

Bachelard, G. (1964). *The poetics of space* (M. Jolas, Trans.). New York: Penguin Group.

Bion, W. R. (1977). *Seven servants*. New York: Jason Aronson.

Bion, W. R. (1990). *Brazilian lectures*. London and New York: Karnac.

Charles, M. (2010). When cultures collide: Myth, meaning, and configural space. *Modern Psychoanalysis*, 34:26–47.

Charles, M. (2021). Creative Transformations: The Establishment, the Mystic and the Aesthetic Drive. In. M. Brown & R. S. Brown (Eds) *Emancipatory Perspectives on Madness: Psychological, Social, and Spiritual Dimensions*, pp. 152–67. London & New York: Routledge.

Cixous, H. (1976). The laugh of the Medusa. *Signs*, 1(4):875–93.

da Rocha Barros, E. M. (2000). Affect and pictographic image: The constitution of meaning in mental life. *International Journal of Psychoanalysis*, 81:1087–1099.

de Certeau, M. (1992). Mysticism (M. Brammer, Trans.). *Diacritics*, 22(2):11–25.

Heriot-Maitland, C. P. (2008). Mysticism and madness: Different aspects of the same human experience? *Mental Health, Religion & Culture*, 11(3):301–25.

Hillman, J. (2005). Peaks and vales: The soul/spirit distinction as basis for the differences between psychotherapy and spiritual discipline. In: *Uniform edition of the writings of James Hillman, V. 3: Senex & Puer*. Putnam, CT: Spring Publications, pp. 67–90.

Johnson, C. L. (1981). Psychoanalysis, shamanism and cultural phenomena. *Journal of the American Academy of Psychoanalysis*, 9(2):311–18.

Kristeva, J. (1986). Revolution in Poetic Language. In: *The Kristeva Reader*. T. Moi (Ed.), L. S. Roudiez, & S. Hand (Trans.), pp. 89–136. New York: Columbia University Press.

Lacan, J. (1997). *The Seminar of Jacques Lacan III: The Psychoses. 1955–1956.* New York: W. W. Norton.

Laplanche, J. (1995). Seduction, persecution, revelation. *International Journal of Psychoanalysis*, 76:663–82.

Leikert, S. (2017). "For Beauty is nothing but the barely endurable onset of Terror": Outline of a general psychoanalytic aesthetics. *International Journal of Psychoanalysis*, 98:657–81.

Lyotard, J.-F. (1985). The Tensor (S. Hand, Trans.). *Oxford Literary Review*, 7(1/2):25–40.

Mancia, M. (1989). The dream as an internal language of memory. *Rivista di Psicoanalisi*, 35(2):328–50.

Meltzer, D. (1984). *Dream-Life: A Re-Examination of the Psychoanalytical Theory and Technique.* London: Clunie Press.

Milner, M. (1987). *The Suppressed Madness of Sane Men: Forty-four Years of Exploring Psychoanalysis.* London: Tavistock.

Acknowledgments

I owe my deepest gratitude toward my companions in this journey—all my research participants who ushered me, sometimes with difficulty, and most of the times trustfully, toward terrains which terrified them and allowed me to carry and create a part-language for their terrors. I wish to thank the ghosts that possessed you and met me with penetrative grimaces, unblinking stares, ear-splitting screams, violent swaying of the body and the shadows that crept into my nightmares, to dislodge my internal processes enough for me to retrieve broken parts of myself which, through much trepidation, also led me to an awakening.

I wish to thank two of my psychoanalytic gurus—Sudhir Kakar and Michael Eigen.

Sudhir Sir—I am grateful to you for always welcoming my curiosities even when I brought them toward you with a toddler-like annoyance and urgency. You have always gently nudged me to pursue my curiosities, a gift so rare to find. Thank you for kindling the idea for this research with your own work and wisdom on similar themes.

Mike Eigen—it is to the ease with which you welcome all experiences and are drawn toward beauty even in most devastating psychic debris, that I owe my questions, tensions waiting to be metabolized and the emergent clarity and especially aspirations for writing this book. Your work is the metabolizing maternal, which has gifted me with many "alpha moments!"

My mentor for the longest time, Ashok Nagpal, for reigniting the "known," illuminating the "not-so-known" and for the tolerance of the "not-yet-known." It is your faith in my creative capacities that helped me face my terrors. Thank you for gathering the scatter and enabling in me a reflective stance. It was your vision that led me to see light in dark times.

I have been blessed by your presences in my life—Epsita and Gagan. Your friendships and love were always helpful in clearing the clutter and expanding my thinking. Your belief in me, especially when it became harder to believe in myself, has sustained me.

Thank you, Dhruba Basu for copyediting this work in other words putting my mad-thoughts into comprehensible order!

My siblings for doing what siblings do best—for keeping me grounded and pushing me toward actualizing my creativity.

My parents, for your balance of love and distance, for teaching me to have faith. I also wish to thank you for the times you could not be there for me. It was in those moments when "thought" could be born and as Bion has enlightened me that thinking became a tool with which to feel.

My new friends (sometimes parent figures) in a new place I now call home—Lisa and Gwion—in your minds I have found a comfortable home. Thank you for holding me in many anxious turns especially during various stages of writing. Your warmth eased my anxieties so I could finish writing this work. I am especially grateful to Lisa, for doing your magic in creating the cover of this book!! I marvel at how you could imagine the enigma of the aesthetic object that is perhaps always experienced as turning her back toward us—her desires lay elsewhere!

Lakshmi Aunty, thank you for your faith in me. Your love and kindness are a gift so rare to find. Thank you for holding me in your mind and always rooting for me!

My best friend and husband, Lawrance, your love has always helped me be my truest self. Thank you for those endless cups of *chai,* for keeping Skylar and Rudy engaged, managing meals and the upkeep of the house when I was immersed in writing. Your presence in my life feels like "being healed by a prayer." Your love teaches me what it means to be possessed by love in a way that I can always return to find myself.

My little girl, Skylar—I have never felt as alive and creative as I have felt ever since you were born. Your love and need for me has taught me to learn from my intuition and reveries. Your curiosities and love for learning has kept me in touch with the playful child in me.

All the psychoanalytic thinkers I fell back on to make my experience thinkable—Thank you for existing!

Thank you also to all my senior colleagues and friends from the field of psychoanalysis who excitedly agreed to endorse this book.

And finally, my deepest gratitude and affection to my friend and senior colleague, Marilyn Charles, who welcomed my ideas and graciously contributed an illuminating Foreword for it. I consider myself blessed that your wisdom is ushering the reader to read and experience this book.

Introduction

"Is it fact or is it fiction?"

At the very start, I would like to request the reader to abandon the above question. I hope you can join me by positioning yourself in the paradox that Winnicott made us aware of when he wrote that, to a child immersed in play with transitional objects, it seems redundant to ask whether s/he created the object or found it. It is the space of play that allows this paradox to remain unresolved while continuing to fuel a quality of "fiction," the same quality that makes it possible to dream in psychoanalytic encounters. Minus this fictional element, the conversation becomes saturated with fact, lacking ventilation for reveries. And this is undesirable, for experience renders itself accessible to our minds through reverie.

The language in this book is close to the language one would use to speak to a child engaged in pretend play. It conveys the stance of a psychoanalytic researcher who is, well, playing along. In writing or, rather, allowing my experience of these conversations to be written through me, I have drawn inspiration from Ogden's (2005a) wisdom on psychoanalytic writing: "Analytic experience (which cannot be said or written) must be transformed into 'fiction' (an imaginative rendering of experience in words) in order to convey to the reader something of what is true to the emotional experience that the analyst had with the patient."

This could well be experienced as a work of fiction. But it is not. The ghosts that haunt the persons discussed herein are as real as the ones you and I flee from in our nightmares. Let me begin with one encounter, the reverie it evoked and their relationship with the thoughts that got woven around the stories I absorbed growing up.

At the time of the "encounter," my daughter was nearly six months old. The night I am thinking of was much like other nights: I was carrying her in my arms as I generally did, gently rocking her, pacing up and down in the room, humming a lullaby. She looked extremely tired but was still curious and wide awake. She wanted to stay awake and continue exploring the buffet of sounds, sights and textures that the world around her offered. I tried to quieten her curiosity and usher her into the world of sleep/dreams. Occasionally, we exchanged glances and smiles; she stroked my face with her tiny fingers and sometimes tried to catch a lock of hair that had fallen loose from my bun. Gradually, she shut her eyes.

I could sense that she was not asleep yet, but was trying really hard. Hours passed. She continued to try, even joining me in humming the lullaby, syncing her melody with mine, humming her own version of it. But, periodically, she would fidget, open her eyes and look around excitedly, even though her body was exhausted and her eyes red and sore. My own exhaustion began to mount, and with it my anger.

Unbridled, my mind went to its repository of countless eerie songs from old Indian horror films, songs that also had a lullaby-like quality, a lure, a deep yearning. They would generally be sung by a woman in vapory white attire; the same eerie melody, repeatedly, just like a lullaby. For the engrossed viewer, this melody served as a signal that something horrific was about to happen in the film. She, the ghost, always stood at the threshold of a door, singing, luring, summoning.

My reverie was interrupted by the awareness that my daughter had opened her big beautiful eyes and was staring into mine. She looked confused. Perhaps she had sensed a shift in the tone of the lullaby I was humming. Realizing that my anger had leaked into the lullaby, I paused.

I had been grunting the lullaby instead of humming it; it had, unsurprisingly, turned eerie. Wide awake now, my daughter was alerting me to this eeriness. I apologized to her. We revived the warmth that we were accustomed to in the space between us. I went back to feeling love for her and humming the lullaby as before. Soon enough, she fell asleep, and I tucked her in. As she travelled toward her dreams, I remained awake, wondering about the ghost woman in white who visited many possessed people I had spoken to.

The ghost is always seen standing at the threshold of their rooms. Could this woman in white be a representation of the mother standing at the threshold between dreaming and waking, between self and the world, between else and else? Could the ghost be the form of the mother that is experienced as "bad" (because, even though she recognizes her daughter's need for rest, she stands in the way of her daughter's epistemophillic instinct, her love for knowing herself and the world around her)?

Quoting Beatrice Beebe, Atlas (2022) writes, "Research is a me-search." My own location, when my research began, was guided by the fact that I am a healer's daughter. I witnessed, from childhood through adolescence and young adulthood, a range of sufferings construed through shamanic perspectives as dislocated faith in need of restitution. Indeed, the seed of this particular line of inquiry into human conditions was sown by a specific childhood experience.

It occurred nearly thirty years ago, when I, along with my siblings and father, had recently transitioned from a nuclear- to a joint-family setup. My grandfather, a priest, was always busy attending to those who sought his prayers and healing. I didn't quite understand then the things people requested to be delivered from.

One night, at the age of four, I woke up for a glass of water. As I walked toward the kitchen, I heard the sounds of a woman wailing, grunting, growling and laughing mockingly. I remember being terrified. With a four-year-old's fertile psychic permeability, I stood there frozen while her screams passed through me. Benumbed, I carried on walking, desperate to link the sounds with vision, to neutralize the terror.

Fear becomes bearable when it has a face. Anonymity, by its very nature, is terrifying. With each step that I took, the wailing grew louder and so did my heartbeat. I reached the living area, which was the space where we, the children, would play in the daytime. That night, it looked different. All the furniture had been moved to one side of the room and a thin mattress had been spread out on the floor. My grandfather and father were kneeling on the mattress, facing a contorted figure that looked like a woman. She was on all fours on the cold, tiled floor, no rug beneath her, groaning as she swayed rhythmically from side to side, her face covered by her hair.

My grandfather laid his hands on her and prayed. She transformed. Her face became calmer.

In subsequent years, I was privy to hushed conversations about cousins or known people who had been possessed by ghosts. When I met them or played with them, it was not without fear. I was scared that the ghost possessing them would show up, harm me in some way. Sometimes I heard fascinating stories about my grandfather or uncles praying and banishing the ghosts that possessed these people.

A few years after the incident described above, we were at my maternal grandfather's funeral when one of his daughters, my aunt, began to exhibit fear and reported having seen the spirit of her dead father. My father prayed, addressing my deceased grandfather directly, and asked him to leave.

I was ten or eleven when my father organized a three-day conference on healing. The atmosphere at the conference was electric with the intensity of the pleas and prayers of the masses, unanimously crying out to the Lord Almighty for divine mercy. Those possessed with demonic spirits began to sway, jerk, roll on the ground, somersault and utter obscenities. Surrounded by admonishment and commands, they gradually turned even more ferocious. For more defiant spirits, even physical violence was resorted to.

Since my childhood, I have witnessed many exorcism rituals in my household. I watched in awe when healers laid their hands on and prayed for the ailing persons and commanded the evil inhabiting spirits to leave. Although mesmerized, I also became curious. I would ask myself a series of questions. *Is this real? How do their bodies feel? How can their bodies acquire such capacities? How can a ritual that seems so violent heal a person, transform them in a way that is reflected in the health of their relationships and interactions?*

These experiences of transformation that I witnessed coalesced into my definition of "miracle" and things stayed that way until psychoanalysis 'found' me later, in adulthood. Today, as a clinician, I find that psychoanalytic work feels like a miracle in slow motion. But before I was found through psychoanalysis, time and again life threw me off balance, pushing me to the edge of what it was possible to experience. I consider myself fortunate to have enough ego-strength to live through, to perceive, to latch on to, to engage with these moments of being "on edge," as a student of psychic reality. It is in these lived moments that a proximity to undefined terror, a taste of what it feels like, becomes possible.

Some of us experience such states vicariously, while others do so compulsively. Our sense of our body shifts, morphing around our affective states—in seething rage, the body hardens like steel; in terror, it seems to evaporate. When affects get blown out of proportion, the body reaches the limits of what it is possible for the psyche to put itself through. Unbeknownst to itself, the psyche extends into the body.

Psychoanalysis teaches us to actively engage with such moments in a bid to learn from them. I grew up with a belief in forces both divine and demonic. I have now, only gradually, come to appreciate the liberation in thought that made it possible for me to have doubts, to question the beliefs of those around me. It is to various experiences that I owe my thirst for knowledge of what, in the violence of possession and exorcism, alters a person—the thirst that provided the necessary impetus for me to undertake my research. Would I have been drawn to spirits and haunting if I had no conception of terrors as "healable," if I had not glimpsed the transformation of the possession state into a healed state? Would I have assumed a technical stance and tried to "understand" states of spirit possession without having experienced, even if only in a vague sense, some dramatization of possession—the swing from one moment to another between radiance and creeping deadness, perceptible in the same set of tissues—and the responses it evokes in others—infectious horror and a limited awareness of one's total helplessness?

Growing up, I heard priests describing how, after an exorcism, the banished ghosts would come for them, seeking revenge. They had to remain watchful and meditative, protecting themselves with prayers. Often, these ghosts rattled the priests by appearing in their nightmares, making them confront their own sins. In hindsight, I recognize that this warning was about the exposure to the intense affective charge of possessed persons and the risk of a thinning of one's own psychic impermeability. My own experience conducting the research for this work was fraught with ambivalence and made me confront, apart from a series of nightmares, the notion of sin—in particular, two major sins pertaining to those parts of me that have respectively found nourishment in spirituality (early on)and in psychoanalysis (later in life). At certain moments, I wondered if my work would amount to blasphemy. At other moments, I wondered about the ways in which my work was not psychoanalytic enough. Until I found solace in Ogden's idea of "the analytic third which is co-created as analyst and patient's unconscious come together," I felt like a ghost, undecided and lost in limbo between psychoanalysis and spirituality, between the shame of challenging traditions and the excitement of exploring modern horizons.

Also pertinent to my feeling like a sinner was my awareness that I was dealing with the forbidden and the ghosts it gave birth to. Our education, even as it enlightens us, also alienates us from all those phenomena that surround and nourish us from the moment we develop a sense of self. This tendency toward alienation is instilled in us by our movements as toddlers away from the suction of the maternal pull—a continuous process of turning our backs toward our mothers. But can we, can anyone who has been mothered, adequately succeed in this venturing forth without generating shadows that grab us in moments of paralyzing terror?

There are a few psychoanalytic perspectives that encourage the exploration of the harmony between opposites or dualities or continuities amongst scary and broken events that span different stages of life, but these preclude the possibility of confidently hoping that we will ever be able to rid ourselves of them or unravel their constituent themes. Spirit possession is one such theme. The literature on spirit possession appears to understand its subject at best as the language of the oppressed and at worst as malingering, emphasizing the regressive movement undertaken psychically in the possession state. Existing research and the directions implicit in them suggest that spirits should be viewed as the reification of intangible or amorphous states charged with pronounced emotions that may play a significant part in deranging potential conceptions/forms in the viewer—they stir vicarious but no less powerful emotional currents in the viewer, turning the latter's nascent thoughts toward culturally-valued understandings of spirit possession that view it in religious terms and strengthen the hold of superstition. Consequently, in the state of possession, we meet persistent nightmarish emotions shaped in large part by social attitudes that view those emotions as mere figments of a deranged mental make-up or as permeated by superstitions that threaten, with utter disregard for all painstakingly constructed rational frameworks, to take control of our lives.

What has been relatively neglected is the process by which parts of the self are retrieved in this regressive turn and can thereafter augment a progressive movement toward self-evolution of some kind. What is cast within religious traditions as "healing" is best understood as an attempt to evacuate all that one cannot experience. Psychotherapy, too, is yet to develop a language that does not merely reduce possession states to complexes and drives or, like religious cures, try to short-circuit the experience of living out one's emotional mess by taking a detour toward evacuation through the body.

This book began taking its current shape in a doctoral dissertation I wrote to express my appreciation of the function served by ghosts and the rituals around expelling them, an appreciation that emerged as I mapped journeys of internal transformation brought about by grotesque states of spirit possession. I have endeavored in my work to restore a sense of ghosts as entities with appetites that are as real as those of living entities.

The research that produced this book was undertaken with a vision of an expanded psychotherapeutic domain that includes clients with religious beliefs, so as to make it more empathic in Indian settings; in this pursuit, I endeavored to learn a language informed by attention to psychological sensitivities and cultural nuances, a language that could be used to converse with psychic states of possession. Sudhir Kakar's works inspired me to tread this uncharted path with less trepidation, sometimes rewarding me with insights I had not imagined before. His early works, *The Inner World* (2012) and *Shamans, Mystics and Doctors* (1991), guided my research plan and grounded it in a unifying thought, which was that reflections on socio-cultural development should not be viewed as divorced from the thrust of individual identity formations. These formations rely heavily on modes and conceptions of local healing practices to generate tales of clashes between the social-institutional and the instinctual-individual, even as these get narrated, at times, from the bottoms of pits of madness and the edges of cliffs of mysticism. Could one reflect on madness as a state of exile from the existing order of mysticism, a state that takes the form of abysmal helplessness but expresses the search for a new path of entry into the mystical?

During the first stage of this research, I gathered vignettes and smaller case studies of patients as well as healers. These tackle issues of tangential but undeniable significance to the spirit of this work—malingering, sexual exploitation as mistranslation by local healers and experiences of transcendence. In the second phase, I used aspects of the narratorial presentation of possession or possessiveness in the film *Devi* as entry points into the cultural psychology of possession. In the third phase, I came across a beautician who lived through her own possession as a young woman. She put us in touch with her healer, who over time also began to draw on the perspectives that I was arriving at through my research, and ended up deciding to rid himself of his alienation from desire. It was in this phase that I also met another healer and a student who used psychoanalysis to make sense of her own experience of spirit possession. Through the course of my research, the "spirit" (or *samkat*) has emerged as that subjective object which is grimacing out through the corner of the eyes. Terrorized, we have only screams with which to convey to the world our need to be rescued. This subjective object is the first signal of an internal world forming. By giving something external its own color, the self evolves. This space of evolution, or formation, is the transitional space where the external and the internal meet.

Confronted with terror, "God" and "hymns" take on the role of the "subjective object" (Winnicott, 1969),while the possessing spirit—the screaming self—is seen as waging a last-ditch battle, with invasions and demands. The researcher evolves into a containing listener, responsive to the creative elements in the screams. Following Winnicott (1965), we assume that the creative nucleus emanates from the true self zone at one end of the continuum of the person and needs to conclude its productions in the form of hymns, dances, prayers, etc., in the court of God at the other end of the continuum. In between lays the strange phenomena of dreaming and reveries. The ghost, as a deformed form of the true self, cries out to God to be preserved "incommunicado" (Winnicott, 1963). It engages with God to divest itself of its false-self longings, longings it feels incapable of de-cocooning itself from. The creation of this communication represents recognition from culture that the unfulfilled yearnings (*atriptaicchayein*) of the ghost, like the emotions enveloped in the song of the ghost woman in white, cannot in fact be fulfilled or find succor.

Writing this book has been about listening carefully to and following the eerie songs of deep yearning that my participants sang, following ghosts and looking them in the eye whilst also attending to all the terrors that emerge from confronting their grotesqueness. I pursued the ghosts until they began to emerge as unfulfilled parts of self, floating in space, yearning to be hosted or housed. But how does one face these demons in others when the psychic permeability inherent to being human makes these ghosts uncannily resonate with and threaten to bring out the demons in oneself? "With love," comes the response from a good object in my internal world.

I grew up hearing countless fascinating stories about my grandmother's fearless encounters with ghosts. She would either calmly sit and chat with the ghosts of deceased people or fiercely chase away notorious ghosts who threatened to harm her and her children. Today, I think of her as having been some sort of a medium, playfully navigating the worlds of the dead and the living. She was gentle, kind, maternal, with a radiant, fierce and tenacious core. Interestingly enough, when my parents named me, they wanted me to have her initials.

I remember my grandmother being very content in her own company; singing hymns, gently clapping her hands, floating from one room of the house to another. She was also my playmate. As a child, I would be amazed by her ability to take one look at me and deduce that I had had a bad day at school. She would do this gently and then invite me to share with her my day's stories.

I wonder if, merely through her manner of being, my grandmother laid in me the foundation for my love of psychic reality. In approaching and conversing with the ghosts of my research participants, I have carried my grandmother's maternal and benevolent curiosity. This has helped me recognize that, perhaps, in the phenomenon of possession by a ghost lies the desire to possess. I wonder if this projected possessiveness stems from love that is hard to relinquish. In some moments, both possession and love appear fused. At other times, love appears to stand in opposition to possession or the desire for ownership. To love is to make room for the pain of loss. The ghosts that emerge from the interpersonal field come cloaked in the agony of unmourned loss. The haunting appears as a longing to belong to the haunted. Gradually, these grotesque ghosts, the haunting parts of the self, begin to emerge as the longing parts of self.

This book allows the ghosts to be heard.

Chapter 1

Allies Lighting Up a Dark Path

Since time immemorial, belief in spirit possession has played a significant role in our efforts to explain madness. In some cultures, like India, belief in ghosts prevails even today. Spirit possession has been understood in various ways. Here, I consider the anthropological and psychological views on spirit possession. What follows is a brief introduction to themes that I sensed might help me understand possession better after I had undertaken a pilot study in this field.

The literature is voluminous and considerably diverse. In psychology, there have been many ways of looking at the cultural phenomenon of spirit possession. Early views reduce religious experience to "illusory wish-fulfillments," linking them to "infantile helplessness in the face of overwhelming powers of nature and a threatening external world on the one hand and the child's ambivalent feelings toward a father who is both a source of protection and fear on the other" (Kakar, 2012). Janet linked dissociated states with spirit possession. When under hypnosis, his traumatized and hysterical patients exhibited multiple personalities. These personalities were aware of each other and addressed themselves as "daimons" (Janet, 1889; 1901). Janet attributed these symptoms to painful forgotten childhood experiences. The dissociation produced a variety of symptoms, and Janet attributed this phenomenon to stress and a constitutional predisposition to this disorder by virtue of a "lack of capacity to unify content specific elementary structures into a singular consciousness" (Fonagy & Target, 1995).

A case that gained fame within psychoanalysis was that of Anna O. (Freud, 1957), a patient who suffered from conversion symptoms. Breuer recognized that Anna O. was spontaneously entering hypnoid or self-hypnotic states. In her normal, alert state, she had no clue why a particular symptom presented itself, but in her self-hypnotized state she was able to discern the origin of and reasons underlying the symptom. When the forgotten episode was revealed and the feelings associated with it expressed, the symptoms disappeared. Breuer asserted that the basis of hysteria was the existence of these hypnoid states that had the power to induce amnesia. The amnesia created an uncon-scious, implying the individual then had three, rather than the normal two, states of mind: the waking state, the sleeping state, and the hypnoid state.

Rejecting Breuer's concept of self-hypnosis, Freud contended that he had never encountered a self-hypnotic hysteria, only "defense" neuroses, and he instead postulated "repression." Breuer and Freud (1883–1885) regarded "dissociation as only one aspect of her hysterical illness, but most contempo-rary diagnosticians would consider Anna O. primarily dissociative rather than hysterical" (McWilliams, 2011).

Freud (1923) offered his first and only detailed analysis of a case of possession and exorcism in 1923. Johann Christoph Haizmann was an Austrian painter who, in 1668, following his father's death, fell into deep melancholic depression, characterized by inhibitions at work and fears about his future. According to his diary entries, the Devil approached him and promised him freedom from the pain of depression in exchange for Haizmann signing a pact that would make him the property of the Devil after nine years. Over the next few years, the Devil often appeared to him, perhaps in the form of hallucinations. Haizmann painted several pictures of the devil as a monstrous creature with female breasts and maintained a diary of his visions.

In Haizmann's devil-images with breasts, Freud saw an unconscious need for a foster father expressing itself. This need initially expressed itself as melancholia, keeping him from enjoying anything. After his pact with the Devil, though, Haizmann began satisfying his desire for material enjoyment.

According to Freud's (1923) analysis, Haizmann wanted all along simply to make his life secure, which he tried to achieve in a pact with the Devil, and when this had to be given up at the end of the nine-year period for which the pact was valid, he tried to achieve it with the help of the clergy—at the cost of his freedom and most of the possibilities of enjoyment in life. In a sense, Haizmann was a man who simply had no luck. Perhaps he was too ineffec-tive or untalented to make a living, and, unable to tear himself away from the blissful situation at the mother's breast, he demanded to be nourished by someone else. He followed "the path which led from his father, by way of the Devil as a father-substitute, to the pious Fathers of the Church" (Freud, 1923). The source of Haizmann's possession is an intense longing for his father owing to his endless material needs. Freud concluded, "Demons are bad and reprehensible wishes, derivates of instinctual impulses that have been repudiated and repressed" and "possession is the suffering and phantasy of a sick man" (Freud, 1923).

Jung regarded spirit possession as "the transformation of the ego-personality" and contended that "it is the condition of this new ego-personality—rather than the process that enabled it—that is considered healthy or unhealthy" (Jung 1921, as quoted by Huskinson, 2010). The cause of the possession was understood by him to lie in the existence of something incompatible, unassimilated, and conflicting, an obstacle but also a stimulus to greater effort, and so, perhaps, an opening to new possibilities of achievement. According to Jung, demonism is a peculiar state of mind characterized by the fact that certain psychic contents, complexes, take control of the total personality in place of the ego, at least temporarily, to such a degree that the free will of the ego is suspended. In some of these states, ego consciousness is present; in others, it is eclipsed (Jung, 1945).

Jung's doctoral thesis concerned a girl named S. W., who was known as a spiritual medium. She suffered from dissociative personality disorder and, while in the grip of her non-default personality state, could communicate with ancestral and other spirits: "S. W. led a curiously contradictory life, a real 'double life' with two personalities existing side by side or in succession, each continually striving for mastery" (Jung, 1959). According to Jung, possession results when archetypal images are not made conscious—escaping from conscious control altogether, they become completely independent. Because a great deal of unconscious material is not integrated into the personality, it will most likely be perceived as an incredibly negative existence of external origin.

William James's view on religious experience and its relationship with possession is relatively expansive. He argued that religion covers far more than one dimension of human life with its unique pursuit of the divine: "Religion . . . is a man's total reaction upon life so why not say that any total reaction upon life is a religion?" (James, 2012) James believed that a prerequisite for the entry of an entity into a person's psyche was a cracked or fragmented self; he saw possession and exorcism as endemic, in a sense, to religious believers whose unhealthy relationships with belief rendered them unable to ignore the existence of evil in their minds. For James, spirit possession was the sickness of a weak soul, more the soul's response to its own fragility than to depriving circumstances. Like Freud and Jung, James did not prioritize environmental influences over human psychological experiences.

On the other hand, I. M. Lewis's (1966, 1978, 1996) "deprivation hypothesis" links possession to subordination or marginality and has been used extensively in the South Asian context. Many writers have tended to view possession as being inseparably connected with the oppression of women by men, socio-economic inferiority, and the inability to express grievances (e.g., Freed and Freed, 1964; Gellner, 1994; Harper, 1963; Ortner, 1979; and Opler, 1958).

Utilizing contemporary psychoanalytic concepts that are missing in Freud's analysis, Bilu (1989) discussed the possession of Eidel, a female rabbi, explaining in his seminal paper the interplay of internalization and externalization in dybbuk possession. Bilu wrote that "unacceptable intrapsychic material is projected onto the object—'the spirit' . . . What is projected is also taken in. The latter, inward-oriented motion constitutes a form of internaliza-tion, albeit a most concrete and primitive one" (1989). Eidel's father had shaped her in line with his own fantasies. Her behavior as a rabbi and during possession demonstrated the extent to which she was engulfed by her father's projected fantasies: "By incorporating her father, she resorted to the most extreme device supplied by her culture in order to assert, in a 'visible,' public manner, her connection with her father." According to Bilu, a cultural device of possession assigns an interpersonal shade to an intrapsychic conflict.

In her book, *Mad Men and Medusas: Reclaiming Hysteria*, Juliet Mitchell (2000) attributed possession to displacement by a sibling that triggered fear of annihilation and evoked feelings like envy, rage, craving, wanting, and so on. Cultural practices favor men by projecting these feelings onto women, who then become possessed by them. In the words of Mitchell, "The 'possessed' thus bears the weight of cultural displacement and expresses the overwhelm-ing want to be reinstated at whatever cost" (2000).

Possession comes to serve as a culturally consonant expression of distress and self-assertion for women. The works of Jadhav (1995) and Nabokov (2000) echo this sense. For Shubha and associates, "possession is an explana-tory model used by those in distress to make sense of a variety of different kinds of problems" (Ranganathan, Battacharya, Parthasarathy, & Gupta, 2008). They link possession with poor coping mechanisms developed in response to life's stressors.

Possession has also been studied from the standpoint of psychoanalytic anthropology, most notably by Crapanzano and Obeyesekere. Crapanzano's 1977 work, *Case Studies in Spirit Possession*, was an attempt to understand the multifaceted significance of possession within the particular contexts in which it occurs. In his introductory essay, Crapanzano suggested that posses-sion be viewed as "an idiom for articulating a certain range of experiences." Seeing possession as an idiom of communication enjoins consideration of how the idiom is constructed and used in specific societies; it requires acknowledgment of the existence of spirits in the believer's world and asserts that possession is about meaning. Crapanzano's heartrending interactive biography of Tuhami (1980), a Moroccan man married to a she-demon whose victims seek healing from the Hamadsha, a popular Islamic brotherhood, required him to question the validity of notions such as projection and the presumed boundedness of the self. Where spirits are consensually understood to enter human bodies, it may be more appropriate to speak of introjection:

> Crapanzano suggests that Tuhami is afforded a "shift of responsibility . . . from self to other" through the possession idiom; he is able to objectify his feelings

"in terms that transcend him"; yet the result of his demonic relationship is a "frozen identity," not curative transformation. (Boddy, 1994)

As far as dwelling on the transformative aspect of possession goes, Obeyesekere's *Medusa's Hair*[1] (1981) is a considerably exhaustive work of psychoanalytic anthropology. The women that Obeyesekere ventured to understand were emotionally struggling and hailed from oppressive backgrounds, but, unlike other anthropologists, he went beyond a static relative status model to highlight the flexibility and ambiguity of the spirit idiom, its capacity to enable personal growth and the optional, manipulative nature of "personal symbols," which are at once both socially and emotionally meaningful. He underlined the complexity of spirit possession by proposing that it not only allows people to give meaning to life problems but also enables them to resolve those problems.

Weaving his fascination with the Freudian model into his respect for cultural nuances, Obeyesekere (1981) suggested that painful experiences seek indirect expression in symbol formation and cultural symbols get created and re-created in the minds of people. His concept of "symbolic remove" describes the transformation of the root meaning of symbols into operational meanings that relate to the social context of the one who avails of the symbols.

Like Freud, Obeyesekere too related symbolism with regression and therefore with psychopathology. However, what is implicit in his work is a recognition of the progressive movement of unconscious thought, which creates opportunities for the transformation of archaic motivations into symbols packed with potential for conflict resolution: the "transformation of symptom into symbol is through the cultural patterning of consciousness, which in turn helps integrate and resolve the painful emotional experiences of the individual, converting Eros into agape and patient into priest" (Obeyesekere, 1981). The symptom of the psyche is replaced by a symbol from the culture, which subsequently assumes a public existence as a cultural symbol, in that the internal experience is staged or performed in a way that allows it to become part of the world of culturally sanctioned meanings. The symbol is thus manipulated by the possessed person and may convey a public message. The cultural symbol of the ghost undergoes subjectification, a "process whereby cultural patterns and symbol systems are put back into the melting pot of consciousness and refashioned to create a culturally tolerated set of images and facilitates 'objectification,' the expression (projection and externalization) of private emotions in a public idiom" (Obeyesekere, 1981) via mechanisms like projection.

The dominant emotion being objectified in Obeyesekere's work is guilt. He described the possession and exorcism experience of his ascetic informants as an objectification and dramatization of their guilt and other feelings associated with it—ambivalence toward parents, projection of the person's hostility onto a dead relative, the demand for love and its negation, reparation, and compensation. All these feelings are projected or objectified in the cultural symbol system.

Let's look closely at one of his case studies. One of his participants, Pemavati, was deserted by her father and adopted by an uncle who turned out to be a loving father surrogate. She had strained relations with her stepfather. Conflicts with her uncle's children drove her to leave home and this move on her part caused immense grief to her loving uncle. Soon he died, causing Pemavati to feel guilt for betraying him. She got married but remained unhappy.

Soon after her marriage, Pemavati began to experience fainting spells. Her community interpreted her fainting spells as possession by an entity they recognized as "the erotic one," also known as the Black Prince.[2] In Freud's time, similar fainting spells were understood to result from the repression of sexuality and were diagnosed as hysteria. However, in the Sri Lankan community explored by Obeyesekere:

> The clinical syndrome isolated by Freud is given demonographic representation. The very act of demonic definition of the "hysterical syndrome" has one consequence: the erotic illness is not the fault of the woman but is caused by a malevolent external agent . . . A society that has demystified the magical world would produce more guilty patients. Freud's patient suffered from hysterical symptoms: in Sinhala culture, symptom is translated into symbol, though in both societies[3] sexual repression is exceptionally strong. Another consequence— whether or not the patient has had erotic fantasies, these fantasies are bound to arise after the demonic interpretation is given, owing to the operation of the self-fulfilling prophecy. (1981)

With the possessing dead relative transforming into a benevolent presence, there occurs an outer transformation:

> She has a new status; she is now a priestess with an, often, idealized goal, the succor of those in need . . . With her new status and role she is now on her own, with a new identity—a relatively independent person, not tied to her family . . . She has abolished the everyday world and has moved into an extraordinary one. She interacts with two communities: the divine beings whom she relates to on the spiritual level, and her fellow ecstatics and aspirants whom she relates to on the human level . . . She has made an enchanted world out of the dirt and dross of city life . . . The calamities that beset her ordinary life have been reversed: her guilt has been expiated; her dead father has been replaced by idealized divine father; her loving relative has been resurrected from the dead, restored in her affections, and made into a minor divinity; her unhappy marriage has been reversed into a good one; and, through her dream visions, a powerful symbol

system, she is married to the gods, their lover and their slave . . . In her possession, she is both good and bad . . . she can abreact her past. (Obeyesekere 1981)

When female ascetics perform such trances, Obeyesekere (1981) wrote,
"they act out the role of the terrifying Kali and simultaneously act out their
own dark aggressions of childhood: abreaction and symbolic action are fused
into a single performance." Key features Obeyesekere (1981) identified in the
environments of his informants were early weaning, the shifting of maternal
affection to another and more desirable child (usually a son), strained relations with the parents, the loss of parental love, parental rejection, being
socialized in a puritanical society with rigid norms about the expression of
aggression and sexuality and the consequent repression of the concerned
impulses—these were the psychological experiences that served as doorways
for possession, often by the spirit of a dead relative vis-à-vis whom the possessed woman harbored intense guilt and/or hostility.

In clinical spaces, one witnesses states like those seen in a possessed person. According to Freud, the splitting of consciousness, a tendency toward
dissociation and the emergence of abnormal states of consciousness were
basic to hysteria. Freud saw the propensity for habitual daydreaming as the
cause of dissociative or "hypnoid" states (1893). Clinical observations suggest that his position was a valid one. McWilliams pointed to evidence:

> that the kind of person who dissociates is innately more resourceful and inter-
> personally sensitive than the norm. A child with complex, rich inner life (imagi-
> nary friends, fantasy identities, internal dramas, and a penchant for imaginative
> play) may be more able to retreat to a secret world when terrorized than a less
> gifted youngster. (2011)

Kluft, a pioneer in diagnosing and treating dissociation, came up with a
four-factor theory of the etiology of multiple personality disorder and severe
dissociation: the individual is (1) talented hypnotically and (2) severely traumatized, and his/her dissociative responses are (3) shaped by particular childhood influences, i.e., dissociation is adaptive and to some extent rewarded by
the family, and, finally, (4) there is no comfort, no comforting presence for
them to turn to during and after traumatic episodes. Typically, they would
have experienced their emotional responses to trauma during their childhood
being punished with more abuse, because "[t]here is often a kind of systemic
family collusion to deny feeling, to forget pain, to act as if the horrors of the
preceding night were all imaginary" (McWilliams, 2011).

Within the framework of developmental psychology, it is understood
that overwhelming childhood traumas may consolidate normative dissociative propensities into rigid patterns of pathological dissociation. This

consolidation is dependent in part upon the qualities of the care giving relationship (independent of trauma) and upon the developmental capacities of
the child (e.g., capacities to self-soothe and symbolize experience through
play or language); as Carlson, Yates and Sroufe put it, "Vulnerability to dissociative coping mechanisms is more likely in the absence of experiences
of reliable support and self-efficacy" (2010). Recent studies on dissociation
suggest that

> the combined influence of experience (i.e., repeated trauma) and biological
> reorganization as a function of experience contribute to pathological dissocia-
> tion. These theories propose that dissociation begins as an individual defense
> against unexpected overwhelming negative experience. The defensive pattern
> becomes entrenched as an automatic and uncontrollable response to stress with
> repetition and anticipation of probable attack. (Perry, Pollard, Blakley, Baker, &
> Vigilante, 1995; Putnam, 1997; Terr, 1990, 1991, 1994, as quoted by Carlson,
> Yates and Sroufe, 2010)

Winnicott (1971), while writing about primary dissociation, sourced
dissociative states to a pattern in the early relationship with the mother;
what characterized this pattern was an abrupt change from satisfaction
to disillusionment and despair, which led to the abandonment of hope in
object-relating. Winnicott's patient, the youngest among several siblings,
was left to look after herself a good deal. The emergence of her ego was
considerably disturbed due to environmental failures, and this resulted in dissociation, which was

> reinforced by a series of significant frustrations in which her attempts to be a
> whole person in her own right met with no success . . . [S]he became a special-
> ist in this one thing: being able to have a dissociated life while seeming to be
> playing with the other children in the nursery. (Winnicott, 1971)

Habitual fantasizing interferes with action and with life in the real or
external world, and, to a greater degree, it interferes with dreaming, with
psychic reality and with emotional aliveness. In the case of extreme dissociation, wherein the environmental failure also accompanies impingement on
the nascent ego, with demands to comply and give up its true spontaneity,
Winnicott suggested that a false self comes into existence. The beauty of the
false self lies in its caretaking function. Winnicott described this as follows:

> At the extreme of illness I see the true self as a potentiality, hidden and pre-
> served by the compliant false self, which latter is then a defense organization
> that is based on the various functions of the ego apparatus and on self-caretaking
> techniques. (1965)

While Freud focused on his theorizing primarily on the freedom from illusion, Winnicott emphasized "the increasing freedom to create illusion" through play. A healing encounter is then regarded as compensation for a significant lack in relationships during infancy and as providing a space for "mutual play" between the analysand and the analyst. With Winnicott, psychoanalysis witnessed an emphasis on the relational.

In *Hysteria*, Bollas (2000) reflected on a good object turning bad if, instead of containing distress, it transforms content to discontent. It utilizes the child as a container for its own evacuative projections, leaving behind an eerie sense of feeling possessed. If circumstances are favorable and the repressed objects do manage to break through the silence, the self is thrown into a state of disorientation like what was known but not thought when the objects invaded the internal space: "The dissociative state testifies to the act of self-interruption" (Bollas, 2000). But one also needs these objects. It becomes excruciatingly difficult to let go of them; the very idea brings guilt.

Moving from Western psychoanalytic texts to psychoanalytic thinking that has emanated from India, Sudhir Kakar's work goes to the heart of cultural conceptions in India around health and illness and what differentiates them from Western ideals. While scholars like Kapferer (1991) and Dwyer (2003) have rejected the psychoanalytic approach, with the latter having opposed Sudhir Kakar's explanations of both spirit possession and exorcism rituals on the grounds that Kakar does not consider the cultural construction of illness and cure, I disagree with these positions. I feel Kakar has stressed the need for a culturally sensitive psychoanalysis. According to him, ghosts are "the reification of certain unconscious fantasies of men and women which provoke strong anxiety in the Indian cultural setting" (Kakar, 1991). His analysis of possession is Eriksonian. He pays close attention to processes that are unique to Indian culture. For instance, he showed through a case study that a man's psychic struggle in an Indian setting is not so much associated with the Oedipus complex as it is a plea for an Oedipal alliance with the father. When faced with overpowering femininity, the boy's efforts at autonomy are thwarted. The father's absence in the face of such suffocation of the self makes the boy want to cry out to and ally with the father, to save himself from the ubiquity of maternal possessiveness.

Kakar's analysis is drawn from a blend of both Western psychoanalytic concepts and his intuitive understanding of processes unique to Indian cultural settings. Through brief case studies, he offers glimpses into the worlds (inner and outer) of possessed persons. Perhaps what motivates the brevity of the case studies was the fact that he writes for the masses and his target readers require him to stop at a certain depth of analysis, beyond which his thoughts will evoke more resistance than reflection.

To an extent, the case studies shared by Kakar explain the causes for possession states. His explanation of how healing happens in exorcism revolves
around the experience of catharsis afforded by possession and rituals of
exorcism. He suggests that, after the terror associated with ghosts is made to
disappear, one experiences catharsis in a dissociated state or while narrating
their scariest dreams to the healer. In the presence of an audience, defense
mechanisms of denial, projection and splitting are employed to repress and
suppress conflicts. Additionally, families are exposed to the distress of the
possessed member and are made to compensate for it through rituals of
various kinds.

Kakar's *Shamans, Mystics and Doctors* evoked in me many thoughts
and initiated a pursuit of deeper knowledge about these matters, which will
become clearer in reflections that follow the case studies in this book. When
I turned to Kakar's *Shamans, Mystics and Doctors*, I realized that his was the
kind of psychology that could provide a hospitable home for my curiosities.
Kakar established a framework pomising a deepening and evolution of my
understanding of possession and assistance in thinking through the doubts
and fears that plagued my mind when I began this research. Most importantly,
Kakar (1991) suggested that internal changes might be latent in possession
states if one were to sustain a gaze long enough.

The lens used by me to understand the phenomenon of possession is, of
course, psychoanalytic. My own "me-search" was facilitated by the discipline
of psychoanalysis. It fostered in me the development of an eye with which to
"see" (and an "I" to see into) and to appreciate the beauty in the complexities
that make each of us human. Psychoanalysis gave me a language designed not
to explain fears away but to engage with them. The weaving together of my
personal world with the cultural world introduced to me by Kakar made me
ask a few questions; I became curious about the kinds of fears that plague the
minds of possessed persons. How were these fears related to the body? Where
in the body did the mind dwell? How did a person transform in possession?
Why are more women possessed than men and what is their status—as wives,
daughters, and sisters? What kinds of babies were they—curious, clingy,
distant? What is so threatening about a possessed woman's frenzy that male
healers must counter it with violence? What does it say about the insecurities
of Indian men at large?

Moreover, I wanted to learn about internal transformations. What is claimed
or reclaimed, lost, nurtured? What is the story of the self that collapses under
duress? What are the origins of the possessed self? If the unthinkable and
unsayable part of the self is being enacted through the body, what is this part
struggling to express? How does it come into being (or nonbeing)? Who in
the possessed person's family is loved the most? Who is nurtured the most at
home? Who is given the most freedom?

My desire to bring out the truth of my research participants' experiences, with an appreciation of the internal and external transformations involved, made psychoanalysis indispensable to me. It was with both doubt and hope that I undertook a pilot study in the first year of my doctoral research. During this period, I visited many churches in New Delhi. I also stayed for a few months in a Balaji temple in the state of Rajasthan in north India. I familiarized myself with the settings of these places of worship and the rituals performed in them and tried to form a rapport with those who visited these sites. I tried to hold conversations with possessed persons, their family members, and their healers. These visits were undertaken to acquaint myself with the complexities I would be pitted against, drawn toward and repulsed by and would still try to unravel in this research.

Based on my literature review and pilot study, I found some features that deserved deeper engagement, reflection, and engraving. I wanted to deepen my understanding of early experiences with the mother, equations with siblings, the dynamics between sets of parents, the sources of nurturance and lack of it and the parts of self that were not allowed birth. Kakar stressed the importance of the early phase of life when he wrote, "As adults, all of our affiliations and intimacies bear the stamp of our particular kind of infancy" (2008). Winnicott, too, explored the consequences of early neglect and disappointment on transitional experiencing.

Transitional space is an intermediate, co-evolving space where the object becomes external to the self. The mother first allows the illusion of omnipotence, which is only gradually frustrated. She receives the child's destruction of her and survives each time. In this destruction, the object gradually becomes an objective or external object. A foundation is laid for its destruction in fantasy and marks the birth of the external reality of the object in the subject's eyes and so the birth of ego; the object can now be seen as an object in its own right, with desires and needs of its own—a recognition that the object can no longer be omnipotently controlled.

The object's survival leads to the capacity for concern. According to Winnicott (1953), if there is a break in the continuity of good-enough mothering, that is, if the child is not allowed the illusory belief that his/her desires create the object of satisfaction and/or if the object retaliates against their destruction or is not there to receive it, the transitional phenomenon becomes meaningless. With the primary caregiver in the mother–infant dyad abruptly bailing out before a capacity to sense and appreciate her otherness has been arrived at, desperate measures are called for to deny the distance between the self and her.

Winnicott (1991) detailed one example to demonstrate such a denial of distance between self and other. His patient, a boy, while playing a game Winnicott referred to as "drawing squiggles," identified all lines as a "lasso," "whip," or "string in a knot." At home, he would string together chairs and tables and precariously tie them to the fireplace. He even tied a string around his younger sister's neck. Winnicott linked the boy's use of string to his mother's postpartum depression and subsequent absence from home during treatment:

> String can be looked upon as an extension of all other techniques of communication. String joins, just as it also helps in the wrapping up of objects and in the holding of unintegrated material. In this respect, string has a symbolic meaning for everyone; an exaggeration of the use of string can easily belong to the beginning of a sense of insecurity or the idea of a lack of communication.

Winnicott suggested that, in primary identification, where the infant experiences absolutely no difference between self and (m)other, this experience of being merged with the mother is rooted in a pure female element; it is this experience of "being" that is brought about by the pure female element. However, as one struggles to distinguish between Me and Not-me, the male element comes into play as part of the process of separation, denoting the capacity for differentiation. According to Winnicott (1991), creative living requires that both the male and female elements be brought together with the corresponding abilities to be and do. The dissociation of these elements prevents one from living creatively.

The inability to take a reflective stance or invest in working and living seemed to point to this dissociation of male and female elements in those I met. I wondered if possession was the string used to keep maternal comfort close. There were difficulties involved in thinking about and acknowledging psychic truth. Where in a person's history lie the seeds of this incapacity? How was I supposed to make sense of spirits emerging from some early maternal failure?

The clinginess to maternal care and the inability to stay with painful experiences that was witnessed in the possessed led me to Freud's paper on melancholia and the works of his successors—Green, Bion, and Ogden—on similar themes. According to Freud (1917) and Ogden (2002a), the ego is initially the receiver of emotional investment. The narcissistic identification allows for an object-tie, whereby the external object is treated as an extension of oneself. In time, the healthy infant develops sufficient psychological stability to engage in a narcissistic form of relatedness to objects; this relationality is premised upon the tie to the object being comprised of a displacement of ego-libido from the ego on to the object (Freud, 1914).

A narcissistic object-tie is one in which the object is invested with emotional energy that was originally directed at oneself. This shift from narcissistic identification to narcissistic object-tie depends on the degree of recognition of and emotional investment in the otherness of the object. A smooth transition requires coming to terms with the lack of one's omnipotence and leads to being able to relate to the object as external to oneself. On the other hand, neglect from a loved object causes the subject to experience disappointment, and the emotional investment directed toward the object is shattered. Loving emotional energy or libido is withdrawn and, instead of being displaced onto a new object, it withdraws into the ego.

In response to the pain of loss, the ego splits and the released emotional energy now serves to establish identification between a part of the ego and the abandoned object, thus allowing the abandoned object to be preserved. The outrage and the erotic love toward the disappointing object are combined and magnified into sadism, which manifests in the internal object relationship, where the sadistic, critical, split-off part of the ego haunts the corresponding part that identifies with the abandoned object. This internal object relationship is marked by a fusion of sexuality and aggression in perversion. The sadomasochistic fantasy and rituals support survival by denying separateness and loss. The persistent attacks by one split-off part on the other leave the ego severely depleted.

This internal abusive relationship is better than no relationship at all and helps in evading the painful feeling of object loss. The painful experience of loss is short-circuited by this identification; the separateness from the object is denied, and it is rendered endlessly captive. Ogden suggested that "[t]here is no loss; an external object (the abandoned object) is omnipotently replaced by an internal one (the ego-identified-with-the-object)" (2002a). Owing to the disturbance of the narcissistic development path caused by object loss or disappointment, the movement from narcissistic object-love to mature object-love with an object experienced as external is skewed toward an incapacity for mourning, i.e., one is "unable to face the full impact of the reality of the loss of the object and, over time, to enter into mature object-love with another person" (Ogden, 2002a). Since there is no loss, there is no space for mourning. Mourning involves living with emotional pain, symbolizing it for oneself (for e.g., in dreaming) and doing psychological work with it. The lost object cannot be disengaged with; the pain of loss is persistently evaded through regression to narcissistic identification, and, by extension, other forms of psychological pain are also evaded at the cost of losing a good deal of one's own emotional vitality.

An interest in the propensity to act out, rather than to stay with the painful emotional states and articulate them, took me to Wilfred Bion's ideas. According to Bion, the mother receives her infant's projected, uncontainable fear, discomfort and anxiety, modifies them and returns them to the infant in a detoxified form so that the latter can assimilate these contents into her self. Through the mother's "alpha function," her child's tensions and anxieties are modified by the creation of meaning out of raw, unprocessed sensory data—"beta elements"—and transformed into thinkable "alpha elements," the food for thought, the material for dreams and conscious thoughts. Alpha elements consist of visual, auditory, and olfactory impressions that are storable in memory and usable in dreams and in conscious waking thoughts. Thus, mother and child form a "thinking couple," which is the prototype of the thinking process that continues developing throughout life.

Bion compares this to the digestive process. The lack of containment in the child's environment causes the projected anxiety and fear to return to the child instead of being contained and modified by the mother, but in a toxic or demonic form, impeding the establishment of the alpha function, which helps one to process and metabolize emotional content for retention in the psyche. As a result, thinking becomes seriously impaired. If the mother's alpha or transformative function is absent, instinctual impulses are left unprocessed. This unprocessed psychic content/beta element is never transformed into a thinkable alpha element; it floats inside the mental space as a bunch of alien persecuting entities. Incoherent and devoid of meaning, these contents cause frustration and are suitable only for evacuation via projection, splitting and projective identification into the body, or into the external world through action. The A6 category of Bion's grid refers to the discharge of beta elements into action:

> it would represent not thought, but action with actions . . . If no thought were possible the individual would go straight from an impulse to an action . . . Confronted by the unknown, the human being would destroy it. Put into verbal formulation of a visual image, it is as if the reaction were, "Here is something I don't understand—I'll kill it." But a few might say, "Here is something I don't understand. I must find out . . . Here is something that frightens me, let me hide and watch it," or if it became braver, "Let me go nearer and sniff it." (Bion 1990, as quoted by Symington & Symington, 1996)

I sensed that the takeover of a body by an entity demonstrated that that body and its desires were being disowned. Disowning desires creates tension that, instead of being metabolized and culminating in the formation of meaning around that which is uncomfortable, is evacuated through the body. Yet, in possession, the mind and body come together.

Freud was of the view that wishing ended in hallucinating. Hallucinations are vivid sensory mental impressions in the absence of an adequate external stimulus. Bion (1958) believed that, when hallucinating, the sense organs function in reverse, in that they evacuate or excrete sensory impressions rather than perceiving them. The one who hallucinates is dominated by intolerance to frustration and an impulse to avoid any uncomfortable and unbearable feelings. Hallucinatory activity is experienced as unburdening the psyche.

I wondered if, in possession, this unburdening happened via the body. Perhaps tension from the uncomfortable psychic content was being evacuated through the body and reality was thereby kept at a distance. Nightmares, too, operate on the principle of not knowing or on giving up the desire to learn from experience (Ogden, 2005b). Nonetheless, I felt that possession required faith in God, who would sanction one's journey into a terrain where all that was forbidden could be lived out. In this terrain, one is not required to make sense of what is happening to oneself. This notion of "going with faith" is very reminiscent of Bion's instruction to therapists (1967a) to enter the analytic session in a state of abandon—without memory, desire, understanding, and expectation. I could tell that only such a letting-go would allow one to touch upon the raw vitality with which forbidden impulses could be lived out, tamed, processed, and would perhaps lead to some internal transformation in the possessed person. The analyst's state of abandon seemed similar to the one a possessed person entered into physically during rituals.

In his more recent work, Kakar has critiqued psychoanalytic views on religious rituals:

> Psychoanalysis doesn't look at rituals as ceremonial forms that deepen the individual's connection with nature, community and the sacred and from which they emerge purified and with a sense of awe and significance . . . for [psychoanalysts,] ritual means the actions of a person suffering from an obsessive-compulsive disorder, someone who is subject to a panic attack if he deviates even the slightest bit from a rigid routine. (2008)

According to him, the psychological value of a ritual lies in the degree to which it contributes to strengthening a person's sense of identity, its personal or group aspect. He refers to the rituals that defend or protect our sense of identity against a perceived danger by closing the psyche as "father" rituals, while rituals that augment personal identity by opening the psyche to novel experiences are "mother" rituals. The ritual of bedtime stories or lullabies and that of possession are "alive" rituals because these

> close certain threatening experiences of psychic danger while they simultaneously open the psyche to experiences that produced a distinct sense of self which is difficult to put into words but is approximately captured by such terms as wonderment, enhancement, awe or a sense of the sublime. (Kakar, 2008)

Which part of the mind of the possessed person made the stance of abandon possible, the kind I noticed in the rituals? I understood that the lived and imagined experiences of the research participants and the cultural processes witnessed by me were both to be studied closely with an attitude that would sustain the complexities of the clinical and the cultural. This undertaking demanded an honest attempt to look closely at the process of socialization that shapes one's sense of who one is and of who one is not, giving equal weight to the psychic and the social.

Keeping the above themes in mind, I ventured in my research into the lives of possessed individuals and healers and also reflected upon alternative ways of looking at this phenomenon, specifically those articulated in the artistic visions of filmmakers. I chose the art form of film in particular because, to invoke Green's (2005) notion of "tertiary processes," I believe films link the primary and secondary processes by augmenting fantasy life, capturing affective moments and opening up space for the imagination of relationships between the inner and the outer in vivid and vicarious ways.

I often wondered how I would "converse" with a person who frequently engaged in the evacuation (rather than the articulation) of difficult emotional states. Perhaps, as my apprenticeship in psychoanalytic psychotherapy has taught me, where verbalizing is not possible, most of the communication happens when the difficult states one can't successfully process are pro-jected onto the listener. The method implicit in psychoanalysis entails that both parties enhance their capacities to achieve a state of mind in which each touches the continuously flowing stream of unconscious conversation with the self, either in the form of dreaming or reverie. Where conversing becomes problematic, we are again rescued by thinkers like Ogden, who, in giving credence to such states as dreaming and reverie, view them as "being generated by analyst and patient at the frontier of dreaming[. They] draw not only on the unconscious experience of analyst and analysand as individuals, but also involve a set of unconscious experiences jointly, but asymmetrically, constructed by the analytic pair" (Ogden, 2002b).

I understood from my pilot work that I was required to ready myself to listen to what was being said, but also to closely and specially tune my ears to what was not being said and what was in turn being evoked in me, perhaps felt through me. I had to constantly subject myself to scrutiny to distinguish between what was being deposited in me from without and that which hailed from within.

One contemporary psychoanalytic thinker who has had a deep impact on my thinking is Phillip Bromberg. The impact of Bromberg's ideas on dissociation runs quietly yet eloquently throughout this book. I have found Bromberg's appreciation of the mind's capacity to negotiate stability and growth aligning with my own stance in this research. Bromberg (1999) explored the relationship between repression and dissociation and explained dissociation as a process that structures the mind as opposed to repression, which pertains to the contents of the mind. While repression takes the edge off psychic conflict, Bromberg appreciates the mind's capacity to *allow* for conflict to manifest in the internal world. He considers the mind's tolerance for conflict as a developmental milestone. In the Freudian framework, all psychic content that could potentially cause conflict is relegated to or repressed in the unconscious. Dissociation works on overwhelming experiences that threaten the cohesiveness of the mind. It operates when a feeling state challenges the mind's capacity to take in experience without fragmenting. Bromberg (1996) concludes that dissociation is a defense against fragmentation of the psyche. One notes that in both repression and dissociation, the mind tries to make sense of psychological distress in a bid to keep the psyche intact and facilitate its evolution.

Bromberg considers dissociation as a process that structures the psyche. Thus, following Bromberg, the process of clinical hour assumes significance as one follows the dissociative process of a patient's internal world. While Winnicott reflected that the inability to be a person stems from the sense of a discontinuity of the self when this self is largely constituted as a response to environmental impingements. Bromberg informs that out of these impingements are formed parts of the self that are complete in their own right. He termed these parts as self-states. Bromberg goes on to lay down an imagination of self that is marked by multiplicity. It is this imagination of the multiplicity of the self that found deep resonance in my mind. When dissociation is seen as a process by which psyche organizes itself, owing to the threat from the environment or the threat of losing the bond of attachment to our primary environment, the most secure sense we have of ourselves, the self-states, gets organized as "me" (self-parts that are accepted) and "not me" (self-parts that are negated). "The centrally defining hallmark of dissociation is the presence of a concrete state of mind, by which I mean that there is thought without a thinker or, rather, thought without the thinker's being aware of the other as a thinker in his or her own right with whom it might be possible to share or reciprocate ideas. Thus, each self-state insofar as it exists in dissociation from other self-states is necessarily an island of concreteness" (Bromberg 2001).

Negation of a self-part out of which "not-me" part got created, is experienced as traumatic. This internal negation is maintained due to the fear of losing the relationship in which the most secure sense of self is anchored. Although secure, this relationship can disallow representation of certain affective states (Bromberg, 2001). A confusion in the recognized Me and Not-me parts ensues impairing one's capacity to believe in what one perceived as their own feelings or affective responses to events (both intrapsychic and interpersonal). The Not-me states exist delinked from the conscious, history, time, space and thus from communication. The experience is exiled into an isolated island, without any bridges to the recognized sense of self.

According to Bromberg (1998), "dissociation becomes pathological to the degree that it proactively limits and forecloses one's ability to hold and reflect upon different states of mind within a single experience of 'me-ness.'"

Bromberg (2001) proposes a way forward through reflection on the "not-me" state as linked to a recognized "me." Chefetz and Bromberg (2004) note that dissociative processes actively work by not allowing any links to develop with parts of self that encapsulate uncontainable areas of experience. My own dazed states during these conversations were evidence of dissociation which become highlighted in conscious experience to ward off attention to the uncontainable experiences of my participants.

Further, dissociation works to ensure that trauma never happens again. There is hyper alertness toward any process through which the not-me self-states can be accessed. Linking with not-me self-states is avoided through dissociative symptoms such as going blank, heightened anxiety, fogginess, and feeling nothing in the here and now situation of the clinical hour (Chefetz and Bromberg, 2004).

Chefetz and Bromberg (2004) posit that recognition of the not-me parts as experience of the self should precede a reflection on them. This recognition is to happen via the therapist speaking about the not-me parts in a manner that has personal meaning for the patient. In their essay titled, "Talking with 'Me' and 'Not-Me': A Dialogue," Chefetz and Bromberg (2004) note that "the dissociated part of the patient's self holding the unsymbolised experience is not in relationship with the therapist, and until the therapist feels its impact as an experience linked to a part of himself that has been dissociated, it stays lost and its existence remains enacted." This valuable insight enable thinking about dissociation as an interpersonal process (Bromberg 1996) where the space for thinking between and about the patient and the analyst is "a space uniquely relational and still uniquely individual; a space belonging to neither person alone, and yet, belonging to both and to each; a twilight space in which 'the impossible' becomes possible; a space in which incompatible selves, each awake to its own 'truth,' can 'dream' the reality of the other without risk to its own integrity."

A year after I was awarded a doctoral degree upon the submission of my dissertation, the relational psychoanalyst Galit Atlas released a book titled *The Enigma of Desire* (2016). Atlas's (2016) work elaborates on Laplanche's (1995) concept of "enigmatic message." According to Laplanche (1995), the unconscious forms during adult–child interactions, during which the parents' sexuality is experienced by the child as implicit and ubiquitous and registered as inherently overwhelming, excessive, and mysterious—frightening and evocative at the same time. This language is present in the various ways in which the child is cared for by their parent. Initially, this enigmatic language of excess exceeds the child's ability to process it in terms of its complex conscious and unconscious messages. However, the child, primarily unconsciously, makes sense of it in their own time.

In this process of sense-making driven by curiosity and creativity, fantasy and reality intertwine and the enigmatic messages from the adult are translated into the child's own slowly evolving world of meanings. This is how, for Laplanche, the excess of adult sexuality forms the unconscious and its quality of otherness. The result is that one develops a mysterious yet othered experience of oneself.

Some doubts I had begun to entertain, about the many ways I, helped by my intuition, had managed to build a language to converse with each participant and the ghosts that haunted them, were addressed when I read about Atlas's clinical work with Danny, who walked into her clinic seeking help in getting rid of a dybbuk that had possessed him. Atlas asked what was being expressed through the dybbuk and discovered that, very much like a ghost stuck in limbo between two worlds; Danny struggled between his longing for the loved and loving part of and his hatred toward the violent part of his father. He also longed for his mother while at the same time harboring rage toward her. His sisters' sexuality overwhelmed him and caused intense pangs of shame. Atlas was struck by Danny's preoccupation with women's clothing, which hid behind it his preoccupation with their naked bodies. All that is forbidden—rage, shame, need, longing—evoked horror, overwhelmed him, and this "too-muchness" was contained in the "not-me" (Bromberg, 2003) part of him, the ghost.

Building on Benjamin's (2004; Benjamin & Atlas, 2015) ideas on the lack of a secure attachment based on affect regulation, feelings experienced as excess and the consequent split between activity and passivity, Atlas (2016) concluded that, in Danny's case, "one part of the *self* is functioning as a container for the other part in order to resolve the problem of excess and failure of self-regulation . . . Danny is the passive-innocent and the dybbuk is the active-sinner." She saw Danny's image-laden, affectively charged language as an "enactment of the contents of 'too muchness' that Danny experiences."

Atlas managed to develop a symbolic language that represented Danny's childhood experience and maintained a fictional quality with which to "talk about the sexuality in the room without reliving his terrifying childhood feelings of overexcitement and dysregulation." In other words, the patient's utterances were taken by her to be messages or communications that needed translation into Danny's evolving world of meanings, not psychoanalytic interpretation. The dybbuk's message carried an enigma, but also performed a defensive function, i.e., these enigmatic messages also carried a pseudo-enigma, unconsciously aimed at protecting Danny from feeling the injuries of his past.

Atlas's work came closest to my own, in that I too tried to converse with ghosts and their hosts while keeping intact the "as-if" or fictional quality in our conversations. The fiction respects the right of the host to remain incommunicado even as their ghosts rage and wail.

Based on my personal experiences, the curiosity that was born out of them, the promise that I found in Kakar's thinking and in the language of psychoanalysis and the pilot study that was undertaken, I became convinced that only with a blend of both a faithful clinical eye and a sensitivity to cultural processes could I hope to illuminate the "beauty in brokenness," the transformations inherent in seemingly horrifying states of possession.

NOTES

1. His research participants were women and men who were once possessed by spirits but, after exorcism, underwent a transformation that turned them into shamanic healers who felt a close connection with divine powers.

2. This means that the girl is suffering from erotic desires, but they are externalized and objectified as the action of a lustful demon rather than considered a product of the girl's own wishes and fantasies (Obeyesekere, 1981).

3. Here, "both" refers to Freud's and Obeyesekere's respective societies.

Chapter 2

Various Beginnings

Based on my personal experiences, the nature of which I hinted at in the previous chapter, I had some sense of the difficulties of connecting with others that a possessed person struggles with. I decided to undertake a pilot study in the year 2008 to acclimatize myself to the research field and the field of experiences it was going to open up for me. I was working as a counselor at the time and immersed in the study of psychoanalytic theory, which combined with the specifics of my upbringing around priests and exorcists to produce a particular set of curiosities and drives in me. I wished to learn how to be around and hold conversations with people who felt possessed by spirits, as well as with their family members and healers. I wondered if it would be possible to establish companionship with the possessed people, whether they would be willing to share life-historical details, whether these details would take both of us down to the kinds of depths anticipated but not reached in Kakar's work, whether I would encounter nodes of beauty or health, however faint, in their narratives, whether their families would allow them to open up to me or whether they, too, would be gripped by suspicion, whether I would encounter antecedent features in the lives of these people, similar to what anthropologist Obeyesekere observed.

I identified a few churches in New Delhi, one church in Uttarakhand and a Balaji temple in the state of Rajasthan as places I would visit. While the temple of Balaji was well-known for conducting exorcisms, choosing churches for this study required careful consideration. Not all churches provide or serve as spaces for healing and exorcism. Fortunately, I could turn to members of my family for guidance, which I did. Unfortunately, these conversations were often difficult because my uncles and father felt that I was using psychology to criticize religion. They were the hardest to convince about the spirit of my enquiry, which was meant not as critique but as appreciation. On some occasions, out of exasperation, they would point me to relevant churches, where I could observe exorcism rituals and speak to priests and possessed persons.

I entered the pilot study feeling both excited and nervous: excited because I thought I would see theory come alive in myriad ways and nervous because I was not sure how to develop a language with which to speak to my potential research participants. I needed to acquaint myself with the language prevalent at healing sites. My training in psychoanalysis had taught me to speak in the language of past traumas, repressed wishes and desires, loss, mourning, etc. However, in the sites that I would be visiting, the language spoken was one of myths and fables.

Moreover, as a Christian in a predominantly Hindu country, I often felt that Christianity was viewed as "Western." I wondered about entering these cultural spaces wearing my identity—a Christian studying a discipline like psychoanalysis, whose theories are primarily anchored in the Western mind. It remained to be seen whether my status as a Christian would serve to enhance or shrink the suspicion at these cultural sites of healing.

It was this very identity, though, that prompted me to begin my study at churches. I hoped that I would find potential participants who would be willing to share their life stories with me, who would help me come to grips with my anxieties and understand theirs, who would familiarize me with healing sites and enable me to feel the texture of the fears, thrills, despair, and joy that possession entailed.

PARVATI

Parvati lived in a slum area in New Delhi. She was thirty-five, married, and a mother of four daughters and one son. She was not able to study and attributed this failure to her mother's death when she was only one and a half years old and her younger brother was six months old. Parvati had no memories of her mother and had been raised by her grandparents.

After her mother's death, her father got married again. This stepmother did not pay attention to Parvati or her brother. When she was seven months' pregnant, she too passed away, and soon after her death, Parvati's father married for the third time. Both parents favored their own children. Parvati's second stepmother had four daughters and one son.

Parvati got married when she was twenty. When she was expecting her first daughter, Parvati began having nightmares in which she saw a woman approaching and strangling her. The nightmare would end with her waking up, screaming. The appearance of these nightmares was attributed to possession by a malevolent spirit. In her waking state she would experience shivers and pain in various body parts, particularly her throat, chest, and stomach.

It was suspected that her aunt had caused her to be possessed with the help of black magic because she did not wish Parvati to bear children and lead a good life. During this time, Parvati was taken care of by her husband. He took her to many local healers, who opined that she was possessed by not one but five evil spirits!

Parvati remained troubled by possession for many years. During this time, she also gave birth to four daughters. When possessed, Parvati would become violent toward her family members, especially toward her eldest daughter, whom she often tried to strangle. There was pressure on Parvati to bear a male child; the elderly women in her family often taunted her over this. The repeated taunts and pressure from outside and the consecutive births of girls probably caused her to experience anxiety and hostility, which she seems to have directed toward her first-born: while possessed, she transformed into the woman who haunted her nightmares and would reach for her daughter's throat with the intention to kill her. Perhaps her murderous anger was away of asking the rhetorical question, "Why were you born?" After all, these daughters were collectively the cause of the taunts she had to listen to, and she found it hard to defend herself or her daughters.

A strange consequence of this unhealthy dynamic was that the possessing spirits would often switch hosts, targeting Parvati's eldest daughter instead of Parvati. I wondered how the daughter came to be possessed by the same spirits that were possessing her mother—had Parvati infused her daughter (and maybe her other daughters) with the sense of not being wanted and perhaps a desire to be owned, claimed, belong, or possessed?

Her healer, Sanjeev, described the experience of exorcising her spirits in a manner that suggested he was quite familiar with the ritual—how the spirit was to be provoked, how its nature and form could be identified, what precautions had to be taken, and so on:

Glory be to God. That day as well, when it was exorcised out of her, I was praying. When Holy Spirit instructed me to ask if there is any such woman who was visited by a sage a few days ago—this sage performed a black magic. As I said these words, the evil spirit came over her. It was revealed to me in a vision during prayer that a sage visited a house and has done some evil magic. I saw this. After that, she was just hitting herself with fists, with all the strength she had in her body. [She] damaged her body by repeatedly hitting herself. Had I not commanded the Satan to stop, she would have lost her life. Then she called her daughter closer, held her by the throat and began to strangle her. He [the possessing spirit] kept on saying . . . "I cannot leave her . . . I have been living with her for many years . . . I won't leave . . . " There were both female and male possessing spirits. One possessing spirit began to seek sympathy toward the end, saying, "I have been with her for past so many years. What harm have I caused her?" I commanded him: "Abandon her body nonetheless! You have no right to reside in her!" Look at her face now. Her face is now lit up. Earlier, this glow was not present on her face. After being healed, she felt pain . . . all

[over] the body . . . intense pain. I mean, it was so excruciating that she was not able to even sit. We gave her water to drink after the prayer. She drank the water and, ten minutes after that, she came back to consciousness. Her joints were aching. This went on for nearly 20–25 minutes. You know what happened after that? Laxmi Aunty and Sharda were very unwell for three days after that. When one is exorcising—there were a few people with me at that time. They shouldn't have been there with me. Are you getting me? They should keep their mouths shut. They were praying along with me. Now, this is in the nature of Satan—his legal right. According to his right, only a selected person can rebuke him. Not any other person. This is his legal right. I did at that time what Holy Spirit guided me to do. God has not given us the right to command like this. We don't have the right.

Parvati described her experience after being healed in the following words: "It feels lighter. Before this, I did not feel motivated to do anything—in eating as well. There was an irritability in [my] body at all times. I did not like anything."

After being healed, Parvati prayed to God for a son, and her wish was granted. The taunts ceased after that. Perhaps it was the birth of a boy, rather than the exorcism, that served to heal her.

The next day, I met Sanjeev and asked him where Parvati was so I could continue my conversation with her. He said that she had already shared with me everything about her life, so he did not understand why I needed to continue interviewing her. He felt that if I wanted to understand possession, then I needed to speak to a healer like him. When I met Parvati, she seemed hesitant and repeated what Sanjeev had said to me.

It seemed that Sanjeev was nominating himself as one of the participants for my research. Although mildly puzzled by his behavior, I decided to speak to Sanjeev.

SANJEEV

Sanjeev was a thirty-six-year-old member of a church near the Delhi University campus. He was introduced to me at a prayer meeting as a person who brought to the church many who sought healing. He preached the word of God in a slum area or *jhuggi* cluster near a railway station in Delhi. Sanjeev and his wife offered tuition at very low fees to the children of the slum.

Sitting in this *jhuggi*, I observed that it was packed with close to twenty students (age group six to ten), who sat on a mattress on the floor while their teachers, Sanjeev and his wife, sat on the bed. The class commenced with the "Lord's prayer," led by a student. As both Sanjeev and his wife assigned class work to each child, Sanjeev said:

Through these children, we also try to bring their families in Christ. Many families out of these have also come into Christ. We do not force them to convert. Ever since these children have begun to come to us, we deal with them in a manner that, through our behavior, changes can come in their behavior, and then their parents can notice this change and try to know Christ. It is written in the scripture: "your behavior should be such that through it people may come to know Christ."

Sanjeev and his wife were Hindus who had adopted Christianity a few years ago, when they were going through many financial difficulties. During the same period, she was visited by a *djinn* whose head was missing—all she saw was the rest of its body. She had begun telling me about this when Sanjeev interrupted her narration. I had started to hope his wife, Sharda, would be a research participant, but when Sanjeev interrupted, I became unsure of whether he would allow it. He expressed his need to be heard and seen by barging into the dialogical space between me and his wife:

Sanjeev: Just two days back I had such a terrible dream, what to say . . .

Me: What dream did you have?

Sanjeev: (animatedly) I saw an extremely beautiful girl. She is extremely beautiful. I have never seen such a beautiful girl. You know what I did in the dream? I am filled with such rage that I tore her clothes, slit her throat and slashed her body all over with a knife. I mean, there was such violence inside me. Everything became bloody and then I woke up and on waking up I was feeling so . . . so . . . (Struggles for words)

Me: Restless? (He looked restless while narrating the dream)

Sanjeev: Yes! Restless! I was filled with a lot of anger and I remained in that state that entire day. Restlessness . . . rage . . . I felt like murdering someone and eating them up.

Me: Hmm. This girl that you saw in your dream, was she someone you knew?

Sanjeev: No. I have never seen her. She was extremely beautiful.

Me: How do you make sense of this dream?

Sanjeev: I asked God, "Lord, please explain to me the meaning of this dream. Why did I have this dream?" Then I prayed for five hours and God put it in my mind that I should observe a fast and pray. For two days, I did not eat anything. Neither did I go anywhere. I only prayed. Twenty-four hours after praying, I felt better, felt that now my relationship with my God had become direct.

Me: So before this there was distance between you and God?

Sanjeev: Yes. I had begun to feel that for some time I had come far from God, and Satan is always waiting and watching for that moment for Lord's devotee to come far from God, even if for some time, so he can then attack. But it is also written that "I have chosen you from your mother's womb." Satan tries really hard to break the Lord's children but the Father always protects his children.

Me: This dream was from Satan?

Sanjeev: Yes. It was (hesitates) related to adultracy.

Me: Adultery?

Sanjeev: Yes, adultery. Satan had attacked me using adultery, and I was so angry that I feared what I might do if I slept next to her [his wife].

Me: What did you fear you might do?

Sanjeev: I feared I may tear her apart the way I tore apart the girl in my dream.

Me: Bhaiya,[1] in the dream there was such immense anger in you that remained even after you woke up. In actual life, do you experience or have you ever experienced such rage? Before you accepted Christ?

Sanjeev: What should I tell you about myself? My life was such . . . [I] don't know where all has God brought me out from. I was such a person that the entire village was scared of my name. There was a time when, with the force of a single staff, I got ten houses vacated. That was the kind of fear I inspired.

Me: (surprised, intrigued, and encouraging him to go on) really?

Sanjeev: I was such an angry person that people called me a goon, and now, ever since I have come in Christ, [my] mind has become absolutely calm. If someone says anything to me, I tell them, "Go brother, my Father who is sitting up in Heaven will decide upon you."

Me: What was the reaction of your family members to this change in you?

Sanjeev: What will family members say? (Becomes serious and thoughtful, smiles a bit) Just two days back, Mother called up. My son has turned five years old, so she was saying that, "We have to organize a ceremony for him, send some money." I said, "Okay, take it. Anything else?" Then she said that, "This ceremony has to be performed by the eldest son, so you need to come over." I told her, "This will not be possible for me to do. I will not come." I told her to get the ceremony done by the younger brother. "I will not do this. You are my parents, you too have your wishes—I understand. You want to organize this ceremony, you need the money—that I can send. But I won't do any such ceremony. Now my head will only be bowed before One." (gestures toward heaven)

Me: How are you feeling after this conversation with your mother?

Sanjeev: I am feeling bad. Mother does not understand that now my mother and my father is only Him [God]. I am the eldest son of the family. She expects a lot from me. Ever since I gained consciousness—meaning ever since I was ten years old—since then a lot of responsibility came over me. Papa's health was not okay, siblings were young . . . so I used to go to the school in the morning and to the fields in afternoon after school.

Me: You had to grow up too fast?

Sanjeev: Yes. Once there was a discussion about making me leave school. So, I ran away from home—went straight to Mama.[2] Dadaji[3] brought me back home, saying, "You come home with me, I will see who dares to stop your schooling." Then I would study as well as work in the fields.

Me: That's a lot of work for a ten-year-old.

Sanjeev: Yes. One time, my uncles came and, in front of me, emptied our mango tree of all its fruit. Not even one mango was left, and I could not do anything. What could a ten-year-old do? . . . But at night I gathered ten to twelve boys from the village, went to my uncles' orchard and emptied it—did not leave a single mango! Then they realized what they had done.

Me: You found a way to show your anger?

Sanjeev: (laughs) Yes. During [my] teenage [years], there was a lot of anger in me. My heart was not in the work. The ox was not able to move properly, so I picked it [the ox] up and slammed it on the ground. (laughs) In the whole village, sometimes in a brawl, at other times something else. I would move around with a gang. Then, when I went to the college, people elected me, I won and became the president. Then there was a conflict with the principal of the college, so I beat him up. He called the police—our boys locked horns with them. It was a riot—there was an arrest warrant in my name. Then I ran and came to Delhi, took admission in Delhi University for graduation. Then, after some time, that case got closed. So, this was my state. And now anger never comes.

Me: Only in dreams.

Sanjeev: Yes.

He responded spontaneously, followed by a pause during which he was visibly thoughtful. He then began talking about getting married at the age of eighteen.

Sanjeev: Everyone thought of finding a suitable bride for me who could keep me in control or change me. That's it, then they got me married.

Me: Another responsibility.

Sanjeev: I was only eighteen . . . didn't know the meaning of marriage. The next day, after marriage itself, I ran to Delhi. Then family members came to Delhi and took me back (laughs). Then they sent her also with me to Delhi. I was twenty years old when I became a father. What is life? What is childhood?

I never knew. There was a lot of opposition after I came into Christianity. Actually, we are from a high-caste Brahmin family. Brahmins are very rigid. Papa did not say anything. My relationship with him is not very close. Since the beginning . . . if I am sitting somewhere, Papa would get up and leave. I was close to Mother. When I came into Christianity, among the family members, Mother was [the] most upset. She would say that, "Now that he is here, spirits of our ancestors will abandon the house. Do not make him sleep close to the temple."(laughs)I said that, "Your gods are cowards. They are scared of me that they would abandon the house on my arrival?" She fell quiet. And indeed, the ancestral spirits left the house. The next day, Mother was staring at me after her morning prayer. I asked the reason. She said that, "Today, the house feels lighter." I laughingly replied that, "It *will* feel lighter because I am here. Your ancestors have fled (laughs)." The village elders were asking my father about me: "What happened to him that he turned a Christian?" He responded by saying, "He must have found something in this for him to take this action. He never does anything without thinking. That is why I am not going to ask him anything. You all are free to ask. I will only listen." Then village elders came home and asked me what I found in this. I asked them a question: "Do you share a personal relation with your gods?" They said, "Yes." I said that, "These Gods are with you at all times?" They said, "Yes, God resides in everything." I said, "No, not in everything. Have you ever experienced that God resides within you?" They went silent. I told them I had experienced it. Then I asked them to tell if they could see any change in my nature. One person said that, "You no longer seem your father's son." I told them, "This change in my nature has come about because my God resides within me. I share a personal relation with him. I have felt it." I asked them to tell me if they have ever felt pity for a poor and miserable person. Have they ever felt like doing something for such a person? Or have they not felt envy toward anyone? Ever since my Lord is with me my whole personality has undergone a change.

Although Sanjeev was not possessed by a spirit, he shared with victims of possession the tendency of disowning his hostile and sexual impulses and treating them as the work of the Devil.

After this conversation, Sanjeev began calling me relentlessly, asking me details about my personal life, my whereabouts, and how I spent my days and nights. I sensed he was being drawn toward me, and not in a harmless way. It was extremely daunting for me to be woken up by calls at odd hours to the sound of his panting voice on the other end of the line, which indicated to me that perhaps he was excited and masturbating. I withdrew and broke off all contact with him.

PASTOR M (P. M.)

I must have been between ten and twelve years old when my father organized a prayer convention at which many sick, possessed, and disturbed people were healed. Hundreds of devotees cried out to the Lord Almighty in chorus in an atmosphere charged with the intensity of their pleas and prayers. Those possessed by evil spirits entered the frenzy of possession—wildly swaying, jerking, rolling on the ground, somersaulting in the air, and uttering obscenities. In this milieu, Pastor M (P. M.), accompanied by his apprentices, went around to each possessed person, chanting the Lord's name. Being enveloped in praise for and worship of the Divine would provoke the possessed person to respond with even more violent, aggressive movements, gestures, screams and cries.

As a young girl, I still remember being gripped by the terrorizing, ear-splitting screams. The louder they screamed, the more determined the priest became—he would lay his hand on the sufferer and pray more forcefully. Some possessing spirits would retaliate for a while and then give up. Some surrendered early, some not so easily, but they all gave up before the persistence of this charismatic pastor.

P. M. was a renowned exorcist in north India, blessed with a very specific gift—the ability to heal possessed persons. I remembered him as a person with an intense personality. His facial structure—hollow cheeks, sunken yet warm eyes, a moustache, and a beard—gave him a striking resemblance to Christ himself (as he is popularly portrayed by artists). As he delivered sermons and sang self-composed hymns to the accompaniment of his accordion, his frail, lanky body would turn into a cauldron bubbling with a contagious aliveness that would seep into the audience as well. His warmth drew large numbers of mesmerized audience members who sought special prayers from him for their specific needs.

I met him again, nearly twenty years later, for my doctoral research. P. M. was now a fifty-five-year-old widower and father of two children. I attended the Sunday service at his church. After his sermon, he encouraged the crowd to lift their hands toward heaven in a gesture of entreaty and to begin praising the Lord loudly, through hymns and words. I, too, raised my hands and began to chant like those around me. Through my partly open eyes, I saw P. M. standing in front of the girl next to me. He entangled his fingers in hers, bent forward and whispered something in her ears that sounded to me like, "The Lord's Spirit touches you." The words had but left his mouth when she fell back into the arms of one of the pastor's assistants—he did an excellent job of catching her before she hit the ground.

He then turned to me and did the same thing, aligning his palms with mine and whispering, "The Lord touches you." I did not fall—I did not, dare I say it, feel touched. He touched my forehead. I did not feel anything but amusement. Those around us had now begun to stare. Witnessing confusion on their faces, I thought to myself, "They have placed their faith in this person as a medium between them and the Lord. The congregation wants me to fall. For them, it is very important to believe that the Holy Spirit walks amidst them. By standing my ground, by my refusal to submit to the Lord, am I questioning their belief? Is the confusion on their faces a sign that something inside them, a necessary illusion, is perhaps on the verge of shattering?"

I had to be sensitive to the situation, to the delicate role of play and illusion that I was getting to witness and be part of. By not responding appropriately, I risked snatching away from the congregation a space that brought their inner and outer lives together in a peaceful paradox. So, I surrendered to the pastor's touch and sat down on the floor.

Looking around, I could see the faith restored on the faces of the devotees. It was as if, through their silent gazes, I could hear them saying, "Indeed the Holy Spirit has touched her. It walks amongst us."

After the service, I met P. M. and told him about the purpose of my visit. I asked him what he thought of spirit possession:

> P. M.: Look, according to me, 99.99% cases of demonic possession are internal. I mean, it is not that there is something from outside of me, something external which is put inside me by someone. It is some old internal wound which one has not allowed to be healed, which is now rotten. Such wounds present themselves in the form of spirits. There is an ongoing struggle inside us, between id, ego, and superego. There is an animal in us. We present ourselves as good because that is what we want to believe the most. When there are riots somewhere, then, whether it is a Hindu temple priest or a learned Muslim teacher, everyone either steps out to murder or steal or to rape. And if we are not able to do any of these things then we gain satisfaction by watching violence on television. I think war is necessary for [an] outlet of this animal instinct in us.

I was, understandably, quite struck by this priest's peculiar understanding of the human psychic condition. He used terms like "psyche," "conscious," and "unconscious" as well:

> Me: So, when a possessed woman is in a state of violent frenzy in front of you, and you know that this is not actually spirit possession, then how do you deal with such a possessed person?

> P. M.: Look, how will it help to be physically violent toward someone who is already internally beaten down? Such a person needs to be hugged. If you look closely into the family history of these people, you will see that either they have

been deprived in some way or there has been some sort of an abuse or they have not received any recognition. Now, only 10% of our mind is conscious—rest 90% is unconscious. When we dream of something scary, we think there is some ghost or ghoul pestering us. But those are the things of our unconscious, which we have not had time or opportunity to think through or to live.

I couldn't help but admire the seamlessness with which his knowledge of the mind slotted into his work as a priest. However, there were many people queued up behind me, waiting for his blessings. Our conversation had to end abruptly. As I was leaving, though, he stopped me and said, "Look, where is beauty? Ugliness is like a huge rock. When we lift this rock and remove all the irrelevant things from underneath it, then beauty emerges from this very ugliness."

It is difficult to express in words what I experienced while listening to him provide me with a framework for my research. At no point in our conversation did I mention my research topic to him—it came to him as if by divine intervention, and a telepathic connection was created between us. Touched by this moment of deep connection with him, I savored my joy in silence before saying, "In this very moment, something strange has occurred. I have not exactly shared with you the topic of my research. It is titled 'Beauty in Ugliness in Spirit Possession and Healing.'"

He said, gently smiling, "Hmm. It is good. The Lord has put this thought in me. It means the Spirit of God is guiding you in the right direction."

Accepting the gift of this auspicious beginning for my research, I took his leave.

Healing is a highly idiosyncratic business. P. M. may owe his understanding of the human condition to books, but his success in helping people deal with their plight lay in his ability to integrate this wisdom with the tradition he belonged to. He told me, "This wisdom has come after one has been through many of life's painful experiences."

I attended his services a few times. To help me know him better, he gave me CDs of hymns composed by him. He did not pick up my calls after this. I wondered if he felt the need to keep his life private. Whatever little I knew of him came from his songs and sermons. He often sang this self-composed hymn, inspired by the Book of Psalms:

> *Whither shall I go from Thy spirit?*
> *Or whither shall I flee from Thy presence?*
> *If I ascend up into Heaven, Thou art there.*
> *If I make my bed in Hell, behold, Thou art there.*
> *If I take the wings of the morning, and dwell in the uttermost parts*
> *of the sea,*

Even there shall Thy hand lead me, and Thy right hand shall
hold me.

Almost all his hymns presented God as an omnipresent, omniscient entity, perfectly in tune with the internal rhythms and states of His subjects—very much like the mother of infancy, sensing the deepest longings of the infant's heart without the latter's having to voice them, invested with powers to make the impossible possible, the bad good, providing protection from the destructive devil and, most importantly, an ever-present presence, found repeatedly without violating the "right not-to-communicate" (Winnicott, 1963). My experience at P. M.'s church service, listening to the recordings of the hymns he composed, singing along with faithful devotion, often transported me to a childlike state of complete dependence, of reverence for the Lord, from which I returned with renewed confidence in my capacities to conduct my research and hope that indeed *all was possible*.

These meetings also filled me with curiosity. Since his hymns asserted God's presence as protecting against evil, I wondered if, perhaps, an evil spirit's fear of encountering the Holy Spirit actually communicated its opposite—a desire for closeness with divinity? Was the desire of union with the mother fulfilled, albeit in a twisted way, by becoming a "bad child" in the state of spirit possession? The *samkat/dusht aatman* or evil spirit can relate directly to the divine one through mutual condemnation, just as its counterpart, a *duta/pavitra aatman* or good spirit, shares a direct and special relationship with the divine one through mutual admiration. Perhaps the idea is: "If I am deviant, the mother will at last look at me. Even if she punishes me, at least she'll relate to me, actively facilitate in me a transformation into a good and obedient child and then reward me with frequent visitations or *darshana*." So, when one says, "The Lord Almighty always finds his children" or that He "does not abandon them," perhaps the hope that is being expressed is: "The mother now won't let me relapse, because she has invested so much in me, to transform me from being deviant into being obedient. She'll now keep me close. Every time I am led astray by my desires, the mother will find me." This would have to continue until, perhaps, the comforting mother had been internalized and could be possessed without recourse to deviancy. In other words: "Her finding me through her presence will pave the way for a generative form of possession."

Reflecting on P. M.'s hymns, the quality that enabled them to transport the devotee into experiencing, with God, the earliest relationship of complete dependence and faith on the mother and the enhancement of self it made possible, I wondered what his equation was with his own mother. He refrained from meeting me personally to talk about his life, but in one of his sermons he did touch on some pertinent details:

Friends, I never saw my father. Whatever I am is because of my mother, who so lovingly nursed my body, mind and soul. She was a poor woman, but she had immense wealth and riches of the love of my Heavenly Father that He has shown through Jesus. Though I lost her, I know we shall meet on the beautiful shore! Her songs that she sang for me while I was in her lap still echo in my ears. Her vibrant prayers that she tearfully offered for me still are my strength. Her gift of a rose flower on my every birthday still is fragrant in my life. Whatever I am today is because of her spiritual mentorship. And on that ship I sail through the oceans of tears called the world. Through this message, I express my deepest possible love to my Ma. Love them, friends, because the time passes by so fast . . . [and then] you realize it's too late.

His hymns were dipped in the love he shared with his mother. He reflected not only on the fertile internal fields nurtured by divine love that took the form of maternal love but also went on to speak about arid internal wastelands:

Friends, Luke 11:24 says, "When an evil spirit comes out of a person, it goes through dry places looking for a place to rest." Please note that this statement was delivered by Jesus himself. It is very important for us to have a deep thinking on it. In one of the translations, it says, "Evil spirits finds waterless places to rest when they come out of a person!" Now I am coming to the statement that our Lord has given. Lord said, "When evil spirit comes out, it finds place of rest in waterless or dry places." What are the dry places? My dear friends, when we struggle in this world, when we sometimes do not get justice, when we are humiliated or hit by incurable sickness, when stung by family disputes, we face [the] pain of the loss of our dear ones, when our hopes are shattered, our hearts get dry. Our life becomes dry. We do not like to pray, read the Word, worship the Lord. If this process is continued for a longer time, we become dry. Remember, evil spirits are in search of dry, waterless places. We need to be watered always, for the Lord has said, "I am the living water." I have heard hundreds of prayers by many when they cast out demons. They command: "I command you to go to pitiless well." Now, [the] Bible does not teach so, and [the] ignorant crowd shouts, "Hallelujah!" Be careful! Evil spirits and demons are not cast out yet! They remain! According to Revelations 20:3, they shall be cast out after the church is raptured! Remember, if you lead a dry life, you are the first target of evil spirits. They are hunting for you, to make you a mental patient, a frustrated person, [a] depressed being. I invite you today once again to come to the fountain of life, which never dries up. Isaiah 35:6 says, "Our lives may be for a short while like a rose but yet God wants to water us with heavenly dew drops."

He was expressing the notion that closeness with God could change the way we looked at our life experiences. Amidst all the disputes, pain, and loss we experience, this closeness will allow us to remain calm and avoid nursing evil forces inside us. The emphasis was on being grateful under all conditions and living a thankful life.

SHANU

I first met Shanu at a church in Delhi whose priest insisted on being present during our interviews. I was irritated by this insistence.

Shanu was a pretty girl. I recall her big sparkling eyes that danced even more as she spoke. When I met her, she was twenty-seven years old. After I explained my purpose to her, she promptly began describing peculiar facets of her experience with possession:

> S: Now, what should I tell you? I have suffered a great deal. I thank the Lord Almighty. I am alive today because of the Priest Uncle (gestures toward the priest behind us, a suspicious witness to our conversations). He brought me closer to God. I was wandering here and there like a lost sheep. I went to consult many healers, tantrics, shamans, Balaji. But, in the end, I found peace here.

It became clear immediately that she prioritized enhancing the church's (and the priest's) glory over talking about herself. I wondered if this was a theme in her life—to put the narcissistic needs of others before her own:

> S: Those other healers made me do bizarre things in the name of healing. For example, they would ask me to take a bath at the crossroads at midnight. This ghost has eaten up all our money. We had to sell our assets and take many loans. This ghost destroyed us completely.

I sensed she was bypassing the experience of her possession and substituting it with an account of the loss her family had had to face due to her condition. It was almost as if her suffering had more to do with the various bizarre healing attempts and with financial losses than it did with the spirits that possessed her. I decided to bring the possessing entities into focus.

> Me: What was this ghost? Who was it?
>
> S: There were two entities, a woman and a man. The man used to make the woman work. He would command the woman to pester me and my mother.

I could tell by her tone that she was trying to lay emphasis on the ghost pestering her mother. I wondered if somehow the mother was being made to compensate for some lack in Shanu's internal world. This thought created a tension in me that I felt driven to metabolize. I became curious about the origins of these ghosts. Where were the cemeteries and cremation grounds of Shanu's internal world?

Me: Where did these ghosts come from?

S: Just on their own. My limbs used to ache a lot. I was not able to do any work, my head would hurt, [my] body would feel heavy. Then we went to various tantric healers and shamans. My younger sister introduced us to someone who brought us to this church. Ever since we started coming here, I have been feeling better. Our heartfelt gratitude goes to the Lord Almighty, for now I am absolutely fine. I do not suffer from any aches and pains. I love the Almighty a lot—He cured me!

She did not seem to want to stay with her pain. In fact, the segue into her feelings of gratitude and reverence toward "the Almighty" felt too abrupt, premature and dramatized. This moment hinted at the difficulties Shanu experienced in engaging with emotional pain while living it out in narration. Instead, she had taken a quick turn toward glorifying those responsible for her healing. She was experiencing God as someone whose glorification, uplift-ment, and enhancement her life had to be dedicated to.

The priest joined in this glorification and immediately began to enlighten me with *his* account of her healing. According to him, the spirits possessing her were so powerful that at least five men had to hold her down and subdue her to keep her from hurting herself and others. The battle between good and evil went on for a long time, during which the priest had his hands on her head and, along with other members of the church, prayed insistently until the possessing spirits gave up and left her body. She was then advised to remain firm in her belief and pray consistently, filling the void left after her exorcism with the presence of Christ in her. That was the only way she could stop the evil spirits from returning to inhabit her body again.

As is no doubt clear, Shanu became a firm believer in Christ. As soon as she adopted Christ as her savior, her life changed. She felt less tense, and, whenever she did feel tense, all she had to do was pray. She now had faith that all her worries would be taken care of. Her account of the glory of her triumph over misery resembled more closely a testimony to God's grace than it did a narration of how she personally experienced her possession and subsequent healing. After some time, I began to feel like Shanu and the priest were together trying to inspire faith in *me*.

I was left wondering what exactly her gratitude was driven by. What had she lived out in her possession, what had she wished to emerge from? What was that state from which her emergence was facilitated by the priest?

In our next conversation, Shanu told me that she was not keeping well. The ache in her body was still there; the residue of her possession illness remained after all. There were still some painful psychic states in her that manifested in the form of painful somatic symptoms. It made me sad that what should have been a deep processing of painful life experiences was being compromised and short-circuited by the wholesale and premature replacement of that process with belief in God. I was witnessing here the absence of the sensitivity that allowed for a state to be inhabited so that one could live one's mess before one experienced the emergence of an enlivening faith. Shanu's capacity to process emotional content was impaired and this impairment was only being reinforced by the church and the beliefs it was foisting on her.

Why were these capacities impaired? I hoped to find some lack in her early experiences that explained her inability to contain psychic states. How was her life before possession?

> S: I used to work. One day, suddenly, my entire body started to ache. It began to hurt everywhere. I ignored it. For a long time, I thought it was due to fatigue. My limbs would ache and contort on their own. How can I describe all the things I used to do? I used to pull my hair, hit my head hard on the walls, my limbs would often be swollen and many quacks have made me do many things in the name of healing. Even then, these evil spirits kept coming.

> Me: Coming from where?

> S: We rented a flat that was haunted. Nobody told us about it. Later, someone told us that there had been many deaths in that house. The ghosts of a mother and her son haunted that house. Whenever I used the bathroom at night, I felt as if someone was watching me, that someone was stalking me.

I was intrigued by the idea of mother–son ghosts haunting her house and later possessing her—an enchanting and exciting dyad. I was curious about how she carried her own mother and brother in her mind.

> S: After she possessed me, I would rarely be conscious. That entity would talk too much, abuse my mother, disturb everyone in the house, [she]would threaten to never leave me that she would take me along. I would often tear my clothes off in public. Once I set the house on fire, stabbed myself, and once I tried jumping from the roof.

I wondered if the close (or closed) bond between her mother and brother evoked murderous rage in her that she turned against herself, probably because her rage was toward a mother she also needed. But the entire family, especially the mother, was also being made to face the brunt of this rage.

> S: My mummy and elder sister grabbed me, they took me to many healers. We were searching for a miracle. Once, I was in a dazed state and trying to jump off a train. My younger brother asked my mom where I was and they went

searching for me. They found me on the last step of the staircase of the train. I was about to jump off. Mummy grabbed me quickly. From then onwards, my mother and brother took turns sleeping—one would sleep and the other would stand guard to make sure I didn't venture out again. They would not leave me alone.

She had mentioned that her initial perceptions of being watched had occurred whenever she would use the bathroom at night. To my psycho-analytic ear, it sounded rather interesting that the state of possession was set off by the body's need to urinate. There was movement here from soma to psyche. Urination is a more frequent, uninhibited, and natural burst than orgasm. The orgasm (even multiple orgasms) is a stimulated pleasure, while urinating is a regular and natural pleasure that provides comfort and content-ment to the body. In terms of the dynamism of unconscious processes, it was perhaps at this time that she was most vulnerable to her own sexual desires, which were unacceptable to her. The spirit entered exactly when she was urinating. It is as if the opening-up of her bodily orifice stirred a correspond-ing psychical loosening and opening up of forbidden desires; both functions of not holding oneself back. Yet again the triad (mother–daughter–brother) appeared, perhaps evoking excitement and rage. The wish was not so much to die but to disturb the peacefully sleeping mother–son dyad, to occupy their minds much like spirits possess bodies and to barge into the space between the mother and her son, driving them to invest all their energies into taking care of her.

S: One time we were travelling in [a] train to the famous temple of Shirdi. It is said about this temple that Sai Baba resides in it. Even in the train, the entities possessing me were making their presence felt. They said things like "she will not get cured here," "she will die" and "she has to live in this world and suffer." The healers have really harassed me in the name of healing. One tantric was making sexual advances toward me. I called my mother and she straightened him out, but my grandmother favored that tantric. She would often fight with mummy and say, "You don't have any idea what kinds of spirits your daughter is taming. It would be better if she died." We lost a lot of money in the process of healing me, and our relatives also refused to help us. Mummy was very dis-turbed. She would often [break down] crying. We also went to Balaji, where a healer twisted my little finger for some reason. We stayed there for six months but there was no change. My mother-in-law also distanced my husband from me out of fear that my spirits would somehow possess him. She does not have a human heart. When we returned from Balaji, the spirits taunted and teased Mummy because even Balaji could not cure me. I used to verbally abuse Mummy—kick her, spit on her, punch her, pull her hair . . .

The mother had to not only take care of Shanu but also endure exploitation by various healers, Shanu's grandmother, relatives, mother-in-law, and husband. For as long as Shanu remained possessed, the mother was protecting Shanu from being exploited by her fears and desires. She was bravely bearing the brunt of Shanu's rage, which was manifesting in the form of different kinds of abuse, as described above—including physical attacks. It seemed as if, through these destructive attacks, Shanu was trying to extract something of and from the mother—her capacity to contain Shanu's hostility and anxieties around sexuality, perhaps? My own sense was that she was employing possession to make up for some elementary lack in her personal history.

Shanu's father had been working and residing in another city for many years. She spoke fondly of him: "Papa is very nice. He understands. But Mummy is also nice. Mummy has really handled me and taken care of me."

Her father was away and not a major part of Shanu's healing. The few efforts he made were unsuccessful. To me it seemed as if the father's intervention was not being sought. The mother's presence and endurance were crucial to the healing process. As Shanu put it, "Mummy has endured the most."

Her bringing the parental couple into our discourse made me curious about the parental couple in her internal world and the relationship between that unit and the two spirits that possessed her. I guided our conversation inward again.

Me: How many entities possessed you?

S: Two. One was a man and the other was a woman. The man would goad the woman, ask her to make me suffer. If she refused, he would beat her. She once told my mummy about this. Then Mummy said to her . . . "You, being a spirit yourself, are scared of another spirit?"

Me: And where did they come from?

S: I was returning from work when I accidentally stepped on an amulet carrying black magic (*totka*). Before all this, I used to be happy-go-lucky. All I was worried about was food and fun. I used to think that, if we have this one life, we should live it to the fullest by squeezing all the juice out of it. But ever since I became possessed, I have not been in my senses. I put on a lot of weight. The spirits possessing me were gluttonous. They would ask Mummy to cook and feed them delicacies.

The gluttony and envy of her evil spirits hinted at her unconscious greedy and envious parts, focused on extracting all nourishment from the mother while at the same time defiling her through verbal and physical attacks. I wondered if the mother had to be attacked because she was also desperately needed.

I had to probe further to get to the roots of the envy that I sensed in her. Her shock at her own gluttony and rage pointed toward the potential use of dissociation by the ego to get rid of unacceptable states. Owing to our limited capacity to process them, such states remain unthinkable agonies (Winnicott, 1971) and are evacuated in the body (Bion, 1976). Refuge in belief in Christ had been chosen by Shanu over the painful process of thinking.

S: After I sought refuge in Christ, I kept getting better (speaks elatedly). My younger sister introduced us to some believers. They once came to our house to pray. As they started singing hymns, the spirits possessed me. I shut my ears. One of the believers held and twisted my ears and said to the spirits, "You will not leave her? Leave her now!" My ear hurt for days. Then we started going to church. The priest at once knew that there were two spirits possessing me. During praise and worship, the evil spirits would really become restless. They would shut my ears. Later, my ears would hurt a lot. I have fallen unconscious on multiple occasions in that church. Many people from the congregation have held me. I was not left alone until I was completely healed. It has now been many days since we last went to church. Sometimes, when Satan takes over, I am unable to go to the church.

Although the painful process of thinking had been avoided, choosing to believe in the grace of God allowed Shanu to receive love from many people. She was elated to share that the whole church, like one big family, was invested in her and had come together to help her heal.

I wondered if and how her needs were met in her marriage.

Me: Did the evil spirits possess you before or after your marriage?

S: It began before marriage. Mummy met some healer who suggested marriage as a way of getting cured of possession. Mummy got me married in a rush. She must have been desperate for my well-being. For the first month after marriage, there were no aches and pains. I used to perform all the chores.

Perhaps the healer intuited that Shanu's distress had to do with unacceptable erotic desires. Marriage and love, providing as they do opportunities for the expression of one's sexuality, would have created a space in which her desires could be lived out and she could be cured. However, her aches and pains returned. There were still some dissociated parts of her causing her to feel scared.

S: But soon the pain returned. I used to feel scared of myself—that there is something inside me. I used to feel terrified, anxious. I used to feel like I was being watched all the time. Light also terrified me. I used to feel that, if I fell asleep, someone would pull my legs off me and take them away. I was too scared to even shut my eyes. Mummy had to assure me that she was awake and near me so that I could sleep. Only then could I sleep.

Even within her marriage, she was disillusioned to find a close(d) dyad between her husband and his mother.

S: I had an arranged marriage. [My] husband was not really supportive. I had many hopes from him, but he was more keen on listening to his mother. Even now, he listens to her more.

Another triad, this time comprising Shanu, her mother-in-law and husband.

S: I am wrong in their eyes because I am unable to carry out household chores efficiently. My mother-in-law used to feel bad that I would be resting when her son returned from office and he had to help himself to food. She used to provoke him as well. We would end up fighting. He should have fought for me.

The husband seemed to lack a spine and a mind of his own supported by that spine. Shanu expected a close bond with him but could not create one because this wish was pitted against the closed bond that the husband shared with his mother, from which Shanu was excluded. She was urging the husband to fight for her, to ally with her against the mother-in-law, just as her possessing spirits had allied with her against her own mother.

Me: You wanted him to protect you?

S: Yes. I used to feel very angry, and in anger I would often not feel like doing anything in the house.

In this admission, the unconscious reason behind her inability to work in the house, one of her symptoms, was made clearer. It was pain caused by her exclusion from the mother–son dyad, the unreliability of her husband and her consequent anger that led her to not work.

S: Now I have been at my mother's place for so long [but] my husband does not seem too bothered. He does not need me. If he did, he would have called me and asked me when I would return.

Her admission of anger gave way to sadness over not being loved and invested in by the husband. She was unwanted because the mother–son dyad was too tightly shut for her to enter and dismantle it. Perhaps she wanted to possess the object of her love exclusively for herself. In a twisted way, possession allowed her to receive her mother's care and in turn possess the mother exclusively for herself. By becoming possessed, she moved out of the vulnerable state of not being wanted or desired toward closeness with her mother, who wanted her and showered her with love and care, the essential juices for one's narcissism. It was perhaps these necessities—love, warmth, and containment—that were missing from her history and being compensated for via possession.

> S: On the other end is my mother, who says that I can stay with her for as long as I want, that I should not worry about anything, that nobody is asking me to leave or go back. This is the difference between one's own mother and mother-in-law. No matter how much they try to treat us like daughters, for us daughters-in-law the rules change. There is a huge gap between saying and doing.

Her making this point about the difference between her mother and other mothers made me wonder—was this difference not perceptible to her earlier? The growing keenness of this perception in Shanu seemed to me evocative of Matte-Blanco's (1988) contention that thinking becomes increasingly asymmetrical as one moves from the unconscious to consciousness.

> Me: And with one's own mother, one can become and remain a child—not handling the chores and the house, just being at rest.

> S: (excitedly)You are right! At my mother's place, I feel I have become a little girl again. When I was a child, Mummy used to beat me a lot, but now she loves me a lot. I feel that, amongst all the siblings, she loves me the most!

At this moment in our conversation, she became as playful and excited as a child. It was the right moment to smoothly venture into her childhood.

> Me: What about when you were little?

> S: I used to be very mischievous as a child. I would eat [the] lunches of other kids in the school. Often, the school authorities would complain to Mummy about me.

Listening to her, I wondered if, in possession, she was still that gluttonous, mischievous, sneaky little devil—in other words, whether possession was a way for her to stage a repetition of or regression into childhood patterns. What became of the mischievous, gluttonous parts of her?

> S: Mummy would get fed up [with] me and beat me a lot. I cannot even tell you how much she used to beat me. On many occasions, she would beat me even when I was not at fault. My grandmother (maternal) would tell her that I was not at fault every time, that she should find out the whole story before hitting me. And I used to be scared of Papa, but he was loving.

The mother failed to perform her containing function when, each time she was confronted with Shanu's defiance and gluttony, she responded with physical beatings. She did not know what to do with these parts of Shanu. One could even say that the mother did not know how to be a mother.

Much later, I was able to better understand this failing on the mother's part, when she spoke to me about the frustrations she experienced because of having to raise her children on her own because her husband was working elsewhere and only providing the finances with which to run the family. Shanu's defiant parts, emanating from her deep wish to remain close to her mother, were the parts thwarted by the mother, who, driven by her assumptions, punished Shanu for mischief she had not committed.

According to Bollas (1987), the premature assumption by the parent that the child is not experiencing a particular psychic state interferes with development of the child's sense of self—"for example, prematurely scolding a child for dropping a glass of milk assuming that he/she isn't feeling sorry already . . . In such scenarios, one is robbed of the moments of guilt, reproachment, reparation and creativity." Perhaps Shanu's mother, by prematurely assuming that Shanu was wrong and punishing her, robbed her of the important experiences of guilt and reparation, the implications of which we come across in her scooping out nurturance from the mother during her possession while remaining out of touch with the "guilt" or remorse around the destruction she was causing. Even while it was narrated to me, it came across as something the family had to accept and go through.

The envious and gluttonous parts of Shanu and the frustrations accompanying them were projected into the images of the evil spirits and were lived out or somewhat tamed in possession. By repeating a relational dynamic from her past (made possible by her possession), Shanu not only enabled her mother to contain her states without resorting to physical beatings but also unconsciously staged what Kohut termed "a corrective emotional" experience for herself. While she was possessed, she could repeatedly destroy her mother until out of this destruction emerged a sense of gratitude toward her mother.

Having learnt her lessons through the beatings she was made to endure by those parts in Shanu that both she and Shanu herself regarded as "evil," the mother now loved her daughter, with all her virtues and vices. Possession gave Shanu a chance to become a daughter and her mother a chance to become a mother.

Having touched on the themes of gratitude and love for the mother, Shanu began to feel freer in our conversations and started referring to other parts of herself without any shame.

S: I have an elder sister. Whenever she visits us, we sit down and chat for hours. We tend to lose track of time, and my younger sister feels jealous and complains to Mummy (giggles).

She had created a closed unit with her elder sister that made their younger sister feel excluded and envious, much like Shanu herself had. She was making her younger sister feel what she had secretly felt—a secret internal script was being staged externally, in the theatre of the relational dynamics shared by the three sisters. The evil spirit of envy now lay deposited in the younger sister.

Me: Listening to you, it seems like you actually enjoy making her jealous.

I was encouraging her to relish the excitement that her wicked parts made possible.

S: Of course! I enjoy teasing her.

Our conversation ended with her expressing her gratitude to me.

S: All this while I felt I was talking to a person close to me. Thank you! Please carry me in your prayers.

I was moved by her gratitude. All she craved was a sense of togetherness, which I had been able to provide her with. Perhaps this desire to come close to the other also brought about a confrontation with her own intense and terrifying needs, which she had defended herself against by retreating into suspicion and withdrawal.

When I tried to get in touch with her again, she did not answer my calls. Soon, she changed her number. Perhaps she felt that withdrawing from the good that she had deposited in the space we co-created even while we were cohabiting it was the only way to preserve the good. Who knows? The researcher in me must suffer not knowing what became of her because I have to respect her need for distance.

Winnicott (1971) informs us that the distance between the child and the mother increases with the arrival of a sibling, bringing on an awareness of the child's externality too early and too harshly for the still-nascent ego. He described the process whereby we first begin to relate to an object by recognizing its externality, its being different from the self and a potential object, to be loved and used: "This moment marks a kind of rebirth for the subject in the recognition of the object's reality." Through the object's survival of the destruction done to it emerges what Winnicott calls "the capacity for concern." Shanu's self seemed stuck somewhere between object-relating and object usage. The problems of narcissism, possessiveness and wanting one's object exclusively for oneself are markers of a failure in the transition from object-relating to object usage. The knowledge of the object's externality is strongly repelled; omnipotent defensive measures are devised to deny all gaps. The possessed Shanu beat her mother, trance-formed into a queen and demanded adulation. For the first time in her life, she found a space—the space of possession—where things could be set right. She could enjoy the illusion of omnipotence that had remained absent in her developmental phase.

This "setting things right" required her to regress back to the state of being a gluttonous infant, gnawing away at the nourishment (lunches during child-hood and food during possession) meant for others, getting even with the punishing mother, pushing the latter to the limits of care and affection she was capable of bestowing upon Shanu. History was being repeated, except that, this time, Shanu was not receiving any impingements from her environ-ment; rather, she was enjoying the power the evil spirits afforded her. In pos-session, her possessiveness was defended, remained disguised and became culturally meaningful. She controlled the outcomes and held the strings to her puppet-objects. Her need for love and recognition was perversely addressed. Her defiance is like the "string" used as a denial of separation from the object. The need for closeness with the mother was satisfied, albeit in a twisted way.

In reversal, one can say that the construction of twisted methods of express-ing and satisfying her needs pointed to Shanu's belief that this was the only way for her to have her needs understood or contained, that the fit between her desires and her inadequately present mother was an imperfect one, that her mother's disturbed "maternal reverie" (Bion, 1962) caused the destructive states to remain uncontained and unintegrated. In the words of Auchincloss (1988), "A subject whose access to the transitional space of inner reality is limited or distorted is forced to use the outside world as a kind of 'transitional stage,' is unable to stage their drama using ideas and words. Their dramas must be externalized in order to be enacted as they are radically affected by primitive object relations and are unable to sufficiently contain and symbolize their psychic scripts."

Despite (or because of) being repeatedly damaged by the possessed Shanu, her mother emerged as a differently perceived object. It was in this shift, the shift in how she looked at and appreciated her objects, that I got a tiny taste of the beauty in Shanu's horrifying experience of possession. Shanu's intoler-ance with triadic equations emerged often and pointed to her possessiveness and her deep discomfort with imagining herself as not-invested-in by others. She was possessed by a mother–son or male–female dyad. The relationship between the parental couple was a strained one. Shanu's father was a quiet and authoritative presence, while her mother remained frustrated and angry, thwarting a fuller unfolding of affects in Shanu. Her father had been absent from the house for the most part and was still working in another city when I began my conversations with Shanu. Shanu's mischief provided her mother an opportunity to perform her own projective evacuations.

I think the mother's preference for her son over Shanu was linked to her hope that he would grow up to earn and share some of her burden. Shanu's possession by a male who never surfaced and a female spirit who wreaked havoc seemed like a transformation of a peculiar equation operating in her actual life—Shanu's absent father calling the shots from the background by providing financial help alone and her frustrated mother at the forefront, shouldering the burdens of the family. The psychosocial matrix laid down for Shanu established the presence of the parental couple as an imbalanced and threatening one. The internal relationship of the parental couple—absent father, frustrating and frustrated mother—imparted a sadomasochistic texture to the equation the two possessing spirits shared, one (male) being a torturer and the other (female) the tortured. This dyad of torturing and tortured spirits made life difficult for the mother.

With limited information, it becomes imperative that we fall back on thinkers to make sense of the kind of Christian healing that Shanu experienced. In the violence (psychological and/or physical) of exorcism, the healer partially joins the striving self of the victim to exorcise the unconscious of its bad possessing objects and, on another level, to gratify the victim's guilt over betraying these internal objects. The healer is made to play a passive role in one's inner drama, while the possessed person has undergone a transformation in status, from being a passive subject (possessed by objects or "done to") to a ferocious, active-possessed person (possessing the other(s) or "the doer").

The relationship between the two spirits was sadomasochistic in nature. The psyche seemed to have masochistically given in but needed evacuation to be able to feel whole and alive. This is where cultural processes became crucial. Firstly, cultural processes made available a language for the representation of that which haunted. Going by Winnicott's theory, reparation can be described as "the environment meeting the infant's experience of omnipotence; allowing itself to be created by the infant as in the area of transitional object and phenomenon, and allowing the infant to make his own contribution toward his caretaking environment" (Khan, 2018). In other words, Khan highlights the capacity for reparation and creativity in utilizing one's environment for growth or evolution, however primitive this evolution may seem to a psychologist's eyes. "Spirit" as a container made available by one's culture comes to bear the label of "evil spirit" when one deposits one's destructive impulses in it. In possession, these very projections are identified with, lived out and, to an extent, tamed in the form of a ghost or *bhuta*.

Although the ritual of exorcism can be understood in innumerable ways, for the purpose of discussion here, I wish to elaborate upon the experience of exorcism as the equivalent of the transitional experience. "The reputation about a renowned healer precedes the healing" (Kakar, 1982). This knowledge about the healer makes way for faith in the existence of someone out there who can prove to be a reliable object, faith in the possibility of a much awaited and needed transitional experience. In an altered state of consciousness, one can break free from the familiar (and familial) and allow an expected entity to enter, or, rather, one is able to possess an unexpected yet somewhat known entity.

From a Christian believer, Shanu heard wonderful testimonies of miraculous healing. I have tried to understand Shanu's healing based on my own experience as a Christian from a family of healers and on my understanding of the link Hopkins (2021) made between Winnicott's ideas and the resurrection of Christ. Hopkins viewed the core of Christian preaching as lying in the passion and death of Christ. For a Christian, Jesus represents patience, kindness, and healing. In his betrayal, crucifixion, death and resurrection, Hopkins (2021) saw an analogy for the destruction of a transitional object and its survival. This basic doctrine of Christianity is conveyed in numerous ways to a victim, through sermons or hymns or the reading of scripture before she is brought for healing. It fits with the possessed person's need for an object in whom she finds it possible to deposit her distress and who will then survive the destruction and yet embrace her, with all her evil, thus transforming the distress and returning it to the possessed person in a somewhat altered form. As Hopkins (2021) put it, "Christ, the healer and now the transitional object, is always surviving, always not retaliating against those who destroy him, he is always waiting and accepting the seeker. He is crucified and resurrects. In other words, he is the embodiment of 'object-constancy,' of trust and love."

Through the lens of self-psychology, Christ can be seen as a cultural self-object. He caters to the need to be "accepted and mirrored":

> There has to be the gleam in some mother's eye which says it is good you are here and I acknowledge your being here and I am uplifted by your presence. There is also the other need: to have somebody strong and knowledgeable and calm around, with whom I can temporarily merge, who will uplift my spirits when I am in despair. Originally, that is an actual uplifting of the baby by the mother, later that becomes an uplifting feeling of looking at a great man or woman and enjoying him or her or following in his/her footsteps. (Kohut, 2009)

In Christian exorcism, a fuller emergence of possession state is suppressed, as opposed to what I observed at the Balaji temple. It is marked by violent protest in the form of the possessed person's angry screams coupled with the exorcist's angry devaluation, the exorcist's determination to cast the demons out and imprint the name of Christ the savior on the possessed person. The violence with which the ritual was carried out indicated that the church was reinforcing its foundational deontological split—between good and evil—in Shanu. Unlike a therapist who creates space for the destructive to emerge into the clinical space, in the Christian healing scenario the destructive is neither encouraged to come forth in its full vitality nor engaged with. The emphasis is on replacing it with the divine force. A fuller living out of one's destructive dissociated impulses is compromised in service of establishing too soon a close alliance with Christ, the perfect object. Engagement with one's deep destructive wishes is replaced with the sublimation of the wishes in the process of serving others.

Today, Shanu is healed but her body still aches sometimes. She is actively associated with the church and its many activities, perhaps in the hope that, by serving the Lord, her deep needs for love and containment will be met, the injuries of the past will be gradually soothed. Her relationships with her husband and mother-in-law cause her a lot of pain, and she mostly stays at her mother's place. Her mother welcomes any opportunity to take care of her. Shanu possesses her mother exclusively for herself alone. Furthermore, she has found an extended family among the church members—her enthusiasm about this discovery was hard to ignore. It radiated through her intense and alive willingness to volunteer in the church's activities and serve the Lord— the one who is forever surviving her destruction of Him.

NOTES

1. *Bhaiya* means "elder brother" in Hindi. It is a way of addressing a male person who may or may not be directly related to you.
2. *Mama* means "maternal uncle" in Hindi.
3. *Dadaji* means "grandfather" in Hindi.

Chapter 3

Engaging with Lives—
Loosening the Grip of Terror

DEVI

This essay uses a psychoanalytic lens to reflect on *Devi*, a masterpiece by the eminent Indian filmmaker Satyajit Ray. The film is based on a short story that bears the same title, written by Prabhat Kumar Mukherji.

Broadly, the plot of the film revolves around the female protagonist, Daya,[1] who is a dutiful daughter-in-law, deeply adored by her father-in-law, Kalikinker. Daya is unfailing in the care she extends to everyone. She is also immensely loved by her little nephew, Khokha. Daya's husband, Uma, is a scientist. Uma's character is a stark contrast to that of his father Kalikinker, who is ardently religious and a devotee of the goddesses Kali, who is regarded as a manifestation of the divine feminine (or "devi"). It is worth noting that the film is set in rural Bengal in the year 1860, which has come to be remembered as the Bengal Renaissance, marked by rapid, radical transformation, and advancements in the spheres of education, art, science, and so on. This serves as a pertinent backdrop to the film's depiction of the tension between tradition and modernity, which plays out through the course of the film in the relationship between Kalikinker and Uma.

The film opens with an image of the face of an idol of Durga. The idol is merely a mold—other than its shape, the face has no distinguishing features. Slowly, this face begins to come alive, as it were, acquiring definition and detail. It comes to be adorned with jewels, and a third eye appears in the center of the forehead. These opening images bring to my mind Winnicott's (1991) insight into what happens when a baby sees the mother—the baby actually sees itself. As the Devi came into being before me, I found the process triggering in me a curiosity about idealization. The view slowly zooms

49

out, and the Devi's face slowly becomes a part of her body. I wonder if this is a pictorial depiction of arriving at the realization that the mother is, in fact, some body.

A beggar and a small boy are sitting outside a temple, singing a hymn for the goddess:

> *I won't call you "Mother" anymore,*
> *You have given me, you have helped me,*
> *You're the light of my path.*
> *I won't call you "Mother" anymore.*
> *I call out to you repeatedly, Mother, Mother!*
> *Have you remained a mother?*
> *You've become my eye,*
> *Guiding me through.*
> *I call out to you repeatedly, Mother, Mother!*
> *Have you remained a mother?*
> *You've become my eye*
> *Provided me with knowledge.*
> *Mother, listen to the pleas of your son*
> *Can a son survive if his mother dies?*
> *I won't call you . . .*
> *I'll go from house to house and beg for food,*
> *I won't come to take shelter in your arms.*
> *I won't call you . . .*

This hymn seems to describe that crucial stage in transitional phenomenon (Winnicott, 1953) when the child is allowed the illusion that it controls the breast. The child's transitional calls, like this hymn, make the breast appear. The child experiences the relationship with the breast as one of inseparability.

It is revealed that the temple is part of Kalikinker's mansion. I step inside Daya's marital home. I am greeted by the visual signs of tradition, represented by idols of Hindu gods and goddesses. My ears ring with the sounds of chants, mantras, chimes, and gongs. High ceilings, wide windows, and spacious rooms in this mansion hint at Kalikinker's affluence—there seems to be enough space for everyone to breathe. I discovered that Uma and Daya are a married couple. Uma is leaving home to pursue higher education. Daya playfully tries to convince him not to leave, arguing that there is no reason for him to educate himself further, as his affluence can get him everything he needs. Uma, however, tries to convince Daya of his love for knowledge. On being asked if she would accompany him, Daya spontaneously agrees but this desire is soon tempered by her sense of duty and worry.

Daya: What if Father [-in-law] does not agree? He won't be able to live without me.'

Uma: Assume that I have convinced Father, then?

Daya: (after a long silence) How will Khokha manage without me?

It seems *Daya's* inner world is shaped by her relational ties to others. When she tries to give in to her spontaneity, she is threatened and held back by an awareness of her duties as an aunt and a daughter-in-law. She believes that the father-in-law's and nephew's lives revolve around her. She is intensely emotionally invested by them; she represents a perfect identificatory fit with their projections. In one scene, Kalikinkar asks Daya if she is unhappy with the burden of managing the house and taking care of everyone. To a psychoanalytic mind, Kalikinker seems like a baby wondering if the mother resents being endlessly consumed from. Although Daya maintains a respectful silence, in the very next scene she responds to her pet parrot's relentless calls—"Mother! Mother!"—in a playful but revealing manner: "Should I be paying attention to you all the time? As if I don't have anything else to do. Don't call out to me when I'm at work. Understood?"

Daya's unconscious resentment toward Kalikinker finds a release in her spontaneous, albeit teasing, response to the parrot. One wonders if she secretly wishes to break away from the roles that bind her and embrace her own desires more fully.

In a crucial sequence, Daya is shown sitting near Kalikinker's feet at the latter's bedtime, massaging his legs with hot oil. In Indian culture, especially during the era that this film is concerned with, it was considered a daughter(-in-law)'s duty to massage the feet of her elders. Touching the feet of elders is even today considered a gesture of respect toward them in India. "Care" remains incomplete without this gesture. However, a psychoanalytic mind wonders about the sexual and sensual undertones of this maternal gesture, which seems intricately tied to the narcissistic needs of young women. As Daya tends to his aching limbs, Kalikinker expresses his deep gratitude toward her. We discover that he once suffered from excruciating pain in his legs. Daya's care delivered him from the pain, enabling him to stand and walk without any support.

Five years back, when I was not able to walk without a stick, had Mother Goddess not been there, I would not have been able to return to this state. I thought that going to the pilgrimage would be a good idea. But that was not to happen. You came into this house. The house lit up. Then the desire for pilgrimage died down. In this old age, when I have got a mother like you, she of course is the Mother Goddess. She can make the impossible possible.

The similarities between his feelings for Daya and the Devi are hard to miss. However, Daya is a human-mother and cannot be controlled by the infant-Kalikinker. His fear closely follows his desire for closeness with her.

Kalikinker: I'm concerned about your husband. Nowadays, it is not easy to handle such a fast-paced boy. You are the only one who can control him. He listens to whatever you say. Does he? Does he write letters to you regularly? Or does he skip that too? Does he write letters every day?!

Daya gets up and leaves out of shyness and the discomfort that is caused by these attacks on the erotic part of her life. Daya is revered by Kalikinker but at the cost of her own personhood. While seated near his feet, she was psychologically exalted to the status of a Devi. Further, it is as if, in Kalikinker's world, the mother is not allowed to be a woman with desire. She is to be idealized and possessed. A desirous mother is a person in her own right. To grant her subjecthood is to risk losing possession of her. Caught in an Oedipal struggle with his son, Kalikinker possesses Daya. She cannot be *like* the mother. She must *be* the mother. Kalikinker appears to be the Winnicottian child, who has experienced a failure in the transition from "me" to "not-me" (Winnicott, 1953).

Daya turns to her nephew, Khokha, who refuses to sleep. Consumed by household chores, Khokha's own mother is unavailable. Disappointed, Khokha reaches out to his substitute mother, Daya. Driven by his hostility toward his own mother, Khokha startles Daya as soon as she enters the room—" Boo!" The need to evoke shock on the mother's face is twofold: it is clear evidence that he has been seen and is also an act of revenge against the unavailable mother. A playful exchange between the aunt and nephew follows:

Daya: What if I had died of shock?

Khokha: Then it would've been very nice.

Daya: It would've been nice? Then how would you listen to stories?

Khokha: Mother.

Daya: And who would have applied kohl to your eyes?

Khokha: Mother.

Daya: And who would've fed you?

Khokha: Mother.

Daya: Then go and sleep with your mother. Why have you come here?

Khokha: Tell me a story.

Daya: What story?

Khokha: The story of a demoness.

Daya: Which demoness?

Khokha: The one that savors the flesh of small children.

Momentarily disoriented, Daya recovers by reminding Khokha of the many ways in which she cares. Khokha remains steadfast in the expression of his anger. He needs Daya because, like a fairytale, she facilitates his entry into the world of fantasies, of deities, and of demonesses. Daya's refusal to allow herself to be transformed into a nobody (or a ghost?) helps restore balance in their relationship.

Khokha's choice of story—the one about the demoness who savors the flesh of small children—is a reflection of his own demoniac need to consume the (m)other projected in the image of the mother-turned-bloodthirsty-demoness. His internal horror is contained in and by the story—an external manifestation he needs to sleep and dream peacefully. The mother is split into "good" and "demoness," and preserved as such. In the film, the corresponding self-object split-off parts are also depicted in the characters of Kalikinker and Khokha. While the reverence that informs the mother–infant relationship is depicted in Kalikinker–Daya dyad, the devouring mother and savored self-parts are depicted in Khokha–Daya. Kalikinker and Khokha both deposit a part of their respective selves in Daya and live out those parts through her.

Possessed, Daya ushers them into the worlds of dreams and fantasies. The next sequence suggests that Daya is telling Khokha the story of the demoness at the very same time when, in another part of the house, Kalikinker is dreaming. In his dream, the idol of the Devi appears and slowly transforms into the face of Daya. Kalikinker wakes up from the dream convinced that the dream was a message—Daya is the Devi incarnate.

The film takes a turn after this dream. Kalikinker falls at Daya's feet. Daya is overwhelmed. Her body reacts to Kalikinker's idealization of her. Her toes are shown to curl inwards, expressing the discomfort she feels about stepping into these shoes, i.e., identifying with Kalikinker's projections.

The clay idol in the temple is replaced by a Devi in the flesh. She sits in the temple and weeps silently, confused, and shocked, while her worshippers remain oblivious to her plight. Many pilgrims and seekers are drawn to her, seeking deliverance from various afflictions. A hymn is now sung in her praise. To my ears, it sounds like a song sung by a child savoring his desire to consume the mother:

> *This time, I've recognized you, Mother!*
> *You're on my lips. O Kali!*

You're in my heart, Kali!
You're in the core of my soul, Mother Kali!
The one who's the essence of life,
I believe in her with all my heart,
I know in my heart, in my souls your grace, O Mother!
This time I've recognized you,
In a new form,
In a new incarnation,
Come and see, Mother,
The personification of mercy, the river of love,
There are no bounds to the joy!
This time, I've recognized you . . .

Daya's transformation into Devi demonstrates the violence inherent in reverence. In other words, it depicts idealization and its discontents.

Devi-Daya is isolated from others, even from Khokha. She has a housemaid at her service. When her husband finds out, he argues with his father, demanding evidence of Daya's godliness. Their argument is really about who has rights over Daya. A sick boy's miraculous healing sanctions Kalikinker's belief in Daya's holiness and momentarily shatters Uma's feeble conviction in his modern ideals. He escapes the scene only to return later to convince Daya to elope with him. Daya agrees.

As they reach a riverbank, Daya spots an idol of the Devi lying there, waves washing over it. It bears signs that it was once worshipped with great fervor. Now it lies forgotten. Daya stops in her tracks and wonders, *"What if I am the Goddess?"* The unclaimed idol has stirred her fears of being forgotten. The megalomaniac part of her surfaces, and she leans into the delusion that she might be the Devi incarnate, the one who healed the sick boy. She is not ready to relinquish her godly status. She urges Uma to take her back. Uma capitulates to Daya's fear.

As a result of the miraculous healing encounter, the Goddess has become even more famous, drawing many pilgrims to her. Meanwhile, Uma leaves for college and discusses this development with his teacher, who urges him to save Daya. He decides to return home.

Back at home, Khokha falls severely ill. His mother summons the local doctor, but others force her to submit Khokha to Devi-Daya's divine mercy.

Khokha's mother: Will you be able to cure him? Promise me, dear. Are you a human or a goddess? Tell me, dear. This is about life and death. I don't believe in you. What can I do? I'm not able to believe it. I would not have let them bring him to you. But even in this fever, he's calling out to you, not once, but again and again. I don't know what's true and what's false. But will you be able to cure him? If you don't return him to me, then I cannot snatch him away from you. Will you be able to?

Daya: Let him be with me tonight.

Khokha's mother: Will you return him tomorrow?

Daya cries and nods in affirmation.

Khokha's mother: Don't cry. You're supposed to be a goddess. Don't cry.

Crushed under the anxious mother's expectations, Daya holds Khokha in her lap while the blessed Devi's *charnamrit*, or holy water, is served to him. Khokha's love and fondness for his aunt has become conjoined with the collective delusional belief in her goddess-like power.

The next morning, Uma returns home to find that Devi has abandoned the temple. There are no hymns being sung or chants being recited.

Khokha has died.

Kalikinker is sobbing in front of Devi's idol, grieving Khokha and bemoaning Devi's role in his fate. Uma is shattered. He harshly confronts his father, blaming him for Khokha's death.

Uma then comes upon the grieving parents of Khokha.

Khokha's mother to Uma: That demoness ate my son.

Uma hurries toward Daya's room and as we follow him, we find Daya dressed as a bride, but her hair is disheveled and her makeup is smudged. She appears disoriented, a breathing replica of Devi's abandoned idol on the riverbank. Her internal conflict—whether to be Uma's wife or Kalikinker's mother goddess—is encapsulated in this image of Daya having gone mad.

Now a madwoman, Daya urges Uma to put a necklace on her neck. She is getting ready to elope, afraid that she will be killed.

In the last shot of the film, Daya is seen running away from the house. Her image fades in the mist, symbolizing the loss of her personhood.

DISCUSSION

Ray's film is suffused with the theme of a reverse-oedipal struggle, a struggle between father and son over whom the daughter(-in-law)/wife belongs to. The father seems not to be able to let go of his daughter, and she seems not to be able to let go of him and take her place in her own generation. The son seems to feel he is the main person in his wife's life, which in some ways he is.

Daya possesses the narcissism of the beloved daughter, which is augmented by her additional role as a substitute mother in the family. She is seduced by this. The bodily contact between her and her father-in-law is part of this seduction, though to modern eyes it is a reversal of the usual situation, in which it is the parent who cares for the child, not the child for the parent.

The transformation of Daya into Devi is an idealizing illusion or delusion, which in fact masks or mystifies the conflict between the difficult choices that must be made. Although being idealized appeals to Devi's narcissism, it is in fact the means by which she is controlled by the family and kept from living her own life or even thinking about it in a way that would enable her and her husband to consider what would be best not only for the two of them but for everyone in the family.

When Khokha dies, it is in part because of this idealization of the Devi—a collective fantasy of divine capacity was given preference over calling a doctor. Then the other side of idealization emerges, with the goddess devalued as a demoness. According to Freud (1914), the origin of idealization can be traced to the loss of primary narcissism. The child is disillusioned about his/her own powers and assigns omnipotence to the parents. Later, Klein (1935, 1940) noted that when primitive love and hate fail to be integrated in a child's development, the result is idealization. An early childhood developmental incapacity is later used as a defense against aggression when all good self- and object-representations are preserved through the psychological act of splitting and kept apart from all bad self- and object-representations. I wonder if the film depicts the failure of this splitting. The mother's failure leads to a crack in this splitting, and the good is contaminated with the bad.

This is also reminiscent of Freud's (1913) view of religion as a projection of human needs on fantasized parental figures. It seems that Satyajit Ray was very astute at representing the deep appeal of this fantasy in emotional, sensory and aesthetic terms, showing that he really comprehended how deeply these different pulls of the traditional family are felt—by the parents or father in particular—and the ideas of the more modern, individualized younger generation, interested in education and prepared, if need be, to move away and become separate.

When the young man, Uma, leaves, Daya is alone. But she is soon invested in by Kalikinker. His idealization of her dehumanizes her. Driven by his unmet desires, Kalikinker frantically seeks a maternal presence in Daya. But Daya is conflicted. She is a wife and a loving aunt. Uma, Khokha and Kalikinker are all trying to pull this maternal presence toward themselves. Kalikinker is persistently calling out to the mother but also trying to enter her erotic life. He fears that his fast-paced son, Uma, will take Daya away.

In one scene, Kalikinker savors a sweet delicacy made of milk, prepared, and served by Daya. It seems as if he is letting his whole body go through a sense of exultation, sustaining through the mouth the image of the nursing mother offering the delicacy. In the next frame, he is receiving a hot oil massage from Daya. Such seductive care arouses a need in Kalikinker to bring this mother closer as a nurse, for himself, first and foremost, but also for the rest of the community. Could this be the origin of his narcissistic fantasy? Out of his need and fear, then, emerges his dream—the only way he can possess the mother is by turning Daya into Devi.

Repetition, like worship, allows us to come closer to a subtle aspect of wanting. Wilfred Bion's (1962b) theory posits that our wants begin to produce a thinker, giving us the chance to say, "*There is a space where I can have nurturance freely. I just have to close my eyes and the offering of the goddess will come into me. I can savor it. I have been chosen.*"

Although Kalikinker's own wishes are savored in his dream, he steals from Daya her chance to dream. Perhaps he hoped that she would gradually become ensnared. Here lies the link between narcissism and possessiveness. Faced by a threat in the form of his son's modern thought, Kalikinker clings to his traditionalist thought, represented by religion. The process of using Daya and his religion to establish the correctness of his worldview vis-a-vis his son's, brings forth the erotic element of Kalikinker's self. Psychoanalysis informs us that Eros surfaces when we are in the grip of dread. One may even say that eros weaponizes our dread to defend us against that which is dreaded.

Uma wants Daya to rebel. But Daya is besotted with her own beauty. Daya too wishes to engage with the delusion of being a Devi. This delusional grandiosity is present in *Daya* from the very beginning. With Khokha's death, this delusional grandiosity comes to a brutal end. With the demise of the dehumanized Devi, her flipside, the demoness, now haunts the mansion.

The tragic end of the film should remind us of the difficulty one experiences in one's early years in relating to one's primary object. This difficulty pertains to the experience of the illusion of omnipotence being brutally snatched away when the child fails to function as an extension of the object's narcissism. One falls from grace, into the abyss of insanity. I wonder if, in Winnicottian terms, Daya's breakdown in the end is, perhaps, the breakdown that has already happened (Winnicott, 1974).

BISHAMBER BHAGAT: FRAGMENT OF A CASE

Two years before I met Ravi, I met another *bhagat*: Bishamber. Here I present a fragment of a case of a local healer or *bhagat*, Bishamber, with a view to discussing the kinds of challenges I was brought into confrontation within the field by the unique psychic constellation that these healers carry. The errors I made with Bishamber were instructive, and they proved instrumental in producing the relative ease with which I was able to orient myself toward Ravi.

This brief story of a *bhagat* I met during one of my research trips to the sacred temple of Balaji is based only on two days I spent listening closely to his account of his lived experiences. I believe, since this work is dedicated to spirits, the profundity of the moments that move our spirits in complex ways and toward some internal shifts ought not to be measured by the brevity or longevity of the moments. It is true that one cannot form generalizations based on having spent a few moments trying to understand a lived experience. But even those few moments can help us develop an understanding of the kinds of experiences that are unleashed in possession and how such experiences may lead to subtle or profound transformations in those who avail of this cultural idiom. It is to acquaint myself with what it is possible to experience and to come to terms with the human and the transcendent-within-human in all of us that I have chosen to preserve the voice of Bishamber Bhagat.

Bishamber is a devotee or *bhagat* of Balaji. This boon of *bhagat*-hood was granted to him after the long and painful ordeal of his own patienthood. He was once possessed by four male ghosts. Traversing the terrain of his own possession enabled him to empathize with other possessed persons. According to him, it was because he had gone through the same pain that he was able to understand the pain of the possessed who came to him seeking deliverance from the evil forces that gripped them.

Bishamber was the second son of his parents, who had four sons in all: one older than and two younger than Bishamber He was bullied a lot by all his brothers but could never retaliate because he was afraid. According to him, it was one of the younger brothers who, out of envy, later used black magic to curse him with a *samkat*.[2]

B: I recall that, in childhood, my elder and younger brothers would gang up and beat me up. The elder one used to beat me a lot, without any reason, all the time. I used to eat my meals separate from them—I was that terrified! Sometimes, they would even snatch away my food. They would be naughty and put the blame on me and then Mum would beat me up.

He never got a sense of justice, because even if he complained to his mother, she didn't believe him. Bishamber said that he always felt his mother was closer to the eldest brother and paid scant attention to Bishamber's needs. The lack of an appropriate response from his primary caregiver, the lack of a sense of security and safety in his own household and his mother's partial treatment of her children caused Bishamber's ego to take form amidst fear and utter helplessness. In most Indian families, the need for love and security are fulfilled by significant others. However, Bishamber's was a nuclear family and he had no one he could turn to. The mother was partial to his brother, but she was also troubled and preoccupied by the father, who was an alcoholic and a gambling addict. When he was home, he caused chaos in the household.

> B: Father was rarely at home. I never saw him sober—alcohol, gambling, drugs, beating up mother, this was all he did. Everyone was tense at home. Due to this, I could not study further. I dropped out of school after Class 8.

To support his family financially, Bishamber gave up studies and started working. He soon became an expert at what he did but was unable to relish the rewards of his hard work because his employer denied him the full share of his salary. Bishamber was yet again denied his share of good objects.

> B: I was twelve years old when I first started working. I would go straight to the flour mill from school. I learned the work rather quickly. When the time came to increase my wages, my employer handed me five rupees and asked me to quit my job. I asked for my dues but he refused to pay me the rest of my salary.

> Me: It seems you received mistreatment from everywhere. Your mother did not pay much attention to you, your brothers bullied you, one brother used black magic to cause you to become possessed, you could not look to your father for any support and your employer, too, deprived you of your dues. It is as if, in every relationship, you were denied your dues.

> B: Yes! That is how it is.

I echoed his sense of having been wronged, of having been robbed of his share of all the essential ingredients that make for a healthy and integrated personality. Bishamber was relentlessly bullied into a corner of loneliness and helplessness.

Bishamber and his younger brother both grew up to become fruit vendors. One day, the brother had oranges to sell at his shop while Bishamber had mandarins, which were popular among customers. Fearing that he would sell more fruit than his brother and cause the latter to lose his customers, Bishamber decided not to open his shop. He kept his stock of fruits locked inside the shop and sat outside. Soon customers started approaching him and asking him why his shop was closed. He lied, telling them that his stock for the day had not arrived, but the customers kept pushing and he eventually gave in to their demands. As predicted, he made a much higher profit than his brother that day, causing the latter to grow envious. The envious brother immediately went to a Muslim practitioner of black magic to summon the ghosts of four men and have them possess Bishamber.

All through his life, Bishamber was a victim—of the closeness between his mother and older brother, of the bullying his brothers subjected him to, of the inadequately present and unhelpful father, of the unjust employer, of the envious younger brother, and of the inhabiting spirits. It seemed reasonable to take Bishamber's position, which was that his brothers stood between him and his happiness.

> B: Yes, daughter, in today's world, who feels happy about the happiness of others, you tell me? People only wonder, 'How did that other person do better than me?'

> Me: You are referring to feelings of envy.

> B: Yes. It is in some people's nature to feel envious. My brother was always like this.

> Me: He has been envious of you since childhood?

> B: Yes. He made sure I was not happy.

> Me: But why you?

At this point, he became silent and started to think.

> B: I never wished harm upon anyone. I was good at studies. Those who are pure of heart get mistreated by others.

Soon after the fruit incident, Bishamber began to change. He stopped working and began gambling and consuming alcohol. His family had to bear the brunt of his new addictions. He never returned home of his own volition. The family went into a financial crisis, because of which his eldest son had to give up his studies and take up a job as a laborer.

> B: The *samkat* would make me spend all my money on alcohol and gambling. I began to stay away from home, my shop shut down, all my money was spent, my elder son had to quit his studies and take up work as a laborer . . .

The affirmation and guidance of fathers shape the identities of sons. His father's absence prevented Bishamber from building up the conviction that his father was a dependable figure he could identify with, learn from, and be loved by. It was as if, in possession, this identification with the father became possible. Like the father, Bishamber was gambling, drinking, wreaking havoc, causing his family financial losses and forcing his son to give up his pursuits and take up the father's role and responsibilities by working. Bishamber was repeating the behaviors that had caused his own trauma.

Bishamber spoke of finding it difficult to fall asleep during this period. He was persistently haunted by a nameless dread. Every time he tried closing his eyes to fall asleep, he felt he was being watched by someone who would attack him and perhaps kill him the minute he lost consciousness. Whenever he slept, he felt as if some entity was sitting on his chest, trying to strangle him, making it difficult for him to breathe. The *samkat* made him dream of his mother and father having sexual intercourse. The only way for him to end the dream was to wake up. It is the dropping of all defenses in the sleep state that unleashes the wish to witness the parental couple in the primal scene, which evokes the palpable anxiety associated with the inability to imagine oneself as not-invested-in by one's objects (Botella and Botella, 2005). The fear underlying this dream is the fear of not being represented, of confronting the unimaginable character of one's exclusion from the closed circuit of the parental couple and later from that of the mother–son dyad.

A local exorcist diagnosed Bishamber's condition as possession by four malevolent male spirits. The moment Bishamber shared with me this image of four malevolent male spirits, I instantly linked it to the presence of four males in his household—three brothers who envied and bullied him and a drunken, absent father. He was taken to the Balaji temple by his eldest son, who stayed there with him for a year. During *peshi*, he often turned violent toward himself and others, and it required the strength of many men to control him. He abused Balaji, rolled on the ground, and often experienced a *gum peshi* (literally translated as "lost presentation") or a state in which the possessing ghost manifests itself through deep despair and stillness. He described this state as one in which "there is no swaying of the head or rolling around on the ground, there is no frenzied movement. But in this state one feels a despair so deep that it makes one suicidal." In other words, Bishamber's possession state had opened for him a small window into depression in the form of *gum peshi*. Could it be that, during such states, Bishamber was being afforded opportunities to process the pain he had suffered at the hands of teasing brothers, a partial mother and an absent father? The *samkat* reportedly implanted strange thoughts into him:

B: The possessing ghost placed thoughts in my head, such as—"drink the water from the gutter" and "do not eat food but eat your feces and rub it all over your body."

After a year of struggle between the stubborn ghosts and the mighty deity Balaji, Bishamber was finally delivered from his possession and experienced a final *peshi* in which he had a vision of Balaji instructing him to follow his path and serve other possessed people. This was Bishamber's initiation into serving Balaji as a *bhagat*.

B: Daughter, even to become a *bhagat*, one has to go through *peshi*. The battle between ghosts and Balaji went on for a whole year! In the end, Balaji was victorious. The ghosts were determined to take me along. Then I asked Balaji if I was worthy of serving him or not, and I experienced another *peshi.* Balaji tests whether the devotee's heart is clear or not. After that *peshi*, I had a vision of Balaji in which he instructed me to serve him. Since then, I have been serving possessed people. My job is to bring such people to Balaji's court—the rest he handles himself.

It seemed the narrative shared with me was that of a righteous man, free from envy and hostility, one that even God had to consider deserving of special status. In his role as a *bhagat,* Bishamber brings "patients of *samkat*" (his words) to the court of Balaji, where they are delivered from the spirits possessing them. He does not make money out of this service. In what follows, I shall try to understand how he might have gone from being possessed to arriving at a "quality in attitude" with which he received his "patients."

DISCUSSION

When I first met Bishamber, he must have been in his mid-forties. He is from a lower-class family in Haryana, a state in north India. He came to Balaji accompanied by a possessed woman named Kanta. A thin and tall man always dressed in a white *shirt-pyjama*, Bishamber had an air of superiority tinged with humility that made him seem both warm and authoritative. He wore a sandalwood *tilak* or mark on his forehead and his demeanor vis-à-vis the possessed was warm, which was a refreshing change from the usual violence and mockery that I was used to witnessing in Balaji.

Bishamber was one-and-a-half years old when his younger brother was born. Later in life the same brother became the reason for Bishamber's possession. This was the first blow to Bishamber's nascent ego. Before the advent of language, Bishamber experienced a drop in attention as his mother began to nurture another infant and then another, who followed a few years later. This can have dramatic effects: "The earliest experience of a 'lack of fit' between mother and infant leads the infant to feel that it is his or her way of loving that is hurtful. This represents the most global and fundamental damnation of self" (Ogden, 1992). Bishamber's self was damned from the start. The breast was snatched away from him too early. The theme of his victimhood to the theft of good objects persisted well into his adult life. The mother who withheld her nurturance had reserved it only for her other children, Bishamber's siblings. She failed to provide Bishamber safety when he was being bullied. Usually, children turn to the father to compensate for unmet needs for love and protection, but Bishamber's father was often drunk and basically insufficiently present as a father. Later, his employer also denied Bishamber his share of a good object by withholding his wages. Since the very beginning, the psychosocial matrix in his household served as fertile ground for the growth of envy, hostility and ferment.

Subsequent life experiences only added heat to the internal cauldron that was already bubbling with unmet needs, desires, envy, and hostility. Could it be, as Andre Green (1986) in his work on "the dead mother" suggested, that "frustrated longings substituted for an unsatisfying object, perpetually frustrating relationships warded off a terrifying gap?" In Bishamber, the gap became scarier when it was time for him to gloat over outselling his younger brother. By making a greater profit than his brother, Bishamber closed the gap between him and a good object, money that his brother desired as well. With the joy of having secured for himself the good object came the anxiety that it would soon be denied to him, leaving in its place only the agony of envy and hostility. One escapes from one's ugliness via projection and splitting—the hostility and envy that lay latent were projected onto the brother.

Green (1986) suggests that, in such scenarios, one's self-representation gets fused with the mother experienced by the person as insufficiently available or actively hostile. I only understood later how being dethroned by a sibling facilitates splitting of the proportion seen in Bishamber. Siblings are born under the same roof and share the same maternal love. If, however, there is a perception of inequality in the sharing of resources or experiences between them, if a sibling robs one of things one desires or brings from outside accomplishments they may have achieved by their own efforts, the other sibling can experience hostility of such intensity that they blame God for having cursed them to take birth in the same house as their sibling and thereby forcing them to encounter inequality. The wronged sibling is pitted in a constant battle against God. Often, those who were discriminated against by their families make sense of this experience of inequality by linking it with the "will of God": "God willed that I be born as a girl/boy in this house, have siblings and experience inequality." Bishamber was possessed by four spirits and via these spirits he hurled abuses and actively fought the source of all beings living or dead—God. Spirit possession is a symptom, but Bishamber's story informs us that it is also about entering a battle against God in the hope that the spirit will communicate with Him, because it has been derived from Him. All the siblings were born under the same roof and yet one of them, Bishamber, had to watch another brother get his share of nurturance. This led to the development of hostility in him toward his parents, who were invested in the other and who were responsible for bringing that other into the world. The ego split under the weight of overwhelming hostility and envy. In possession, he was battling his own creator.

In our conversations, Bishamber gave evidence of his unconscious hostility through constant complaints against his family members, who always came between him and what he desired. But beneath all the hostility and envy was a void. He had avoided a confrontation with this emptiness, unconsciously afraid that it would bring forth the painful realization that he had not been invested in by the other. To me, this void perhaps became most real when a slight shift in my gaze, from him to a wailing possessed woman nearby, offended him.

> B: (in a reprimanding tone) Now look, daughter, I am talking to you and all my attention is on you!

I had momentarily become the mother about whom Bishamber had said earlier, "My mother never paid any attention to me." When I returned my gaze to him, it was clear that he was upset about not being looked at or paid attention to by me. In my defense, I told him the truth.

> Me: (apologetically) my attention was also on you. For a brief moment, I looked at Kanta as she was wailing in pain.

> B: That is supposed to happen. She is now Balaji's headache. I only bring patients here, the rest he handles.

I struggled for words with which to rescue myself from his complaining stare. I was looking the void right in the face. It threatened me with abandonment. Fearing the severance of the bond that had formed between him and me, I began to think of something to say to him to resume the conversation, to quickly fill the gap that had been created by the slight shift in my body. But before I could say anything, he spoke.

> B: Okay, then. Namaste. It was nice talking to you. We will talk again if you are here for the next few days.

He then left without letting me respond to his "goodbye." I felt abandoned. He was exhibiting his life's pain before me. The shift in my body away from him was perceived as my not investing in him and was responded to with withdrawal. Like him, I too was not supposed to worry about the possessed woman who was being beaten by Balaji. Like him, I was supposed to have faith in and leave all miseries in Balaji's mighty hands. I was supposed to mirror him and contain his distress, and, unlike his mother, I was not supposed to avert my gaze toward an other.

I stood there, wondering if I, with my questions, was evoking subjectivities in my research participants, compelling them to look at their pain even if they lacked the relevant psychic equipment to undertake the task. Bishamber's desire to be heard and his taking offence at a momentary lack of investment made me aware of the fragility of his self and prepared me to deal with the same in other possessed people I was to meet during my research. Dissociation in possession saved him from experiencing, but he was no more possessed. Expressing displeasure was better than not-experiencing facilitated by dissociation. Disturbed by the anger his life experiences evoked in me and interested in gauging the extent to which his anger was still dissociated, at one moment I had asked him if he felt angry toward those who had wronged him.

B: I have never felt anger. I only feel extremely sad.

I think that, while the hostility and sexuality were somewhat tamed by having been lived and relived in *peshi*, the sadness beneath it was being felt and processed repeatedly in the intermittent silent states of *gum peshi*. In narration, the account of the depressive state of *gum peshi* was soon followed by a number of repulsive images.

B: This *samkat* produces such obscene images that it feels shameful to even describe them. Thoughts of drinking sewage water, eating feces and covering oneself in it, and images of parents having sex—and I could not even close my eyes. Then I would wake up from my sleep.

Me: Out of fear?

B: Yes. (Pauses) I mean, who would like to see their parents like that? But *samkat* forces one to see it!

This narration revealed the content being visited and revisited by Bishamber in *gum peshi*. The *samkat* that made him think of consuming and covering himself with feces is the damned and self-spoiling part of him. It is as if it is saying, "Eat shit! This is what you are good for! Nobody wants you! Look! What are your parents doing! They are procreating! This is how they brought you a brother—the reason you had to de-possess the mother! You were not born! You were excreted!"

It seemed that the irrepresentable and unimaginable character of his absence in his objects' eyes was being visited and painfully processed in *gum peshi* or a lost presentation. In the deep despair that marked the state of "lost presentation," there was a potential for this absence to be positivized or represented and made culturally meaningful. My sense was also that I was being drawn in as a voyeur. He shared the obscene image, from his dream, with me at a time in my life when I was battling my own anxieties. I was all alone in a research field swarming with men looking for an opportunity to take advantage of young girls—possessed or not. Once, I was stalked on my way to my guest house. I was told that I was possessed and could be healed in exchange for cash and sexual favors. There were stories of young girls being kidnapped, raped, thrown out on the streets, and left unattended. It was a scary time for me, and in Bishamber's authoritative persona I found a protective father figure. In fact, when I was with him, the other men stopped bothering me. Going back to the image from his dream:

> Me: In this dream, would the *samkat* appear next to you (I had in mind the image of a voyeur) or in the guise of your parents?

> B: No, the *samkat* tells me to look but does not appear. It only shows things. I do not know. Perhaps it appears in the image of my father because the four ghosts that possessed me were male, but I am not sure. It would only show me things.

At that time, I sensed some resistance in me. On reflection, I could see that this resistance on my part hinted at a failure to imagine that a father-like figure could be sexual as well. I had not worked through my own anxieties, which were affecting my capacity to receive the ugliness he was sharing with me. Instead of working with the images he shared, I let the conversation drift toward his experience of bullying and the associations around it. It was only later that I had a chance to look into my resistance in personal analytic work and supervision. This experience taught me not to get horrified but to receive the perverse parts in other research participants I met later (for instance, Ravi).

The image he shared with me can be understood on another level. The mother who was desired and whom one wanted to control was always outside one's omnipotent control; hence the feelings of helplessness, over one's failure to force the (m)other to be alive to one's needs. Now the same mother was being held, reached repeatedly in penetration, and controlled by the father who remained passive in reality. However, this passive and weak father, when he appeared in the dream, possessed enough vigor to pleasure the mother. I think, in watching this sight repeatedly and in becoming like his father while possessed, Bishamber was addressing a need to align himself with this power of the dream-father and metabolize it until it became a part of him. One way this working-through was made possible was by being possessed. The image the *samkat* made him endure during possession underwent a transformation in his *bhagat*-hood. I understand the obvious excitement with which he watched the possessed being beaten by Balaji as a transformation of his private fantasy—"objects that have wronged me are being beaten by Balaji/ Father"—into the public reality of his culture. In *bhagat*-hood, this fantasy can be enjoyed endlessly.

His individual fantasy was being played out through the collective fantasy of his culture. His hostile and erotic impulses were being tamed. In *peshi*, his impulses were contained and culturally meaningful. Owing to the "protective father part and the transformative mother part of the ritual" (Kakar, 2008), the self becomes capable of opening itself up to novel experiences that allow the difficult parts of the self, not otherwise embraced, to be lived. But this is done in the guise of possession and, so, does not threaten one's personal identity. One can be saved from the shame attached to seemingly bizarre parts of the self and remain of pure heart, not intending anyone any harm. Envy is unacceptable as part of the self. Also, culturally freeing a full-blown expression of anger in a relational culture like that of India can evoke anxiety related to the possibility of losing relational ties and reinforces one's fears of abandonment and estrangement. With repeated experiences of *gum*/lost/silent *peshi*, the unmetabolized parts of self could be gradually metabolized and made part of the healer-self. Bishamber could now use these parts to continue the process of healing through the healing of others.

Bishamber's possession and healing gave him a context in which to place and actualize his wishes. The cultural belief in spirits worked as a container, holding unwanted and unpleasant psychic content and transforming it into a content that, in his context, was now more acceptable. The mother, who was parasitically possessed because of her absence from Bishamber's life, was now the other—the done-to. Bishamber had now turned into the doer. A shift was facilitated in possession, from passivity to activity. Could it have been possible without a third element—the possessing spirit?

It was his *seva bhaav*, or the sentiment that drives him to serve others, that Bishamber used to nurture the deprived parts in himself and others and thereby feel worthy. He had become a figure carrying both the authority of the father and the warmth of the mother. He was no longer in need of his mother, for he had found both his parents in Balaji, just as Balaji carried both *his* parental figures—Rama and Sita—in his heart. This became clearer when Bishamber said, "Now I do not feel sad when I think of my mother. She is not with me, and that is okay. Now, Balaji is my mother, father, my brother and my boss." All those who had deprived him of his share were now found in and provided nurturance through Balaji. Furthermore, Bishamber emerged out of possession with a quality in attitude that allowed him to look at his distress differently: "I feel that Balaji filled my life with misery so I would detach from everyone else and join him." In this statement, I found a resonance of how I had understood the implication of inequality in the sibling bond. It was God who was experienced as the one responsible for filling Bishamber's life with miseries. In possession, he could battle God and communicate with him via spirit, which is an essence of God. The battle ended with God replacing everyone he had saddled Bishamber with since birth, everyone who had wronged Bishamber. Only God, who was responsible for the inequality Bishamber had experienced, could make right his own wrong. He now nurtured Bishamer in the form of riches, well-behaved children, respect, love, and satisfaction with whatever he had.

B: Today, he has filled my house [with joy]. My children have no ill habits. They respect everyone. My new daughter-in-law is a teacher in a school, but she too is very humble. She also gives us a lot of respect and cares for everyone. There are no problems in the house. Earlier, I was only focused on earning more and more money and gathering wealth. Now, I do not have this worry. I feel content with what I have.

No complaints, only gratitude. When I asked him if his brother was still envious of him, he replied, "Yes, he must feel envious. But now, I have Balaji. Even if my brother sends an evil entity my way, it will backfire on him." Balaji, as a joint-parental figure, fulfilled Bishamber's deep need for empathic response. Balaji cared for him in a way his mother could not.

B: No matter where I go, I know he is with me. He is watching over me. I have conversations with him all the time. He is always smiling. Ever since I first sought refuge in Balaji, I have not been worried about anything. I have surrendered all my worries to him.

The paranoid watchful gaze of ghosts had transformed into the benevolent gaze of an omnipresent god.

I never met Bishamber Bhagat again. He did not leave any forwarding address or contact information with me. Perhaps he was threatened by our closeness, and I had to respect his need for distance. He shared quite a lot with me in the two days that I spent listening to him. It is certain that his issues have not been completely resolved. The residues of his psychic difficulties still lingered. But he had managed to live a good and satisfying life. Perhaps this is the farthest one can go in an attempt to lead an authentic life in a relational culture like India's.

Freud (1905) wrote, "There are many ways of doing psychotherapy. All that lead to recovery are good." To recover in the Indian context means to be able to connect with the personal as well as the cosmic. I am sure that, today, Bishamber Bhagat from Haryana is helping others toward some form of recovery. He will always be grateful to Balaji for creating a space through possession where his hostile and sexual impulses could be tamed. Through the lost *peshi*, he was offered moments of reflection in which his pain could be felt and processed. The taming and processing of his evil was a part of the containment offered by Balaji. The taming, processing, and containing continues in the form of his experience of *bhagat*-hood—the thrill of watching possessed persons being penalized or feeling driven to help and bring troubled individuals to Balaji's feet. Balaji teaches us that, in *peshi*, one can dive into one's own depths. From this diving in, all that is negative and not metabolized can become meaningful and positivized.

LINGERING IN POSSESSION: BEFORE AND BEYOND

Shubha was a student of psychology at a university in Delhi. When a common friend of ours told her about my research, she expressed excitement and the desire to speak to me about her own experience of possession. I got in touch with her, and we decided to meet on the campus of Delhi University. At the time, I had access to a small room on the campus where I held counseling sessions. Shubha and I decided that the room would serve as a good setting for an uninterrupted conversation in which she could plumb the depths of the experience she wanted to share with me. Contrary to what I had imagined, though, I discovered considerable resistance in her. In our first meeting, she made it clear that she wanted to speak about the "illness" of possession, not her experience of it.

> S: I actually had this problem when I was in Class 11 or 12, at the peak of adolescence.
>
> Me: Do you mean you felt that an entity entered your body, causing you to do things you had no control over?
>
> S: Yes. I was possessed. I used to have fits, I used to say bad things to everybody at home, utter obscenities.
>
> Me: Did you notice whether these fits were triggered by particular events?
>
> S: At times when a situation demanded something of me, especially like an emotional response. Like when a teacher would tell us an emotional story and I was asked to respond or when I had to respond to a group of friends. I would faint and my jaw would tighten. Then I was taken to Manheru. There is a Balaji temple there that is also very famous. There, all of a sudden, when I saw my parents were troubled because of me, that they were trying to take care of me, I realized that I was not possessed, I felt very guilty—because of me, my parents were troubled. I realized that I was not possessed, but I liked that everyone, especially my mother, was taking care of me. I became conscious at that moment.

She had jumped too early to her experience of healing, completely bypassing her ordeal, her journey, the experiences that led to her possession and the details of her possession experience. She did not seem very keen to talk about her life; rather, she seemed to want to get our meeting over with. I gently tried to coax her possession experience into a dialogical space.

> Me: During fainting fits, were you aware of what was happening to you?
>
> S: I was aware, but I could not control it. It was like my body responded to the situation by fainting.

Me: Your body responded to the demand of emotional response?

S: Yes. All this I am able to say now, after having studied psychology.

Me: Perhaps we should also try to see how and why the notion of emotional response became so demanding that it led to fainting fits.

She remained silent. Sensing her difficulty in thinking about this, I decided to mobilize some thoughts for both of us.

Me: Has emotional response always felt difficult? What do you remember about your childhood?

S: I was a lonely child. I used to be very stubborn and demanding. I always wanted Mommy. When my words were unheard, I would get extremely angry. I used to grab my mother's arm if she tried to hit me. I would not eat anything until my parents would pacify me. I used to really relish it when Mommy fed me lovingly, took care of me. I never got along with my siblings or cousins. Ours was a joint family. When my aunt [father's sister] would come home for her holidays, she would say about me, "Such a bad girl, doesn't listen to her parents." My cousins would not speak to me. I was a very bad little girl. I was a very bad girl.

Me: Do you still feel like a bad girl?

Her juxtaposing the "little" with "bad" in her self-description made me wonder if perhaps she continued to be haunted by the "bad girl." She was quiet for some time. Then, in a rather timid tone, she responded.

S: Everyone around me told me that.

At this moment in our dialogue, I felt that I was looking at a timid little girl. My tone became gentler.

Me: I gather you used to long for your mother's affection. Can you tell me more about her and about your relationship with her?

Sensing her discomfort, I thought it best to leave the "bad girl" unperturbed for the time being. I did not consider it wise to bombard her in our very first meeting with questions about an experience I was not sure she had the capacity to contain.

S: I don't know . . . it's a very difficult question. I don't know how to describe her. She is very complicated. Ummm . . . I always wanted Mummy. I would always seek her in everyone—in friends, in boyfriends . . . But she was always busy taking care of others.

I noticed that she emphasized the word "I" every time she used it. I wondered where the mother was. Was I looking for the mother too soon? Was Shubha asking me to wait? It was obvious that there was hostility in her toward her mother, but I had little sense of who the mother was. However, the hint of an early maternal lack was telling. I wondered if Shubha's experience of it was related to a sibling's arrival.

Me: Who were the others?

S: Siblings. Especially my younger sister. Mother is very inclined toward her. I was a year old when she was born.

Me: Hmm. And the mother might have gotten busy with her.

S: It might have been like that. Even today, when my younger sister and I fight, Mum always sides with her, and I get punished. I remember, in our childhood, my sister used to lie about me to Mommy and Papa and I got punished. My mother would believe all the lies and my father used to beat me. After a while I stopped trying to prove myself right. I would say to her, "Yes! I did it! So? What will you do?" I became all the more rebellious. But I was punished anyway.

Her anger and hostility toward her mother could be sourced from the loss of maternal love to a sibling at the tender age of one. There may have been intermittent spaces and phases in which she was provided love, which made it possible for her to express her anger, although it was never contained and always responded to with punishment. The punishment only served to enhance and harden this anger further—into rage.

Me: Who punished you?

S: Papa.

Me: Can you share more about your relationship with him?

S: (after a long pause) that is a very difficult question. I don't feel like relating to him or even to my mother or anyone in the house. I don't feel the need to relate to anyone. I have very few close friends. And everybody thinks that I am arrogant.

When the mother and father were brought into the conversation, there was silence around them. I understood the silence as a manifestation of rage. So intense was her rage that she did not even feel like relating to them in the act of talking about them.

Me: Have you thought about why it is that you cannot relate to anyone?

S: I don't know. I feel the demand for emotional response is too much.

The resistances I had initially encountered in her were becoming clearer. She did not want to, or could not, engage with the emotions aroused by her parents and siblings. This reminds me of something Eigen (2011) said: "Our ability to produce states is way ahead of our ability to process them." Since Shubha had been studying psychology for five years, she understood my language, and I felt comfortable being upfront with her, something I avoided with other research participants.

> Me: Could it be that, from too early on, an emotional response in *you* was not understood correctly? Everyone was telling you how bad you were because you craved your mother and got angry when not attended to. Your emotional reactions were stunted. Perhaps that is why producing any emotional response becomes difficult for you?
>
> S: Yes. I feel so.

In summarizing her experience for her, I was trying to come somewhat closer to her states yet remain distant enough to articulate them. It was the beginning of rapport formation. She remained silent for some time. Could she be helped in getting around the difficulty she experienced in thinking about her father?

> Me: You said you don't feel like relating to your father. Can you say more? Can you describe him? His personality?
>
> S: It's difficult. I don't know what to say.
>
> Me: Perhaps you could tell me about the times you were beaten by him?

Her evident incapacity made me feel that it would be easier for her to express anger and hostility than to think through it. I felt it would be best to take the route of emotional expression—I had to connect with her at the level of affect rather than push her hastily into thinking.

> S: I used to be very stubborn, as I told you. I used to misbehave with my mother, and then, when Papa used to come back after work, he was told about my behavior and he would slap me and beat me. He used to tie me with a rope to the water tank on the roof at night. I would keep crying, but he would not untie me.

She was quiet. I sat there imagining a little girl tied to a water tank and surrounded by darkness, pleading to be untied, to be taken in by the warm light of maternal comfort. I felt terror settling inside me, making me shudder in a bid to shake it off.

> Me: You were surrounded by darkness.

S: (very matter-of-factly) yes, and there was fear of monkeys, that monkeys would come in the night. In the beginning, it was very scary. After some time, I stopped being scared. I knew they would come after a while and untie me.

All this time, the conversation had been marked by a generalized sense of impoverished affect. Experience was being presented to me without the accompanying affect. I had to rely on my apparatus alone to feel this dissociated effect. I had tried, with my question, to invite her to express her anger, but here she was depositing her terror in me. In her case, terror had hardened into anger. But in that moment, I palpably felt like I was tied to the water tank in pitch darkness, fearing that monkeys would appear like ghosts from nowhere and perhaps claw at me. The longer I stayed with this image, the more my body experienced goose pimples, trying to escape the terror through tiny pores in my skin. Clearly, Shubha was not feeling the terror. She was relatively close to anger. I had to carry this terror in me until I had gained sufficient confidence in Shubha's own capacities.

Me: Did it affect your behavior in any way?

S: No. I became all the more rebellious.

Me: I see. Is your father an angry person?

S: Yes, he is. He always wants his commands to be followed.

Me: Did he beat your mother as well?

S: Yes. If she didn't listen to him or didn't do as he told, he would beat her. Otherwise, he is very spiritual and all. He is a devotee of Balaji. I remember, he used to travel ten kilometers every week to that temple for a glimpse (*darshana*).

Not only Shubha but her mother, too, had to bear the brunt of the father's anger. Shubha chose to become like the father and rebel against his anger instead of taking the beating like the mother. There was a discord between his angry temperament and the zealousness with which he worshipped Balaji.

Me: It seems you are bringing out a contrast in his personality. At home, he beats your mother and you, demands obedience, and the same person is so spiritual that he travels so far every week for a *darshana*?

S: Yes. I noticed it, too. At home, he would have all the children sit in front of him and lecture us on values, but it never affected us.

Me: It seemed hollow because he was not following those values himself.

S: Yeah. There has always been this double-bind communication.

Our conversation ended here, leaving me in emotional pain as I thought of Shubha's difficult relationship with her punitive father. I began our next conversation by asking about her bodily experience during the state of possession.

Me: At the temple in Manheru, or during fits at your school or at home, did you enter a trance-like state and become unaware of what was happening around you?

S: No. I knew what was happening around me and what I was doing, but I had no control over my body. I knew I was lying on the floor. My body would become stiff, especially my jaw. But I couldn't do anything to control it.

S: In that Balaji temple, I saw, when the *kirtan* (worship) was happening, that many young women and girls started swaying and dancing. They had no inhibitions. I thought, "Now that I am here as a possessed girl, I should also start dancing, because if I don't, those around me will think that I am not possessed, that I am just faking it." So, I also started dancing.

Me: You played along.

S: Yes.

Me: It seems possession provided you with a language with which to articulate difficult experiences. You would faint perhaps in much the same way that you might have briefly switched your mind off when your aunt kept rubbing it in that you were a "bad girl" or when your father left you alone, tied to a water tank on the roof. To me, it seems like a language you learned.

S: And I learned it from my family members. From my grandma, I learned how she used to have fits. Her jaw would also tighten like this (she demonstrates). From my aunt I learned how she behaved when she was possessed. Once I saw my grandmother trying to exorcise ghosts out of my aunt. (Smiling) It [the exorcism] was very violent.

There was an incongruence between what was being said and how it was being said. Her smirk while recalling the violence her aunt was subjected to hinted at some sort of sadistic pleasure.

Me: Was this the same aunt who used to tell you that you were a bad girl?

S: Yes. I don't interact with her. Like I said, I don't feel like relating to anyone. I get tired of being social. Usually, I prefer to spend time alone in my room. Everybody thinks that I have a major attitude problem.

Me: Is there anyone you allow into your space during these moments of being alone?

S: I have a boyfriend. He is very loving and caring. He knows everything about my life, every small detail. He is the only one who knows about my life, and now you know.

Me: (smiling) and how has he received it?

S: He cried for me and responded with love. It felt very nice. (Smiles)

Me: Your need was reciprocated. Tell me how he reacts when you are in one of your phases, when you want to be alone, cut off from social life?

S: I love studying, so sometimes, when I am studying, I get lost. I put my phone on silent and then forget about it. Then, after four or five hours, I realize that I haven't told him. Then he gets very angry and says, "You could at least have informed me that you were studying!" Then I apologize. But in my heart, I don't feel it, because I really like being alone.

After a brief pause, she asked,

S: Ma'am, can you tell me what you understand about me?

This question felt abrupt. I wondered if there were things that she did not quite understand about herself, capacities she sensed she lacked, and whether my apparatus was required to bind, into meaning, all that was not understood by her.

Me: It's too soon for me to say anything. A few things in your narration that stand out starkly are, for instance, what you shared about your need for your mother, how, when you were a year old, the mother could not be available and had to cater to the younger sibling, how hard it always was to get to her, to access her. The younger sister would lie so you didn't receive your mother's affection but got punished instead, turning you into a rebel and seeking your mother in everyone.

S: I even imagine her in my life after marriage. My boyfriend and I are living in a house—and my mother is staying with us. I often tell her, "I will keep you with me after marriage." She ignores it.

This was a crucial conversation because it established that the residues of intense yearning for the mother were still present in Shubha. I wondered whether the mother was being rescued from the dominating father or this intense seeking hid behind itself a contrary wish to disengage from the mother and get closer to the father instead.

Me: Somehow, your father does not come up until I bring him up.

She was taken aback by my remark.

Me: When you began talking about him, the first thing you remembered was how he used to punish you. He seems absent, both from your narration and from your imagination.

She thought for a few minutes about this.

S: I don't even feel like relating to him.

Her rage toward her father was intense. Beneath the anger, I could sense a vague discomfort that I could not quite understand then. We met a week later, and I asked her if our last conversation had provoked any thoughts in her.

S: It did. For the first time, I was thinking of my father, how little I talk about him. I don't feel like talking about him.

Me: Talking about him brings back old memories of being beaten by him?

S: Yes.

Me: And perhaps it also brings back the experience of pain?

S: Hmm.

There was silence in the room. I noted that her hands were folded across her chest and her legs, too, were crossed. Her body was stiff. It was as if the body remained true to the need to keep the painful psychic content from entering the realm of experience. Observing her body closely, perhaps I came close to her experience, and the words that came out of my mouth next seem to me, in retrospect, to represent an attempt to become a spokesperson for her body.

Me: When it comes to experiencing pain, I turn stiff.

She looked up instantly and smiled as if my remark had struck a chord. Her hands slowly unfolded. Receiving resonance caused her body to slide into greater ease.

S: Yeah. I can't stay with pain. When it comes to . . . like, when something painful happens, I turn inwards. I turn cold. When I talk about my father, I don't really feel much pain.

Me: I have noticed that, even when you have shared the experiences you have had with him, it is as if emotions are absent.

S: Yes. I usually turn inwards.

It was not just anger she felt toward her father. It was as if an internal agency was prohibiting her from relating to the father.

Me: I wonder if that is why you prefer being alone—to bypass the experience of pain?

S: I don't know. I generally like being alone. I know we live in a society and that, no matter how hard we try, we can't live in a vacuum. We passively keep interacting with society. But I like to be alone, doing things that I like.

Me: Like what?

S: (smiles) that is a nice question.

Why was it a nice question? Did she know what she liked? Or was "doing things I like" just an excuse for remaining socially withdrawn? A few minutes passed before she spoke.

S: When I am alone, nobody is guiding me, instructing me or interfering in my things—"do this" or "do that" or "don't do this" or "don't do that."

The nice question evoked in her the sense of freedom that came from being alone.

S: My father . . . he used to keep pushing, keep saying things to me, and keep instructing me on every little thing. I know he is very knowledgeable and caring and all, but it is not care. This happens with my boyfriend as well. He and my dad, they are very caring, but when they care like this, I feel suffocated.

Her hands moved toward her throat in a gesture of self-strangulation.

S: I feel the pressure. I feel that, now, I have to return it.

Me: Yet you liked it when, during your illness, you were receiving care and love from your parents. So, perhaps, it feels good if you get to take, but you don't feel you have the capacity to give.

S: Yes! You are absolutely right! I have never thought of it this way but what you are saying feels right!

We stayed with these thoughts for a few minutes.

Me: Being alone means not being in a giving position. Giving is tiring. Giving involves responding emotionally.

S: You don't know how I finished my master's dissertation which was around the theme of spirit possession.

Her capacity to give was restrained because she did not feel understood.

Me: It must have been hard to speak to your family about your theory?

S: Yes. They are convinced that it is spirit possession. I decided to let them be. Like you said last time, it is their "language." I have noticed that, after my dissertation, I started adjusting more with them. After speaking to you, I went back to my work and I felt there was no direction in it. I don't know what I am rejecting and supporting. Initially, I was being sympathetic, and later I was being critical.

Nobody understands her, and, in return, she refrains from responding emotionally to anyone. In the context of her dissertation, her coming closer to something and then withdrawing from it was an enactment of the fear of not being understood. Although her creative work helped her appreciate the language prevalent in her family and brought her closer to them, our conversations were opening windows through which she could see the discord inside her, prompting her to be sympathetic to and appreciative of her family and its language and values—and to criticize them. This was her struggle. I wondered if her association with psychology contributed to her criticality.

Me: Do you feel caught between two cultures?

S: Yes, and I even mention this in my work.

Me: Caught in the question—should I listen to my parent's [and submit to] the culture they have raised me in or the wisdom I have arrived at through psychology?

S: Yes. Even Kakar mentions this in his work . . . that he felt that he was at the margins.

Me: Yes. How does it feel, being in this in-betweenness?

S: It gets uncomfortable. Everyone in my family is obsessively religious. My brother goes for *kavar yatra*[3] every year before Maha Shiv Ratri[4]. For the last two years, I have not been attending the festival. My father and others touch my niece's feet to take her blessings. Recently, they were watching the news about that woman in Punjab who is always dressed as a bride, and many celebrities come and worship her. They don't let her feet touch the ground. They carry her in their arms and dance. So my parents were watching it on the TV and criticizing it— . . . "These people turn anyone into a god." Then I replied, "You do the same." I tell them that they too take blessings from my niece.

Hold on to the old (the family and its values) or make space for the new (the modern, psychoanalytic, theoretical wisdom she was receiving through her education)? Was her struggle also related to choosing between her mother and her father?

Me: And how do they receive your remark?

S: They don't take me seriously. (Laughs). Nobody takes me seriously.

Me: Has it always been so?

S: Yeah. It was always like this, but it has intensified ever since I stopped praying and worshipping and especially after I started studying psychology. Nobody takes me seriously. Since [I started studying psychology], everybody [has concluded] I am mad. They are anti-psychology.

When she tried to make her family aware of new perspectives, her efforts were not received well. There was a lack of containment for the "new" that Shubha was trying to bring into the household. Not listening to her and labeling her insane were ways to blatantly negate her attempts to discard her family's beliefs and replace them with modern and rational ideas.

S: [All of this is] also because I am unemployed. My father often taunts me. He has given me two options: "either you find a job or you get married to a rich man." But I somehow convince him that—"Now I am dependent on you. When I get married, I'll be dependent on my husband. Let me have something of my own, let me stand on my feet, and then I'll get married."

From thinking of herself as the daughter who was not taken seriously and considered insane, Shubha had moved to considering why she was not taken seriously—her being unemployed. Confronted with a father who did not take her seriously and did not attempt to understand her and even taunted her, Shubha assertively expressed her opinion to him and realized that, by doing this, he helped her be understood by him. I acknowledged this achievement.

Me: So you are able to present your thoughts to him without fear.

S: Yes. This confidence has come because of psychology. There are so many women who can't verbalize—they gossip or watch soap operas and get an outlet [for their feelings].

Those who don't have the capacity to effectively assert themselves choose to do so rather violently through possession. In Shubha's case, the discipline of psychology facilitated the emergence of a capacity to verbalize what earlier seemed like difficult emotions. She felt more able to express her mind firmly and assertively without instigating a conflict that could become crippling. She called this capacity "confidence."

Me: What about men?

I asked this question because, tonally, there was a great deal of emphasis in her use of "women."

S: I think women don't get a chance while men don't use their chance, they act out.

Me: Are you thinking here about your father as well?

Although seemingly spontaneous and bizarre, this remark was an attempt to bring her father into the conversation. I got the sense from Shubha that something was giving way in her.

S: (Smiles) Yes, I was. My father acts out his helplessness, his weaknesses.

Me: Why is he helpless?

S: (looks away and thinks hard) He has struggled a lot and he is never praised for his struggle. He feels punished.

Me: For what?

S: When we were in Bhiwani, he always wanted to come and settle down in Delhi. He was the first one in our family to come to Delhi, and then he brought his brothers too, but he has never been appreciated for what he did. He struggled a lot in his life. My grandparents never appreciated him.

The subtle introduction of men who "act out" into our discourse gave me a glimpse of traces of empathy in Shubha toward her father, which I had only faintly sensed earlier. In the above account, those traces became more profound. The conversation gradually turned toward the identification she feels with her father.

S: I am exactly like my father—the way he reacts or expresses [himself]. I have noticed this, and everyone in my family says, "You are exactly like your dad." I don't want to be like him. I want to change my orientation. He can't be on his own. He can't be alone.

Me: You are the opposite.

S: Yeah. I like staying alone.

She was like her father. This identification suggested that she was at the very least finally relating to her father. It was clear that identification and closeness were desired but also caused discomfort and were therefore denied. The mother was to be kept closer; the father was to be actively kept at a distance.

S: People say that he is biased toward me. Mummy is biased toward [my] brother and Papa is biased toward me. At times I feel I am taking advantage of him. He gets me everything. Whatever I ask for, he gets it for me. He agrees to everything I ask.

Me: But you find it difficult to agree with him?

S: Yeah. When it comes to listening to his instructions, I close myself or isolate myself in my room. Also because my mood is very inconsistent. When I am happy, I'll do anything they tell me to. But when my mood is off, I don't care about anyone.

She was gradually opening up about the joy of being a father's privileged daughter. While the elder brother had the mother, Shubha had the father. She seemed to experience joy when she "received," and this made me wonder about the corresponding part of her that felt "pressure" when required to "give." She "closed" herself when it was time to listen to her father or to "give" him an experience of being received. She reminded me of goddesses who were only benevolent when pleased by their devotees. Receiving from others pleased her. What else did?

Me: And what makes you happy?

S: I don't know what makes me happy.

Me: Sounds similar to what you were saying about your father.

Through this remark, I wanted to bring her identification with her father to the forefront. I sensed that she possessed enough ego strength to reflect on the conflictual relationship with her father that I was inviting her to look into.

S: He too finds it troubling, being happy. He can't handle jokes. Whenever Mom or we children try to joke with him, he ends up scolding us. I don't know what makes him happy. I don't know what makes me happy.

Me: I am thinking here about your boyfriend. Does not knowing what makes you happy affect your relationship with him or others?

S: (thinks for a few moments) He is a lot like my father. He is very demanding and possessive. Initially, I found him very open-minded—a mix of tradition and modernism. But now I realize he is very possessive and conservative. He doesn't like my talking to other guys or wearing short dresses. He is just like my family.

Me: Was this similarity the reason you were drawn to him?

S: No. Initially, he was very open-minded. We were together in school when I was in Bhiwani, and then we got transferred here and he went to IIT Delhi. Then we met [again], and I knew he liked me but it was I who voiced it for both of us.

Me: Are you also possessive?

S: No. I am not possessive. I let him be. He is not very attached to his parents. His life revolves around me.

Both the father and boyfriend were conservative. Both were not accepted by their families. Both were insecure. Perhaps Shubha sought both her parents in her boyfriend. Both the father and boyfriend came to Shubha with a need to possess her and to be received by her. There was a digestive pause during which she gazed at the curtain, processing her thoughts. I let her be.

The next conversation began with her thoughts on possession.

S: Ma'am, I think the kinds of fairy tales or bedtime stories you listen to as a child—they take on a reality of their own.

Me: Were you also told such stories when you were little?

S: No. But in our family, almost everyone was affected by *samkat* at some time or another. I saw my aunt behaving unusually.

The fairy tales were not *told* in the household but enacted.

Me: Were you told what *samkat* looks like?

S: No, never. There was a fear around it, that one is not supposed to talk about ghosts. But the fear was always sustained, to scare the child—"if you don't do this, the ghost will come." For me, there was always a question—"Is this real?"

Me: When you were tied up, all alone on the terrace, surrounded by darkness, did you never fear ghosts?

S: I don't recall. I remember being afraid of monkeys, but not really of a ghost. And I knew that my parents] would soon come [untie me], but at that time it felt like a long wait.

Me: And how did you deal with this long period of forced isolation back then?

S: I guess I mothered myself. I used to start talking to myself.

Me: What would you say?

S: I don't remember. I guess I consoled myself—"don't worry, don't be scared." And I also had an imaginary friend. It was the corner of my toilet. I used to share things with it. Whatever happened with me at school or through the day, I would come and share with it.

At this point in our conversation, I was overcome with deep despair. The corner of her toilet was where her states got contained. I felt her sadness and loneliness while she went on narrating her experience matter-of-factly.

> Me: I am extremely alone. I have no one to talk to, to relate to, and no one who can understand me. I am extremely sad.

Without realizing it, I had slipped again into an active voice. It was as if I was in touch with the unthinkable, unbearable, and unsayable in her. I had articulated it. I was feeling a state she was not allowing herself to feel. For a few moments, we remained blanketed in heavy silence. Reclaiming what was dissociated in her allowed her to loosen up and share more.

> S: There is one thing about me I have not shared with you yet. I don't go to any relative's house alone. I make sure my parents are with me.
>
> Me: Why is that?
>
> S: I don't feel like adapting to others.

I thought a child would want her parents to accompany her to feel safe and secure. I was intuiting a possible experience of abuse in her history. She remained silent. But the texture of this silence seemed like the non-verbalizable aspect of experience, calling for another apparatus, someone else's tongue, someone who could put the experience in word-containers. I was experiencing a conflict—should I ask her? Or wait for her to tell me? After a short period of internal struggle between my intuitive sense of the need for the moment and my intellectual understanding of the traditions and ethics of psychoanalytic encounters, I decided to side with the former.

> Me: Was it a relative?

Tears welled up in her eyes. This was the closest she had come to experiencing pain in the course of our interactions. One of her hands was clasping the other by the elbow while the other hand was playing at her chin. She was trying hard to hold her tears back.

> S: Yes. My cousin brother.

We remained quiet for the longest time. Then I summarized my understanding of her pain. She had been violated on many fronts—emotionally, physically, and sexually. She was not crying anymore, simply nodding in agreement. My momentarily becoming her and articulating that which she could not bring herself to experience had opened up the possibility for her to imagine me as her imaginary friend. I *was* the toilet corner, containing her state, not replying. Her violated body had palpably entered the dialogue.

A week later, I opened our conversation by expressing my curiosity about the body's experience in possession.

> Me: How does the body feel during *peshi*? When you were rolling your head violently or swaying back and forth rhythmically, how did the body feel?
>
> S: You know, you feel free. You are completely free. You can do anything, and it is acceptable there [in sites of indigenous healing]. It is even encouraged.
>
> Me: So the body is uninhibited. When you were in *peshi*, were you there? Were you present? Did you know what you were doing?
>
> S: I knew what was happening. I knew what I was doing, but I couldn't control it. After some time, even if I tried to control my body, it didn't happen. I knew what I was doing but I couldn't control it.
>
> Me: What about the music?
>
> S: The music is so loud. And most people close their eyes during *peshi*. I remember I did, and just started swaying to the rhythm of the music, and after some time, it feels like it's coming from inside you, you know, like, it feels the music has entered you and passed through you.
>
> Me: Like you have become permeable?
>
> S: Yes, permeable. And one with the culture.
>
> Me: When in this state did you feel any pain?
>
> S: At that moment, one does not feel anything. Later, it aches everywhere. My mother used to apply pain relief on my neck every night.

A confluence of mind and body in *peshi* is achieved, a state of utter, pain-less bliss that Shubha described beautifully. When the body is uninhibited and fuming with eros, it moves in a frenzy, seemingly free from the agency of the mind. But they are linked in this moment, for it is through the body that the mind touches bliss and raw vitality. Freud saw the body as being closest to the source of instinctual impulses that do not tolerate postponement of discharge. Shubha's description confirmed vividly that the possession state, horrific though it may seem, is nonetheless often a beatific experience, an experience of free fall, with all bodily inhibitions lifted; in possession, she became "one with the culture" and those around her. It was a painless state. She could do anything—"it was encouraged." The life of the body may have been restricted at home, but here all restrictions were lifted. This fuller bodily experience in possession offered a chance to discharge and tame instinctual impulses by living them out in their raw vitality.

Me: What happens just before the state of *peshi* sets in? Do you remember what happened right before you felt *samkat* come over you or enter you?

S: I remember the first time I felt possessed. It was before my cousin's wedding. A few days before her wedding, she got possessed. She used to get possessed by a *duta*—a goddess used to possess her. Whenever she got possessed, we children were told to leave the room. I used to be very curious. Whatever the elders would prohibit us from doing, I used to feel like doing exactly that. I used to wonder why they were keeping us from doing this thing, what was happening? I wanted to see, so I would hide and peek to find out what was happening. I saw that my cousin was reprimanding everyone. She was telling them about their future. All my relatives were sitting around her with their hands folded. I found it very fascinating. As she became okay, at that very moment, the electricity went off. Everybody got so scared. It was a coincidence, but everyone was already so scared when she got possessed. When the light suddenly went, everyone started thinking it was because of the ghost. It was dark, and everyone started searching for some light. I was also very scared, and I started looking for Mummy. Then I started making myself possessed. I thought, maybe if I became possessed like my cousin, then everybody will also gather around me like they had gathered near her. So I was intentionally trying to become possessed, and then, after some time, my body started feeling very light. I started feeling like I didn't have a body. My eyes were closed. I don't know when my B. P. dropped and I fainted.

Me: You were trying to induce a possession state—you were scared.

S: Yes, but I also liked the attention my cousin was getting. I think now that, as a child, I used to fall sick a lot. Something or the other was always happening to me. And then, when Mummy would take care of me, I used to like that a lot!

Me: So, you, your cousin brother, cousin sister, all experienced possession?

S: Oh, there came a time when, one by one, everybody was becoming possessed. When this incident happened, when I fainted for the first time, I had applied *heena* to my sister's hands. I was sitting with her and her friends and they were talking about sexual stuff—all the double-meaning things. They thought I could not understand, but I could understand everything. I was pretending that I could not understand what they were talking about. It was very pleasurable for me.

This event was during her adolescence, a time when sexual urges are in tumult. Listening to elder sisters' sexualized conversations would only have kindled the incipient sexual desires that marked this phase of her life. However, I was yet to understand why this surge led to an intense seeking of the mother.

S: Everybody had warned my mother not to let me apply *heena* to my cousin sister. Everyone asked for me to be kept me away from all these things so that

I would not be possessed by *samkat*. I had heard them say these things, and I acted upon [the prohibition]. When I fainted, everyone started blaming my mother, saying, "We told you to not allow her to apply *heena*." I knew everyone was already anticipating that I would become possessed. I did not know what to do (laughs). I would merely faint—I did not know what to say or do. I would not even realize that I had fallen unconscious.

Me: It was like a short-circuit. As if the system could not take the load of emotional voltage, so the electricity went off. The only response left was to faint.

S: Yes, but after some time it began to happen automatically. I would faint automatically whenever the situation demanded something of me.

Me: It was your way of saying, "I can't take it."

The conversation gradually drifted back to the point where we had broken off the last time, when she had briefly brought up her abuse.

S: It was my cousin. He used to come and lie down right beside me as I slept. He would come, excited, from somewhere else and ejaculate inside me. I now think it was a perversion. Back then, after some time, I would touch myself and find something slimy.

Me: How did you feel?

S: I used to feel nice—"there is somebody who has come to lie next to me, I am not sleeping alone." I did not realize what was happening with me. I must have been ten or twelve.

Me: When did it stop?

S: I don't remember. It stopped on its own.

Me: Did you ever confront him?

S: No. I never had the courage. I did not understand what to say.

She decided to share with me an assignment she wrote as part of her master's thesis on her possession experience that constituted an attempt by her to come to terms with her emotional pain. She believed it would help me with my research. In the process of reading it, I met her several times to discuss what she had written and understand her experience better.

Shubha wrote:

When you find yourself alone you can feel a sensation of pain . . . Eyes melt with tears of pain . . . heart cry in grip of pain . . . such an intense relation of pain yet unknown what is pain midst the loneliness it's again pain . . . that makes you feel alive with the painful part letting you survive . . .

Her use of phrases like "eyes melt" and "heart cry in grip of pain" struck me as unusual, and her fainting awakened in me a curiosity about the relationship between psychic pain and the body.

S: The body helps to manifest the pain in the form of "symptoms." During my periods of psychic pain, I experience restlessness, pressure to act out—and sometimes the sense that I have a body flies away.

The notion of the body flying away when confronted with psychic distress and fainting every time she was required to respond emotionally pointed to an inability to process difficult emotional states and a pull toward evacuating unmetabolized emotional content through the body. It seemed her ability to articulate, rather than completely evacuate, had improved substantially since. I wondered if her possession experience was instrumental in the development of these capacities in her.

Me: Were you able to feel and process emotional pain prior to being possessed?

S: I used to feel pain, but I think I did not develop the capacity to process it, and maybe possession was one culturally appropriate context—not medium—for venting out all the pain that had accumulated over the course of my growing years.

Me: Were you able to communicate your pain or anxiety then?

S: Yes, at that time my possession state was [like] crying out loud, exhibiting my pain in all its hues.

Me: Has this ability undergone any changes since your realization that you were not possessed?

S: Yes, I am slightly better at acknowledging my pain and stressors. And, rather than defending myself through denial, I accept it and I am now in a better position to increase my capacity to tolerate it, to process it instead of acting out, because acting out can become painful for others, creating a vicious cycle of actions and reactions of anxiety, anger and guilt.

Me: Has your ability to deal with pain become better because of your experience of possession or do you think it is because of your study of psychology?

S: I would say it has to do with psychology. Possession gave me the space to take new birth as someone "special," to be one with my family—they provided me with needed love, care, affection, attention. But studying psychoanalysis became a tool, drilling deep into my possession, obsessions, fears. Also, I was able to appreciate the intense relationship between freedom and escape.

Me: What was the image of a ghost in your mind? What were ghosts to you? Where do they come from? Why do they come? Whom do they possess? What should one do in order to safeguard themselves against ghosts? What prayers should one say?

S: I had no image of a ghost. I used to think ghosts were aggressive, free-floating winds. I learnt, from my family and culture, that ghosts used to come from cross-roads or from consuming something sweet or from wearing perfume or during menstruation. One should obey the family elders, worship Lord Balaji, not step out of the house wearing perfume. Hanuman Chalisa[5] helps, and a few hymns.

That night, when I first became possessed, at my cousin sister's wedding, a ghost came upon one of my cousins, and all the other children were isolated from her. Then the electricity went off, and it was dark all around. I was sitting in a group with my other cousins, males and females, and other relatives. The male members of the group were trying to scare us with references to ghosts and thieves. They were poking fun at each other, playing pranks, trying to scare each other. I was constantly searching for my mother, calling her while talking and playing. But every time I was told that she was downstairs and could not come until the electricity returned. Like a three-year-old, I thought, "How can Mummy be so bad and uncaring. She is busy chatting! Can't she come?!" Suddenly, somebody opened the gate of the balcony and a chilly wind hit me. My heartbeat increased—I started breathing fast, very fast, my head started hurting like hell, my hands went numb and, in minutes, I found myself falling unconscious. I was sleeping, with tightly shut eyes and constricted breathing. That was a mystical experience for me. I could hear what people around me were talking about—"She is also possessed now! She was applying *heena* to the bride, that is why she has become possessed now!" Suddenly, I heard my mother crying and calling my name with a lot of love and care. I thought to myself, "Now that Mummy has come, it's time to get up." I was about to open my eyes when my mother took me in her lap, so delicately that . . . I could not open my eyes. I remained sleeping like that for a few more minutes, until my mother became restless. I got up. She hugged me and kissed me. She asked, so tenderly, "What happened?" I replied, "Mum, I feel scared," and she pressed me more tightly against her breast than before. She didn't enquire any further, and I was enjoying all the love, care and attention, surrounded by a huge crowd. People around her were alerting her to the fact that I was possessed. I really did not notice all those comments at that time, but they lingered on my mind like unattended, disturbing sounds. My uncle scolded my mother for having let me put *heena* on a girl who had been possessed in the past. She was apologetic. I was feeling bad for Mum and good for myself. I was happy with the intentional hurt I caused her. It was as if I was angry with her for leaving me alone in the dark and not attending to my constant cries. When Uncle was scolding her, somehow I felt, "Good! Now she will realize! She was chatting away, having left me with others! Now she is getting reprimanded." I was getting irritated and angry with my uncle as well—why was he scolding Mum? He was not very wise himself. She is my mum. She knows how to handle us.

While I listened to her, several images appeared in my mind—her tied to the water tank all alone, talking to the corner of her toilet, turning cold every time her father was brought up, falling unconscious while possessed. Since the very beginning she had lacked a source of containment. Her father brought coldness instead of containment. In the account shared above, I found it interesting that, as she had sat there with her cousins and desperately waited for her mother to appear, she had been met instead with the coldness of the breeze, just as her childhood needs had been met with cold responses from those around her. Her compromised capacity for containment caused her psychic apparatus to collapse again, but this collapse was not into the cold abyss of loneliness; she fell this time into the state of possession, from which she was gathered up into her mother's warm embrace.

Me: Listening to you describe your experience of spirit possession, I find myself thinking about a child whose family members are perfectly adapting to her needs. Knowing that my family members can now finally allow me to "be"—to be angry, aggressive, alone—that such moments were finally allowed to me, moments in which I could come in close contact with parts of myself, and my experience was not going to be interrupted or interfered with.

S: Yeah, part of that is apt, but it's not the entire truth. Possession of course gives you the space to be free, to unconsciously be yourself, but within limits. When wishes get fulfilled, you have to pay a price, too. Possession introduces a lot of guilt and stigma in the life of the one who is possessed, and now, along with your already existing conflicts, a new birth takes place, new conflicts emerge, tying you to an endless loop. And, sometimes, I feel that becomes the reason so many people do not get cured for years and relapses happen. It's an escape from freedom.

Me: Guilt I understand. It is the stigma I want to understand more. I used to think that people get possessed because "going insane" carries a stigma in our country. Please help me understand the stigma. New birth, new conflicts—my impression is that you can now articulate your needs to your father better. However, could there be a wish in you to never be born? Perhaps birth brings conflicts. Birth also separates us from the mother.

S: I agree. And with me, I request you to work like a therapist, not as a researcher; the therapist in you relates to me better and enlightens me. Yes, I do harbor guilt within me. Perhaps, with the acknowledgement of your actions, your superego haunts you. And it was for the same purpose that I my dissertation was focused on this. I wanted to give cultural healing space and respect, but I ended up criticizing it, which says a lot about my conflicts—that I carry a binary, a split, and I am still looking to develop the capacity within me to make myself familiar with those splits. Also, as things have two sides, positive as well as negative, possession as a cultural illness gives you the space to go culturally mad and live your conflicts through the ghosts of your desires, but, along with that, it makes you disabled, snatching away the tag of being "normal." When there is unguided knowledge, one constructs the logic behind things with one's own limited knowledge, experience, and fantasies. Myths are born. These dramatic possessive states were not new things for me. I had witnessed them earlier, too, so many times, but only partially, never fully. My grandmother used to get fits. She used to go unconscious during her fits, with her jaws closing so tightly sometimes that they cut her tongue, leading to bleeding. Only my aunt could open her mouth, by pressing her nose shut forcefully. The closing of the nose pressured Grandma to open her mouth to breathe, and the moment she would open her mouth, my aunt used to pour water to bring her back to consciousness.

Me: How is the general female voice in the family?

S: The voice of the women in the house goes unheard. Their existence is invisibilized. Our family is typically patriarchal, with males dominating and ruling. But I remember my grandma's sons used to give her respect and attention, because of which she used to get the space to exhibit her wishes. She was much younger than Grandpa, so he forcefully established physical relations with her. My aunt was the only daughter in the family and got married much earlier than others, to someone who was older than her. My father was also dominating. Even today, he cannot tolerate my mum saying certain things.

I have always been fascinated by the question of whether or not a human being can be possessed by a spirit, and whether or not spirits really even exist. Often, I have seen that, during prayer meetings, family functions or at other ceremonies, the "ancestral spirit" or "family deity" enters the body of a family member, often female—she becomes possessed. If it's the first time, then she becomes the site of further visits by ancestral spirits in the future. That is to say, the spirit visits her every time it has to converse with the family. It generally comes to scold the family for misdeeds or for mistakes during rituals or for the incomplete performance of rituals or for forgetting them or not giving them their due respect. I used to wonder how people could trust and worship a crazily dancing madwoman. Whenever a spirit visited her, everybody would be at her feet. She would be considered the most powerful and revered of them all. It's considered more important than even idol worship—everybody rushing for a glimpse, touching her feet and seeking her blessings. If a goddess descended on or possessed a person, everyone would line up to present their problems and seek divine intervention. All this used to make me feel that you could suddenly become a god, all-powerful, loved, respected, sacred, anxiety-provoking, with each possessed person exhibiting a different and unique yet similar drama. These possession states and persons were always fascinating to me. After witnessing such incidents, my mind would get consumed by curiosity. I always wanted to *feel*—how does a spirit actually enter? Does it actually enter or is the person faking it? How does the possessed person's body feel—as heavy as a mountain or as light as air? Are spirits harsh or soft? It is not just that curiosities haunted me—I always wanted to be the subject of this cultural experiment. I always used to pray for a goddess to possess me. Why don't I get possessed by a spirit? While wishing and fearing simultaneously, I wanted to study the death rituals of Hindus and explore the possible links between "dramatic" possession states and the restoration of "lost members" through these states.

Me: Something lost is restored in possession—who/what was lost for you? Was it restored in the state of possession?

S: Maybe possession becomes a site of collective mourning. Mourning lost maternal love. While mothering myself, I was performing my own death rituals.

Me: You spoke of feeling guilty about being possessed. How did you deal with that?

S: I had this desire to do something for my parents. I was feeling obligated to them because of what they were doing—guilty also, but at the time, the pleasure was overpowering. So I never had a boyfriend before Naman. I didn't even look at guys. My friends were enjoying their teen years differently, and I was different. While concentrating on my studies, I took an oath to not disgrace my father and family and scored 90%. Though things have changed and I am a very different person now, I still miss my mother, I still want her love and I still do not like my father. But, somehow, to an extent, Naman has become the father and the mother.

I realized I was feeling guilty, and the next morning I was taken for an exorcism. All I felt was excitement! I had visited the temple many times, but this time it was entirely different. I felt special, as if my wish had been granted and I was a part of the world of supernatural forces, my family and heritage. I was very calm outside but excited inside. I guess, apart from all the attention, I was also enjoying and amused by the elders' foolishness. After reaching the temple, I started getting nervous, thinking—what if the priest told them the truth, that I am not possessed? What if Lord Balaji got angry with me? Because, like me, he knew that I was not possessed. I started feeling anxious. I sat for the exorcism ritual but was constantly praying, saying, "I have not told any lies, please God forgive me, my intentions are not bad, all I want is love. Grant me that the priest will tell my parents their daughter is very sick and that they should take good care of her."

In minutes, my world changed when the priest declared that I was possessed and prescribed treatment for me. I was not an ordinary child now, but a special one who could scare anybody and ask anybody to follow my commands.

I wondered if dissociating a part of herself was a way to associate with her community. I sensed that behind this fear lay a belief that the priest was omniscient, that he would be able to see through her falsehood and discover the truest part of her that only a priest or God could find. Confirmation of her possession led her to take on the much-desired status of a little dark goddess.

S: When we came back home, I was asked to only rest, eat and sleep. All throughout, I kept on thinking, "How can this be? What if I am really possessed and I don't even know it?" I was oscillating between fears and desires. It was time for a wedding in the family—again, I got lots of attention and affection from a huge crowd, not just my family. But it was not so fascinating and pleasurable. I was asked to follow certain rules prescribed by the priest. I could not eat sweets at the wedding. Nobody was sharing their eatables with me. I could not wear perfume and make-up like the others. Then it remained with me like a habit or excuse. Whenever some difficult situation would arise, I would exhibit my possessed dramatic state by falling unconscious. My blood pressure would drop, be it school or at home. People around me, family members, doctors, or teachers, used to refer to my condition as "fits." No kind of treatment, medical or traditional, was working for me. Only the way my aunt used to treat my grandma worked—or, rather, I should say, being a conformist to my group, I let it work on me. My mother learnt it quickly from her. It would be practiced on me and became my "medicine." My parents were the most affected. My mother, father, brother, sister, and other family members loved me the most and prayed hard for me, trying various rituals only to cure me. I used to feel alive through them, in them. Sometimes, due to news reporting and media awareness programs, my father would get suspicious of my state, but I and other family members were able to bypass his suspicions. My father tried so many times to talk to me alone, about my problems, any love affairs, academic pressure, family trouble, etc. I used to like the special time and space I was getting with my father. I used to answer all his queries with a "no" and a smile. My school counselor also tried to have a word with me a few times, but I never gave her a chance to burst my secret desires.

Unlike other possessed individuals I had interacted with, here was Shubha, attributing her healing and a sense of aliveness not to God directly but to the investment by her family in her cure. In this investment, her father's role was of special importance because, going against his otherwise strict demeanor, here he was giving space to his daughter's sexuality—something she seemed to desire and relish. As a result of all the investment that was coming her way from all those who had wronged her in the past, Shubha had now arrived at gratitude toward them.

S: I was never conscious of my symptoms and sickness. Never sought help or let anybody help. After two years of all this, finally I bid goodbye to it when my family's problems were getting unmanageable. Once again my parents took me to Balaji, but this time I decided not to fail both of them—my parents—and our cultural beliefs. By participating or, rather, letting the traditional healing process work on me, I tried to relocate myself and restored the faith of my family. This time, I let my family and myself celebrate my cure.

I recall, before I began working on my dissertation, I had a dream in which I saw my mother and Chachi fighting. Some tantric was practicing some ritual on me and I was going deeper and deeper into the mud. I was trying hard to fight against the tantric's power, but he had trapped me by tying a rope around my waist. One end of the rope was in my mother's hand and the other in the tantric's. I could see that if my mother let go of the rope, I would be able to free myself from the tantric's trap, but I was feeling annihilated by the sight of my mother holding the rope. I was shouting for help and pleading, but firmly, with anger, asking my mother to support me. I kept saying, "Support me! This man is a fraud, but at least you support me!"

The lie of my being connects me with my disavowed desirous self. I was dissociated from my own desirous self. Admitting to one's desires is very difficult, almost impossible. Excitement and anxiety go hand-in-hand. Maybe what I repressed, my mind and body tried to recover through possession. Hence, the truth of it was what I wanted to live through my dissertation, creating a hospitable womb in myself to something known and lived but yet unthinkable, unsayable, to something in background, running as a script yet not consciously attended to: did I betray my parents? Was it a joy to be hidden but a disaster not to be found?

Perhaps the tantric in her dream represented the enchanting erotic desires she harbored. To undertake psychic work, the internal mother must be surrendered so that one can sink into the mucky business of thinking and processing the "unthinkable" and "unsayable." Shubha seemed to be getting ready to undertake this plunge into muckiness. The dream expressed Shubha's struggle with letting go of the internal mother, with creating distance between the self and the (m)other to allow the function of reflection to emerge. Being in the state of possession was like being in the mother's lap. Was this the fictional part of Shubha's possession experience? However, the academic exercise of writing her dissertation allowed her to engage, to some extent, with her psychic truth. It seemed she was using the space of our conversations to continue thinking through her emotional experience.

S: The seeds of my mental sickness were sown in my childhood. I was a bad kid, sadly. I have been hit and punished by elders since childhood for being mischievous and notorious. I took birth in a joint family and, as I have seen, in joint families, there are so many kids and not all can enjoy special attention—only a few. After my birth, my mother got pregnant within three months without her knowing it. When I was about one, she gave birth to my younger sister. Because she was in her post-delivery resting period, I was attended to by my grandma and aunt. If I was ever mischievous, they would hit me. My mother would bring up these instances in later years and add to my pain, and I cannot stop myself from fantasizing about how it must have felt to the one-year-old me. My imagination helps me reconstruct what was repressed. My mum would say that she used to feel helpless, that she could not defend me from them or stop me from being mischievous. One day, when she was sharing this experience with me, I was looking for my mother's nonverbal expressions to understand how she felt about it now. Thankfully, she could still feel the pain and continued to complain about my grandma and aunt. I was always fighting with my siblings and cousins. They would hit me, take my things and complain about me. But the elders would not notice. When I would hit them back, then the elders in the house used to scold and beat me up. Everybody would stop talking to me. And I used to feel that everybody was so bad, especially Mummy, nobody loved me. I started withdrawing within myself, not talking and playing with others, only with myself. I made an imaginary friend—a corner of my home's toilet became my friend. I used to talk to it, sharing my grievances, happiness, and sorrows. It never replied, but I never forced it to. I always used to say, "I will wait for you to say something to me someday. Until then, you listen to me." If Mum ever scolded me in front of any guest, I would turn more wild, aggressive, and bad. Slowly, I was turning into a rebellious animal. My father's punishments and beatings stopped having an impact on me. He used to get tired while beating me, but I never accepted defeat. When left alone, I used to cry hard and tell myself, "Cry as much as you can right now—later you would have to be tough as iron." Growing up meant greater physical strength—now I could hit back at my punisher. I started hitting back at my parents, especially my mother. After a fight, I would stop eating food for days, until my parents got on their feet, begged me and won me over. There is much more to say, but now I cannot. It's too heavy to take. I am sorry!

A few weeks later, Shubha wrote a letter to me, informing me that her mother had expressed joy because she thought Shubha was now an adult and did not need others to care for her. Her mother also expressed regret over not having taken care of Shubha in her childhood. On meeting her, I asked her what the interaction with her mother had made her feel.

S: I don't know. It was like . . . I felt bad about it too. As in, why did it happen—why, why did it happen only with me? But also a kind of freedom. Now I know that something happened with me at some point in my childhood and my mother was not available for a long period of time. But now I understand that and so I can bypass it instead of thinking about it and letting it impact me. At least now she can acknowledge it.

The acknowledgment and apology from her mother seemed to add validity to Shubha's experience. It had really happened. She was not crazy. It also eased the hostility that Shubha harbored against her mother and freed Shubha's mind to also reflect on potential identification with her mother.

S: It's like, if you identify with the mother, the depressed part that identifies with the mother, that somehow becomes the medium for you to live life. The model mother showed you how you should be living. When you try to evolve, then your pain reaches your mind. Your mind can feel the intensity of the pain. You evolve. So I was able to bypass that internalization, although I still have it within me. In the kind of relationships that I establish with people—as she acknowledged that she has been absent, I too acknowledged that there come times in my relationship when I am absent, not always present.

Me: And what is it like to be present, to be a body and not a ghost?

S: You know, um, for the moment, for a few moments of bodylessness within me, as if I am not born out of that pain—that was comforting for the time being but I could not stay with that for a long time. I had to come out of it. After a while, I almost got invisibilized. I wanted to come back after having, after feeling, after touching that pain, after feeling that sensation of bodylessness, but I wanted to come back to be heard.

Me: Screaming and wailing in the state of possession did not seem enough to be heard because of its fictional quality.

S: From not having a sense of my body to an experience of possession in which the body is so alive—swaying, dancing along with other possessed people—it was very overwhelming and scary. Like something is not in your control. Almost as if I had surrendered myself to somebody and that somebody was making me move. After an entire session of having a *peshi*, my body would be in severe pain. I could not talk and my neck would hurt for a full day. After each encounter with the *peshi*, I would experience severe pain in my body and would sleep for one entire day, but after that, I would feel much freer than before. But, yes, it was like menstruation, like you wait for your periods to come and then, when it goes, you feel lighter, as if your body has become clean of some kind of dirt from the inside.

Me: As if the dirt of the mind gets evacuated via the body?

S: Almost as if somebody else is inside you and that you have to remove that person from your body through these cultural paths. I am thinking about the fact that, you know, when people are not healed for years, they keep on getting possessed for years.

Me: Maybe because it is pleasurable? In your case, it led to a good need satisfaction—your mother was with you, taking care of you. It seems fainting replaced thinking and processing emotional pain. And possession consolidated this mechanism. When we can evacuate emotional pain, we do not have to suffer thinking through it.

S: Yes, exactly!

Me: You spoke of a moment when it all became clear to you. You saw that your parents were taking care of you, they were troubled because of you. After this sight, there came a realization—"I am not possessed"—followed by guilt. In this journey from fainting, being possessed, not being in control of your body, to becoming self-aware, you did not have psychology. How did the capacity to look inwards develop?

S: (Laughs) Hmm . . . that is a very interesting question. Because, you know, all through this time I have believed that psychology made me look at things this way. Then how . . . ? I am not sure. I have seen people getting healed. They tend to be more devoted to Balaji or to their parents. When they became ill, they were in their own shell, but when they came out of possession, they somehow changed toward their families, toward themselves, toward people around them.

Me: It is almost as if you, too, were able to shift the gaze from yourself toward your parents. You were, for the first time, able to *see* them.

S: Yes. And from there the desire emerged in me to understand this phenomenon better and make it accessible to people. I wanted to bring out the beauty in my experience, but I ended up criticizing it. I think I would say . . . guilt . . . perhaps it was because of guilt that I realized how my parents were suffering because of me. I think first there was guilt, because I always felt that I had somehow created all this to get attention. I had used the language I could understand, the language my people could understand. I utilized that to get what I wanted, to create. Almost like a mischievous child.

Me: And a creative one! Finding ways to create the breast wherever and whenever she wants.

S: Yeah, but not everyone can appreciate it in that manner.

Me: To me it seems like it was your self's way of surviving, of reclaiming what was lost.

S: And that's why my mother appreciated it—or, you know, in a mixed tone, she appreciated and acknowledged it also, that, you know, there was a time when I went away from her. Now she is distant, but she is still close to me. She is becoming interdependent.

Me: Maybe . . . (pause) in your experience of possession, were there any hymns, chants or prayers that especially spoke to you?

In asking this question, I was allowing myself to be guided by what my intuition was telling me about the cultural process that made her journey to guilt and reparation possible. I wondered about the significance of her repeated visits to the temple, of others praying and organizing rituals for her cure, of hymns that facilitated some processing of painful emotional states, of interactions with the healers and conversations between the healer and the possessing spirit believed to have been inhabiting her.

S: No, it was my family's belief that was much more instrumental than other things. Them praying for me—my mother used to sing hymns in the morning and in the evening, for me, and even when I used to enter those possession states, my father could not believe for a long time that I was possessed. He used to think that I was doing it intentionally, to get all the attention, and he even tried to have a word with me many times. He would ask if there was something else troubling me, as if he could sense . . . He was counseling me at those times. He had no knowledge of psychology but still. You were asking me where that language came, allowing me to see this other side of possession. It came from my father. He kept on trying and asking me if there was anything troubling me. Although he had seen his mother, sister and everybody getting possessed, when it happened to me, he was curious about whether it was something behavioral or related to the mind.

Me: It's very interesting that your mother's lullaby-like prayers coupled with your father's being able to see your truth even if he had been domineering— when you were possessed, he was able to sense the truest part of you—I think these two things contributed to your healing.

S: Yes! Exactly! It made me realize that I had to get well as soon as possible. And even though he could see my true self, he was there with me in the temple. He kept sitting the entire night. He became another mother to me. So he was there, letting me explore parts of myself with freedom.

Me: He sensed the reality of your state, but he was still letting you enjoy this illusion that you were possessed, powerful and uninhibited.

S: Yes. Now, after talking to you, I find myself able to make sense of these things. All this started, unconsciously, because there was a lack of warmth, and ultimately the wish is to fetch that care. Even Kakar talks about this, right—that healing is possible through the care that comes from the family.

Me: For some people, illness becomes a way of getting others to care. In child-hood, you would often fall sick and then relish your mother's care and warmth, and now that you have started working, taking care of yourself, your mother's care and attention are coming your way without your having to fall sick.

S: In fact, now she tries to possess me by constantly calling to see how I am doing.

Me: I wonder if your possession or illness enhanced her sense of worth. You were the one she was supposed to take care of, and now you are not possessed but independent, you are not in her possession.

S: Yes! Exactly!

Me: So, while you felt you could possess your parents through your episodes of possession, that you could get their love and care, through your possession, your parents also possessed you. Perhaps, deep down, there was guilt in them that they had not given enough—

S: (Interrupts) Care!

Me: Yes, due to your sister's illness. And your possession gave them a much-awaited chance to reclaim what *they* had lost, a chance to form a deeper emotional connection with you.

S: Yes, exactly, exactly, exactly, yes, it makes a lot of sense!

Me: I am also wondering about how, during your possession, when you lost your sense of possessing a body, and when, in your possessed state, your body felt alive and lighter, how your parents also acquired a body for you. They became somebody to you, they became "persons" for you. And now that you are invested in your career and are becoming a person yourself, perhaps they are feeling threatened, perhaps they feel that they are losing their own bodies, as if they are becoming invisible.

S: Yes, exactly. (Thinks for a while) Yeah, and also one more incident. When I was possessed, so, my sister got operated that time—hand surgery for her burnt hand—so, you know, one day, she had her stitches and she was resting, and I became possessed and I took a pair of scissors and I went very close to her, as if to scare her, and I said, "Today I will cut your stitches and that will be very painful to you." I scared everybody. My mother came and she started shouting. Because I was in a possessed state, they thought that I could do it. So they got very scared and my mother came and one of my cousins gave me a very tight slap and my whole cheek turned red and I was in a lot of pain. I fainted after that because it was very painful.

The possession experience opened up a space for her to live out her hostility toward the sister who had taken most of Shubha's share of parental love. I asked her if her experience of possession made her feel more "real."

S: I would say yes, if true means more alive and intense. It was more of a true experience than any other illness, as I was much closer to my deeper layers of self and could learn more about my desires and struggles. It was like a child's make-believe play, but I was playing with my family's beliefs.

Me: This play allowed you to come close to your desires and to your body. What haunted earlier was embodied. The rage toward your sister, the lifting of inhibitions during possession states and bodily closeness with your father who had become a mother for you, all these moments and perhaps more allowed space for your body to reclaim its life. The body and mind could come together, rather than collapsing under the demand to relate to each other—the body could now feel alive and be gradually integrated with the mind. You became more assertive. I think we have understood now the beauty in your possession experience—by giving the passions of the body their due space, a chance for the aggressive part to be voiced and the seductress part to be lived, possession created the much-needed space for the establishment of a link between the dissociated body and mind.

She took on the role of a supervisor here and helped me understand her even better, this time through theory.

S: Every day we live with both our mind and body, but we don't acknowledge that they are interrelated. They seem like two agencies working parallel to each other. Winnicott's dependent stage, the "I": a new baby's initial formation is entirely focused on to the body—the needs, desires, impulses. To a baby, these things are granted and not forbidden. The mother and other members of society happily lend their breast (or life source) to a baby so he or she can "be," grow, play, live. The independent stage, "I and you": but when the baby matures, the society that at first gave now slowly takes it back from the growing baby and expects to develop its own breast (or objects of gratification). Here comes the role of the mind, that is, symbolically the baby needs to create an image/memory or imagination of having developed breasts or other parts that offer gratification. The interdependent stage, the "we": now, after further growth, society expects the baby to function with both dependence—relying on the maternal provisions—and independence—relying on the memory of the mother, but this is not a smooth passage, and, as we have gathered from my childhood experiences, some conflicts occurred during my developmental stages, and it seems my gratifications could not be accomplished optimally. But fortunately, I could relive my split-off parts and reflect on them through my possession experience, in trance form. I will share with you a similar experience I had today, which I had during a trance or an altered state. I am an auditory person, music touches me. Today, I was missing Naman like hell, I had tears thinking about him. After a long bout of a depression-like state, I got up, switched on music and started dancing like a crazy woman who is madly in love. I untied my hair and began dancing like possessed people dance in their *peshi*—free, alive—I touched myself, I felt myself, as if Naman were touching me and had entered me. After a few minutes, I went to the washroom and, while urinating, I simultaneously began wondering whether I could be with him. Then I felt I had grown up and started laughing at the thought that now I'm old enough to no longer want to stay with my parents. I could sense my desperation for Naman, along with the frustration of not being able to be with him, of still being with my parents.

I guess the beauty of this mutual dialoguing between mind and body lies in the fact that their play allows the much-needed space of living and reliving. Living with the body—in actual acts, impulses, snatching the breast, illnesses, madness—and reliving with the mind—in reflections, memories, imaginations, bearing the breast. To acknowledge their conglomeration, I had to let go of my fears—bodily shame—using my own cultural props, the very sources of such shame and dissociation, and then I was able to access the guilt and acknowledge the presence of others and my own incompleteness without them. It's like breasts are the life source and they are the source of death, too.

DISCUSSION

The function of maternal reverie is to transform the infant's unpleasant psychic states into less toxic experiences. Infants deprived of access to this fail to develop the capacity to think through psychic content. According to Bion, "if no thought were possible, the individual would go straight from an impulse to an action. . . ." (As quoted by Symington & Symington, 1996). In Shubha's case, an inability to recognize the external status of her objects and a tendency to avoid experiences were repercussions of the lack of access to maternal reverie in her childhood. On many occasions, listening to Shubha casually describe painful events from her life, I felt her sadness and loneliness. As noted before, it was like I had become her imaginary childhood friend, the toilet corner, and yet different enough to feel and articulate the unpleasant emotional states that she dumped in me. Interestingly, she linked her possession with her need for maternal love. Her frequent illnesses in childhood are today understood in a different light. I have now understood that the effect that imbued our conversations for the most part was associated with her strained relations with both her parents, who were experienced as insufficiently present.

Drawing from Ogden (1992), we understand that the father's dominance and mother's victimhood establish the father's presence in the daughter's mind as a threatening one. The transition from the dyadic relationship with the mother to a triangulated, oedipal one with the father is compromised. Sexual feelings that mark the oedipal phase are dissociated from. As a result of the threatening father's image being reflected in the mother's victimhood, the body is not erotically invested in. The father cannot be imagined as a love object. This failure in Shubha's transitional oedipal relationship took the form of a paralysis-like incapacity to relate to him in any way. Her father never appeared in the narrative until I brought him up. She did not even feel like relating to him. It was not many interviews later that she realized how little she spoke about him. Talking about him caused her to turn inwards. He was someone she could not have or be like. Coming close to the father meant betraying the victimized mother.

Interestingly, her first possession episode was provoked by a sexually charged atmosphere. In her adolescence, the resurgence of repressed sexual content in a sexually charged climate stirred the palpable anxieties surrounding the notion of betraying the internal mother by entertaining lascivious thoughts. The pull between sexual desires and associated anxieties was resolved by punishing the mother. By laying down a model for her daughter through her victimhood, Shubha's mother unconsciously kept her from relating to her father. Shubha's possession allowed her to punish her mother for creating this gap between father and daughter and demonstrate her to be uncaring. Shubha's private perception of her mother was made public through possession—"She is in fact a bad mother who led her daughter into possession."

Although becoming a loner seemed like a defense against the wish to come closer to and identify with her father, Shubha continued to experience a pull toward relating with him, which brought him back into her narrations. Much later, she expressed her gratitude to me for enabling her to talk about him. She realized that there were many things she did not know she felt toward him and still many more things about him that she did not know but wished to know. It was the image of the troubled parents invested together in her healing that gripped me, leaving a tension in me that had to be metabolized. What followed was a process whereby the therapist-researcher in me gradually metabolized the tension created by this image and developed an understanding of beauty in Shubha's experience of healing.

Her wish to come close to her father was gratified through her possession-illness on the many occasions when he, suspecting that it was not anything supernatural, tried to initiate conversations with her. She received all his questions with a smile. It was as if, in smiling, she was admitting her desire for closeness with her father. When asked about the factors that may have contributed to her healing from possession, the image that came forth was of her mother singing lullaby-like hymns and her father's presence, his efforts to give space to her sexual and hostile wishes. While the pre-oedipal internal infant could be soothed by the mother's lullaby-like prayers for her ailing daughter's recovery, the oedipal father could be related to in private conversations with him. He had indeed become a mother-in-father.

Perhaps, sensing intuitively that her daughter would benefit from this reorganization of interpersonal (and internal) relationships, the mother, too, facilitated this relationality between father and daughter by letting them be, by not intervening. The father's questions to his daughter about her sexual conflicts and anxieties were expressions of his readiness or openness to perceive his daughter as sexual, as becoming a woman. This initiative on his behalf gave the dissociated hostile and sexual impulses their due space. The father's love and acceptance, his allowing his daughter to "be," was a much-desired and much-needed ointment on the wounds caused by the violence he had committed upon her in the past. His investment in his daughter made available to Shubha the necessary supplies for her self and led her toward the path to recovery. For her body to move endlessly, uncontrollably, and uninhibitedly in possession, it required the presence of both the parents, who were hitherto perceived as having intensely invested in other children. The mother was required as an active presence so that she could generate an experience of dreaming through lullaby-like hymns, while the father could now enable the evolution of the imagination of a lover. Nothing in this was threatening because nothing was actually entering the body. The mother's lullaby and the father's reference to sexuality were turning the woman into a sexual being.

To sum up, there are two images of Shubha. The first is of her missing her mother in the past with such intensity that she would faint. The second is of her missing her boyfriend with such intensity that it led to her "touching" and "feeling" her body the way he would have touched her, felt her, known her. In between these two stations is her experience of possession, defined by the experiences of being held by the mother's lullaby-like hymns and of sexual growth in the space offered to her by the father. These two components in her possession experience caused her to be embodied or, in other words, caused her "erotogenic body" (Botella and Botella, 2005) to begin to form. With Naman's arrival in her life, this development was only furthered, as he listened to her with warmth and touched her with love. So, these three components—the mother's investment in her healing, the father's readiness to imagine his daughter as sexual and ushering her toward imagining another man as a love object, and the reception of love and touch from the boyfriend—facilitated the transformation of her non-erotogenic body into one that was now erotically invested.

PERVERSION OVER POSSESSION, FRAUDULENCE OVER FAITH

When I met him, Ravi was a twenty-nine-year-old man running a tea shop in Balaji village in North India. In his spare time, he welcomed possessed persons and their families, listened to their malaises, and told them about rituals and ceremonies they would benefit from. I first met him when I, another researcher and a friend were sitting in Ravi's tea shop discussing ghosts and spirit possession or *samkat*. We were talking specifically about Indian philosophical notions of suffering. Before I knew it, Ravi had also become part of these discussions. He was bright and shared his knowledge of the scriptures. My sense while listening to him was that the knowledge he was sharing with us and the links he was drawing with various Hindu myths had emerged from his having survived some painful life experiences. I asked him how he had come to know so much.

R: When one has truly experienced misery in life, experienced it closely, only then is such wisdom awakened.

The day after that, when I met him again and expressed my curiosity about what he had said the previous day, Ravi shared with me his story. Some years ago, he was "mentally disturbed" (his term) and was taken to the nearby city for psychiatric treatment. He was prescribed certain medicines, which he took for a year. Although they brought his problems under control, they made him feel sleepy and lethargic all the time. The doctors recommended that he remain on medicines his entire life. Unwilling to do so, Ravi discontinued the medication and suffered the side effects—fainting spells, problems with sleep, etc. It was a difficult time for him, a time during which he was helped by his belief in Lord Balaji and what he calls his "own willpower."

R: I began to motivate myself, telling myself to change my negative thoughts into positive ones.

When asked what these negative thoughts that needed to be replaced were and where they originated from, he told me that he had once performed a *kanak dandwat* right up to Balaji temple. *Kanak dandwat* is a ritual that involves travelling a certain distance by repeating a specific set of actions: lying face-down on the ground, making a mark on the ground with one's hands, standing up again and then repeating the set from the mark made. This ritual is to be completed in one night. On completing it, Ravi felt his mind being suddenly flooded with thoughts. All he felt like doing was running toward Lord Balaji. He became irritable and eccentric. His description of this episode and its impact on him was very vague, but I sensed that these recurrent thoughts he suffered from were of a violent nature. He was taken to a psychiatrist, but a plea (*"darkhast"*) was also submitted in Balaji temple to Lord Balaji for his divine intervention.

It was in his determination and what he called his "willpower" and the consequential emergence of wisdom that I located the aesthetic value of his suffering. It seemed to me that Ravi considered his mental disturbance to be synonymous with *samkat*, i.e., it was the literal translation of the word *samkat*—a misfortune. It was not an experience of losing control over one's body and mind to an alien malevolent entity. I was also intrigued by the selflessness with which I saw him helping other possessed people. It was this empathy and drive to do good that made me want to understand Ravi.

R: My *samkat* began, according to me, with a dream. Later, I tried to understand the dream. I saw the temple located on the highest peak of the three mountains. Then I saw myself simply wandering in a jungle. Then I saw a cow. As I walked on, I saw a strange idol. At its base it is one statue, but at the top it branches into three different faces, one on top of the other. I pick a tiny straw and poke the eye of the face at the bottom, and suddenly it comes to life. Then I leave the idol there and continue walking. I see that cow again and, this time, I run after it. The cow runs through a flock of partridges. I follow her, but I cannot catch her. Then the dream ends. When I reflected on the dream, I realized that, in my search for *dharma*[6], I had arrived at Maharaj Ji's doorstep. I had followed *dharma* for him, fulfilled all my duties, but his eyes could never see my pain. I tried to open his eyes to my pain, but when he finally opened his eyes to my pain I left him there and moved on. I paved my path through many sorrows. Only by going through the sorrows of others will I be able to follow *dharma*. Mother cow is the symbol of *dharma*. The flock of partridges is like the many sorrows. I have to keep following *dharma*. That idol symbolized three generations—the idol on the top is that of Lord Balaji, the next idol is that of the first supreme priest, Ganeshpuri, and the one at the bottom is that of Guru Ji, in whose eye I poked a tiny straw.

Ravi then showed me the image of this guru on a banner that was pasted on the wall right behind me.

R: I did a lot for this Guru, but a person like him can also betray. When he wanted to build his temple here, he approached me for help. I invested some money in it, gathered a few boys and we carried bricks and cement on our heads and climbed uphill. It took us the entire night, climbing uphill and downhill. I do not know how many times. My head wasn't screwed on right. Some people here had an issue with his temple, but he did not tell me anything about it. Then, one day, the police came looking for me because, in the entire village, I was the only one who helped him. People were angry with me. I called him, but he did not answer my calls. The police took me into custody for a few days. My family somehow managed to gather enough money to get me out on bail. I felt quite bad that he had trapped me and disappeared. When I called him again, he answered and called me to Delhi for a religious conference. I left my younger brother in charge of the shop and went. On reaching Delhi, I felt that his behavior toward me was different. He was surrounded by his followers, so he did not pay any attention to me. I felt awful about having endured so many difficulties for this man only to find that this is how he was treating me. I told him that I wanted to go back. He said that I should. I disappeared for fifteen days. I lost my mind. I felt that Guru Ji had betrayed me. I had invested Rs. [Ten thousand] in his temple. People here filed police complaints against me, everyone was angry with me—my mind was all over the place. While returning from Delhi, thoughts of suicide repeatedly arose in my mind. I was hoping that Guru Ji would stop me, that he would ask me if I had eaten anything or had money or not. On the way, the bus stopped at a hotel where passengers could have food and freshen up. I got down to have some food. I do not know where my mind was, but I got into another bus and reached some place far away. Then the bus conductor told me that I was on the wrong bus. They dropped me on the way, saying that my bus was behind them, that I should board it. All my stuff was on that bus—my mobile phone, wallet, clothes . . . but my bus did not come. For fifteen days, I was just wandering aimlessly on the roads, living on the roads. I would keep sitting in front of any roadside food stall. Visitors would see me and find me pitiable, wounded, but with some capacity to think and understand. They would feed me. There I met a priest. We spoke and he took me to his home, took care of me, fed me, bathed me, gave me clean clothes to wear. Then he called my brother. My family came to get me. My brother was very concerned about me.

Ravi had a good relationship with his elder brother, but he did not talk much about their father. Giving in to my probing, he revealed that his father had died of illness. He would fall ill every year or two. This had made Ravi aware very early on of his responsibilities toward his family. He began working to support the family and earned Rs. 150 a day as a laborer. His academic performance deteriorated, and he decided to complete his schooling through distance learning.

After completing his schooling, Ravi went to Delhi to attempt the Delhi police selection examination. A day before he left, he took his father to the city for a medical check-up. When the doctor advised them to undertake further blood tests, Ravi asked if it would be okay to wait four or five days, as he had to go to Delhi. The doctor responded affirmatively, and Ravi left for Delhi the next morning.

It was just after he had taken the exam that he remembers having felt that something was wrong (a premonition). He soon left for home and reached his village to find his shop closed. On arriving home, he was told that his father died. He reached the cremation ground just in time to see his father's face before the flames consumed it. Today, Ravi blames himself for his father's death.

R: If only I had missed the trip to Delhi that day and taken him to the doctor, he would have been alive . . .

After a long silence in which I sensed that I was being pulled into the role of a counselor, I tried to console him and brought to his notice what I considered to be his way of dealing with his loss.

Me: It is very sad. Perhaps that is why you regarded Guru Ji also as a father. It is as if you are searching for a father figure. What Guru Ji did to you caused a pain so deep perhaps because you saw a father reflected in him.

R: Yes, madame. I regarded him like a father. I felt awful about what he did to me.

Me: Your *samkat* began after that?

R: Yes. A few days after returning home, I finished the *kanak dandwat* and reached the Balaji temple. Soon after attending the morning prayer ritual, I don't know what happened to my mind—suddenly I started to hear voices . . .

Me: What were these voices saying?

R: I don't know . . . to die and to kill. Negative thoughts would often come to my mind. I would feel like dying. I did not feel like working. I would just be lying in bed. Sometimes I used to get up and run out of the house. Family members were very disturbed. I was experiencing terrible depression. That was when they took me to the psychiatrist who prescribed the medicines.

Me: What was the diagnosis?

R: He diagnosed me with depression and gave lots of medicines and said that I was supposed to take them for the rest of my life.

Me: Did you experience any relief after taking the medicines?

R: What relief? I felt sleepy all the time. I stopped going to the shop, felt lethargic the whole day.

Me: Are you still on medication?

R: No. In the name of Lord Balaji, I stopped the medication. I took a vow to somehow live my life without the medicines. Partially due to my own willpower, partially by grace of Lord Balaji, I am absolutely fine now.

Me: What caused your depression, according to you?

R: It was *samkat*. Usually, people experience it when someone uses black magic to cause them to become afflicted by spirit possession. I feel there is something in the air in this place. You have come from Delhi, madam. Don't you find the environment here polluted?

Me: Polluted? Hmm. Many possessed people visit this place, so I am picking up on a lot of sorrow and pain in the environment here. But that is my experience.

R: Yes. I feel that—as is mentioned in the scriptures—all of us are made of this very soil, air, and water. God resides in every tiny grain of this universe, and we are also made from the same grain. This *samkat* is also made from the same grain. When it departs from a body, it goes back into this very soil, air, and water. So my theory is that the air and water here are such that *samkat* can easily enter someone. I feel there is something strange in the very air here, it can corrupt the mind and then cause depression.

Me: So, according to you, is depression caused by this air and water or by life's painful experiences and negative thoughts, like you had mentioned before?

R: Both. *Samkat* comes from the air. Then come negative thoughts. *Samkat* causes depression, and Balaji delivers us from *samkat*.

Me: But there are many people who have been here for many years and still not been healed of their *samkat*.

R: It also depends on one's own *karma*. Now, in my case, it was Balaji's grace and my own willpower that instructed me to get better somehow. Deliverance from *samkat* is possible when your own power and Balaji's power come together.

Me: Hmm. You have gained wisdom from living through your sorrow. Now I am better able to understand what you said earlier.

R: Madame, when we are beaten down by sorrow, when we live through our sorrows, only then do the mind's eyes open up.

By now, it was clearer to me that there was a lot of sadness and guilt in Ravi stemming from the nature of his father's death. This pain had not been evacuated but was being lived and felt. In his search for a father substitute, I could sense he was attempting to deal with the loss. I became curious about the other relational dynamics in his house. His mother, brother, brother's wife, brother's children, and his own son stayed with him. After a quarrel, his wife had left him and taken their daughter to stay with her parents. His was a child marriage.

R: I must have been in Class 3 or 4. My family members got me married. At that time, I did not know what was happening. We were very happy that we are getting married, like dolls. I could never get along with my wife. We were always fighting. I used to like a girl in school when I was in Class 10. She was in my class, and she also used to like me. We used to write love letters to each other. Then my family brought my wife home and I learnt that we had actually been married off during our childhoods. I told my family members that I would not accept her as my wife. Then they also found out about my affair with the other girl in school. That girl's family came home to beat and threaten me and forced me to call her "my sister." They began to ask her to either accept me as a brother or beat me with slippers. She refused to do either of the two. Even amidst all these problems, both of us were trying to save each other. Then we decided to end it. Now she is a teacher in a school in the city. I met her once. She invited me and my wife home. I could never get along with my wife. I tried everything. She does not understand me.

As I was leaving, I thanked Ravi for speaking to me about his life experiences.

R: Madame, it is not that I did not gain anything from talking to you. The kinds of questions you were asking made me think about myself. My knowledge has also been enhanced. There is that saying—when a wise person meets another wise person, the wisdom multiplies, and the boundless Divine (*Paramatma*) resides where one soul meets another. In conversations, one soul converses with the other soul. So, I also enjoyed talking to you. Now, after you leave, I will sit and reflect on all the wisdom I gained from you. I will discuss my reflections with you the next time you come.

It seemed to me that Ravi was deeply invested in trying to find ways to serve possessed people. Not only was he driven to help them, he also offered his help without any hope of any materialistic gains.

R: I know what they go through. That is why I want to do something for them. It is good if something good can happen to someone through me.

Time and again in our conversations, he would thank me for awakening him to many aspects of his inner life. I had successfully established a link for him, between his disappointment and his perennial search for a father. This made him grateful. His persistently thanking me carried hints of idealization that made me very uncomfortable and, to some extent, intimidated. The discomfort I felt was a product of my own relationship with being put on a pedestal. It felt dehumanizing and infected me with anticipatory anxiety— *What was to come?* Would the pedestal suddenly be pulled from underneath me? Would I suffer a massive fall?

I met Ravi after a few weeks. He was doing well. He had become involved with the welfare of the people of his village and had expanded his business, going from running a small tea stall to distributing mineral water canisters to vendors in nearby villages. I congratulated him on his growth and wished him luck with his future endeavors. Rather than accepting the wishes, he gave me all the credit, claiming that I had given him the motivation he needed to achieve everything he had. This puzzled me, because I did not feel like I had tried to motivate him at all. I had only expressed admiration for the determination and willpower with which he had triumphed over distress. Was he starving for this kind of mirroring? Was this validation the fuel he was waiting for to excel in life, in order to emerge with all the compassion and empathy he had for others? Why was he idealizing me? What were his relationships with his parents like? Which part of his self was being lived through me and what had I done to facilitate this?

In our next conversation, my questions began to find answers. Almost a month later, I was travelling somewhere from Delhi when I received his phone call.

R: Ma'am, I have been facing a difficulty for the last few days. I have thought a lot about whether I should speak to you about it or not. I felt maybe you would be able to help me understand why this is happening to me. For some days now, whenever I see a young woman or girl, I get obscene thoughts about them. (Hesitates) I mean, I get aroused. My state becomes such that I fear I might end up doing something.

Me: What do you do then?

R: I mean, I look for a place where I can be alone—I have to relieve myself.

Me: Does that regulate the arousal somewhat?

R: Yes, for some time. But then, when I see another woman, the arousal returns. I have tried very hard to control it, to distract myself. I tried meditation. But the issue still remains. I have been very disturbed. I could not understand whom to seek a solution from. I don't understand what is happening.

I could not think of any way to fix this then because he had called at a time when I was travelling. He was sharing this perverse part of himself with me either because he genuinely trusted me and hoped that I would contain and detoxify it or because I too evoked this feeling of arousal in him. Either way, I was slightly intimidated. I told him that we would need to think it through and figure out how it was linked to the life experiences he had discussed with me. He also informed me that his wife had come back to him from her parents' home and had been compulsively washing her hands ever since. I suggested that he speak to her and find out what was going through her mind when she felt the need to wash her hands. I offered this suggestion as an attempt to connect the dots between his state of arousal, his wife's return and the subsequent compulsions they were both feeling.

My sense was that his wife's return had evoked sexual desires in Ravi that he could not satisfy with her because she was experienced by him as emotionally incompatible. I had not met his wife so I could not say much about the anxieties that were being dealt with through compulsive washing. But I felt that if both husband and wife came closer emotionally and tried to straighten out their relationship, their respective compulsions would be taken care of. I carried his anxieties in me until I met him again in Balaji village after a few weeks.

R: My wife's condition worsened. We had to take her to see the doctor in the city. The doctor prescribed medicines but even with the medicines did not help. Now we have consulted a local healer here. We submitted an appeal to Lord Balaji. That brought her some relief. I feel she will get relief only when she is told that there is a ghost inside her.

Me: Maybe that is why the doctor's treatment did not give her any relief?

R: Yes. If one believes that one is possessed, one's treatment must also be like this, through traditional methods and rest. I am trying to talk to her just like you had suggested, but she does not understand me. She is not literate, so our ways of thinking are not compatible.

Me: Did she suffer from this condition before marriage, or has it only come up now?

R: She was fine before marriage. Then she left for her home. She has been like this ever since she returned from there. She left for home after she got into a fight with my younger sister. My younger sister is differently abled. Somehow, we got her married, but her in-laws began to trouble her and stopped her from studying further. So, I brought her back home and now I am somehow trying to help her finish her studies. My wife often taunted her. She has even commented on the fact that I am doing so much for my sister, more than I have done for her so far.

Me: Does your wife also wish to study?

R: No, ma'am, she does not have any such wish. She is always whining just for the heck of it. She said something to my sister that made me mad. I slapped her. As a result, she took our daughter and left for her parental home. She left the son with me.

Me: And this difficulty that she is reporting, this feeling, that a force is possessing her, this has emerged ever since she returned from her parent's home?

R: Yes, ma'am.

Me: When you took her to the healer, it must have been comforting for her to know that you believed her and were concerned for her well-being. You chose to consult a healer and not a doctor, just as she has wished.

I was trying to validate his efforts to fulfill his wife's needs and reinforce to him the impact this seemed to have had on her condition. I wanted to show him that one way to resolve his wife's distress was for him to give her the space she needed.

R: Yes, ma'am, it is possible. She has been feeling much better ever since we came back from there.

Me: Do both of you still have fights?

R: Yes, ma'am. She still fights with Mummy and my younger sister. I don't say anything to her.

He was experiencing difficulties negotiating the various needs of his sister, wife and even mother. His wife was displaying her displeasure with this by pointing out the imbalance in the way her husband treated his family members on the one hand and her on the other. She did not want to study like Ravi's sister, yet her displeasure was evidence of her disappointment over his failure to fulfill her needs. This unsatisfied and incompatible wife failed to arouse Ravi, who was instead aroused by other women outside the house. This part of his character lay in juxtaposition to another part that emerged in his accounts of his work as a healer. For instance, in one conversation, he narrated how he had been able to restore a possessed girl to health.

R: Ma'am, at first I spoke to her the way astrologers do. It is only when you speak to them like you know everything about them that they believe you know a lot as a healer, that you possess some supernatural power. So, I just shot an arrow in the dark and it hit the target (laughs).

He was aware of the need for the possessed person to be known in gentle ways, to feel like her experience was understood and heard by someone without her having to voice it. Perhaps the mother of infancy is being sought, the mother who is intensely in tune with her infant's states and is experienced as omniscient. Ravi seemed to know too well how to manipulate this universal need for an omniscient m(other).

R: Ma'am, I told her that she was part of a group of four very close friends. I just went on and on until she began to talk. She is in Class 9 and must be around fourteen years old. She has lost everything. She had an affair, and when she woke up to reality, she became depressed. The guy stopped responding to her calls. She became irritable, would often erupt into angry outbursts at family members, experience spells of crying. She stopped talking to people. Her family members became worried and attributed her behavioral changes to possession by a malevolent force.

Having extracted her truth out of her, Ravi then moved toward intervention, taking the stance of a father who spoke with understanding and authority.

R: I spoke to her like a friend, told her that she was only seventeen or eighteen years old, that things were still not too bad. "You have your whole life in front of you, there are many things you are yet to achieve in life, spend time reading books." She liked how I spoke and what I said to her. She is still like a delicate clay pot——-breakable. I made her aware of the realities of relationships. I told her to consider all the pros and cons before making friends. I considered it important to have this conversation with her. Now, if a person has a tummy ache and we are treating her for fever, the treatment is bound to be useless. I did not share anything with her family members. I told them what they wanted to hear——-that she was possessed—and prescribed a few mantras and rituals.

He seemed to be sufficiently in tune with the needs of possessed people and their family members. I felt tempted to ask him how he would handle someone like Riya. He told me that a person like Riya would need some rituals and ceremonies to prepare her to take the stance of an opponent and confront the force possessing her. His intuition told him that whatever possessed Riya would abruptly leave her body. He felt that we would need to make her realize that the force possessing her had been cast out of her and was being held captive inside an object, that it would never return to possess her again. Ravi emphasized that, since Riya was convinced that she was possessed, she would have to be spoken to in this language. He went on to describe how, on many occasions, he dealt with similar cases by mildly torturing the possessed person—for e.g., by twisting one girl's finger. He firmly believed in not charging any fee for his interventions because, according to him, when money is involved in the performance of such rituals, faith gets shaken.

R: Money should never come in between [the healer and the sufferer]. I try to receive the other's love. I do not want wealth. Love is the greatest source of wealth. And I give you all the credit for whatever I am able to do today. Ma'am, I was nothing. When I came in touch with you, you shook the Ravi in me. Then I realized that I am someone, that I too can succeed in life.

His idealization was continuing to make me very uncomfortable.

Me: Thank you for considering me responsible for all these positive changes in you. However, here I am reminded of your dream, the one in which you poked the eye of one of the idols and brought it to life. Perhaps you also allowed your mind to be poked by our conversations and created space in your mind for the realizations brought about by our conversations. You opened up the doors and windows of your mind. Only that could have made any of this possible.

R: You are right. Nonetheless, I remain grateful to you. Today I am handling so many cases, talking to so many possessed people. It is as if all these cases are your cases. You have become a part of my mind. Everything that we have spoken about has stayed in my mind and that is why I have been able to help so many people. Today, my work is going well. In the entire village, only my children are going to an English medium school.

He then advised me to tell Riya about my conversation with him and said that he could instantly tell she was possessed by the ghost of a child, that she saw images of a woman and of snakes, that the child ghost provoked her with sexual images, that she sometimes experienced sleep paralysis and felt like someone was sitting on her chest. I must admit that I was surprised at this point because all of these images and sensations were in fact being experienced by Riya. When I shared my surprise with Ravi, he remained calm and told me that these were common experiences for all possessed people. He conveyed to me his willingness to help Riya while at the same time expressing regret over not being able to help his own wife.

I decided to take Ravi up for his offer to help. When I spoke to Riya and her family about what Ravi had said, they expressed a keenness to meet Ravi. I arranged a meeting between them in a guesthouse where I was staying in Balaji village. But I could not be present for it as I had to return to my family in Delhi. Later, Ravi informed me that their meeting lasted a few hours. He listened to Riya and her parents closely. After the meeting, Ravi asked me to weigh in on a treatment plan for her. Without sharing details about her life, I explained to him that I thought she would benefit from both her parents somehow being made part of the rituals meant to heal her. Ravi took my advice and recommended to the family that Riya recite the Hanumat Kavach with her mother and that her father take her to the temple, where he was to circumambulate Riya with certain sacred offerings seven times before presenting them to Balaji. This ritual, which can involve money or any other offering of value, is often performed by elders in the family. It symbolizes the extraction of a malevolent force from the person for whom the ritual is being performed and its containment in the offering, which is then surrendered, to be dealt with by divine forces.

Ravi then began to talk about his guru, a father figure he had trusted who had betrayed him by not paying attention to his needs:

R: Ma'am, I keep close those who hurt me. Somehow, these injuries guide my path. Guruji hurt me at every step. He abandoned me in a place I could not find a way out of. I understand how he thought—I am unable to forgive him or turn him into a completely negative person. Every time he has done something wrong to me, I have felt it and told him so, but even then, I am unable to view him in a purely negative light. He was selfish. He could not really see anyone else or anything other than his own selfish needs. One should carve one's own path and tread it. I have learnt from what he did to me, somehow.

Me: What was his response when you conveyed to him that you felt wronged by him?

R: Ma'am, humility (*shaleenta*), innocence. He would ignore everything with displays of humility.

This reference to *shaleenta* or humility seemed like a veiled reference to me, "Shalini." Perhaps he was hinting at his sense that, like the guru, I too was using humility to overlook some of the needs he was bringing to me.

Me: It seems there was no space for your resentment in that relationship.

R: Yes, ma'am, it was exactly like that. After each such exchange, I would feel very restless, I would feel enraged. Ma'am, I am saying all these things to you because I am able to comprehend these things. Now you watch, I will not let him enter the premises of the Balaji temple. I cannot tell you how angry I am. I did so much for him. I do not know why he treated me like this. What do you think?

I hesitated, but he persisted. He wanted my opinion.

Me: Having spoken to you a few times now, I feel you are searching for something in these relationships, whether with your guru ji or other older men. It seems you are searching for an image of your father in them. Not finding it makes you restless.

There was a brief pause. He was quiet and thoughtful.

Me: You don't speak much about your father. I wonder about the emotions attached to that relationship.

R: Ma'am . . . (sighs, pauses for a few seconds) . . . you do not realize that what you have just said is 100% correct.

Me: Would you like to share something about your father? How was your relationship with him?

R: Father used to work as a porter at a railway station in Delhi. He was rarely at home. You are quite right. I think, for a child, the love of both parents is important.

The conversation had to end abruptly, as a large group of customers entered his shop and needed to be attended to. We spoke again after a few days:

R: Ma'am, I thought a lot about what you said. I realize that perhaps I am the one who is at fault. My own desires were attached to that man [the guru]. I thought a lot about this, and then I called him. I asked him for forgiveness and I told him that our relationship could not go on any longer.[7] "Both of us were at fault . . . you took advantage of me and I allowed you to do so." As I said this, ma'am, all his poison began to spew out. He said nasty things to me. He said, "Ravi, you don't know your place." I responded by saying, "Fine, I don't know my place but you are also hiding behind a mask." He said that he was not the kind of priest (*bhagat*) who would come to the Balaji temple [to deal with cases of possession]. I told him that he is not a *bhagat* but he is not god either. The conversation turned into a heated argument. Then he apologized. I said to him, "Now I know my place. Until now, I was living in an illusion. Now my illusion has shattered. I attached my desires to you." Ma'am, if I am doing so much for someone, I can at least expect a "thank you." Soon after this conversation, I erased all the traces of him in my life. Now I am feeling very relaxed.

Me: What were these desires that you had attached to him?

R: Ma'am, I have always been financially weak. When I heard him speak of his plans, I thought that, if I could be connected with him, the boat of my life will also find its shore, I would become something. These desires deepened and I began to drown in them.

Me: Is there a connection between your father and all these desires?

R: Until I was thirteen or fourteen years old, my father used to work in Delhi. I do not have even the vaguest memory of having sat and spent time with him.

Mother tried to make sure we didn't feel the lack of a father, but she was bur-dened with many responsibilities . . . raising children, her own younger siblings, farming. Whenever Father came home from Delhi, he would bring with him sicknesses. I have always seen him sick, hospitalized. Mother could not even take care of herself. We somehow grew up. Even today I cannot ignore anything Mother says. I really respect her.

Me: And how's her relationship with your wife?

R: They don't get along at all. In fact, neither of the two daughters-in-laws [his and his younger brother's wives] gets along with Mother. If my wife says something to Mother, I feel offended. For this reason, there is always tension between us.

Ravi then began to attend to customers. I was left wondering about a poten-tial link between his breakdown and his father's death. When we resumed our conversation, I asked him about it:

Me: I was wondering about the demise of your father and the *samkat* that fol-lowed. It is as if your *samkat* was born with your father's death. Perhaps, with his death, a lot inside you was left unexpressed? I am also reminded of your relationship with your guru, wherein you felt that there was no space for your feelings of resentment, which led to restlessness in you. But perhaps this rest-lessness does not transform into a haunting *samkat* because, like you said earlier, you are now able to comprehend these things and verbalize them.

R: Ma'am, all that you have said fits my experience quite aptly.

Me: Then I would wonder what became of the desires you attached to the guru. Where are these desires directed now? Could they be driving the excitement you experience every time you see a woman and desire to attain her? These desires have just emerged, right? Perhaps, earlier, these desires were attached to your guru ji, and before that to your father. Like an unmet *samkat*'s unmet desires?

R: (looks thoughtful and lets out a sigh) Yes. I am yet to reflect over many things.

On the next occasion we spoke, I asked him about his bodily experience of the state of possession.

R: Ma'am, I have never experienced that state of frenzy caused by the appear-ance of the ghost (*peshi*). I went crazy. My mind lost its sense of balance. Those who experience *samkat* do not actually go mad. Their agony comes out of them swaying and dancing. In madness, one does not have any control over oneself.

He was making an important distinction here between his understandings of the mentally disturbed and the possessed, respectively.

Me: I recall you once said that it is when we are beaten down by sorrow that the mind's eyes open up. Would you like to elaborate on that now?

R: Ma'am, in order to get past any situation, a person needs to confront reality. When one is in misery, I believe that one has a chance to know reality, to know the reasons for the misery. He might think, "Why is this happening to me?" Through such questions, he becomes aware of reality, gains wisdom about what is good or bad for him.

Me: What did you come to know during your own period of misery?

R: While I was in that state, I thought a lot, but those thoughts were mostly negative. Nobody meant anything to me. Later, I realized the value of relationships in my life.

Me: I wonder if that wise Brahmin priest played a pivotal role in bringing about this realization. You returned very forlorn from Delhi, hurt by Guru Ji, and then landed up at the house of this priest. He took the place of the guru and cared for you, perhaps restoring your faith in relationships?

R: Exactly, ma'am. He did a lot for me. I remember, when I entered that village, many people hit me, threw stones at me, because I had gone crazy and I would often bother passersby. I would get after people and ask them to help me. I was grabbing hold of people and giving them telephone numbers to call. But I did not receive any support from anywhere. My condition was deplorable. One night, I slept in hay. Someone gave me some clothes to wear. At another time, someone gave me some food. The kids of the village would often chase me, pelting stones. That old Brahmin scolded the children, and then I shared my whole story with him. He called my family members and informed them of my whereabouts. He then bathed me, gave me clean clothes to wear, a cozy bed to sleep on, and warm food. He spoke to me and asked me many things. He spoke about many spiritual themes. Even then, I was talking a lot about *dharma.* He conversed with me for three hours. He gave me evidence of humanity. So, from all of this, I learned that it is foolish to forget about our experiences in life. Now, give me a resolution for my problem [the problem of experiencing sexual excitement at the sight of a woman].

Me: I wonder if that "problem" has anything to do with how you, perhaps, find it difficult to live out your relationships fully. I wonder about the intimacy between you and your wife—perhaps it is affected because your desires are still attached elsewhere? And perhaps she senses it too, and then resents you for not being fully present in that relationship. This is my understanding, but I could be wrong. What do you think?

R: Hmm. That sounds right. The reason for it is that, after my breakup with my girlfriend, my family members brought my wife home. It made me furious. Why did they bring her? I would avoid going near her. I remained troubled for one whole year. Then I went to meet my ex-girlfriend. I wanted to meet her once. I reached Jaipur. She did not treat me well. She asked me why I was there, told me not to come see her again, that there was nothing left between us. She said that she did not have any feelings for me. She complained to her father, who stopped me while I was on my way somewhere in the village and began to interrogate me. I told him that I had not even touched his daughter, and after some convincing, he let me go. But I felt awful that she did not love me the way I loved her. I began hating women.

I was never attached to my family members. There was always a tension between me and Father. I wanted to study further after Class 12. I was the smartest in my class, too. I told my father that I wanted to study further and that, if he did not have the money to sponsor it, I would work alongside too but he did not approve. He said he could not do anything about it and that I would have to study here in the village. I began to blame him for every setback. My peers were working respectable jobs. I tried to fulfill all my responsibilities but I remained frustrated, fought and felt dissatisfied thinking about my father's limitations. After he passed away, I used to think about how, if I had been present, I could have done something for him. He was asking for me in his last moments. He was the one who encouraged me to appear for the police service examination. In my last conversation with him, he expressed regret that he had not been able to do anything for me. When I returned, he was already gone—I could not meet him.
He remained silent for a few minutes.

R: I don't think any parent is wrong. The circumstances are to be blamed. I realized this after losing him. I would have done everything in my power to save him if I had been there. Today I try to compensate for his loss, satisfy him somehow . . .

Our conversation ended here. Since then, we have spoken only to find out how the other is doing. His work, at the tea stall and as a *bhagat*, is flourishing, and I make sure I appreciate his attempts at restoring many to health, as it seems an attempt to restore the abandoned and angered part of his self.

DISCUSSION

Ravi's father was absent throughout his childhood. During this time, the mother was present but was burdened with the care of her other children and household responsibilities. When his father was around, Ravi had to address his health issues. He was, therefore, stuck between an absent father and a preoccupied mother whom he grew up to idealize. I am reminded of a similar psychosocial matrix unconsciously laid down by Indian mothers for their sons, understood by Kakar (2012) as an oedipal alliance. A son captivated by the mother's overbearing presence craves alliance with the father, who is expected to rescue him. The father is expected to guard and sponsor the son's separation from his mother when the son's need for autonomy surfaces. His affirmation and guidance shape the son's identity.

> Given the intensity and ambivalence of the mother-son connection in the Indian setting, the need for the father's physical touch and his guiding voice becomes even more pressing, the necessity of oedipal alliance often outweighing the hostility of the Oedipus complex. (Kakar, 2012)

His father's absence in his life prevented Ravi from developing the conviction that the father was a dependable figure to identify with, learn from and be loved by. There was in him a long-buried resentment against the father who was not sufficiently there, who frustrated Ravi's desires for further education and forced him into child marriage. When Ravi did move toward a stable future, his father died, leaving him with feelings of hostility as well as guilt. The desires Ravi harbored for his father and later directed toward the guru were the desires to ally with them and to make up for the loss of the former through paternal substitutes.

One figure who emerged as dependable, who momentarily took charge of Ravi's life, was the old Brahmin priest that Ravi met. He was a person Ravi could depend on when he was at his most vulnerable, and he did a good job of not frustrating Ravi, who did not highlight any words of wisdom uttered by this revered figure, but did allude to an intense sense of having his materialistic needs fulfilled by being put in touch with his family and being offered clean clothes, a clean bed, food, nurturance and protection from humiliation.

Soon after being betrayed by his father-like guru, whom he thought he could depend on for sustenance, Ravi experienced a breakdown. In this account, he performed the *kanak dandwat*, a ritual marked by a sentiment of utmost submission, requiring one to repeatedly and completely prostrate oneself and thereby gradually reach the Balaji temple. After enacting this sentiment and submitting to this divine figure through the entire night, when Ravi finally reached the temple, he "lost his mind." The urge to run toward Balaji was driven by his desire to merge with the dependable father, to be hugged by him. It was the self's attempt to undo the loss of paternal love that it had had to deal with in the form of the father's death and the guru's betrayal. In Balaji, there was hope—hope that the reliable father could still be found. This hope was fueled by having lived through an intense experience with a priest who temporarily allowed Ravi to depend on him.

After his breakdown, Ravi regressed to a state of unemployment and became unconcerned about others. With his vulnerability stirred by the perception of closeness with Balaji, his unconscious hostility was unleashed.

He began to hear voices that conveyed to him destructive desires. Medicine helped bring his condition partly under control, but it did not seem reliable enough to depend on for the entirety of his life. A near-concrete reliable paternal presence was needed. So, with the help of his willpower and belief in Balaji, he discontinued the medicines, and today he does not need them.

I think of that image from his dream—the idol with three faces arranged one above the other. The top-most face was of Balaji, followed by that of the "supreme priest" Ganeshpuri, and the last one was of Ravi's guru. In my opinion, the one in the middle also represents the priest who helped Ravi and was positioned (in Ravi's yearning psyche) between the betraying guru and reliable Balaji. It was his generosity and humanity that linked the disappointed and disheartened Ravi with the unfailing god Balaji. In his *bhagat*-hood, Ravi identified with this newfound father and took on Balaji's function of alleviating the distress of those suffering from *samkat*.

Balaji, helped by the generous priest, was established as a "selfobject" (Kohut, 1984) and served the purpose of supporting Ravi's efforts to maintain internal cohesion, strength and harmony. He was not possessed but mentally disturbed. He had expunged the layer of faith, yet his faith in humanity was held in place by the impact of his encounter with the priest. Ravi kept himself at a certain distance from this benevolent figure who had urged Ravi to live his life and straighten his relationships.

My efforts, too, were aligned in this direction when I suggested to him a way of resolving his problem and then punctuated it with the caveat that I, too, could be wrong. Caught in the performance of some form of unconscious theatre, like the distanced, almost mythical brahmin and the lost father, I, too, was keeping myself at a distance from him. Like the father who did not allow him to study further, I was also saying that his enlightenment would commence with the wife, that he needed to connect emotionally with her, that mere physical intimacy would not give him a wife. This movement toward enlightenment that I was trying to encourage was resisted, leading to sexual arousal and a detour via perversion.

Ravi's perverse streak operated underneath the garb of *bhagat*-hood. I tried to understand this side of him. His wife demanded that he pay attention to her needs, stirring internal remnants of the mother of childhood who demanded adherence from her children so she could control situations at home effectively. By not getting close to this needy wife, Ravi ended up bringing forth his unconscious hostility toward his mother (whom he worshipped in reality). There was a split—the mother was idealized, whereas the wife, as a bad projection of the mother, was subjected to hostility and neglect.

Freud and Ogden have informed us that the ego is initially the sole receiver of emotional investment. A tie with an external object is facilitated by a narcissistic identification that treats the external object as an extension of oneself. Gradually, one develops sufficient psychological stability to engage in a form of relatedness with the object that is largely based on a displacement of ego-libido from the ego onto the object (Freud, 1914). A narcissistic object-tie is one in which the object is invested with emotional energy that was originally directed at oneself. The shift from narcissistic identification to narcissistic object-tie is facilitated by a recognition of and emotional investment in the otherness of the object. If this transition is smooth, it leads to the achievement of relating to the object as something outside the realm of one's omnipotence. However, as in Ravi's case, the overbearing presence of the mother who frustrates the boy's attempt to establish autonomy fuels hostility toward her, which is defended against by idealizing her. The ego split and the released emotional energy serve to establish an identification of a part of the ego with the disappointing object, thus allowing it to be preserved. The outrage and the erotic love toward the disappointing object are combined and magnified into sadism, which manifests in an internal object relationship between the abandoned, sadistic, critical, split-off part of the ego and the part that identifies with the disappointing object. Sexuality and aggression are pathologically fused in perversion, with sex mobilized in service of the aggressive drive.

The sadomasochistic fantasy and rituals support survival by denying separateness and loss. The painful experience of loss is short-circuited by this identification, the separateness with the object is denied and the object is either rendered endlessly captive or possessed. Owing to a disturbance—object loss or disappointment—in the process of narcissistic development, the movement from narcissistic object-love to mature object-love with an object experienced as external is skewed toward an incapacity for mourning, i.e., one is "unable to face the full impact of the reality of the loss of the object and, over time, to enter into mature object-love with another person" (Ogden, 2002a).

In my opinion, Ravi's compulsive masturbation is linked to his disappointments with his objects. An internal object relational dynamic between the disappointing object and abandoned object plays out in his work as a *bhagat*. By pretending to be omniscient, manipulating the minds of possessed persons and twisting their fingers to exercise power and control and compulsively masturbating, he manages to hold the image of the disappointing unattainable object he could not omnipotently control. This object can be held or possessed in the fantasy and penetrated repeatedly in the hope that, with each forceful thrust, one's unconscious hostility and rage will come closer to being contained.

In perversion, the mother is forgotten as an object in her own right. Sharing with me his perversion and his discomfort was a way for Ravi to share his movement toward meaning. This movement toward meaning and away from the mother, who was consciously worshipped, provoked in him anxiety.

Although he claims that it was through an encounter with and acknowledgment of external and internal realities that he gained wisdom, it seems that his compulsive masturbation and investment in paternal substitutes were evidence of the failure of his attempts to process the pain of the loss of his parents' presence, as was desired for the development of healthy personality. The picture is of a narcissistic regression in which the lost object is not disengaged with, and the pain of loss is persistently evaded.

Ravi seemed to have chosen perversion over possession. In perversion, one experiences no attachment, whereas in possession one is gripped by a force—there is fear, but there is also a struggle with the entity that is experienced as residing in one's body. Possession is like a spike nailed into the self to stop the flight into perversion, causing the self to spin round and round in the same spot. One may formulate that possession is an antidote to perversion. It allows for the raw vitality of horror to be lived. It is only traversing this horror that makes relationships begin to feel real and leads to the emergence of compassion, empathy, and a drive to repair the relationships one had damaged, externally and/or internally. In Ravi, it seemed as if the horror had split. In his relationship with Riya (another research participant), he made sure that money was not involved; his good, not-sexual part was presented to her. With me, his perverse part was brought forth. As a result of this split, he was closer to shame than to an admission (and "living") of desire in possession.

Neumann, a Jungian analyst, suggested that the "integration of the shadow . . . cannot take place . . . unless one admits the tendencies bound up with the shadow and allows them some measure of realization . . . [T]his leads to disobedience and self-disgust, but also to self-reliance, without which individuation is unthinkable" (1973). Based on a clinical study, Khan (1984) reached the conclusion that allowing evil tendencies some measure of realization by committing actions in accordance with them, could have severely demoralizing effects on the personality. In the case of Khan's patient, self-disgust was unleashed by the enactment with a partner of a beating fantasy he had long enjoyed, with no loss of self-esteem, in the form of solitary masturbation. The enactment precipitated his revisualization of himself as an "evil man" and his depression, which required psychoanalytic treatment.

It is important for ugliness to be excreted. It leaves through the most intimate sexual places and comes out in an unidentified form, though its foul smell reinstates the notion of ugliness as something foul. In this kind of self-realization, all the boundaries between fantasy and reality seem to disappear. It is similar in this sense to the practice of *tantra*, invoking in particular the *pishachini sadhana*. As Kakar put it, "The pollution fantasy underlying the stringent Hindu social regulations that govern what is to be touched or eaten . . . is no longer buried in the depths of private psyches but becomes publicly shared in tantric practice—actual or imagined" (1991).

Tantric practitioners would explain the unmetabolized ugly parts in us as "'undigested karma'—act[s] or affect[s] or experience[s] one was not able to experience fully in the past and so such experiences lay unintegrated in consciousness" (Kakar, 1991). Both the feces and the *bhuta* represent ugliness. While the former belongs to the body, the latter belongs to both mind and body—the self. Possession is, then, like smearing shit all over one's body because that allows one's ugly parts to be lived and, to an extent, tamed. In *tantra*, the practice of smearing and consuming one's own shit and urine is believed to eventually lead to an unbreakable alliance with Karna Pishachini, a demoness who unlocks one's wisdom, reveals the secrets of time and allows for a transcendence of boundaries and an expansion of one's consciousness that provides one access to knowledge of the past and the future of the other.

Unlike ideal "tantric," who arrive at wisdom after a lot of contemplation, wisdom that does not promote the manipulation of sexuality but uses it to attain higher knowledge, Ravi harbors desires. He brings those desires into his so-called services (*sewa*) as a *bhagat*. Balaji sanctions a living out or, rather, a taming of our sexual and hostile parts in the frenzied state of possession. The *bhagat* whose own sexuality is split and dissociated mobilizes such impulses in the possessed persons and vicariously lives these out in themselves. This is done in non-threatening conditions, with the involvement of families and without anything actually being thrust inside the body of the sufferer. It is as if the family, by participating, sanctions a taming of the *bhagat's* unfamiliar and unacceptable sexual and hostile parts.

Ravi created a dichotomy between insanity and *samkat*, which for him is merely the appearance of one's agony (*dukkha*). He went insane; he was not possessed, for, to be possessed, he would need to have faith. He replaced faith in any higher power (internal or external) with determination. I now see this determination as the perseverance that characterized his engagement with his agony. His *samkat* did not manifest externally and sway like that of a possessed person. It was an agony nurtured by him, rather perversely, and emerged—to an extent—in the space of research relationship between him and me, in the form of the erotic part of his personality.

It seemed, in sharing his perversion with me, Ravi's aspiration to venture into the realms that lay beyond shame was coming forth. He aspired to be with a woman like me, whom he perceived to be educated and enlightened. A part of his "excitement" was directed toward me because I had become a more tangible presence than Balaji. Unable to actualize his almost adolescent aspiration and desire, he remained in the domain of horror, shame, and compulsion. He was urging me to guide him so he could be rescued from this entrapment.

Although intimidated, I tried not to judge him. I preferred to remain intimidated, while keeping him in a position from which he could offer the researcher in my knowledge. Confronted with his demand for guidance and resolution, I encouraged him to strengthen his relationship with his wife. It is only now that I have come to understand that a close relationship with god does not entail simply stipulating morals. Godliness is also saying, "You have to live through this mess!" To god, bad and good are equal. S/he accepts all and can appreciate beauty in most broken and ugly parts. It is this ethic that my suggestion to Ravi lacked.

Ravi's claim to being a *bhagat* can be seen as the claim of a malingerer, but my experience with him made me aware of the malingering and stable parts in me. The motivation for this research—to be able to appreciate beauty in brokenness—expresses an awareness of the godly ideal. But, intimidated as I was by Ravi, my inability to empathize with the perverse parts of his self took me far from that ideal. I was able to offer him some "godliness," insofar as my presence was able to evoke goodness in him and I was able to temper my fear, but I lacked the spontaneity of Eigen (2011), who, when confronted by a patient's desire to have sex with him, responded—"Wow! That's a beautiful image!" I was yet to embrace sexuality, to learn to enable emotional aliveness by receiving the other's states with spontaneity and awe.

POSSESSION: A PLUNGE IN FAITH

I met Riya for the first time in the *samadhi sthal* (shrine) of the temple of Lord Balaji, situated in the village of Mehandipur, Rajasthan. As one steps onto the premises of this temple, one is immediately hit by the smell of the holy fire that is kept burning round the clock, the sounds of pain, anger and seduction—moaning, wailing, pleading, grunting, growling, shrieking, laughing—and the (somewhat ironically) painful sight of rhythmic movements everywhere—swaying, jerking, heads spinning, bodies beating against walls or rolling violently on the ground, chaotic running, somersaults, heads being bowed repeatedly before the shrine and pilgrims revolving around the *samadhi* or tomb in postures of worship. I sat under a banyan tree, soaking in the vibrant "climate" of the place, tuning in to the rhythms that were being stirred in my mind and body.

Riya found me. She came and sat next to me. Swaying slowly, watching me out of the corner of her eyes, her pale white face partially visible and partially hidden behind a cascade of her contrastingly pitch-black, scattered hair and her lips curled into a sinister grin. Her features were sharp and body slim. I was drawn in and at the same time repulsed by the sinister, grotesque ghost in her. Scared and disgusted, I averted my gaze. We simply sat, not talking but still communicating, she through her swaying, and I by averting my gaze.

Another possessed man came and sat next to me, and we began to talk. He knew Riya and asked her how she felt. She (or her *samkat*) answered in a child-like voice, "No, brother, I have not left yet. I will not go just now." Scary, yet there was something about her gaze that seemed inviting. I was gripped by fear, evoked by her grimace.

The next day, she approached me accompanied by her elder sister. She had learnt from other people at the temple that I was a researcher trying to understand *samkat*. She expressed a willingness to participate. One day, I was invited by her to meet her family. It was this instinct in her, to accord value to my research with an expectation that she would gain something, that eased my fear.

In her normal state as a twenty-five-year-old girl, Riya first came across as extremely jovial and talkative. In her and her elder sister Neetu, I sensed an urgency to relate to and be heard by a person who was interested in looking past the scariness and grotesqueness of ghosts, willing to accept those as features of the language of ghosts and to try and decipher what was being said through the presentation of scary and grotesque elements. We met in the premises of the *samadhi sthal* and sat on a thin plastic mat spread out on the ground. The girls sat facing me, blocking a silent woman behind them. It was only later that I realized this silent woman was their mother. I was greeted very warmly by the sisters and made to sit between them. After the preliminary questions about her condition were out of the way, Riya animatedly shared with me what she was told by a priest—that "there is a little child and a djinn" inhabiting her. In those first few moments, her manner of talking gave me the sense that I had to be a playful and enthusiastic maternal presence around her from the very start to tune into her animated self. Perhaps mirroring her animated self was a way of knowing what animated her.

In our first conversation, Neetu offered a brief insight into what she thought was the reality of Riya's possession.

> N: Because of her *samkat*, things become very difficult for us. For instance, it's like she is possessed by the spirit of a little child—if it is not obeyed, it gets very irritated. Her own nature is also the same. She gets irritated over small things. She gets really angry.

Neetu was actually suggesting that Riya and her *samkat* were one; it was another part of Riya, a mirror image, a reflection, only with slightly enhanced features. I used humor to gauge how far Riya would be able to undertake a journey into the labyrinths of her inner world.

> Me:(looking at Riya,) So her *samkat* is like her!

We burst into laughter, which indicated that she could receive some self-knowledge with good humor. The girls then shared with me that Riya's *samkat* wanted to transform into Balaji's *duta* or messenger, but the celibate god Balaji was not letting it do so because of the *samkat*'s sexual and hostile character. Riya had been possessed ever since the age of three. She and her family believed that her paternal aunt, who was envious of Riya's beauty and her work as a beautician, caused her to be possessed with the help of an evil tantric.

> R: I recall, when I had my BA second-year final exams, I was doing threading for a customer in my beauty parlor, and I just suddenly fell unconscious. After some time, I gained consciousness and resumed my work, but again I fell unconscious. I kept fainting in this manner repeatedly. I couldn't understand what was happening to me.

Despite many investigations, it was concluded that there was nothing medically wrong with Riya. On the advice of a doctor, she was taken to a local healer, who diagnosed her as possessed by an entity and even deduced that the entity had been sent by a Muslim tantric. Her fear of what was happening to her indicated the presence of something "unthinkable." Her family was advised to take her to the temple of Lord Balaji.

> R: I told Mummy that I felt scared when Lord Balaji was mentioned.

Many healing attempts were made, much money spent on local healers. Riya and her family were often exploited by local healers in the name of healing. Both the sisters spoke about one tantric healer asking for 35,000 Rs and sex in return for healing. Even while sharing this, the girls spoke in hushed tones, bodies turning toward me, blocking the mother behind. There was a pause during which they could not bring themselves to say the word "sex" and instead looked at me intently. I sensed that perhaps my capacity to receive and release the taboo term ('sex') was being evaluated. The presence of an educated, independent girl closer to their age (than their mother) could go a long way in allowing the forbidden to live in the space of gossip. So, I subtly encouraged it.

> Me: Sex?
>
> R: (emphatically) Yes! That was how obscene that tantric was! At that very moment, we told our father, "This man is not right."

Riya was tormented not only by healers but also by Lord Balaji, who punished the *samkat* during the state of *peshi*. In her very first encounter with
Balaji, a repulsive image made its way into her mind.

> R: The head priest gave me some holy water. I had to sip it every evening.
> The first time I drank it, I saw an extremely filthy thing inside my stomach,
> as if, inside my stomach, two entities were having sex, and then I saw a very
> filthy-looking baby wandering in my stomach. This is why Balaji was not
> accepting it. How can he accept such a filthy thing? That holy water given by
> the priest was going to slowly diminish the *samkat*. Only then would Balaji
> accept it.

On listening to her describe this image, I experienced not fear but instead
a sense of hope, for an image of a couple having sex and producing a child,
albeit a bad one, was a sign of stifled creativity that could later prove to
be influential in her healing process. I did not know how the two elements
would come together to heal her, but this image of procreation gave me hope.
The elder sister explained to me that, in a state of possession, Riya would
behave and talk like a child. Riya was looking elsewhere while this was being
explained, her eyes dreamy and a faint smile on her face, as if she had been
transported to some other world.

> Me: Well, she is a child herself!

As if my statement revealed that I had caught a glimpse of the child in her,
lost in daydreams, Riya abruptly looked right at me and smiled before immediately becoming conscious and giving evidence of her compliant self.

> R: I would have been in BA third year if this *samkat* had not possessed me. My
> parlor work was also flourishing. I had many plans for my business.

Although she was possessed by the impulsivity of a child, she wanted to
consciously present herself as a grown-up person capable of handling a business on her own. It was the envious aunt who had "caused" her to be possessed
by a child's ghost and paralyzed Riya. There was a split in her—not-working,
daydreaming, fantasizing, and not-living through emotional experiences were
attributes associated with the machinations of the possessing spirit, while
conscious Riya wanted to actively run her business and do well. She excitedly
shared with me her plans for the expansion of her beauty salon.

> R: But the aunt could not take the idea of me getting ahead of her own children.
> I fell ill. My hands would contort on their own (brings fingers of both hands
> close together and turns them inwards, toward her body) like ghosts' hands?

Everybody would keep trying to straighten them, but to no avail. The aunt was conspiring to keep me from doing my job. I was not to get ahead of her children. We were not to have more money than her.

The aunt is a hated figure in the family, for she had selfishly used all her relatives for their financial resources and today enjoys all the luxuries that Riya and her family have to struggle for. The sense I got from listening to Riya was that she desired the luxuries for herself. But more significantly, the aunt was envied for representing the drive to get what she wanted.

Riya told me that the aunt had intended to kill her before her birthday.

R: Papa goes with me everywhere. Ever since I became possessed, Neetu has also been facing some issues in her family.

It was as if, for her to survive and take birth as a new person, it was necessary for her to seek her father's presence. The implications of the juxtaposition of the image of being accompanied by her father in her potential rebirth experience and of the problems in her sister's marriage struck me today, while writing. It was like Riya was saying, "In possession, I can enjoy closeness with my father, whereas my sister has to struggle with her marital family."

I wondered if Neetu's attractiveness was a cause of Riya's envy. It was only much later that this envy became clear to me. It is clearer now why I was made to sit between the two sisters. Before meeting me, they knew that I was a researcher and the very endeavor of my research might have seemed akin to trapping a jinni in a bottle. I sensed a palpable urgency in them, which I now understand as pointing toward a need to be understood and heard. Making me sit between them like a screen allowed for a certain distance to be maintained between the envious Riya and the envied Neetu. From where Neetu sat now, she could safely say about her envious younger sister that "her own nature is also the same. She gets irritated over small things. She gets really angry." This statement carried seeds of knowledge—"my younger sister is not possessed"—and apprehension—"How can I tell her that?" Passing through me, this confusion of knowledge and apprehension reached Riya and was received by her in the form of humor.

Neetu required a screen through which her confusion could be metabolized, processed, and conveyed to Riya in a non-toxic form. On the other hand, Riya required an object that could appreciate her feelings of envy toward Neetu, that could replace the elder sister and would not evoke envy or a sense of lack because this object—I—came with a promise—to understand *samkat* and all the inner brokenness that it represented. With me as a processor between them, they could negotiate their respective states and reach the other in a non-toxic form. I asked her about her experience in possession.

R: When in a possessed state, I feel that my body has become very heavy, that someone else is seated inside me, as if the body is mine but the voice is someone else's.

Me: And you are able to control that voice?

In hindsight, this question seemed to have stemmed from my own anxieties and fears around ghosts. I found it difficult to imagine a body and voice that were not mine. My fears ensued from an apprehension of the lack of agency over one's self that Riya was inviting me to empathize with and experience. My anxiety was also a revelation—that I was by this time sufficiently in tune with Riya's states. I, too, felt as scared as she was. Perhaps she too could intuitively sense my fears because subsequently, she began to probe me about my professional convictions.

R: So do you believe in ghosts?

A clinical stance on my part would enhance her sense of estrangement, so she wanted to make sure that I shared her beliefs and was not looking at her as pathologically ill.

Me: I don't know. I am still figuring that out. There is something there.

R: So, people suffering from mind's tension visit you?

Me: Yes.

R: Do you prescribe medicines to them?

Me: No. I am not a psychiatrist, I am a psychologist. We converse with people, listen to their stories and then try to show them the possible reasons for their suffering.

R: (intrigued) And people get better?

Me: Mostly. Who would not want a space where they can share all the secrets they have not shared or can't think of sharing with anyone else? In many cases, this is enough for people who wish to feel better.

I tried to establish that I occupied a position somewhere between rationalism and tradition. My profession required me to carry an aesthetic appreciation of the beliefs of my patients, to "listen." My "listening" stance could be likened with the stance of the priests and healers at the Balaji temple, who patiently listened to possessed people describing their malaises, putting me in a transitional space between the modernity of a psychologist and the traditionalism of an indigenous healer.

Riya thought quietly for some time before bidding me goodbye for the day, as the evening worship had commenced and Balaji was summoning her *samkat* for *peshi*.

I was left standing with Neetu, who then shared her story with me. At the age of eighteen, she eloped from home to get married to her husband. Seven years had passed since then, and Neetu had not been able to conceive a child. Her early marriage meant that she could not complete her education, and her husband prohibited her from pursuing further education and employment. Recently, she developed an intimate relationship with a young unmarried man in her neighborhood. Even before making love, he had been decent enough to remind her that she was married—it was her insistence that had led them to make love. Later, with the onset of Riya's *samkat,* the situation at home had turned unfavorable for Neetu, as her husband had learned about her extra-marital affair and asked her to leave his house.

Neetu came to her parents' place and visited the Balaji temple along with the family. I gathered that the entire family attributed her problems to the *samkat,* but she seemed to have a different opinion. She was aware that she was much better-looking than her husband and felt that his insecurities had prevented her from being independent. She got involved in an extramarital affair because her need for love and attention were not satisfied by her husband. Her family was not ready to assign desires to Neetu, but she seemed in touch with her desires. Neetu was also made to consume the sacred offering blessed by Balaji, but in her it did not trigger the state of *peshi*, indicating that she was not possessed. They arrived at the understanding that it was Riya's possession that was affecting the lives of others in the family.

Later that evening, Riya asked me if, after being cured, she could talk to me about her "mind's tensions." I told her I welcomed it. There were two tracks running in the narrative—conservative Riya and bold Neetu. Like the envied aunt, Riya's elder sister also had the drive to get what she desired. The difference between her and Neetu's ego strengths pointed at differential treatment by parents in their growing years, something I had to explore. Riya's propensity for daydreaming pointed at some environmental failure in the early years of life, impingement and perhaps even demands to comply. Her relationship with her father also had to be explored. What was the effect of a silent mother on Riya? What was the meaning of fainting, of the image of a couple having sex and of a filthy little child wandering inside her internal space?

I approached subsequent conversations guided by my curiosity. In hindsight, I realize now that, after having been shut out by many possessed persons, I was anxious about the possibility of being shut out by Riya, too, if I did not establish proper contact with her. I called her and was told by her mother that Riya was resting. She called me later.

R: How are you, *didi*? You called the other day, I could not talk. When I do not feel like talking to someone, I do not talk to them. I thought you might have felt bad.

Me: No, it's okay. Talk when you feel like talking.

R: But not everyone is like you. I have a bad habit. Sometimes, when a customer calls, I hand over the phone to Mummy. Many people get offended by this.

While I had been anxious, she had been expecting a call with ambivalence and was admitting it by informing me that, when she was not in the mood, she handed the phone to her mother. I asked her if she was feeling better.

R: No, visiting the high priest also did not help. The *samkat* is repeatedly saying, "My *'buddhi* (wisdom) is locked." Balaji, please unlock my *buddhi*. *Samkat* is saying, "I do not remember anything, please just unlock my *buddhi*. Only then can I be seated in your holy presence." I was in a very bad condition. Balaji would repeatedly throw me into sewage water. I used to drink that dirty water. When I gained consciousness, everyone would tease me, saying, "Today, you drank a soft drink." I told you that, once, as soon as I sipped Balaji's holy water, I saw a very filthy thing. I saw two entities having sex inside my stomach, and then I saw a very filthy-looking child. I feel scared that, because of the *samkat*, something wrong could happen.

I was drawn into a disgusted state imagining how it would feel to drink the gutter water and, upon returning to consciousness, be led by people to remember it as a soft drink. A leading question, guided by innumerable scenes from Hollywood horror films, flung itself out of me at Riya. I was scared and disgusted to have come upon this question.

Me: Do you feel that the *samkat* can get you pregnant?

Later, while thinking of Kakar's description of the mythology of the Balaji temple, in which he mentions the birth of Hanuman, I was able to see how spontaneous processes of curiosity and thinking sometimes produced apt questions while drawing, seemingly without my knowledge, from traditional mythical reservoirs of culture. Balaji, too, was the result of forced pregnancy when *Vaayu* (god of air) raped Hanuman's mother, *Anjani*. My unconscious was operating with an awareness of the theme of my research, looking for aesthetic resonance in most grotesque states. For this reason, the recurrent wish of the *samkat* to turn into Balaji's *duta* or messenger led me to unconsciously look for similarities between Balaji and his potential *duta*, the *samkat* possessing Riya. I wondered if this *duta* would be born of a forced pregnancy, just like Balaji himself.

R: Yes, I have heard from many people there that, if one is possessed, one shouldn't even consume any medicines. The *samkat* might turn the meds inside into something else. When I start my work, I begin to feel terrified. I call Balaji's name before I start working. Even while I work, it seems to me that it is not me but the *samkat* working.

Me: The *samkat* is a child, right?

So stuck I was on the demonic image of the child in her and my accompanying associations, that I, rather erroneously, brought the child back when she was displaying the qualities of an adult, albeit one with a tendency to take flight into child-like states. Riya made me aware of her difficulty in owning and expressing anger.

R: Yes, it starts throwing tantrums. I am also stubborn, but he is very stubborn. Sometimes, when I am in a normal state, I ask my brother if he has brought anything for me when he returns from his travels abroad. I ask this jokingly, but the *samkat* starts a fight and complains to Mom and Dad that he [the brother] gets things for himself but never gets anything for me.

Me: Do you ever feel angry at your brother for getting things for himself but not for you?

R: No. I don't feel angry. I ask him jokingly. It is the *samkat* who gets angry and says, (Riya imitated her possessing spirit's seductive tone) "Why have you kept her locked inside the house? Let her get out of the house," meaning that the *samkat* wants me to step out of the house.

I chose to pursue what she had last said about the *samkat* wanting her to venture out of the house. I chose to refer to her in third person to create an experience which was twice removed, mindful that my question might create anxiety.

Me: I wonder if the *samkat* desires that Riya should look good and step out of the house and that people should look at her in admiration.

R: Yes. (pauses) Some people are possessed by ghosts who make their faces look ugly, but my face did not become ugly. The other day in the Balaji temple, during *peshi,* he [the *samkat*] was saying, "I will make her fairer before I leave."

Me: Your aunt sent this ghost using black magic because she was jealous of your beauty?

R: Yes. Another reason was that she wanted my parlor work to collapse.

Me: Neither should Riya look beautiful herself, nor should she beautify others. But the ghost she has sent to possess you wants you to look beautiful and to be admired by others.

She remained silent for a long time.

Me: Is there someone who admires Riya?

R: You mean a boyfriend? (sarcastically) Ya! Papa will break my legs.

Me: He must have become strict after Neetu's wedding.

R: Yeah. He said clearly, "She did it, but if you ever do something like this, I will break your legs." (speaks in a hushed tone after pausing for a few moments) I get many propositions, though. There was this teacher in my computer coaching classes. His mother was my customer.

She said that she would share more later, as her father was hovering near us, and then went quiet.

She wanted to talk to me excitedly about all that was forbidden by her father who evoked fear in her by brutally banning the experience of excitement. Although the sexually expressive sister escaped the confinements of this forbidding father, if Riya dared to do so, her legs would be broken—she would be made immobile. Between her fear of her punitive father and her wish to revel in forbidden terrains, there emerged the possessing spirit, who offered Riya the chance to be mobile while acting on forbidden desires. This possessing spirit would rescue her from the confines of the restrictions imposed on her by the fear-evoking father; it would make her fairer, more appealing, it would draw attention toward her. It was as if the people having sex in her stomach were two parts of Riya—Riya herself and the spirit, which stood for all that was desired and forbidden. It empowered Riya vis-à-vis her father, for the father would not be able to render Riya immobile by breaking her legs because the desire was projected in the image of the ghost. She was merely its hapless "puppet."

Riya's rebelliousness was required to maintain a tension within the family—neither could they exercise complete control over Riya, nor could she achieve triumph over them. In the state of possession, she referred to her parents as "uncle" and "aunty," creating greater distance between herself and her controlling objects. I felt that Riya secretly wished to be her aunt's spoiled child. This is the "healthy" function of possession: we need possessing spirits to scare away our controlling families and our internal versions of them.

After a month and a half, I called her for a telephonic interview, but she did not answer. I began to feel anxious and wondered if something had been stirred by our last conversation on account of which she did not want to speak to me. When she called later, my anxiety was evident.

Me: Oh, I thought perhaps today you are not in a mood to talk.

R: No, it happens often. I told you, if I speak a lot to someone, I don't feel like talking after that. I feel angry.

I wondered if, with time, as we talked more and came emotionally closer, she would reach a point when she would also shut me out. It seemed to me from our subsequent exchanges that she had perceived my anxiety.

R: Earlier it did not happen so often. Ever since I became possessed, this has become frequent.

Me: I wonder if the spirit also fears that Riya and Shalini might come closer.

R: Yes. (Thinks for a few minutes) If that happens, then I will speak to you in my normal state.

Me: When we converse, where is the spirit? Can it listen to our conversations?

R: Oh yes. It listens to everything. It does not have any problems with you. If it has a problem with someone like Papa, Mummy, or my brother, it says so.

I was anxious about the prospect of this alliance with her breaking due to the fear of intimacy I had sensed in many possessed persons during my pilot study. I understood this recoiling as resistance to encountering parts of themselves that my questions were inviting them to visit. Riya, too, was grappling with this fear, but I was not a scary presence because my questions and comments evoked sentiments closer to those of the possessing spirit. I was acknowledging the force that desired to be desired by others, to look beautiful and venture out of the prison built by her father. My questioning was oriented toward the erotic element of her self.

But Riya's definition of health was different from her family's. Her ambivalence toward me stemmed from a fear that I would evoke these parts in her and then leave her to align myself with her family. I felt a need to go to her beginnings. She had been told by the supreme priest that she had been possessed ever since the age of three. On further probing, it was revealed that that time of her life coincided with the birth of her younger brother. An abrupt halt in our dialogue occurred when she could not recall anything from that time beyond this detail. It was as if her memory or unconscious wisdom (*buddhi*) was locked too, just like that of the spirit that possessed her. She became somber at this realization.

Me: It seems there are many similarities between you and the spirit. Both are stubborn, but the spirit is slightly more stubborn than you. Both get angry easily, but the spirit gets angrier. Both of you have memories (*buddhi*) that are locked, but at least you remember things that happened after the age of eight. The spirit wants Riya to look beautiful. And you? What do you feel about adorning and beautifying yourself and others?

I was speaking in a flow here. It seemed she did not see my question coming. She looked taken aback. By now, I had summarized for both of us that there were similarities between her and the spirit, as if it was only another part of Riya. I was now moving closer, to know the extent to which the body was invested. There was enough ego strength in her to recover from her surprise at my question in a bid to engage with it.

> R: I really love my work, sister. I actually wanted to become either an engineer or a doctor, but because of this spirit, I was not able to study anything. If I tried to study, I would feel as if nothing was going into my brain. I would study at home and forget everything during the exam. I also had a dream to study a lot and become an engineer, but the financial situation at home was not good. So I started the parlor. For my future, I plan to get training in a beauty course and open a big beauty salon of my own. At the Balaji temple, many women used to come to our guest house for threading, facials, and *heena.* I can tell merely by looking at someone's face for a few minutes what kind of facial treatment they need! In Balaji, many people sought my advice. I offered beauty treatments to many. A lot of the time, when I am working in my parlor, I feel it is not me but the spirit that is working.

The possessing spirit and the concept of beauty seem to be intricately connected. The possessing spirit feared deeper thinking and knowledge, and in it Riya projected all her failures. I tried to ease her fears by implicitly conveying that it was not necessary to be a doctor or engineer.

> Me: It is as if the *samkat* is another part of you. It is not clear if you like to look beautiful and beautify others or whether it is the *samkat*'s desire. The similarities between you and the *samkat* are many, as if it is but an exaggerated version of you.

> R: Yes, sometimes I also feel the same. I don't know . . . whatever it is, it needs to go.

Until this point, there had been great tentativeness on my part. I had been able to perceive Riya's envy toward her aunt and sister, to form a rapport with her, to establish a certain ease with her and to sense the intensity of her resistance to and ambivalence toward me. Some things had become clearer— her father was forbidding, her mother was silent and was not talked about much, her sister was sexually expressive and envied, Riya had trust issues and wanted to look appealing and be desired, and she too had arrived at the recognition that the spirit seemed to be a part of her self, similar enough to share many traits with her yet different enough to live out the anger and sexuality that Riya was prohibited from expressing. I had come some way from the first sense of disorientation I had experienced on meeting her. I now knew some of the themes I needed to focus on.

A year of knowing her had elapsed. One day, she called me while I was travelling to tell me that it was possible she would visit Balaji soon and that she wanted me to be there. I was deeply moved by this gesture; her need to relate to me was evident. I thanked her for the call and assured her that I would see her at the Balaji temple on her next visit. Since I was travelling, I apologized for not being able to speak to her for long. However, soon after this, I was overcome by guilt. I sensed that she would take offence. My fears were confirmed when we spoke next.

R: That day, when we spoke, when you were on the train, that very night the *samkat* wreaked havoc. I fell on the bed and then kept falling repeatedly. My body was not in my control. I kept getting up and then falling, again and again. I was not able to recognize anybody around me. Dad and Mom held me. I thought that perhaps my blood pressure was low, but I ate well. Soon after finishing my meal, I felt dizzy and fell unconscious. This morning, soon after breakfast, the *samkat* began to create trouble. It kept telling Papa, "Please take me to Balaji. I want to go to Balaji's court. Why aren't you taking me to Balaji? You are lying!" And there, at the temple, it says, "My *buddhi* is locked. Balaji, unlock my *buddhi*."

I was made aware that not receiving the desired response from the other brought about a state of collapse in her, a way of expressing that—"I suffer minor deaths (that take the form of fainting) when I am made to confront my status as someone who is not-invested-in by the other." The incoordination of her body had been aggravated after our last, very brief conversation. It was becoming clear that our conversations were loosening the tight grip in which her desires were held. Given that I had mobilized an unleashing of prohibited yet exciting sentiments in her, she had perceived my not speaking to her as an abrupt withdrawal of my investment in her. The fears she had mentioned earlier were provoked. Repetitive fainting and the inability to recognize anyone were like the effects of enchantments or spells, brought about by the resurgence of her sexual impulses and her hostile impulses, which were directed toward me. Exhibiting these impulses was an antidote to disappearing in the other's eyes (Botella and Botella, 2005). The *samkat* was urging Balaji to let her out of the house because this arousal of desires was incompatible with the presence of her family—around them, she could not *live* her arousal. Going to Balaji meant at least getting out of the house and then hoping that Balaji would unlock the *samkat*'s *buddhi* or wisdom so it (and Riya) could understand its beginnings and come to own the animating temptations, desires and wishes.

In subsequent conversations, I told her about my visit to another healing site, which was located in central India and hosted an annual ghost fair. I told her that I had never witnessed the frenzy of possession that I saw in the Balaji temple.

> R: Here, Balaji beats people a lot. I told you how he beat me up and made me drink water from the gutter. One healer asked us to come during Holi, because that's a time when many spirits are exorcised. I hope that my *samkat* also gets exorcised on Holi. Because of it, I am locked indoors and cannot go anywhere. There is a wedding in the family, but I cannot attend that. The other day, I was watching television when my mom asked for some help in the kitchen. I started helping her, and I don't know what happened to the *samkat*, but suddenly it made me mute. Papa kept on asking me what had happened, but my mouth just wouldn't open. Then Papa put some ashes in my mouth, taken from the temple in our house, and the *samkat* let out a loud scream and began to murmur, "Balaji, I want to be in your divine court . . . please summon me . . . " My uncle and aunt were also present. They were alarmed and told everybody else in the extended family.

She shifted swiftly from one state to another. First, she described her ordeal in Balaji and recalled hoping that Balaji would de-possess her. Then, she recounted the disadvantages of possession—she wished to go out and attend the wedding, but in accordance with the rules laid down by Balaji, possessed persons are not allowed to be part of such events. On the other hand, she felt fine while working and could be of help at the wedding. Besides, the *samkat* could possess her at any time, even while she was engaged in the most mundane activities, like watching television at home with family and helping her mother with chores. Then why prohibit her from being part of an event so exciting? When she told me all of this, I sensed that we were circling around her need to be taken care of.

> Me: I wonder how it feels to see that there are many people around to take care of you in this time.

> R: Yes, everyone is making efforts to get this spirit to leave me (pauses). Last night, the *samkat* came again and my legs began hurting terribly. I cannot even tell you. It comes at any time. When it arrives, my body aches all over. The pain is so excruciating that I burst into tears. When I consulted doctors before going to Balaji, all my reports came out normal. When the doctor was examining my hands contorting on their own—like the ghosts' hands—they asked me to get my calcium checked, but all my tests came out normal.

Me: This pain cannot be understood even by the doctors. It is beyond a doctor's expertise.

R: Yes!

Me: What else happens when you try to sleep at night and a *samkat* comes over you?

R: Dreams happen. I do not see ghosts in dreams. I only see myself drowning in water and calling out to everyone for help, but no one is listening. Everyone has moved ahead. I think to myself, "Riya, what is happening to you?" I don't really know what happens. Now, it's been a long time since we submitted our plea in Balaji's court, but nothing is happening. Their rules are also extremely strict. I am supposed to consume plain *chapatti*. They say that, if you are determined to get this thing out, then you have to starve yourself. This *samkat* has to be starved, only then will it leave the host's body.

After a pause of a few seconds, she continued, abruptly changing the topic.

R: Oh! I forgot to tell you, the supreme priest passed away. Now his grandson will see the possessed persons. A tomb is now being constructed in his name. He was very powerful. It is said that he would take others' *samkats* upon himself. The temple priests would refer all the tough possessing spirits to him. These priests don't even speak nicely. I have heard a lot about the supreme priest's grandson . . . He sits in the temple of Lord Shiva. It is said that he also speaks to the *samkat* very nicely.

She found it difficult to own any emotion and, as a result, the emotions she was scared of were handed over to the possessing spirit. She was aware of the death of the supreme priest. I think her scream emerged from this awareness. Becoming mute was a reaction to the memory of what the deceased priest had stood for. In his worldview, there was no place for sexuality; in fact, the rules laid down by him stifled the open expression of sexuality. Riya wanted to flail her limbs like she was drowning in water and thereby experience body-life fully, but she was trapped by various rules and regulations. Meanwhile, those of her age were getting married and moving ahead in life. Riya also felt that, although the supreme priest was an exalted being, he too had been unable to see her needs for what they were. It was as if she was saying, "I respect him, but he is taking a lot of time to hear my cries and give space to my desires." And before he could actually do anything, he had passed away.

From expressing the perception of the loss of an understanding presence—body aching with the desire to be heard, helpless, turning mute and wailing—Riya next moved to relating via projection to a part of herself that desired and felt envious. This was a sign of health. She could not stay for too long with the pain surrounding the priest's death and the fear evoked by her unconscious hostile impulses toward him and sense of hopelessness. The difficulties of mourning were immediately followed by the vitality of envy. Through envy toward her aunt, she was able to get closer to her desire instead of remaining in the painful state of mourning and feeling increasingly vulnerable.

> R: My aunt was once very poor. She didn't have money for the education of her children. She took a loan from my father. Now her children are educated, but she does not ask about our well-being. Because of the *samkat*, the financial condition of our house turned quite bad. Now, with Balaji's mercy, everything is slowly becoming better. Papa used to drink alcohol. After we started going to Balaji, he stopped.

He who had made Riya follow his rules was now made to adhere to Balaji's rules. What a high this must have given Riya, I thought. The father who prohibited was being forbidden from indulging *his* appetites. Hope was on the horizon, as she planned to further her education as soon as she was cured. This hope ran parallel to the ache of unmet desires. Riya could not remember anything about her computer course and the computer teacher who had expressed interest in her:

> Me: Perhaps it is painful to recall that time because that was when someone showed interest in you but your father forbade any imagination or reciprocal action. It is better to forget periods of time that we associated with any kind of pain.
>
> R: (hesitates) No, no, actually I used to address him as "brother." His mother was my customer. She still is, but now women from his house have stopped coming to my parlor. Ever since they found out that I was possessed—because of this *samkat*, many of my customers have left. Now they go to some other beauty salon.

She had still not mentioned anything about that computer teacher. We were still talking over the phone when she abruptly disconnected. When we resumed the conversation a few minutes later, she told me that her brother-in-law had been calling her while she was speaking to me, and, when she had not answered, he had gotten suspicious and begun to trouble her sister, Neetu, with questions. This had disturbed Riya.

> R: I am feeling so enraged. I told him that my papa never forbade me from speaking over the phone. Why was he trying to stop me?

This was the first time I saw Riya angry outside of a state of possession. I felt relieved. I was glad that her suspicious brother-in-law (another version of her father) managed to evoke an anger that she could own. It was a very real moment for both of us. This suspicious and controlling brother-in-law was also causing Neetu many problems.

> R: Yes, he was continuously cribbing to Neetu. Neetu has told him about you. He feels there is no need to talk to anyone, that I am forever on the phone. I told my brother. He said, "You know how he is, he is a suspicious type." Now my sister also regrets marrying him (giggles).

Although a micro-expression, her giggling at troubles in her sister's life revealed her latent envy and the joy she was allowing herself in that moment. The sexually expressive sister who got away from the forbidding father Riya feared evoked envy in the latter, but the heaven Neetu's bold step had promised did not exist. Moreover, being invested in by a male, unlike her sister, who was being tortured in her marriage and discovering the fallacies of her fantasies, boosted Riya's sense of self. It brought her closer to owning her desire at a moment when this owning served to enhance her own narcissism—"I am loved and admired, my sister is not!" Next, she finally spoke about the computer teacher.

> R: The other day, you were asking about that computer teacher. I will tell you now. I used to address him as "brother," (in a hushed tone) but he used to keep staring at me with admiration. He did not propose to me, but he would say, "Don't consider me your teacher, think of me as your friend. Then you will understand the lectures better."
> We laughed.
>
> Me: You did not like him?
>
> R: I would call him "brother."

This juxtaposition of her sister's misery with information about Riya herself being admired by another male was noted earlier as well and provided an essential window into her envy. The desire was disowned and projected on to the computer teacher. I nonetheless tried to reach the source of this disowning.

> Me: And Father would also have been strict, if he had found out then—
>
> R: (cutting me short) Papa has been strict since the beginning, but my younger brother doesn't even let me stand near a window. He starts scolding me—"What are you doing there near the window?" Meanwhile, he himself keeps chatting with random people on the internet all day and night behind closed doors. I don't know what all he does behind closed doors. He has security codes on both of

his phones. If someday I put a security code on my phone, then he will create a scene. He has a girlfriend. Everybody at home is aware.

The presence of punitive and forbidding males in her life—her father, brother, and brother-in-law—had led her to disown her sexual and hostile impulses. It was becoming clearer to me that the differential treatment given to siblings was a significant factor. Could Riya process this difference in the ways she and her siblings were invested in by their parents?

Me: He has a girlfriend, and you are not even allowed to stand near the window?

R: They scold him also sometimes. Papa also knows that I have some male friends. Mom gets angry at my brother, says, "All night long you are with your mother behind closed doors!"

She lacked the capacity to acknowledge that she was not privileged and invested in by her objects and took to quickly protecting them against whatever hostility she might have harbored against them. I was being given (unconvincing) proof of her father's sense of justice and her mother's anger, which was not potent enough to stop her son from objecting to Riya from standing near windows and breathing in her desires. She wanted me and most of all herself to believe that she was in fact invested in, that she knew how to claim her due by throwing a tantrum.

R: The other day, my father called. He was asking me what he should get for me. Whenever anyone goes out somewhere, they get something for me. Someday, if they don't get something for me, I will eat their heads.

At least in this narrative, she could live the illusion that she was intensely invested in by her objects. Interestingly, after this, she turned the conversational spotlight toward me, asking me questions about my life. Did I cook before marriage? Was mine a love marriage or an arranged one? How long had the courtship lasted? How did I first meet my husband? Did my parents know? I patiently answered all her questions, as they were essential to her getting to know me. I sensed then that I was being seen as a role model, with the hope that there were things she could learn from how I led my life and managed gratification. I again asked her if she had found someone.

R: I want to stand on my own feet first. Until then, I will not get into all this. I also liked that computer teacher, but then this *samkat* came and after that he, too, stopped speaking to me. Now we rarely speak, and. as friends. Other people—relatives—have also stopped talking to me. All my friends have also left me. It makes me sad.

Me: This period of time in your life will also tell you who can accept you with all your imperfections, your ghosts.

R: Yes. What you are saying is absolutely right. Since the *samkat* came, this much I have definitely learned about relationships.

My being able to resonate with her experience of being held captive by the punitive father and brother and the self-disclosure on my part led to greater closeness between us. As a result, after having denied her interest on two previous occasions, Riya for the first time owned her desire, admitting that she too liked this teacher of hers. But her *samkat* had taken over. This *samkat* was a *dharma samkat* or a moral dilemma—was she to remain captive as an ideal daughter, run her salon and restore the family's lost honor or take flight into her own intoxicating temptations?

The germination of desire in Riya's consciousness was followed by the onset of the *samkat*. Now, in conversation, the acknowledgement of desire led to accounts of greater arousal, attributed unfailingly to the work of the malicious spirit and incompatible with the ideals that prevailed in the household.

R: Last night, the *samkat* came over me again. These days, it troubles me a lot. It presents itself at any time, and, whenever it arrives, it urges my father to leave it in the Balaji temple.

Me: And there, in the Balaji temple, he is beaten by Balaji. It's as if the *samkat* likes being beaten.

R: (laughs) But because of his being beaten, my condition deteriorates. My whole body breaks. I would feel it while asleep. There would be pain everywhere. Now I am menstruating. I am forbidden from the temple and from taking offerings. Because of this *samkat*, my menstruation cycle has also become erratic.

While she was talking about her aroused body, I, not knowing how to contain the body in words, rather erroneously brought it closer to the punitive superego reflected in Balaji. Today, it seems to me that I was too struck by the juxtaposition of arousal and pain that characterizes perversion and was trying to find glimpses of perversion in her enactments. Now I feel that all she was doing was bringing her aroused body, kicking, and swaying with aliveness, into the narrative. Her *samkat* was wildest during menstruation, the period when body is confused yet alive with a multitude of sensations running through it like endless clouds casting vast shadows over a landscape. My inability to recognize this excited body was reminiscent of the dream she had had, in which nobody around her was able to see her drowning body or hear her screams. I had colluded with others. This collusion led to my perceiving her sexually aroused body as a child's body.

Me: Perhaps because your appetite and eating patterns are also going awry.

R: Yes, Mummy was also saying the same. It could be because of a lack of appetite and weakness. In possession, there are so many prohibitions that I have to keep in mind. Even if I eat well, my stomach is never full. I would eat ten *parathas*[8] and yet feel starved. It was then that I wondered whether perhaps there was something inside me that ate all the food. Everybody would be shocked when I would eat so much and still feel hungry, because the *samkat* was eating all the food! Sometimes I feel a strange pain near my liver. It feels as if something is eating me from the inside. I feel terrified. I tell Mummy, "Please take me to the Balaji temple and exorcise this spirit out of me, otherwise it is going to eat me!"

Like the mother, I too had misrecognized her hunger for living out sexual desires as her hunger for food. As a result, she was never satiated, because the mother and I were catering to the wrong needs. Her aroused desires were eating her, pressing for some evacuation or articulation.

Me: Its hunger is scary.

I now feel I was speaking for myself here. I was scared of her greed and did not know how to contain it. Confronted with the ugliness of not knowing what to do with her intense sexual needs, I continued with the line of thought that framed her as a baby in need of maternal nurturance. Perhaps I was able to unconsciously receive what she was trying to communicate and sensed what I had done wrong, because in the next conversation I kept her sexually charged body at the forefront.

Me: Perhaps in Balaji, the *samkat* gets the space to say anything, to do anything.

Giving her aroused body its due space in our dyad led deeper into the sexual side of her experience.

R: Yes, it's true. (Pauses for a few moments) Now it is saying that it will be exorcised in the temple of Goddess Kali.

Me: Why in Goddess Kali's temple?

R: Because it is in her temple that all filthy spirits are exorcised. In her temple, even alcohol is given as an offering. And I am possessed by a *masan*. A *masan* is a filthy spirit. It will be exorcised in Goddess Kali's temple only. Balaji is a celibate. I am told that all filthy and obscene spirits are exorcised either in Goddess Kali's temple or in Lord Bhairava's temple.

Her *samkat* was not a child but an overly sexualized ghost, so filthy that a celibate deity, like Balaji, would not even touch it. Interestingly, it was this ferocious mother goddess, Kali, who appeared with the promise of containing her uninhibited body, which had now become a cauldron of seductive and destructive desires.

I took a break of 3 months for my wedding. When I met Riya after my break, she looked more radiant than before, in a bright red Indian ethnic shirt-and-pants combination. She rushed toward me and greeted me with a tight and warm hug. It seemed that she found me as beautiful as I found her—she complimented me on my looks repeatedly. She asked me how my married life was going.

R: If I ever get married . . . the relationship that is to be established after marriage with the husband . . . I feel I will not be able to fulfill it.

I was glad to see that something inside her had loosened, allowing her to share her deepest fears with me. I tried to ease her fears by sharing with her that I, too, had lived the experience and that we would talk more about it. She asked me why I had not applied *sindoor* or a red mark on my forehead as a sign that I was now married. I told her that I was Christian. This surprised her.

R: You are a Christian!? Oh! I thought of you as a Sardarni[9]. That is why I never cracked Sikh jokes with you. I did not know that you are a Christian. You look like a *S*ardarni.

She then asked me to accompany her to the evening ritual of *peshi*. I agreed, and we left for the temple immediately. I wonder now what in me surrendered to being led by her to a ritual so overwhelming. We managed to make our way through the thick and ever-growing crowd at the temple to the front row, very close to the barrier at which all the possessed people stood, some holding the barrier firmly and swaying mildly and some waiting for the hymns to begin.

R: When I enter the state of possession, please be behind me. Some possessed people start to beat and pull others by the hair. Please be with me. I feel terrified. Just make sure that nobody beats us. One cannot really predict other people's *samkats*. Once, here during *peshi*, I slapped Neetu (laughs).

I must admit I was experiencing mixed feelings. On the one hand, I was somewhat apprehensive of her slapping or punching me during her frenzy—and of being possessed by her *samkat*! I also sensed that this was a test to see if I could contain the destructive part of her. We sat on the road in front of the temple gate and were talking when the temple bells began ringing loudly to indicate that the worship of Balaji was about to commence. Instantly, the atmosphere became charged with devotion, everyone visibly stirring in their spots, the clapping of hands and cries of "Balaji Maharaj ki jai!" (Hail Lord Balaji!) echoing across the temple premises.

Riya, too, sprang up to her feet. She turned around once, making sure that I was right behind her (I was), then turned back to face away from me, tied her stole around her waist, opened her hair out, gripped the barrier, and began swaying slightly. Her eyes open and glassy, gazing up at something far beyond the evening sky, her hair swinging from side to side, her face pale. And suddenly, she entered the state of frenzy. Her body twisted beyond recognition and rhythm. As I stood right behind her, watching her for a while in this frenzy, and it seemed to me that she was being held by the hair and tossed around in every direction possible by an invisible force. It was like watching her body container crumble and go into pieces—whatever it contained was spilling out and over.

Fearfully, I wished for the omnipotence of a goddess. If only I had multiple hands (like Kali) and the ferocity of Riya so I could catch all the crumbling pieces and put the broken character back together again, rescue it from formlessness. I stood there receiving her while she fell "on me," "at me" and, certainly at the level of affect, "into me" as well. The body that otherwise looked timid and constrained now seemed like it was experiencing an internal fireworks display! In her drowning dream, Riya was enveloped by water, frantically flailing to survive—or perhaps out of a desire to be seen. In possession frenzy, the water was replaced by the *samkat* that enveloped her.

The possessed people on either side of her now stopped and looked at her. I was holding the barrier on either side of Riya. She fell back on my chest, held in place by my arms. It was like a game of trust! Perhaps I had already become a reliable object in her mind; she simply needed to test it, bodily. In an analytic setting, the client lies on the couch while the analyst sits outside the former's view, usually behind. The healing site is like a couch. At this moment, I became the couch for Riya—she could fall on it repeatedly, enact her misery and frustration and, perhaps, see if I could withstand the magnitude of her emotions. During this episode, she had her back turned to me (literally and, I think, also metaphorically). But her "frontal spine" (Pollak, 2009), with its functions of seeing, verbalizing, and communicating, was also turned away from me, toward the deity's eyes. Although communicating her refusal to actively relate to me, she sought to be held like a child would of a mother.

The ritual (*aarti*) went on for an hour. There were bodies of other possessed people around me, rubbing against mine, their and Riya's hair lashing my face and arms, their wailing screams splitting my ears, their spit and sweat on me as they displayed the frenzy of possession.

Standing there amidst what seemed like an ocean of affect, I too responded at the bodily level, with cold sweat, palpitations, and chills alternating with hot flashes. I was scared and felt suffocated, both bodily, due to the crowd closing in, and emotionally, carried along by the wave of feelings I was being exposed to and the feelings evoked in me. It ended after what seemed like an eternity, after which it was time to receive the holy water, sprinkled by the head priest. Despite constant requests being made through the microphone to not push, the crowd still pushed and pressed in its eagerness to receive the divine blessings of Balaji in the form of a few droplets of holy water. Little children cried out from being crushed by the crowd. Riya and I were also at the mercy of the crowd behind us, but we held on firmly to the barrier in front of us and managed to keep ourselves safe.

Riya then held my hand and took me closer to the shrine of the first priest of the Balaji temple (the *samadhi sthal*). We sat surrounded by many possessed people who were at different levels of trance states, from the mild to the frenzied.

R: (sorrowfully) How painful it is to watch all these possessed persons. I used to feel really scared earlier, but now I feel pity.

Me: And do you also feel pity toward yourself?

R: Not pity, just immense sadness. I just want this spirit to leave me. That aunt really trapped me.

Fear of disowned sexual and hostile impulses had turned into sadness, a feature which had been absent before.

Me: And she has everything.

R: Yes.

Me: And you have to struggle so much for everything.

R: Yes. (thoughtfully) She did not think about anyone. She went after and got whatever she wanted.

Me: Like your *samkat.* It gets what it wants.

R: Yes, you are absolutely right!

Me: The spirit sent by your aunt is like her, as if it is her dirty, filthy child.

R: I have never thought about it like that. It makes a lot of sense. This ghost is like her. Anyhow, I don't know when it will leave.

The sadness surrounding the thoughts of her *samkat* and rich aunt indicated to me that some internal processing was underway. She had begun to experience it as sad that the aunt enjoyed all the luxuries Riya desired for herself. Envy and hostility were giving way to a depressive state that would take her closer to a sense of lack. All the while, she sat firmly holding my hand in hers. I sensed that the contact communicated warmth.

After this experience, Riya began frequently entering the possessed state. Her body was aroused.

This reminded me of a patient Bollas (2000) wrote about, who, at the beginning of each therapy session, would be well-behaved but would abruptly "burst into provocative and scathing verbal attacks, for which she apologized." Her therapist understood such attacks as tests of his capability. "She then became more infantile and acted out physically in sessions by trying to grab his penis. For a very long period of time, she was preoccupied with the analyst's genitals and when trying to grab them would be met by his physical holding of her." Bollas considered the therapist's physical intervention in this case as serving an important symbolic function of bringing his own body to the patient for the binding of sexual states of mind.

Being physically held seemed "to release [the patient] to intensified hallucinatory states, for example, she talked about a persistent vision of her genitals rotting away." In the case of Riya, after the recent encounter between us, she began to clasp my hands in hers during our conversations. Our palms were held together even when they became sweaty. This sensuous feature was absent from our interactions earlier.

After this experience, I had a series of dreams in which I saw myself as a man—the face was mine, but the body was that of a man. I wondered if, by repeatedly falling on me, Riya had stirred in me a latent desire to imagine myself as a man.

We next spoke a few days after her return from the temple. She told me she felt increasingly terrified and found it difficult to be alone:

R: Recently, something happened. One day, I was alone at home. I felt as if something was stalking me, standing next to my bed. I told it that I was not scared of it. I have complete faith in Balaji. It was a Sardarni. She stood on the threshold of the door and wore a turban around her head. Papa was saying that it must have been some random spirit that followed me. Those who are possessed often see such things. My aunt made all kinds of plans to kill me. It is good that we sought refuge in Balaji.

There was a change in her symptomatology. The contact between our bodies in *peshi* had led to a textural change in our conversations and aggravated her symptoms. The spirit possessed her more often and she was being followed by a Sikh woman. Since my marriage, our meetings had precipitated the following sequence of internal events in her—she had perceived me as beautiful, shared with me her fears around sex, thought of me as a Sardarni and entered a *peshi* with me. It was as if her compliments were directed toward someone who, like a Sardarni, had the drive to successfully establish sexual intimacy in marriage. In Punjabi culture, Sardarnis are thought of as being more sexually upfront and bold than women of other cultures. They are known to use their bodies well, to wrestle their ways into having possible intense sexual experiences. In other words, a Sardarni in Riya's culture represented someone with an ability that she (Riya) feared and lacked but desired. Her deepest fear coincided with her imagination of a sensation that her body would primarily experience, the sensation of having the penis enter it, tear it apart and damage it, like the baby-*samkat* that, she felt, ate her insides.

A Sardarni could handle the feared penis. This Sardarni haunted her but also tempted her with the promise of an experience that would open the body to numerous sensations and the mind to exciting images—but also to corresponding, palpable fears. By entering a bodily experience with me, a "Sardarni," was Riya trying to evoke in me the Sardarni she perceived me to be?

Receiving her need at an unconscious level, I sensed a certain loosening in my own body and mind as well. I noticed that I began to throw my limbs around while walking, became more vocal and upfront, touching in our conversations on various vistas of experiences that I would invite her to experience and talk about. This led to further awakenings of desire in her—and an aggravation of her symptoms. The upsurge of desires evoked corresponding fears. I wondered if she had invited me to *peshi* because she sensed some inhibitions in me and sensed that I had the capacity to become the Sardarni who would let her talk openly about sexual matters. While Riya experienced heaviness in her body, fainting spells, aches, the space given to her body in *peshi* and our conversations also led to the return of her ability to work, as she felt empowered and began stepping out to attend beauty seminars and trainings.

At this point, there appeared a promise—the celibate god Balaji spoke through one of the healers and conveyed to Riya the information that only the goddess Kali could consume the sexual and hostile *samkats*. This was a promise of the possibility of the destructive impulses being metabolized:

R: There, in the Kali temple, a priest asked me to adorn the goddess with gar-
lands and red drapes. When I began to perform this ritual, my hands started
trembling! I was extremely terrified!

Me: What thoughts were racing through your mind?

R: It felt as if Mother Kali would step out of the idol and kill me. My *samkat*
is bad, and all the bad and filthy ghosts are scared of Goddess Kali. Balaji is
pious. Mother Kali is feared by all. I don't know why. Actually, I have always
been scared of everything.

Her hands trembled because she felt impure, filthy, and unworthy of touching the pure and holy Mother Goddess owing to her sexual and aggressive
desires. The fear evoked by these desires was further enhanced in front of the
Mother Goddess, who would punish her for carrying such filth. The desire
was to clasp the other, but it evoked strong fear and resultant panic, which
caused the body to recoil inward. In panic, the body that desired was pulled
into itself. The dirt and filth got lodged in images of dirty/gutter water, a
filthy child, a filthy penis out to tear the body apart. And the cultural image
of Kali as a goddess capable of curing one of the derangements brought on
by the filthy child-*samkat* was transformed into both a fear—of Kali's ferocity—and the faith that only she—*not the celibate Balaji*—could touch the
samkat, contain the filth.

The aggravation of her symptoms pervaded Riya's body and mind—her
body felt heavy, hot; it ached and collapsed in fainting spells, while the mind
was afraid of the *samkat*, an alien entity, controlling her body. She resumed
working. When she remained idle, her mind was flooded with thoughts that
led to the *samkat* taking possession of her body.

Subsequently, the *samkat* emerged in the form of a penis, shifting from
inhabiting the stomach to pulsating in her genitalia, trying to force itself out
during urination. Her forbidden desires were opening up. No more was she
holding herself back.

R: Now it tells me that it is beneath my stomach. Earlier, it was in the stomach.
Now it is sliding toward my legs.

Me: And that is how it will gradually leave?

R: Yes, it should just leave now. Actually, now the *samkat* does not disturb me
when I am working. The other day, I was attending a seminar on a new airbrush
makeup technique. Throughout the duration of the seminar, the *samkat* did not
trouble me at all.

Me: It seems like the *samkat* is under your control, not the other way around.

R: Yes. There is more relief now than there was before.

It was a relief to hear that she was doing well in her career. Just as she had subtly made me aware of it, I am certain she also made her family aware of a pattern—the *samkat* possessed her only when she was idle. It logically followed that the only solution was to let her remain occupied with work she enjoyed. Allowing her to "be"—to attend a beauty seminar—seemed like a step toward this understanding. As expected, the result was that the *samkat* lost its grip over her.

Riya seemed to have found a way to get what she wanted, but not like the selfish aunt had. She was merely trying to fight a vicious spirit by becoming active and taking charge of her career. The spirit was the only entity that allowed or empowered her to "do" things in the first place—to hurl abuses, to raise her voice against the punitive males of the house, to work skillfully in her parlor. The joy of feeling empowered that she may have experienced in possession had now seeped into her normal waking state. The split was being bridged. From completely disowning her anger earlier, she was now gradually moving toward embracing it. The aggravation of her symptoms, the experience of empowerment courtesy the *samkat* and the newfound belief that Kali alone could contain her destructivity were gradually enabling her to embrace her virtues and vices. Amid all this, however, the empowering force, the *samkat*, continued to make attempts to assert itself.

R: I am very disturbed. The *samkat* showed itself to me in the afternoon. Balaji was directly addressing it. He was asking it when it would leave my body. It was asking to be left at the Kali temple.

Me: Balaji talks to it directly?

R: Yes, of course. Balaji comes, he takes good care of me.

Me: How does it feel when he speaks directly to the *samkat*?

R: At that moment, it feels okay. But, after a while, the *samkat* comes back. Mother Goddess Kali will devour it, because it is a dirty spirit. it flashes sexual images at me.

This was the first time Riya had uttered the taboo word—"sex." Soon, bold sexual content began to enter our discourse. I could sense her inhibitions falling away. She did not need to enter the state of possession to express herself—she was now articulating her internal content even in her normal state.

Me: Oh really? What does it flash?

R: A penis stalking me. It can change its form into anything. Sometimes, while urinating, I feel as if the thing inside me wants to come out.

Me: How?

R: From where we urinate.

The sensuous contact between our bodies in *peshi* had, it seemed, unlocked the stifled sexuality in her—from being haunted by sexual desires in the form of a Sardarni to being promised by the *samkat* that it would be metabolized by Kali alone to sensing the *samkat* shifting from the stomach toward the genitalia to finally perceiving that it was a penis stimulating her vagina, trying to force itself out. The child-*samkat* was now a penis, and this shift had been facilitated by a sexually bold Sardarni. The symptoms were getting aggravated because now there was a promise—that in Kali she would find a suitable container for all that she felt was destructive and filthy in her.

R: One cannot share such things with one's parents, although Papa says, "I know this *samkat* is very obscene." Do you know why it flashes sexual images? So that I receive slander. My confidence has also become extremely low. I feel there is nothing I can do well. I feel useless. Sometimes I wonder why my aunt sent this spirit to me. She must have seen that I was beautiful, timid, that I had all the qualities.

Sexuality was being linked with a sense of being damned or cursed. The mother's silent presence and the father's humiliation did not leave any space for her desires. Sexual and hostile impulses were unacceptable and assumed an ugly texture. I tried to link this force in her with the lack of maternal nurturance that I sensed had come about because of her dethronement by her younger brother. It was this lack that I think caused her to disown parts of herself in the first place.

Me: Sometimes, when you talk about the *samkat*, describing all that he does, I feel a lot of tenderness toward it. It does have a tendency to tease, which is very child-like. It throws tantrums like a toddler. All this sometimes evokes tender feelings in me toward the *samkat*. If it were my child and threw tantrums like this, I would hold it in my lap, listening to its concerns. I would try to reason politely with it about the kinds of demands that could not be fulfilled and why. The way your *samkat* weeps, plays, throws tantrums, fights—it makes me wonder if it actually needs love and a sense of belonging. I wonder where it came from. How were its parents? I wonder if they loved it. What do you feel? What do you imagine is the story of this ghost?

R: Papa asked. It said, "I don't have parents. I am an orphan." Oh, sister, it has such a massive appetite. It always feels hungry. The other day, it gobbled up so much food!

With some nurturance, her sense of being orphaned or left alone very early in childhood came forth palpably. There was no sense of belonging to someone. There was only hunger and an intense craving, accompanied by the hope that being fed well would undo the sense of being damned that pervaded her being. Unacceptable sexual and hostile impulses only enhanced this sense of being condemned. Sexual impulses were projected into the possessing spirit. Even the elder sister's sexual expression—following her desires and eloping with her lover—was attributed to the *samkat*. In my attempt to establish the reason for her sense of feeling damned and cursed, I asked her if her elder sister was friendlier than she was. Who among the two experienced less difficulty in establishing interpersonal relationships? This would tell me if the sense of being damned was Riya's alone.

> R: She makes friends easily. Even as a little kid, she used to talk a lot and engage everyone. I was always a reserved child.

Although Neetu had charmed everyone as a child, there were now people who were drawn to Riya's charm and skill as a beautician.

> R: A new client came with her daughter. She told Mummy, "Your daughter's nature is very nice." I am only scared of doing haircuts. One day, I had to do bridal makeup for a housemaid. (Her tone expressed panic) Something went wrong, and her face became black. I felt very scared and received a lot of humiliation for what I had done. Neetu often encourages me to not be scared, to practice bridal makeup on her.

Her panic expressed that she had accidentally lived out her envy in the scenario narrated. Although she had learned how to charm people with her skills—unlike her elder sister, who used merely her natural chirpiness—there lingered a fear that those charmed would soon leave her if her envy slipped out inadvertently. She had to remain skilled and offer something to the others who would otherwise abandon her.

I could empathize with her fear of being abandoned. I suggested that, to hone her skills, she could practice on some friends. But she did not have or make friends. No one could be trusted to help her develop the capacity to keep the desired object close. Underneath the envy was a fear that others would want what she desired and, instead of helping her, would snatch her desired object from her, that, if she went with her vulnerabilities to another person, she would turn away disappointed because nobody had the capacity to "give." In other words, she felt others also harbored the envy that she did. Her panic was soon replaced with guilt and self-loathing. I listened to her helplessly. There was no way I could enlighten her about herself. A part of me perhaps prayed for her *buddhi* to be unlocked, which would help her gain some clarity about why she felt damned and why she needed praise as narcissistic nutrition for her damned soul.

We had to patiently wait for Balaji to unlock her *buddhi*. I had entered the free state of a faithful devotee; however, like Eigen (2004), my faith was in the "unknown reality that feeds unconscious processing." I immersed myself in the unknown reality, led by the meeting of our respective unconscious minds, to retrieve haunting parts of my own self. Her envy, panic and self-loathing had stirred in me similar fears that I too grappled with. I thought it best to cater to her narcissism, to bind the destructive force with life force:

> Me: It's as if the *samkat* does not want you to feel good about yourself, to live life's good moments. You feel sad about being stuck, but it seems the *samkat* also wants this. Whatever it wants is happening.

> R: Yes. This is true.

> Me: That you should remain distant from all those people and experiences that can bring you good feelings about yourself, that Riya should feel confident—perhaps, if you allow yourself to live and receive good moments, the *samkat*'s grip on you might loosen?

> R: Yes, you are right. I feel I am useless in every sphere of life. But what you are saying makes sense. I am doing exactly what the *samkat* is making me do.

In hindsight, I realize today that my encounters with the brokenness in her stirred my own fears. My sense of stagnation was taxing my containing capacities and using the therapist in me to prematurely appropriate the brokenness it experienced as grotesque. I was really taking on her difficulties. I was not sure it would work, but at that moment it was the only way I could come up with of binding the badness that was unleashed by living out envy. I realized that both Riya and I shared similar fears. I carried out these interventions with faith that something would unlock her wisdom—and mine too. To me, this faith meant what Bion considered a "psychoanalytic attitude," faith in the stream of unconscious to take us where emotional truth would raise its head, where frantic attempts at mastery, at helping, are discontinued. And the faith did pay off. In facing my own fears, unknowingly replacing the beautiful work of culture with that of a therapist, the price I had to pay was in terms of the limits I came to face in myself. The next night, I had the following dream:

> I am sleeping. My husband is sleeping next to me. Suddenly, I hear my brother-in-law calling out to me from the adjacent room. I wake up to go check on him. He asks for a glass of water. I go to the kitchen and bring him a glass full of water. Then I go to the living room to check if the door is bolted. As I reach the door, some force grips me . . . I am possessed! No matter how hard I try to move my body, it refuses to move, I am frozen. I try to scream but I am not

able to open my mouth, to make any sound. I try to say "Jesus," but no words or sounds come out. I am terrified. My husband and brother-in-law are looking at me but no one is able to see that I am immobile. How can I call for help? I start beating the wooden door with my palm, hoping that perhaps someone will hear the noise and come to my rescue. I woke up startled, not knowing whether it had been a dream or it had happened for real. My first impulse was to call my father and ask him why he hadn't been there on so many occasions when I needed him.

Another dream the night after that:

I am in a strange village as a researcher, to understand the lives of the children there. I manage to form a bond with one boy who runs a candy shop. We walk around the entire day, talking about his life. In the evening, we reach his shop and he gives me some candies. From a distance, two women—one young, the other old—are watching the two of us interact. The younger one says to the older one, "We told her not to venture into this village. We told her not to come. Now, she will need to be taught a lesson." Suddenly, I wake up startled, as if I have been dreaming about being in the village, and venture out of my room to see if everything is fine at home. I step out of my room to find a woman bending and feeding on that little boy's corpse. She raises her head. She has my face. I woke up again, terrified, disoriented and not knowing if this time I had woken up for real.

Both the dreams left my faith in my own capacity to derive sense out of them deeply shaken. I could not understand what my unconscious was telling me. Momentarily, the distinction between real and dream was erased, causing me to experience terror I had not known until then. I felt that I had burned my hands trying to contain the destructive in Riya. I was reminded of the countless words of caution the men in my house received whenever they ventured out to perform rituals of healing and exorcism. For a brief moment, I even wondered if evil forces were threatening to possess me as revenge for my closeness with Riya.

In the second dream, I woke up startled. Had the engagement with the "destroyer" in Riya evoked the destroyer in me—a part of my self that erased all meaning? I felt so. My dream experience of not being able to move and not receiving any help echoed Riya's dream experience of drowning but not dying, while people were watching but no one was offering to help. My own containing function had deserted me—perhaps this is what terror does, it robs you of all resources.

Our dreams spoke volumes about our helplessness. I had stepped in to rescue her. In internally letting go and shifting from knowing possession to being possessed, I was confronted with my own split-off part—the young boy. Something in Riya got released during our brief conversation, but at the same time, something possessed me—the devil in me had been unleashed. I identified with Riya's tendency to not-feel life, the frustration that erupts when creativity is blocked. I had experienced a regression. If I had been able to recover some intelligibility, then this movement would have become what Botella and Botella (2005) described as a "retrogressive one."

It was only many months later, when I brought all the material together, that I was able to make sense of these two dreams and how they helped me discover essential truths of Riya's experience of possession and usher her gently toward healing. What I realized was that this had been an instance of brokenness being used to recover beauty. I had indeed taken on her *samkat*. It spoke to mine, shook it until it was symbolized in my dreams and came to haunt me. Would I have been able to dream this unthinkable part of my self without having been open to parts of. Riya's self? I don't know. I had begun to identify not only with parts of her self but also with her beliefs. The position that "we had to patiently wait for Balaji to unlock her *buddhi*" demonstrates that I had also entered the mind state of a devout *bhagat*. I had experienced sufficient internal letting go by this point to dream these nightmares that I had gradually unlocked using *my* Balaji—the thinkers I referred to. While I could not make sense of these nightmares back then and felt I was grappling with sheer meaninglessness, some processes of representation were beginning in Riya. For the first time, the *samkat* had taken a visual form.

> R: Two days after talking to you last, I began to see a child for the first time. He was very filthy and ugly, dressed only in underwear. He looked starved and impoverished. When I am asleep, he stands beside my bed. It is a very filthy thing, and it shows me filthy images.

Was it a mere coincidence that a boy had emerged in my dream, been eaten up or assimilated by me and had now appeared in Riya's images? Through the image of this split-off boy part, both Riya and I had become entwined in the other's history. It was this male, split-off part that caused both of us to feel damned and cursed, perhaps on account of being born as women in a culture that favored the male child. In the nightmare, I had stuck my face into the corpse and eaten it; in life, this male part helped me venture into healing sites alone and persist with my research while constantly being exposed to threats of various kinds. This was the first imprint on me of the process of dreaming set off by this first layer of images that the terror of the possessed person had yielded, images through which the dream had taken its own form.

It was as if Riya was in tune with my internal processes in the same way that I was with hers. She knew I had taken on her *samkat*.

> R: Did you get disturbed in the Balaji temple by me?

Me: (surprised) What made you think that?

R: When I was in the state of possession, it must have been extremely inconvenient and disturbing for you.

Me: Are you a *samkat* for the other? A disturbance?

R: I feel this way because of the *samkat.* It has really caused me to lose my self-confidence. I feel unable to think any good thoughts about myself.

Me: and to receive any good feelings.

R: (After a brief pause) You are right. I have to face the *samkat.* The other day, it was crying. It gets easily annoyed. It is very melodramatic, a coward. I don't feel like stepping out of the house. I always need someone beside me. It is Neetu's baby shower today and I don't feel like going. Now, while I am talking to you, the *samkat* is listening to everything. The other day, it created a scene. I began to cry and said, "I don't have a mommy or daddy. I am three years old. Celebrate my birthday. My name is Ranjeet Kaur. I am both a girl and a boy. I have been living in this house for the past eighteen years." It's been two nights since that happened. I haven't slept. My limbs feel lighter. It feels as if my legs and arms are not my own. I don't feel hungry.

In the image of Ranjeet, both the male and the female elements of her self had come together. This change was indicative of some assimilation of the hitherto split-off male self, an assimilation that involved considerable conflict.

R: Sometimes it comes at night as well, to unburden its head, when the entire body feels heavy.

Me: Whose? Yours or its?

R: I mean mine. He must also experience it as heavy, so sometimes, even at night, I enter the state of possession. Then everything feels light. Oh! I dreamt that my aunt was conspiring to kill me. I felt terrified. She is in India these days. She is miserable, hospitalized. My brother was trying to get a visa, but it was not approved. This aunt has sent such a nasty *samkat* to prevent us from moving ahead in life.

It was as if the heavy burden she felt was a burden of envy and hostility toward the beautiful sister and the aunt, who were connected with their desires—they enjoyed all the riches. When the body expressed hostility, it felt lighter. This lightness was only temporary, because the weight of envy remained untouched and thus returned in the form of the *samkat.*

From mistrust to trust, inhibition to arousal, derangement to some clarity, discomfort to ease, fear to hope, paralysis to activity, tripping over to regaining balance, Balaji to Kali, from researcher to Sardarni and from child-*samkat* to penis-*samkat* to androgynous-*samkat*, both Riya and I had covered great distances. We were to wait patiently to see if we could also move toward some evolution—with the help of either Balaji or psychology.

Riya's inability to look inwards was beginning to cause me frustration, a feeling that I had learned as an apprentice to value in the clinical space. I sensed that I was hitting a dead end. When we spoke, she told me about a Muslim shrine (*dargah*) that she had visited for her healing but been disappointed by because she had not witnessed or experienced a fuller and more frenzied state of possession than in the Balaji temple. The priests had not attended to her and her family well. Her need for a fuller bodily experience and for her pain to be taken seriously had not been met—the body and mind were not invested in by the healers. In Riya's prayer at this shrine—"Oh, Saabir Paaq Baba, free me from this *samkat*, make my body healthy!"—there was a lot of emphasis on the body not getting the space it needed for a more charged expression in the state of possession and on the body wanting to feel healthy and alive. Riya also told me of a new development.

> R: Sister, my *samkat* has revealed a new form. One day, after dinner, everyone was just sitting around when a girl began to speak from within me, began singing, "My name is Chameli, I have come from far, far away." She began hurling filthy abuses at Papa, Mummy, my brother, Balaji. Papa made me sit in the temple. She abused all the deities. She had a heavy voice. Then my brother played the Hanuman Chalisa on his phone, and I began to sway wildly in *peshi*. At first Balaji kept observing it quietly. Then he held it by the neck and made it apologize to everyone, and it apologized. Only then did Balaji let go of its neck. When I returned to my senses, I told Papa that this spirit had revealed another form this time. This thing changes form. I feel a very loud voice will come out of me, like they show in the films. There will be a loud scream and then this thing will leave me.

Another shift: from Ranjeet—encapsulating both male and female parts of the self—to Chameli, who, in challenging the hostile policeman—father and Balaji himself, had announced herself to be as bold as the character in the song with which she introduced herself! There was another temple closer to Riya's house that was frequented eagerly by seekers and pilgrims. The priest of this temple might have looked at her frail and attractive body and perhaps sensed that she harbored the unconscious desire to seduce with her beauty but experienced *samkat* in desiring and wishing to be desired. Interestingly, he too opined that her *samkat* could only be cured by the ferocious Kali, not by the celibate Balaji, thus confirming her belief that only a ferocious form of the mother could metabolize her destructivity and cleanse her self, by devouring all the filth represented by the *samkat*. It was a movement toward evolution, as the child-*samkat* had now taken the form of a seductress. However, the emergence of the seductress and the resultant confidence that accompanied the hope of her disowned self-parts being metabolized by Kali brought about a sense of doubt in Riya. I am reminded of Eigen's (2019) words, "It is not true that the devil never appears in a mirror; sometimes bits of self-knowledge do come through."

> R: The day the *samkat* showed me its new form, it was abusing me as well. Sometimes I wonder if I say these things on my own.

At this point, I eased her doubt, saying that it was okay even if she did.

With the appearance of Chameli, eros had begun to inhabit her body. Abuses served as a raw way of articulating her hostility and sexuality. Although these elements were still disowned, her doubt gave me hope that the split parts had begun to come together. In other words, with the emergence of eros, she had begun to take the stance of an analysand.

> R: Papa asked it when it will leave. It said that it would take me along. Papa told it to first seek salvation for itself. It began to demand chicken, alcohol, sacrifices of children. In anger I often grab children of friends and relatives by their throats. I have even grabbed Mummy and my younger brother by their throats.

The *samkat* demanded alcohol and sacrifice, the very elements associated with the worship of Kali. She was validating her unconscious sense that it was Kali and that Kali alone could match and contain the filth of the *samkat*. From doubt—"Am I capable of abusing?"—to inhabiting her own body, another shift was underway.

> R: On the festival of Rakhi, one of my aunts got supplies from the other aunt's place. I spoke up and told her to take everything back to that witch! Then Papa backed me up and told her that there was no need to bring stuff from that aunt's house. She [the aunt who had brought the supplies] said that there were no such things as ghosts. That witch aunt of mine has brainwashed her. She [the witch aunt] took money from everyone to construct her house.

Riya was very much in touch with her hostility toward the envied aunt. Like the aunt, Riya's *samkat* too sucked all the good feed it could get from her family members. After this, the conversation moved to her education, which had been held up by the *samkat*. I could sense that her inability to process emotional content, to undertake deeper thinking and to establish interpersonal relationships had to do with a significant failure of her environment in containing her states, which had by now assumed diabolical proportions and for which Kali's metabolism was now being sought.

I did not share the language Riya understood—the one that involved ghosts, deities, rituals, and so on. Nonetheless, I wanted to help her find a way to move past the hurdles she experienced, in a language familiar to her. For this reason, I sought help from a local healer I knew—Riya. He agreed to help Riya and I introduced the two of them.

My mind had latched on to an image Riya had described in our first meeting—a couple engaged in sexual intercourse. This image had flashed in her mind when she had taken a sip of the holy water and had been followed by an image of a filthy child roaming around inside her body. I could sense in this image some healing potential. Later, after becoming familiar with thinkers like Green (1986) and Botella and Botella (2005), I understood that the primal scene works like a cure for the internal unresponsive mother. It brings into the frame "the logic of, 'because daddy'" (Botella and Botella, 2005). Finding a cause for the mother's disappearance from the primal scene is preferable to the unthinkable withdrawal of her love. Bringing in the father makes the mother's absence thinkable—"Mother not around because of Father." This is how I understood the assimilation of data. It became "thinkable" for me.

At the time, I could only sense in this image the potential for healing. My sense found resonance when the appearance of this image was followed by the expression of the *samkat*'s ardent wish to transform into Balaji's messenger or *duta*. I wondered if the image of a man and woman having sex will ever transform into an image of the peaceful coexistence of the father and mother (and the tendencies bound up with maternal and paternal elements), like we see in religious iconography—Balaji carrying the image of Rama and Sita (the ideal Indian parental couple) in his heart and revealing it to Lord Rama as a proof of his love. I had witnessed an elaboration in Riya's experience that was describable and left a tension to be metabolized by me. Before I was familiar with these thinkers, I looked at Riya's experience in terms of the language of hallucination. Much later in our conversations I was able to use the healing potential of this imagery.

Meanwhile, the therapist in me tried to appropriate the disruptions I sensed in her self. In my interactions with Riya, I tried to heal parts of her through the discourse I had faith in, the one that helped me see my not-so-integrated parts. All this was undertaken so that I could offer her a nudge toward healing. However, looking back, I now realize that it was my dream experience that had marked a turning point in my understanding and the transformation of her possession. It offered a stark reminder that one can't hope to touch parts in the selves one hopes to mend if those parts haven't been visited in oneself. Without this necessary ordeal, healing will be incomplete. At worst, it will be another repetition of the patient's experience of being met with disappointing objects. Right before my nightmares began, I had cultivated faith in the need to patiently wait for our unconscious wisdom or *buddhi* to be unlocked. It meant taking a plunge into what Botella and Botella (2005) would call retrogressive thinking, what an Indian like me would certainly think of as "faith." I surrendered myself to forces, leaving myself with no way out. It was important to live the terror and disturbance to be able to dream Riya's nightmares and arrive at some intelligibility through them. It was an extreme form of empathy.

It took me some time to metabolize the states that were evoked in me through my dreams and interactions with her. It was a letting-go facilitated by faith that led me to a state of possession in my dreams. Our dreams sometimes depict the frustration we feel at having to fill up the empty spaces in another person. For Riya, that empty space was her father's pride; for me, it was others' need for nurturance (water for my brother-in-law and good feelings for Riya), while I was left thirsty. I learned I had to allow myself to be "used" by her. Through the fine-tuning of our respective unconscious minds, facilitated by the deep empathy I felt toward her, my apparatus was now being used to get closer to her experience and to revisit in me what had been pushed into oblivion.

Through dreaming, I was able to feel the fear she experienced, the fear of not having agency over one's own body. In a way, then, Riya and I came together in our respective healings, opening vistas of experiences for each other. I stepped in to rescue her but had to deal with my own not-so-integrated parts being unleashed. Faced with the terror of this dream, I fell back on the beauty of my culture—to call out the name of Jesus in times of fear. The first dream was an expression of my sense of stagnation, manifesting as bodily immobility. It evoked in me the urge to get closer to the father, which was satisfied by becoming a "tom-boy" in the second dream. Figuring out how I could get her father closer to her in a non-threatening way had also been my struggle with Riya. I tried to achieve this goal by attempting to bring a thinking agent between "I" and "me" and becoming the father-in-mother (Ogden, 1992), admiring Riya's power and beauty.

It was much later that I realized she needed the father to be more tangibly present. My sense was that the mother was also a silent victim of the father's tyranny. As a daughter, Riya identified with the mother's sense of being flawed and weak. This did not, however, enable her to come close to the father in the manner that is characteristic of the oedipal phase. A lack that I sourced to the mother caused her to feel damned, while the one associated with the father caused the sexual and hostile impulses to be deemed unacceptable. As a result, bodily sensations that hinted at aroused sexual impulses assumed a scary quality. The dynamics laid down for her made it impossible for Riya to cultivate a male part that would empower her to be "active" rather than a passive recipient of all misfortunes or *samkat*s. My sense was that she would benefit from "the" father, not with someone "like" the father.

I was able to make use of my intuition to facilitate a bringing together of the parental couple in her healing when Ravi consulted me and asked for my advice. I refrained from sharing details about Riya with him but suggested that she would benefit from her parents somehow being involved in her healing. Thereafter, he recommended to the family that she recite Hanuman Chalisa and Hanumat Kavach for seven days with her mother and visit the temple every Saturday with her father, who would have to perform a ritual by moving a plate of offerings in a circular motion around Riya's face seven times before offering them to Balaji. The tension from my nightmares and my frustration at the lack of a reflective function in Riya led me to advise Ravi to bring the parents together in her healing. Psychoanalytic thinkers I relied on helped unlock my unconscious wisdom. Bringing the parents together in the enactment of Riya's healing would force the mother to stop remaining aloof and engage with her daughter, while the father who forbade would be made to care for his daughter, allow for intimacy between himself and her and understand her needs as she lived out her sexual and hostile impulses in the state of possession. The parental couple was now together—in her healing. I felt that this reconstitution of the internal parental couple would facilitate Riya's rebirth or the birth of a male part in her that would only gradually be assimilated. I had to wait to watch the repercussions of the ritual on her.

Meanwhile, significant content related to the relational dynamics in Riya's household emerged from her in our conversations:

R: Before seeking refuge in Balaji, we were non-vegetarians. Papa used to drink. He is an angry person, and now he does not drink. Balaji will beat him so much if he ever drinks. Mummy is diabetic and suffers from hemorrhoids. She was okay before my brother was born. After his birth, Mummy's body deteriorated. Mummy has a master's degree, but Papa did not let her work after marriage. Before she married Papa, she was a schoolteacher, but he did not let her continue with her job.

Me: That's sad. And after your brother's birth, her body deteriorated but you also became quiet and reserved.

R: I became reserved because of the *samkat.*

Me: Okay. And your mother's body?

R: That began to deteriorate soon after my younger brother's birth. Papa also started drinking frequently, and Neetu was charming everyone in the house.

Subsequently, Riya began telling me the extent to which she identified with her mother's victimhood.

R: If my demands are not met, I fight.

Me: It was like this even before you were possessed?

R: No. Before I became possessed, I used to remain quiet. If my brother ever teased me, I would hide behind Neetu for protection. Now I give it back to him. (Immediately corrects herself) I mean, the *samkat* fights back. He is always online. Even right now, as we are talking, he is listening to everything. The other day, you mentioned something about your PhD and thesis. While I was in the state of possession, it was saying about you, "What does she think of herself?"

Me: (Laughing) That's alright. My work won't stop because of his envy.

The slip—in the matter of whether it was she or the *samkat* who was fighting for space—revealed that she could own her aggression. There was a certain ease between her and her aggressive parts now. She had had to take cover behind her sister in her childhood and behind the *samkat* in adulthood to assert herself, while here I was, a person seen as possessing sufficient internal freedom to be able to express my thoughts in writing and to share them with the world. Understandably, my position aroused envy. Nonetheless, that she could share it with me made me feel privileged, because she may have sensed that I could handle her envy of me. I could playfully receive her envious part.

R: The *samkat* wants me to remain miserable. It distracts me, from work, from worship.

Me: It still seems like what it wants is happening, as if you have bowed down in front of it. After some time, even slavery begins to feel comfortable. Perhaps the question here is, "What do I get from the *samkat*'s domination over me?"

She thought for a while.

R: It is trying to dominate me. I pray to Balaji for a stronger heart so I can face this thing.

Me: What if we rephrase this prayer a little bit?

R: How?

Me: Try saying what I am about to suggest and tell me how you feel. O Almighty Balaji . . .

R: Wait, I will forget. Let me grab a pen.

Me: O Almighty Balaji, I welcome you into my heart so we may together face this force. Please transform all harmful forces in me into benevolent ones.

She wrote and then recited it a few times. Each recitation was followed by a pause. I sensed she was allowing herself to "feel" the prayer. Suddenly, she spoke.

R: Sister, this is really good. This prayer that you have given me is exactly what the supreme priest would have come up with—the one who passed away. He would also make people write down prayers like this.

Me: How did you feel?

R: Reciting it a couple of times made me feel good. Anyway, today, after talking to you, I am feeling lighter.

Me: Like you would feel after *peshi*?

R: (laughs) Yes. I will try to think good thoughts. As soon as I feel better, I will enroll in a specialization course. This *samkat* is trying to distance me from everyone.

Faced with the brokenness in her, the therapist in me tried yet another way to promote her journey toward healing. In a psychodynamic setting, we work with the patient's preconscious to bring to consciousness the unconscious. The aim is to foster a transition from primary to secondary thinking. Green (2005) introduced the notion of the "tertiary processes," which help in establishing links and pave the way for this transition between primary and secondary thinking. For many, the alliance with a higher power in a stance of prayer facilitates this movement. My hope was that the meditative state of prayer could mobilize unconscious processes and facilitate the desired transition as Riya defenselessly opened herself up to the omniscient and benevolent deity. In this state, questions are asked, problems presented and, almost instantly, the answer emerges from within like reveries, as if God had planted it in one's heart.

Prayer can initiate internal processes without being intrusive. These cultural processes offer a gentler working-through through the patient's preconscious which is largely constituted by one's culture (Kakar, 2012). In Bionian terms, prayer, if framed appropriately, can serve as an alpha function, transforming the un-metabolized beta-elements into thinkable alpha-elements. In fear or terror, the meditative state of praying with carefully chosen words can help mobilize the memory and even perceptual traces of that phase of life when the mother's benevolent presence caused all monsters to disappear. Although Riya could be the physically powerful and notorious *samkat that took over her* in her possession state, in prayer she could get in touch with her needy and vulnerable self.

The memory of this early object relation manifests itself in the person's search for an object, person, place, event, ideology that promises to transform self. The transformational function of the object is evident in many religious faiths when the subject believes in the deity's actual potential to transform the total environment . . . We see how hope invested in various objects (a new job, move to another country, a vacation, a change of relationship) may both represent a request for a transformational experience and, at the same time, continue the "relationship" to an object that signifies the experience of transformation . . . [O]ne feels a deep subjective rapport with an object and experiences an uncanny fusion with it. There is a sense of being reminded of something never cognitively apprehended but existentially known. (Bollas, 1987)

I hoped that, through prayer, she would be able to remember her origins existentially. Although this intervention on my part may be subjected to criticism, it is not devoid of clinical sensitivity.

A few weeks of prayer passed:

R: Sister, I have to tell you something. After talking to you the last time, I had made up my mind about trying to be happy in all situations. I used to get scared and let this *samkat* dominate me. I decided not to be afraid. I will do what the *samkat* stops me from doing. I even stepped out of the house two or three times. And the *samkat* has not possessed me for a week. I have told my father to take me to the temple every day. It makes me feel relaxed. Everything is fine, but whenever I sit down to pray, the *samkat* flashes before me images of penises in place of images of deities in the idols.

I sensed the confidence in her tone as she became more determined to stand up against the persecuting and damning part of herself and felt increasingly relaxed in the company of God. She was beginning to allow herself to stay with the good. This time, too, my being able to receive her states and offer some containment in return had led to the appearance of an image. The dread of the *samkat* had transformed itself into a visual image—it had a face. I was reminded of what Symington and Symington (1996) had said about alpha functions: "One indicator of alpha function is the transformation of the raw data into internal visual images."

Riya was sharing with me her experience of being re-born and expecting me to make some sense of the penis image that was replacing the images of idols. Today, I can do this. Placing herself closer to the punitive father evoked the image of penis; the desire was to come close to the father sexually, but, like the punitive father, the celibate father Balaji did not leave any space for such desires. Back then, however, I could not respond to her adequately, because I myself was experiencing a downturn in my health and consulting a doctor at the time. I felt bad for not being physically capable of echoing her excitement over this shift she had experienced in her internal state. By our next conversation, she had become worse.

R: The last time I spoke to you—that very night, the *samkat* came upon me, wreaked havoc, abused everyone, abused Balaji also. I was miserable.

From having felt better after talking to me, she had now swung to the other end of the spectrum—she had gotten worse after our last conversation. This was not a new pattern in Riya. When she did not get the desired response from me, she or her *samkat* became violent and wreaked havoc in the house. Her aggression had to do with an inability to imagine herself as not-invested-in by me. It also told me that the disappearance of maternal care from her life might have been brutal and accompanied by a sense of hopelessness that love from other objects would never come her way.

Riya went to see Neetu's newborn children and described them as very adorable. I could sense the sadness in her tone and brought it to her notice.

R: No. I am happy. But because of the *samkat*, I feel like crying all the time.

In the past, Riya had giggled at her sister's misery. Today, watching her be happy with her life, Riya was experiencing not envy or hostility but sadness. Although this sadness was partly disowned, it was sufficient indication that she was closer to a sense of lack than to harboring destructive envy. This shift was manifested in her *peshi*, which was akin to a reflective, depressive state rather than a violent one, as had been seen on previous occasions. The depressive state, being in touch with a sense of a lack and vulnerability, was unbearable and was soon countered by the emergence of a powerful male force, another form that the possessing spirit took.

R: I was fine there. But, on our return, I entered a violent possession state. Every time I ate anything, I would go into a state of possession. This time, during *peshi*, I felt a man inside me. He seemed very heavy, like an elephant. And a deep, loud voice came out of my mouth. I could not breathe properly. I was panting like this (demonstrates). It said, *"I salute all the gods and goddesses of the Hindu religion. Balaji is the most powerful being in the whole universe. I have never challenged him. Neither did I say anything to Neetu's babies, but you did not give me anything to eat."* At that party the other day, "I did not eat anything, I did not feel hungry." And then the *samkat* changed into a child, it was crying and terrified.

The emergence of the heavy man represents the realization dawning on the *samkat* that its wishes would not be indulged. It was seductively reminding Riya that "I am changing—I pray to all the deities and yet I am not rewarded enough." But it was also arrogance: "I am huge and perhaps don't need others to take care of me!"

R: The *samkat* has made my language very rough. I try to be polite but I get angry easily. One customer owed me some money for a service I provided. She started negotiating and asking me to lower the price. I told her my rates were the lowest among nearby parlors. She persisted with her request. I got annoyed. I asked if she was in a vegetable market. She got offended. This made me anxious about possibly losing another customer. The very next day, the *samkat* appeared and started saying, *"That woman spoke rudely to me—I mean, that woman spoke rudely to your daughter. She was not giving your daughter her due, so I spoke to her angrily."* I was extremely tense—what if she got offended and now I lose a customer? What should I do? Was I wrong?

It was clear that, with the empowerment she experienced through this man with the heavy voice and body, she was beginning to find her voice and assert herself. Since she was not used to asserting herself without the *samkat*, this was causing her some problems.

Me: I don't think so. You were asking for your due. And you did try to reason with her at first. I don't find anything wrong with asking for what you deserve for your work. And to run a business and get people to pay you, one has to be a little strict for this kind of work. If you are too nice, people might take advantage and your parlor will shut. You felt angry because she was not giving you your due. This makes all of us angry, but not many people can handle our anger, so we have to be selective about whom we express our anger to.

She was asking me to validate her step toward self-assertion. I tried to ease her troubled mind, to join in her struggle to claim what was due to her. However, behind this assertion lay an aspiration to accomplish something big and perhaps get ahead in life. Getting in touch with her vulnerability in the depressive state of *peshi* had first evoked the beautiful part of her self that tried to figure out ways and means of undoing the sense of a lack that she perceived. This was followed by a progressive step, as she chose to assert herself and claim what was hers instead of taking cover behind the *samkat*. And nestled amidst these moves was the realization that her aspiration to move ahead in life would not be fulfilled through enactments in *peshi*—a more real force was required.

I had to encourage this progression so it could consolidate in her. Her doubts over what she had done revealed that she possessed a faint awareness of having found her voice but was not sure the voice was claiming the right thing. In my response, I failed to identify the heavy voice as her voice. However, she soon gave me (and herself) another chance.

R: Yes. I only asked what was owed to me. I was tense when she got offended. The next day, she sent the money. When she called, I apologized to her for speaking to her rudely. She said that she was not offended, that she wouldn't have called if she were offended. She forgot about our conversation. The next time she comes to avail some service in my salon, what should I say to her?

Me: Just convey how things are—"I try to deliver the best service at the most reasonable rates, so when someone demands a concession, it does not feel good. The other day, I got angry because you demanded a concession. From now onwards, let's try to understand each other."

R: Yes, that feels right. I will say it. On another occasion, another customer was not paying me for my services. Papa began to taunt me, saying, "Riya, you cannot handle such a small problem." At that very moment, the *samkat* came over me and began to abuse Papa. Papa thrashed the *samkat* brutally, with kicks, punches, slaps. He hit the *samkat* so much that, even now, three days later, it hurts everywhere. I have not spoken to Papa for the last three days. I mean, the *samkat* is not talking to Papa.

Me: But you are running a business on your own at such a young age. One only slowly learns the strategies by which to get people to pay on time.

R: Yes. I will only learn these things gradually. Papa hit the *samkat* quite a bit.

Her rage against the father was so intense that, at the slightest hint of humiliation, it exploded. In this one conversation, she had shifted from sadness at her sister's prosperity to finding her voice to claiming her due to rebelling against her humiliating father—and now, to the image of a phallus.

R: I still see the penis.

Me: What other images do you see?

R: Earlier, I used to see two people doing it.

Me: And who are these two people?

R: A man and a woman. I can't see their faces. Then I see a penis. A few days back, I dreamt that I was passing my neighbor's house and she was standing outside it, without any clothes on. I was surprised—why was she not wearing any clothes?! In another dream, I saw that I was part of some rally. All of us were climbing a hill. Then a large group of men came running up from behind us, and none of them was wearing any clothes. All of them are running up the hill, and I am surprised that they are naked, and then my body began to tremble. My vagina was throbbing—my entire body was throbbing!

Unbeknownst of me, these words came out of my mouth—

Me: When did this happen? While dreaming?

R: No, it happens just like that. While sitting, when the whole family sits together and has meals.

Why did I consider these vivid states parts of her dreams? On many occasions, she entered the state of *peshi* while eating food or when others were eating food. In this case, too, the images of naked women and men, the sensations in her body and particularly in her vagina, erupted when everyone was eating. Why were these images and sensations being evoked by the act of eating? When she was narrating her experience to me, it struck me as a dream. I owe it to Bion, who "shifted the focus from the symbolic content of thoughts to the process of thinking and from the symbolic meaning of dreams to the process of dreaming" (Ogden, 2005b). According to Bion, we are always in the state of dreaming—that is, unconscious psychological work is always happening. It is as if one is saying that "although I am awake but I am in a dream state." In Riya, this waking dream state was taking a very particular form—"when everybody is eating, I am not drawn toward receiving food." Her mind was structured to receive things from openings other than the mouth—for instance, from the vagina.

Receiving and giving were to be performed through openings other than the mouth—this showed that psychic change had begun in her. Her mouth did not consume gutter water anymore, it did not spit abuses in states of rage. Rather, as will be seen soon, she was able to enter the space of kissing. She was talking vividly—one could sense that she was struggling to put her experience (or her alive body) into word-containers. Reading this account today feels like reading about a dream. Riya's psychic constellation was characterized by its potency at causing surges of affects, bodily sensations, rage, sexuality—storms in the body and mind. In Balaji, with the emphasis on a fuller bodily experience in *peshi*, there was space for the expression of all the excitement evoked by the psychic content that was yet to be rendered intelligible. However, her attempts to bring these sensations and images into her narration were bound to be accompanied by struggles and hesitation. She had taken a long time to arrive at this stage, a stage in which she was able to recount these vivid states in her narrations—and I responded by thinking of it as a dream.

What was the unconscious process guiding my sense? My seemingly spontaneous question shows that I was trying to create a dream state for her by entering that state myself. It is in this internal state that one can listen to the other dream. If she had said that she encountered these states in her waking state, things would have been awkward for her and for me as well. In my spontaneous question lay a structure. The question: "When did this happen? While dreaming?" reveals an unconscious sense that people are always dreaming and one has to possess ears with which to listen to the dream. Simply put, it is because I framed it as a dream (or fiction) that she was able to arrive at the truth. The value of the question lay in ushering the other into a space created unconsciously, a space created by the "language of dreaming"—a space I hinted at having already entered. It was then that she was able to narrate to me her vivid states.

Asking her directly why concepts or thoughts associated with sex evoked fear in her would have been evidence of a split. Resolving this tension required me, the researcher–therapist, to enter the dream state myself, retrieve the language of the territory and create a space where the other could use that language to share her deepest fears. Her fear was not that she couldn't name the term; her fear was of the forbidden term flashing before her images of a procession of many naked men flaunting their penises and of the nudity appearing right at her doorstep. It was her spontaneity that had her describing the vivid states as appearing before the act of eating food, which meant that her other orifice—the vagina, stimulated by all the sensations she was feeling—was beginning to open up, perhaps for procreation or for nurturing something more meaningful, perhaps for pleasure. Here lies the method—one can only tread toward intimately knowing the self and the desire of the other along with one's own self and desire, without letting it become a sexual relationship. We were creating a thinking couple—a couple in understanding.

From describing various sexual images, she had moved to describing the bodily arousal she felt that could not be lived out in the presence of a restricting family. She visited her childhood.

R: And my head hurts. Ever since the age of four or five, I have been a scared child. I would avoid visiting any relatives. I was always scared of going any-where alone. I always wanted Mommy. I always wanted to be close to her. Wherever she went, I would be with her. I was scared of being alone.

Me: Did something happen when you were alone?

I was thinking here of sexual abuse.

R: No.

Me: Have you ever kissed?

I must confess that, internally, I was rolling my eyes and asking myself, "Where did that come from? Who is asking these questions?" I was uncon-sciously being guided by my intuition that all these images were hinting at her desire to have a man.

R: No. I was never into all these things.

Me: What do you feel about these dreams?

R: I was very surprised by the fact that all these people were unclothed. I never used to get such dreams. I used to dream about my wedding. I would see myself decked up in bridal attire, adorned in bridal jewelry, wearing a garland of shoes around my neck, and looking at my reflection in the water. Now I don't see all of this. I see all the images I shared with you, and sewage water, and myself drowning in water. I would dream that I was drowning, not that I had already drowned, and people were watching but not coming to help.

Me: Is it an image of helplessness?

R: Yes.

Her internal imagery had transformed. The couple having sex, the filthy child wandering inside her, the Sardarni haunting her, the dream image of herself drowning, her reflection in sewage water, dressed as bride and wearing a garland of shoes—each hinted at her desires and how they were met repeatedly with humiliation from the males in the household. The childish voice, the tactile sense of her body being eaten from the inside, the fear of the *samkat* getting her pregnant, the belief that the *samkat* had made her fairer, the part-male, part-female Ranjeet, the bold, wholly female seductress Chameli, the heavy man and the image of the penis—which first replaced images of deities, followed her and distracted her from worshipping Balaji—and finally the naked bodies of men and women.

After having endured a state of vulnerability and sadness and countered it with a powerful assertion of her needs, she moved to the next stage, in which she actively rebelled against the father for humiliating her. In running the business on her own, she was trying to claim a phallus—which her father had repeatedly denied her, but this time she fought him. The fight between the father and the daughter was over the phallus. The penis image she was seeing did not evoke disgust but surprise. She wanted to consume the phallus, or rather the powers associated with it. The manhandling she had been subjected to by her father had aggravated her desire for the phallus. Her desires were now becoming increasingly sexualized due to the multiple opportunities she had had at the Balaji temple to live them out. Like free association, which allows the mind to wander in any direction possible, in *peshi*, her body could move freely, making forms and poses, experiencing the flow of aliveness she had not known in her suffocating household.

This free mobilization is facilitated by Balaji. He fosters regression to such elementary states, in which the repeated sensation of bodily satisfaction is instrumental to the continuity of one's being. Balaji does this by implicitly saying to the possessed person, "You can be free with whatever desires you have. I am here." In the past, Riya's father had stifled her mother's independence. Now, he was mocking Riya's attempts to achieve her own independence. It was as if the father spanked her because, in becoming independent, she had taken his phallus. He tried to claim it back by humiliating her, and Riya again tried to devour it orally by verbally abusing him.

It was this penis that the child in Riya wanted to consume, in the hope that the incorporation of this phallus into her self would make her a man. By abusing through the medium of the *samkat,* she was symbolically making the father impotent—to which he reacted with more violence. The change in imagery after this bodily tussle revealed that the contact with the father had unleashed raw sexual content, which took the form of naked bodies. One previous incident had also involved bodily contact leading to the unleashing of sexual content—her *peshi* with me, which had also aggravated her symptoms and caused her to start fainting, perceiving her body to be burning with fever or desire, seeing a Sardarni, fearing and believing in the containing capacity of Kali, and feeling her *samkat* come further down from her stomach to her legs. In Riya, the desires of a woman were now gradually emerging, manifesting in surprise at (not fear of) naked bodies. She had the phallus that made her raise her voice against her customer, claim her dues and fight her father, abuse him, and take his beatings.

The celibate Balaji was like the punitive father who was repelled by the *samkat*'s hostility and sexuality. He would not even touch it. Like the father, Balaji too would merely punish Riya. Kali represented the hope and the desire that only the mother could consume or metabolize or touch and contain such intense destructivity. The mother's presence was being sought, as it had been in childhood. An appeal was being made to the mother, to contain the fears of the father's penis and of Riya's own destructive wish to eat and retain the penis in herself. Becoming part of this containing process, I asked her something I was not sure made sense—"Have you ever kissed?" This spontaneous question puzzled me for quite a while, but now I understand that the progressive movement through the internal mapping in her images, the snatching away of the father's penis and the call to the mother for containment had influenced my mind. Though spontaneous and surprising, my question was guided by the effect on my unconscious of this progression I had been witness to for so long. The penis that could tear the body was now to be consumed tenderly through the mouth.

Kissing was in line with the theme of Kali consuming the *samkat* and of orally consuming the father's penis through abuse. Kissing could make way for a tender eating up of the penis. Kissing (or the thought of taking the penis in) was repulsive, but the penis was no more a source of fear. It was as if the saliva, smells, hard skin, and thick hair that were repulsive at first were now being savored. This fusion of smells and saliva was desired. Kissing is a tender form of sex. There is no thrusting. It lubricates other openings of the body. The penis that was once scary required the presence of a mother who would say, "You should live this experience. There is no danger in it, only ecstasy." By sharing with me the emergence of sexual content in her, Riya was bringing forth the evolved and beautiful part of her self. This beautiful part that I received unconsciously transported me into a state in which I could become the sexually upfront Sardarni and mobilize a "Kali-like" taking-in of the penis or the *samkat*, tenderly, through kissing. Although the dream of drowning and the reality of not having a phallus caused her to feel helpless, Riya had learned to deal with this sense of helplessness effectively. It was as if she was beginning to consume or incorporate the phallus. It showed in the confidence with which she was planning her future, in dreaming and doing.

R: After I last spoke to you, I made up my mind to focus on worship and try to get out of this situation, maybe go for further training as a beautician. I also have got my visiting cards printed. I will put up a board outside my salon. I have called a girl for an interview. She is trained in bridal makeup. Now I want to gradually get better.

Me: Don't worry, things will gradually become alright. And if they don't, then we will think about how to make them alright. I am around.

This was another response of mine that surprised me. I was being assuring.

R: Yes, true. You are here. You have really supported me. First comes Balaji and after him it is you!

Me: But I have not done anything.

The moment she began to idealize me, I was overcome by discomfort. She was entering her belief through me, and I was struggling between being assuring and doubtful. Spirit possession or the psychic constellation of a possessed person opens zones for the researcher/therapist marked by a constant tug-of-war between these two states: being assuring and being doubtful. At the time of the above interaction, I was actually puzzled. I was not aware of what I had done to make her feel comforted. It was as if I had snapped out of a spell, as if until that point I had been unconsciously receiving her communications and allowing her to use me to play the role of an upfront Sardarni.

R: No, you have explained to me many things. That day, after talking to you, I realized that I was letting the *samkat* win, letting it dominate me, doing whatever it wants. Now I have decided I will not obsess over things. Truly, you have really helped me. It is true, I now believe completely in Balaji, that he will send someone or the other. He sent you for me.

Her internal parental couple was on the verge of forming with Balaji as a variant of the father who, although punitive and distant, allowed Riya to live out her desires and Kali as the mother who contained her distress and mobilized in her a tender incorporation of the phallus—and I was the messenger (*duta*) sent by Balaji.

> R: Balaji is my guru and has opened my eyes. Earlier, I was scared to go anywhere alone. Now that's not the case. I can go to the market alone and not feel scared.

> Me: Just like during your childhood you held your mother's hand to get through darkness, now you are holding Balaji's hands and he is getting you through this dark time.

From feeling confident about the newfound phallus in the presence of both the mother and the father, Riya jumped to relishing her beauty. It was as if the "guru"—an image of the combined parental couple—offered her a mirror in which her beauty was reflected. She excitedly told me about her sister's party, at which every guest had been amazed to see the dissimilarities between Riya and her sister, noting that Riya was fairer and her features were better than both her siblings.' She was acknowledging her beauty and also jokingly acknowledging the *samkat*'s role in keeping her fair and slim. Her symptoms were transforming and offering greater space for the expansion of her self. The acknowledgment of her beauty led to her *samkat* revealing its true form.

> R: The other day, soon after finishing dinner, the *samkat* came over and began to abuse everyone, including me! Balaji held him and made him puke out the truth!

Having said this, she waited for me to reciprocate with a similar level of animation in my tone.

> Me: What truth!?

> R: The *samkat* is actually a penis!

Although the content she was bringing up was becoming increasingly sexualized and her inhibitions were disappearing, the penis still caused her discomfort and excitement (not necessarily in that order).

> R: It changes form. Sometimes, it turns into a child, at other times a girl, sometimes a man.

> Me: Oh!

In this account, there was no fear, only a sense of having achieved something. The penis was being brought forth with its procreative function—it could give form to a man or a woman, it could empower her against the controlling males in the house and it made her look beautiful! However, this procreative function had not yet been recognized.

R: That aunt of mine sent such an obscene ghost.

Me: Was she always like this?

I was entering the phase of the phallic-*samkat*.

R: There was an altercation with her. She used to interfere a lot in our family's matters. Another aunt of mine went to the U.S. and handed over her beauty salon to Neetu. After a month, this witch aunt of mine came to ask us for accounts and collect all the income. Papa was always suspicious of her intentions. Neetu also used to feel insulted. Actually, after Grandmother passed away, everyone gave her the status of a mother and she became proud. Some years ago, she used to visit us every day and bring various delicacies, like *kheer*. This penis-*samkat* entered me after I consumed *kheer* offered by her.

Kheer is an Indian sweet dish made using milk, rice, and nuts. In many parts of Northern India, *kheer* is also slang for semen and vaginal fluids. The *kheer* was consumed orally by Riya. The *samkat* entered orally, was born as the baby of a couple engaged in sexual intercourse inside her, inhabited her body, stimulated her vagina and finally revealed itself to be a penis. In line with her fear of the penis that would enter the body and tear it apart, this child-*samkat* was gnawing on her insides. The pulsation in her vagina due to its transformation into a penis was a form of excitement Riya could not make sense of—the feared penis was now causing the body to experience excitement! Offered by the phallic-aunt, it had been taken in through one opening (the mouth), remained contained in her body, empowered her against her family, let her live out her desires in the state of possession and begun lubricating or mobilizing another opening (the vagina) with desires before it was to be delivered out. Riya had breast, baby, and penis confused.

Earlier, she had feared the phallus. The fear had been so deep-seated and all-encompassing that, in a state of terror, Riya became the thing she feared the most. In other words, it was as if, in Riya's mind, to orally consume a phallus (through *kheer*) was to become it. Consuming the phallus was a defense. The culture around her revered the male child and the phallus. Born as a girl in a culture that openly idealized boys, perhaps it felt to her like nothing inside her was good and nothing good would come out. A penis seemed like the best thing to be. But her insides were full of shit—the space where the seed was to be nurtured was dirty, that is to say, anally constructed, meaning there was no space in her internal landscape to receive anything nourishing. She received at her will and offered at her will because, like with anality, there was greater pleasure in withholding. Until this mechanism changed, what was inside would also fuel fear. So, to take it orally was in a sense a regression—"I am all penis." But this penis was not going to procreate because she still nursed the sense of being dirty or impure. Balaji had made her drink the sewage water, cast as the toxic opposite of semen to punish her for envy and the other vicious emotions she harbored. Now, it was Balaji's holy water that calmed the *samkat* down or gradually diminished its filth and toxicity.

In a playful exchange, I tried to explore the empowerment that the phallus brought about in Riya.

> Me: I am thinking about the fact that, when the *samkat* takes over you, it also makes you so powerful!
>
> R: Oh yes! Once, during possession, I slapped Neetu really hard!

She laughed. I could tell that she was relishing the power that came with the *samkat*. I sensed it was the right time to facilitate an "indwelling" of her destructive desires in her body, instead of moralizing about her/the *samkat*'s actions.

> Me: Really?!
>
> R: Of course! Then, at the Balaji temple, Neetu got really angry but she did not say anything to me.
>
> Me: How powerful the *samkat* must be!
>
> R: He says that he is a hero and Balaji is a zero.

We laughed at the *samkat*'s childlike sense of omnipotence.

> R: It says to Balaji, "Wait and watch how I leave this girl in a miserable condition."

Although Riya had come a long way, from fearing her *samkat* to beginning to embrace the parts of self it represented, living its omnipotence evoked guilt owing to unresolved conflicts. In this scenario, she could only briefly relish the effect that accompanied her raw bodily performances in possession states. The defiant part in her sought embodiment through the mirroring it hoped to receive in possession or in conversations with her healer and me. The body had entered the world of words for the first time with all its aliveness; the mind-body dissociation had momentarily broken. It was evident that the self was striving to establish a stronger mind-body connection here. If the manipulative mind could integrate the desire for destructive actions, the right to "be" would be unquestionable and lead to a relatively integrated human. A closer and better mind-body relationship was being hoped for. Once accomplished, the energy released would take its place as a part of her total personality, forcing the deep-seated dissociation to diminish or be overcome. An important tendency that had earlier been left out of her process of development could now be assimilated into the self, worked with, and perhaps converted into effectiveness and self-assertion.

Phases of psychopathic acting out were meant to repair chronic narcissistic injury or the sense of injury. Such acts, attributed to the *bhuta*'s work, actually helped the damaged and constricted ego to enter and experience embodied life more thoroughly. All the behaviors Riya was describing to me indicated reparative work: persistent attacks on family, either verbally or physically, bringing about in them a transformation whereby they became devoted to taking care of Riya's needs and demands and actively performing various healing rituals; expressions of anger *qua* possession when refused a privilege or offended by family; awe-struck descriptions of her own physical power during possession states. We get a glimpse of the reparative drive of the self in the seemingly asocial manifestations of the possessed person—in line with Winnicott's theory, reparation can be described as "the environment meeting the infant's experience of omnipotence; allowing itself to be created by the infant as in the area of transitional object and phenomenon, and allowing the infant to make his own contribution toward his caretaking environment" (Khan, 2018).

Gradually, many "developing" sides of Riya were emerging. As she dreamed of and worked toward seducing customers, the charming Chameli, for instance, blossomed.

> R: After I am exorcised, my new life will begin. I have many plans—to open a bigger parlor, to receive training, to hire more people, there is lots to do!
>
> Me: Good! Dreams help us move forward.
>
> R: I have also decided that, whenever we pay a visit to the Balaji temple for a glimpse of Balaji, I will appropriately guide other possessed persons there.

Here Riya was emerging as god's messenger or *duta*, marked by empathy, capacity for concern and a desire to serve others, strikingly unlike the *samkat* inspired by the selfish aunt.

> Me: That's a really good thought.
>
> R: Thank you! I am told that Ankur and I are very good-natured people.

There had been a textural change in the dynamics between Riya and her brother. Ankur had hitherto been presented as a junior version of the

disciplinary father, who teased, humiliated, and prohibited Riya from following her desires. But now, things were different. A bond was beginning
to develop between the two. For the first time, I sensed not Riya's hostility
toward Ankur but an ease.

> R: By the way, the *samkat's* mind is twisted. I also used to feel that I would go
> crazy, but talking to you has really helped. It is true, talking really brings about
> change.

I should have explored how talking had helped her. Unfortunately, before
I could think of doing so, she resumed her associations.

> R: Once, when we went to the Balaji temple, we saw a possessed girl being
> dragged by her hair by her brother. He was beating her. Everyone around paused
> to look at them. It was such a violent sight. The daughter of one of my custom-
> ers is also possessed. Her brother is in Australia. He was telling their mother,
> "She has gone crazy, abandon her on the streets or in the asylum." That poor
> mother was saying, "How can I leave my own daughter?" I felt extremely sad
> listening to her.

Riya was conveying that it pained her to witness violence and humiliation.
She was identifying with the girl and the humiliation her brother was making
her endure. Witnessing this reminded Riya of the horrors of her own possession. The pain she felt, which was accompanied by silence, was a sign of an
ongoing internal processing of her experiences of violence and humiliation.
There was also something else at work beneath the silence.

> Me: What are you thinking about?
>
> R: I was thinking about the fact that my *samkat* has slapped Mummy, Neetu, and
> Ankur and abused everyone at home, but my family has never stopped support-
> ing me, they never abandoned me. They have stood beside me. Ankur is better
> than the brother of that possessed girl. Seriously. My eyes have opened after
> visiting Balaji. I have seen and learned about the world.

The processing of the humiliation had produced the realization that the
samkat had made it possible for her to see the truths she had hitherto remained
oblivious to. She was now beginning to appreciate the presence and efforts
of her family members and the loyalty and tenacity they had shown in surviving her destruction. The very people toward whom she had harbored
such immense hostility were now becoming more real, such that she was
beginning to see their other parts. It was the space created for her and in her
at the Balaji temple that had allowed her to repeatedly destroy her family
members in *peshi*, forcing them to cater to her needs as if they did not have

needs of their own. I, too, had had to face the brunt of this destruction on occasions when I had not been available to her in the ways that she desired. It had caused her to get angry and led to an aggravation in her symptoms. Repeated destruction had led her to a stage at which she was now able to see clearly that those who had wronged her in the past had also stood beside her. Her newfound appreciation for them and tolerance for ambivalence, a stance that bridged the chasm she had perceived between the all-good and all-bad worlds, had indeed been brought about by her faith in Balaji.

When I first wrote about this, I was driven by an appreciation of her faith. Balaji had provided her with a space in which to live out her forbidden parts until she could reach a position that allowed her to appreciate her relationships. In other words, my gratitude to Balaji was gratitude to this cultural healing space. I had become a believer in the culture and the various ways in which it provided for individuals, non-intrusively helping them deal with the 'psychic.'

Riya's inner eyes were now open, as she was beginning to see clearly and appreciate the various colors of what had earlier been viewed in black and white. She had moved from a fear of the penis (of establishing sexual intimacy in marriage) and consequent blatant reluctance to even entertain the idea of a relationship of love to imagining and sharing with me the attributes she desired in her partner. Some thinking and imagining around the penis had begun.

> R: I want a man for myself who does not have any problems with my work. There are some men who mind if their wives work, especially if she runs a beauty parlor. He should also be well-qualified. Beauty is not that important to me, but he shouldn't be ugly either.

It was refreshing for me to listen to her describe the right man for her. Interestingly, the first attribute she had mentioned was one that contrasted with a position her own father had taken. She was making it clear that she did not want to suffer like her mother had when she had been prohibited by her husband from working as a teacher. Looks were important but were secondary to a good education, open-mindedness and understanding—qualities her father lacked. She was hoping for the penis that would not invade her inner space and tear it apart to make space for itself, the penis that would only bring with it experiences of being embraced and empowered.

A few months into following the rituals recommended by Ravi, which involved the presence of both her parents, Riya reported a significant change in her state.

R: I bathed in the morning and cleaned the temple. The minute I sat down to chant the Hanuman Kavach, Balaji held up all those obscene images in front of me and removed them from my mind's eye. Then I completed the entire ritual peacefully. Now I pray every morning and, after that, I look into Balaji's eyes and tell him everything that is in my mind, and he listens. I feel very relaxed. I am able to work well the entire day. Only when I am sitting idle, does the *samkat* come.

The Hanuman Chalisa and Hanumat Kavach prayers are considered extremely potent against evil entities. The sentiment captured in these mantras is such that, in reciting them, the devotee becomes the idealizing, adoring child submitting to the protection of the omniscient Hanuman. They are prayers for strength, intelligence and true knowledge, the only tools that can relieve one's pain. The deity's image is intensely glorified, like a child perceives the mother's beauty—"Your golden color and beautiful attire make you shine, with you wear earrings and curly hair"—and the father's masculinity—"You carry in your hands a lightning bolt and a victory flag and wear the sacred thread on your shoulder." Hanuman is constructed as a repository of learning, an ardent listener, and a compassionate parent whose bravery is unparalleled. Like the mother who transforms the unpleasant self-states into pleasant ones merely by the way she holds and sings lullabies to the child, Hanuman uplifts all pain, suffering and burdens, cures all diseases, grants all happiness and worldly and divine comforts and, most importantly, alleviates all the fears one's own destructive urges may evoke.

> *Bhoot pisach nikat nahin aavai,*
> (Ghosts, demons and evil forces dare not come close)
> *Mahavir jab naam sunavai.*
> (When they hear your name, O Bravest One)
> *Nase rog harai sab peera,*
> (All diseases, pain and suffering)
> *Japat nirantar Hanumant beera.*
> (Disappear when Hanuman's holy name is recited endlessly.)
> *Sankat se Hanuman chudavai,*
> (Those who remember Hanuman in their thoughts, words, and deeds)
> *Man karam vachan dyan jo lavai.*
> (With sincerity and faith, are rescued from all crises in life.)

By being present every morning during the recitation of the Hanumat Kavach, Riya's mother gently ushered her daughter toward her father, who took Riya to the temple every Saturday and performed his part of the enactments devised to cure her.

Riya was taking baby steps toward becoming a woman and I was delighted with the progress she had made. What came next, however, was like an explosion, an experience that shook her and brought her inhibitions to the fore again.

Ravi had a word with Riya and found that, although the *samkat* had been weakened, it was still there. After speaking with Riya's father, Ravi got them in touch with a healer who was well known for his ministrations. Riya and I spoke about this when we next met in Balaji village.

> R: First he asked me to untie my hair and then he began to accuse me of fanta-sizing about obscenities. He said that the ghost possessing me is very lusty and will not be exorcised by Lord Balaji. I felt terrible when he said that. And then he began to talk to me in an obscene way. He said, "Just come near me once, let me take a closer look at you." I was so scared. He was saying all kinds of dirty things to the ghost. I did not say anything to him, but the ghost began to abuse him. Even then, the healer persisted. The ghost went on verbally abusing him and getting really angry at him. I was not able to say anything. Whenever something like this happens, I am unable to speak. I feel that this ghost is speak-ing. Even now, it is the ghost who is talking to you. Sometimes I see the Riya inside me sitting in a wheelchair, gagged. She is watching everyone, begging them to stop the ghost.

Riya was sobbing bitterly.

Listening to her reminded me of my own immobile body in the nightmare I had and have mentioned earlier. I could understand how terrorizing this image must have been for her. She was paralyzed waist down in the dream, as if incapable of mobilizing any thinking around sexuality involving the lower half of her body. Sitting in a wheelchair, not being able to speak about sexuality, she was helpless, at the mercy of her forbidden desires, which the healer had threatened to evoke and which, if they broke into her conscious-ness, stood the risk of being exploited. She lacked the capacity to fight this evocation.

This encounter also offers a glimpse into the "seduction" of possessed per-sons by healers, a practice that pervades healing sites like the Balaji temple. On the one hand, it is true that the healer was addressing the ghost in Riya, seducing it, provoking it, and trying to control it. The *samkat* was indeed lusty and could only be scared away with such advances. As I understand it, what drives the commitment to this approach is the belief that perverse advances can be instrumental in initiating growth. A corresponding benign image is of the kiss of true love that awakens the unconscious princess. In this case, what Riya feared was that obscene advances were being made toward her, *not* the *samkat* possessing her. Though it was the *samkat* that defended against these advances by abusing the healer, it was nonetheless Riya's fear that was being evoked. She sensed danger. So, it was not a conversation between the *samkat* and the healer—it was a communication between Riya and the healer.

On other occasions, the all-powerful *samkat* had been able to gather Riya's fears and channel them into aggression in the household. However, here it had failed to do so. Usually, healers control *samkats* by evoking sexuality until it is sufficiently lived and internalized, after which the possessed party realizes that there is no need to be afraid of the *samkat*, for it gives pleasure. The *samkat* remains a problem until one can see that it gives pleasure. Healers and tantrics are supposed to tame sexuality. They are not afraid of it. The understanding driving their healing endeavors resides in a conviction that sexuality needs to be sufficiently fueled for one to stop seeing it as unclean or impure and capable of creating horror.

After Riya described her experience with the healer, I, having understood her helplessness in dealing with such advances and the manner in which the *samkat* compensated for that helplessness, waited for her to calm down before speaking.

Me: I have noticed how, when somebody humiliates you, your ghost comes forth. Your father said something to you the other day, this healer humiliated you. In both cases, the ghost turned up and lashed out at them. It abuses those who humiliate you while you are left gagged in the wheelchair. This ghost seems to be getting back at them on your behalf.

R: Yes, that is true.

Me: Right now is the ghost listening?

R: Yes.

Me: Can I talk to him?

Riya looked down for a few seconds. When she turned her face back up, it seemed I was looking at somebody else. A smirk danced on her lips, an ominous look in her eyes, piercing, directed right at or into me. I was mildly scared, but invoking the image of my healer grandfather's and the warmth of my grandmother gave me some confidence.

Me: Now that you are listening, tell me if you wish to leave Riya's body.

Perhaps because I appeared externally unfazed by the ghost, Riya's/its expression softened. I watched her/its eyes turn from eerie to worried. She/it spoke again in what sounded like a little child's voice:

R/*samkat*: Yes. I want to leave.

I was feeling more confident now.

Me: Then why do you fight on Riya's behalf? Whenever she is humiliated, you come forward while she is left helpless in a wheelchair. If you keep on taking over on her behalf, how will she learn to stand up and speak up?

I waited, anticipating a rebellious response. Riya turned her face away from me, looking elsewhere, and somewhat perplexed. I could tell she was thinking. She/it then turned back to face me.

R/*samkat*: Yes. You are right.

Me: Now can I talk to Riya?

Riya/it looked down. While all of this took only a few moments, back then it felt like the experience was unfolding in slow motion. Time seemed stretched to me, perhaps because of my own stretched capacity to endure the horror of the exchange.

She looked up. There she was again. I was relieved to find Riya back.

Riya: Yes?

Me: I was speaking with the *samkat*. As long as it keeps speaking and fighting on your behalf, you will not feel the need to learn to do so yourself. I am wondering if this feeds into why you feel nobody takes you seriously. Because you think that *they* know that it is not you who is talking but your ghost, and he is to be evacuated.

R: Yes. I have never thought like this. I do not know how to express my opinions.

Me: That we will learn slowly. Sometimes, when Papa or Ankur speak rudely to you, you can say, "Do not speak to me like that. I do not like it, and I do not like to fight either."

R: Yes. I will have to try.

In my desperate attempt to contain her anxieties and respond to her dependence on me, I took a didactical, motherly stance. With a mix of warmth and authority, I tried to give her a glimpse of the capacities she lacked. I realize now that I could only have done this as a mother. I wonder if, in this dialogue, I was consuming the *samkat*, telling Riya that it was not needed any more. Like a mother who has put away the stroller to teach her toddler to walk, I was trying to enable Riya to use her psychic limbs or capacities. I did feel sorry for and guilty about this intervention on my part.

In our next conversation, Riya told me that she was feeling better and had made up her mind to turn to the goddess Kali because she felt only Kali had the capacity to consume the unclean *samkat*. Had my desperation and tenacity in the role of a mother-like figure mobilized her belief in Kali?

After a few more days when we met again, Riya spoke more concretely about the fears she associated with the body. It became clear that she was ready to look at her body and even embrace it if someone could help her see beauty in it.

R: I fear that someone resides inside my body.

Me: What do you feel about your body?

The motherly stance from the last conversation still prevailed, and I could sense intuitively that it had worked for her and was also desired. She seemed to want me not as a therapist but as a mother with whom she could share all her secrets.

R: Meaning?

Me: Meaning, do you think that you look beautiful?

R: (hesitantly) No, I don't think so. I don't pay much attention to it. (blushing) Everyone says that I have good features. I also feel that I am okay.

What was the extent to which this beauty was owned and lived?

Me: Do you ever get ready, apply makeup, try out different outfits, adorn yourself and admire yourself in the mirror?

R: (amused) No! I don't do all these things. I don't really care about my body and beauty much. Neither do I apply makeup or get dressed up at home or when I'm going out. I don't give my body much attention. Neetu does. Earlier, I, too, used to. I used to wear jeans and get dressed before heading out, but not too much. And then, when this spirit possessed me, I had to stop all of it. Possessed persons have to live simply. Now I don't care for any of it. I stay shabby.

Me: But your profession might demand that you stay nicely dressed and try on yourself all the makeup that you want to use on your clients, no?

R: No, I never do these things. And even if I do deck myself up, dress myself up and adorn myself sometimes, like when I am attending some social gathering or during some festival, Ankur and Papa start policing my choices. And then I drop everything. I don't like to be scrutinized.

Whenever I had seen her in Balaji, she had indeed been dressed shabbily—not "decked up" at all.

Me: And Mummy?

R: What will Mummy say? She never says anything.

Me: Well, it's difficult to feel beautiful when people around us do not allow us to look beautiful.

R: Yes. Anyway, I cannot get into all this because of the *samkat*. Possessed persons are prohibited from all this. They have to live a simple life. The *samkat* also wants me to look beautiful and men to stalk me.

Me: If a house is not owned by anyone, thieves can easily enter and make it their den. The body that is not being owned becomes available for the *samkat* and other destructive forces.

By using a metaphor like a traditional healer, I was subtly trying to introduce the idea that the estrangement she felt vis-à-vis her bodily needs could only be done away with by owning her body. She had to chase away the thieves and reclaim her body, embrace it so all its needs, which she attributed to the *samkat*, could also be embraced and celebrated.

R: (after some thought) I have never thought about it like this. Are you saying that I should do all the things the *samkat* wants me to?

This question needed to be handled very delicately. I continued with my metaphor.

Me: All I am saying is that, if you don't own your body, attend to its needs, beautify it, admire it and allow it to be admired, then the *samkat* will consider such a body its own and inhabit it. It is also possible that it is taking advantage of the fact that you are not accepting your body.

R: It makes sense. You mean I should accept that . . . I am beautiful!?

Me: Yes! It is also required of your profession that you *feel* beautiful so that you can make others feel beautiful.

I knew she would only embrace her beauty if she thought it would help her get ahead in life.

R: Then Ankur will pick on me and spoil my mood.

Me: Well, then you will have to learn to quiet him down or to block him out.

She wanted to feel beautiful but lacked the capacity to deal with the forbidding presence of her brother and father. She needed to develop psychic limbs (assertiveness and perseverance) so she could keep all interference at a distance as she embraced the beauty of her body and claimed her desires. Having gained some encouragement from our dialogues, Riya had already

begun to invest in herself and her womanhood. The prospects of her investment seemed to excite her.

R: I have a brand-new makeup kit locked up somewhere. I will take that out.
In any case, I have to learn how to do eye make-up. I will try it first on myself.

Me: Good!

R: Also, I did not tell anyone, but I cut my hair the other day!

There were ways in which she was secretly allowing herself to feel like
a beautiful woman. She was becoming that woman in bits and parts. This
secret space of self-love was not discussed with anyone else because people
around her lacked the capacity to appreciate and understand it. Touched that
she allowed me into this secret garden, I asked her to teach me something
about make-up, partly because I really did want to learn and partly to give
her a sense of agency or joy, the sense that she could offer me something, to
enhance her perception of beauty in herself.

R: Now, only my head feels heavy. I do not experience full-blown possession
states. Mummy circles a coconut around my head seven times, and I feel better.
A few days back, I had such a horrible dream. I was in the Balaji temple, and
my brother came and told Papa that my *samkat* would be exorcised in the next
two hours. "Take her for *peshi* quickly," he said, and my *samkat* heard this. Papa
asked me to get up, and I followed him. Then, suddenly, Papa fell to the ground,
and I was saying, "What happened to my father?" But inside me, the *samkat*
was delighted. Some people took Papa to the hospital. For some reason, I didn't
know where he was, so I had to ask around to find the hospital, where Papa was
lying in bed. On the bed next to him was Ankur, also lying down. I asked the
doctor, "What happened to my Papa?" The doctor said, "He is mentally a little
disturbed, so please don't disturb him." Then the *samkat* intentionally started
to trouble Papa, asking him to get up. I began to shake Papa, to wake him up,
saying, "Papa, wake up! Papa, wake up!" Papa suddenly woke up and stood on
the bed. He was holding a dagger in his hand. I got terrified and hid behind the
curtain. The *samkat* was very happy that Papa had gone crazy. Then Papa moved
toward Ankur and stabbed him in his ankle. At that moment, I let out a loud
scream and woke up. I was terrified. I couldn't stop crying. Mummy slept beside
me, so I tried to wake her up. She shoved my hand aside. Then I called Ankur,
and he woke up immediately and began to ask me with concern, "What happened to you, Riya?" He switched the lights on, quickly got Balaji's holy water
for me, along with ashes from our *puja* room, and made me drink the water and
consume the ashes. I then told him about my dream. He patiently listened to the
entire thing. Then I felt a little lighter.

Now my parlor is also running smoothly. Recently, I got a friend ready for a
party. Did her make-up and everything. She did not pay me then and said she

would pay me later. I did not push her because I trusted her. Later, when she called and I asked her about the payment, she said that I had not done a good job and that everyone was saying so. But I dressed her up and decked her up really well. Ankur was listening to our conversation. I understood that she was not going to pay. She was just trying to manipulate me. In the end, she only paid half. I learnt a lesson—in the future, I will always ask for advance money. I became extremely anxious, though. I even thought about not installing the board outside my parlor for marketing purposes, but then both Papa and Ankur encouraged me. They said, "Such things happen in business. Why are you scared because of such a small thing?" They themselves installed the board.

Until this point in her life, her father and brother had been obstacles for Riya, humiliating her for and discouraging her from trying to become an empowered, independent woman. This dream indicated that the part of her *samkat* she wished to get rid of was the part that represented her hostility toward the two of them; she wished to attenuate that hostility. Now, she was planning to enroll in a leading beauty institute to polish her skills and had plans to publicize and expand her salon.

Riya remains convinced that worshipping Kali will help her, so, today, she worships both Balaji and Durga. She recites the Hanuman Chalisa as well as the Durga Saptashati. The celibate Balaji offers her chances to feel empowered through the *samkat*, while the tenacious and warm Durga consumes and transforms her distress into capacities that enable her. Durga, after all, has many limbs, and perhaps one day, like her, Riya too will develop multiple psychic limbs that will help her deal with her multiple relationships. Her *samkat* has lost its intensity. It only surfaces occasionally, mainly pestering her in the form of headaches.

DISCUSSION

Spirits do not appear out of nowhere. They appear where there is authority, where family, society and relationships control and punish sexuality and desire. Although anthropological traditions, too, share the same understanding, Riya helped me to arrive at it through a personal path. My role was to ease her fears. More critically, I was able to touch a hallucinatory level on many occasions to retrieve from the deep recesses of our unconscious minds our respective relationships with the split-off male parts in us. In Riya, the struggle with this male part led to images of a filthy *samkat*. In my dream within a dream, this male part enabled me to "do" things—to conduct research. In touching this hallucinatory level, I was able to open a language of dreams in which Riya could share the truth with me—her spontaneity gave way to a link between consuming food through the mouth and receiving the penis through the vagina. This link created space for further exploration and a corresponding easing of her fears. "Kissing" was one such space that was created by these dream states, a space in which we developed an imagination of sexual pleasure, led to arousal in the most intimate place on Riya's body—the vagina, which was not involved earlier. We had affected a shift from the oral to the genital. Her fears were easing. I was able to point her toward the procreative function of the penis, gradually creating more space for her to process herself as a bride and imagine the right man for that bride.

In the last dream she shared, she was actually able to erase the phallus, represented by the brother. In my case, the contact with the "negative" in the dream had brought about a state of disorientation; in Riya this negative was now being positivized in the hostility with which the brother in the dream had been erased. What had occurred was a transformation. Although the mother was yet to come alive to Riya's needs instead of shrugging her plaintive hand away, the support of the father and the brother would in the end facilitate these processes. She had decided to take on bridal customers once again, to invest in their beautification, which doubled up as an investment in herself as well! In all of this, Riya's fundamental wish was for a family of her desires to be constituted, which would allow her to move toward an imagination of sexual union with a man. But she could not have done it all by herself, not even by swaying in front of Balaji. This was possible because I could bring myself to be used by her, to welcome her projective communications, feel her states, to experience her and to experience my own fears, my nightmares, and my ability to touch the hallucinatory level of thinkability.

I come from a family that believes in ghosts and ghouls, so the inquiry undertaken here was deeply personal for me, causing me to venture into transitional spaces between the subjective and the objective. I had my own fears when I entered into a dialogue with Riya. But, as is evident, I refrained from actively splitting my fears and included them to some extent in the dialogue. During these dialogues, I could on many occasions intuit the unconscious-to-unconscious communication and, on some occasions, I colluded with her unconscious needs. In doing so, my method wavered toward a slant. But it was this slant that helped me dream Riya, to carry her throughout and, guided by her progress, to nudge her toward further transformation.

Right before entering the research field, I spoke to my father about my anxieties. He said to me, "Go with faith. Empty yourself. Things will emerge only if you don't try frantically to reason. Where there is reason, there is no faith." Today, this brings to my mind Bion's (1967) instruction "to enter the analytic session without memory, desire, understanding and expectation."

Riya also taught me that I had to learn to appreciate faith. She may have been possessed for various unconscious reasons, the kind of reasons that psychologists would love to talk about at conferences and other forums. But I think, most importantly, she was possessed because she was faithful. Her faith was in god, who made it possible for her to live her mess. Riya, I myself, and the thinkers I was drawn to dive into the unconscious with the faith that it is a necessary ordeal, the only one that will make our states thinkable.

Today, Riya and I share a special friendship. Although she felt aided by my interventions, which were more like prayers recited in a state of anxiety, I shall always be grateful to *her* for teaching me some important lessons—to receive the inchoate and horrific, for instance, in dreaming; to contain the brokenness and not interpret it away; to wait until the other develops the relevant capacities; to be sensitive to my own psychic and bodily states; to appreciate the glimpses of beauty in most grotesque parts of self; and to do all of this with faith.

My attempt throughout this work has been to refine the existing under-standing of possession by using playful communications and by charting how, through such communications, one can only gradually and non-intrusively be ushered toward healing. This steering toward healing is devoid of any questioning of faith. As Winnicott (1953) taught us, a child who is engaged in play—a space where inner and outer realities meet—should not be asked, "Did you conceive of this or was it presented to you from without?"

NOTES

1. The name Daya in Hindi means mercy.
2. *Samkat* literally translates to "misfortune." However, in many parts of north India, *samkat* also means "spirit" or "ghost that has possessed someone."
3. *Kavar yatra* refers to an annual pilgrimage undertaken by the devotees of Lord Shiva, who fetch "holy water" from the Ganges and carry it on foot across hundreds of miles on foot to dispense it as an offering in their local or specific Shiva temples.
4. Annual Hindu festival in honor of Lord Shiva.
5. Hanuman Chalisa is a prayer in praise of the Hindu monkey god Hanuman, also addressed as Lord Balaji.
6. *Dharma* means "moral or religious duty."
7. Objectively there was no contact between them. The guru ji refused to answer his calls before this conversation. It was strange for me also to receive this informa-tion. The relationship was more alive and intense in Ravi's internal world than it was objectively.
8. Indian flat bread.
9. A Sikh woman is referred to as a Sardarni.

Chapter 4

Between Dread and Meaning

Italian psychoanalyst Giuseppe Civitarese (2016) wrote, "The price of meaning is a struggle against ghosts. Someone who is too afraid of ghosts gives up meaning. He feels the absence which the name recovers." Drawing inspiration from Civitarese's wisdom, this chapter explores the space between dread and meaning in the context of our relationship with ghosts. I ask if ghosts help in the recovery of meaning. An intuition guided me through this research: the feeling that ghosts are the mind's first attempts to make sense of an unthinkable emotional experience; they step in to rescue us from a complete collapse of thinking. With psychoanalytic thinkers as my allies, I will now return to that iconic image from Indian horror films, the one that appears like a recurrent nightmare: the ghostly woman in white, standing on the threshold, singing an eerie, luring song. I will follow my curiosity about what this image may represent about the human mind and the epistemophillic instinct that drives it to search for meaning in unthinkable experiences.

I would like to return to the scene I described at the start of this book—the one where I was trying to put my daughter to sleep by singing her a lullaby. As stated, my anger at my daughter for not falling asleep had imparted to the lullaby an eerie quality. I feared then that something haunting my internal world would creep into my daughter's internal world—a danger and eventuality that Atlas (2022) has made us aware of through her work on the emotional inheritance of generational trauma. Nudged by my reverie and grateful to my own love for knowledge, I was drawn toward the image of a ghostly woman in white. I wondered what she represented: the m(other), no doubt, but which m(other)? The one at the threshold between dreams and wakefulness? Between self and world? Between knowledge and cluelessness? The bad mother, standing in the way of her child's conquest of the knowable?

I was angry because I was tired, hungry, and sleepy—I wanted to gratify my own needs, which is pertinent because "ghosts are born where there exists a conflict between needs" (Atlas, personal communication, 2021). This was a moment of rupture in "primary maternal preoccupation" (Winnicott,1956), the state of heightened sensitivity and attunement in which the mother is preoccupied with her infant to the exclusion of other concerns. Later in his elaboration on the ego–object relationship, Winnicott (1969) proposed that this state facilitates object-relating, wherein the baby perceives the mother subjectively rather than as a person outside the baby's omnipotent control. The space shared with a mother in this state is experienced as a non-intrusive holding environment for the infant.

With the help of Bion, I zoom into the moment where the mother receives or fails to receive the infant. According to Bion (1967), the baby begins with a preconception—a sense of the breast—and in its search for that breast, it meets a realization—it finds the breast, with some help from the mother. Repeated experiences of this realization help the preconception develop into a conception. The rhythm of seeking and finding is crucial to the evolution of the capacity to think. In other words, the infant seeks the object and how s/he moves from this point will depend on the object's receptivity and its capacity to allow itself to be found. If the preconception of the breast is met with a negative realization of the breast, it is experienced as a no-breast, or "absent" breast inside. The next step depends on the infant's capacity for frustration, on whether the frustration is evaded or modified. The internal tolerable sense of hunger can either be transformed into thought or if this sense of the no-breast is intolerable the frustration is modified into action. Bion distinguishes between a conception and a thought. He explains that, while a conception results from the sum of a preconception and its positive realization, a thought is the outcome of the sum of a preconception and its non-realization or its negative realization. A thought then forms out of frustration around the absent breast. "In this case the infant is not confronted with an absolute void. Put simply, s/he fails to find the breast he is seeking, but her or his mind retains the memory trace of the breast" (Civitarese, 2019).

In reflecting on the frustration that follows an encounter with absence, Bion (1967) writes,

> If intolerance of frustration is not so great as to activate the mechanisms of evasion and yet is too great to bear dominance of the reality principle, the personality develops omnipotence as a substitute for the mating of the pre-conception, or conception, with the negative realization. This involves the assumption of omniscience as a substitute for learning from experience by aid of thoughts and thinking.

Winnicott, in his reflections on the mother's mirroring role and its impact on the baby, makes the case that, if the baby looks at the mother but does not find a reflection of itself, it develops a propensity for predicting the mother's emotional states. Perceiving to keep itself prepared and guarded takes precedence over perceiving to learn from the world. As this scenario persists, the baby's need for a predictable structure hardens. This makes prediction easier. When one knows what is coming, one does not have to suffer learning from experiencing it.

Reflecting further on the relationship between the baby and the breast, I draw on Klein's understanding of projective identification as a mechanism by which the bad parts of the self are split off and projected into the mother, who then is perceived as hostile. Initially, Klein (1921, 1928) explored the epistemophillic instinct and the ways in which children's anxieties interfered with their curiosity. In Klein's view, curiosity begins with the mother's body. The child has phantasies of exploring the insides of the mother's body and destroying its contents. These phantasies provoke anxieties, which, when repressed and displaced to objects in the external world, produce a symbol (Klein, 1930). Alternatively, if the anxieties dominate, symbol formation is thwarted.

Bion elaborated on the communicative and evacuative aspects of projective identification (1959) to envisage the development of the thinking apparatus as originating in a state of disturbance (1962a). Thought develops in the absence of the other, which gives rise to disturbing raw emotions that the mind must cultivate an apparatus to process. Thoughts precede the thinker or origin of the thinking apparatus. These raw emotions are protothoughts, what Bion referred to as beta elements, discussed in Chapter 2. To recap, these pre-reflective beta elements are "on the boundary of somatic and psychic" (Britton, 2003). They create frustration and are evacuated into the mother. She makes use of her reverie to contain the infant's experience and return it in an altered bearable form. Bion wrote, "Reverie is that state of mind which is open to the reception of any 'object' from the loved object and is therefore capable of the reception of the infant's projective identifications whether they are felt to be good or bad." Through the mother's alpha function, then, raw beta elements are transformed into alpha elements. The infant not only re-introjects his or her own altered experience but also the mother's transformative containing function, which in turn enables in the infant a tolerance for frustration and a capacity for thinking—the unbearable experiences become bearable. The tendency to evacuate is replaced by the ability to experience.

Of course, "[f]ailure in this process can occur because of the object's lack of capacity for reverie and alpha function, but failure can also occur because of the individual's envy and intolerance of frustration" (Spillius, 1983). If a failure occurs, the infant receives his or her own experience in a more unbearable form. What we have then is a state Bion called "nameless dread." Spatially, being in the state of nameless dread is akin to standing frozen at a threshold. This threshold marks the site of paralysis of the thinking apparatus. One can neither stay with the experience, nor escape.

How does one go from being stuck in "nameless dread" to changing when any change can also feel catastrophic? Bion (1966) noted, "Some aspect of the personality is stable and constant, and . . . this is maintained as the only force likely to contain emergent ideas which express new awareness of reality of the self the world." If the relationship between this continuous self and the changing, emergent self is one of mutual enhancement, development takes place. He described this relationship as *symbiotic*. If, however, that continuous identity is disrupted by new kinds of self-development or self-discovery, psychic change will be experienced as catastrophic, since the changes will cause the sense of self-continuity to disintegrate. When this happens, the subjective experience is one of fragmentation and, in these circumstances, preserving a sense of continuity of existence requires *all* change to be resisted and no new experience being allowed to emerge. This mutually destructive relationship between container and contained has been described by Bion as *parasitic*, and by Britton (2003) as *malignant containment*. Britton posited that "faced with these two catastrophic alternatives—incarceration or frag-mentation—some people remain paralyzed at the frontier, on the threshold."

According to Britton, if a mother fails to receive her infant's projective identification and resists all attempts by the child to know her mind, she creates for the child a picture of a world that does not want to know the child and does not want to be known. From this point, "taking things in" becomes catastrophic, the manifestations of which Bion (1958) found to be arrogance, stupidity, and curiosity.

> Other fears result from a phantasy of the projected self being taken in and then destroyed, of one's nature being taken in by another's devouring curiosity and consumed in the process, of oneself being comprehended and nullified during the process. (Britton, 2003)

Equipped with Bion's and Britton's frameworks, I now turn to look at the ghostly woman once again. She possesses radiant beauty and is depicted as standing at a threshold, singing a repetitive, eerie, luring song, which contrasts starkly with her cold, distant expression. I consider her beauty and horror and wonder if this image can be understood as the moment of what Meltzer called "aesthetic conflict" (Meltzer & Williams, 2008). Donald Meltzer (Meltzer & Williams, 2008) proposed an idea of an essential "aesthetic conflict." Reflecting on the ambiguity inherent in an infant's meeting the mother, Meltzer defined aesthetic conflict as "the aesthetic impact of the outside of the beautiful mother, available to the senses, and the enigmatic inside which must be construed by creative imagination. Everything in art and literature, every analysis, testifies to its perseverance through life." For Meltzer aesthetic conflict causes pain because of the uncertainty inherent in it. This uncertainty is best greeted with a desire to know, Bion's K-link. Here lies the path to learning from experience. "In the interplay of joy and pain, engendering the Love (L) and Hate (H) links of ambivalence, it is the quest for understanding (K-link) that rescues the relationship from impasse. This is the point at which Negative Capability exerts itself, where Beauty and Truth meet." Bion, inspired by Keats, considered that the tolerance of aesthetic conflict lies at the heart of "negative capability": a capacity for tolerance of uncertainty, characterized by not having to irritably reach for facts and reason. Unknowingness hovers above all encounters between self and other interpersonal as well as intrapersonal. This unknowingness carries a special intensity in psychoanalytic encounters.

The ghostly woman perhaps represents the aesthetic object that one is drawn toward in order to know her, but her mysterious internal world turns her into a threatening ghost. Therefore, those who follow her die, their death symbolizing the paralysis of the thinking-knowing apparatus. I am reminded of Rilke's words—"For Beauty is nothing but the beginning of terror, which we are barely able to endure, and it amazes us so, because it serenely disdains to destroy us" (1989).

My proposition is that sensing the presence of a ghost constitutes the first attempt, perhaps even a feeble one, to make sense of the nameless dread. With the appearance of a ghost, the nameless dread acquires a name. But is there space for an alternative understanding of ghostly apparitions in a discipline founded on ideas of psychic reality that are based on the European mind?

Taking his cue from Freud, Britton (2003) regards psychic reality as created by belief, or our judgment of reality. According to him, a belief is the

function that confers the status of reality on to phantasies and ideas . . . Belief is to psychic reality what perception is to material reality. Belief gives the force of reality to that which is psychic, just as perception does to that which is physical. (2003)

Further, he considers belief to be a component of the epistemophillic instinct. Beliefs require confirmation from reality to become knowledge: "Reality testing occurs through perception of the external world or through internal correlation with already known facts and other beliefs" (Britton, 2003).

While Freud viewed the unconscious as the unknowable, containing unreconciled fantasies uncontaminated by beliefs about the outside world, psychoanalysis is also "a product of its own history and culture, primarily Western, and no cultural product can be quite free of that 'embeddedness'" (Kakar & Sarin, 2008). As I embark on the journey from individual psyche to cultural psyche, I turn toward my own culture, that is, Indian culture. Based on decades of reflection on the Indian psyche, Kakar views the unconscious

> like an engine running on parallel tracks of desire and the spirit. Desire and spirit move in a common psychic space . . . The two may never meet, but in our most creative and alive moments they tantalizingly brush against each other in the empty space that otherwise stretches between them.

In contrast to the well-bounded ego of the West, Kakar speaks of the relative fluidity of the Indian ego:

> With the Indians, the boundaries to the ego aren't as rigid. That comes from the corporeal, the body itself is open. The image of the body that one has in ayurveda, for example, is that of a permanent exchange between the ego and the environment. If the body is open, the boundaries to the ego are also open. The body forms the basis of the ego. One views one's body in the same way one views one's ego, and in the Indian view this ego is more fluid. For an Indian, mental illnesses come from spirits that force their way into the body; one falls ill because of evil spirits. In the West, the ego is a fortress—that's why in psychology many biological approaches are taken. What happens in the fortress is important and not what comes from outside. Here in the West, it would be considered esoteric to say that sunlight or stones can influence the character, because the view of the ego is different. The exchange between environment and ego is emphasized much more strongly in India. (Holl & Kakar, 2006)

I wonder how the idea of a fluid ego that cannot be split sharply affects the way psychosis is conceptualized. The image of the ghost, often understood as hallucination that marks psychosis, is as much cultural as it is intrapsychic and a carrier of deeper meaning. Ego feeds the psyche a sense of reality. Ghosts are part of everyday reality in the Indian view of things. In one of his works on indigenous healing traditions, Kakar reflects on the preoccupation with the role of the "therapeutic" in Indian culture, bursting as it is with a plethora of healing traditions as well as an emphasis on care more than on performance or equality in social relations.

> There is a god for every psychic season, a myth for every hidden wish and a legend for every concealed anxiety . . . Incorporating all possible fantasies around core human concerns—birth, love and death, body and bodily functions, relationships with parents, siblings and children—Indian myths, through a process of creative listening, reading or watching their enactment in folk plays and dance dramas, are readily available to the person for the lifelong task of strengthening psychic integration and maintaining continuity of the self. (Kakar, 1982)

Psychoanalytic thinking around ghosts, spirit possession and healing in India (Kakar, 1982; Kumar, Dhar & Mishra, 2018) has revealed a picture where "personal idiom" (Bollas, 1989) is displaced into bizarre symptoms of spirit possession. The rhythms of Wilfred Bion's thinking on K links translate into Kakar's (2001) ideas on "maternal enthrallment" that plagues the internal world of men in Indian culture. According to Kakar, the Indian male infant relishes a brief period of jouissance as he begins to discover his own and his mother's sexuality. This blissful state persists until the father, the potential rival, intervenes this blissful state. Even after this state is interrupted, the wish to go back to that original erotic field and taste the luminous feelings that marked that field lingers on and gives birth to an unconscious fantasy of perfect eternal sexual excitement with the mother's bodily and psychic presence. However, in the real world, the prospect of sexual intimacy with a woman is experienced as an attempt to have intercourse with the mother and it feels incestuous and severe the pleasurable unity with the mother in fantasy world. In Kakar's view, the Indian male remains in a state of "maternal enthrallment" in which he, like an infant, seeks the woman sensually while adult female sexuality is split-off and evokes dread. Going by Kakar's framework (2001), then, the nymph-like ghost woman who suddenly turns grotesque and devours man's virility represents the enthralling mother and his own split-off phallic self-representation. According to Nagpal (2000) the threat to the male identity posed by woman's sexuality is warded off "by drawing strength from a life-long dependence upon spiritual gurus and family patriarchs," a trend we witnessed in Ravi and Bishamber.

Kakar's work demonstrates how an unconscious fantasy gets socialized in possession. In other words, an individual myth is projected on/into collective myth and thus made culturally intelligible, minusK meets meaning and loses its dreadfulness. The abstract, unfamiliar, unconscious content is rendered familiar as one enters the known world visited in daily rituals and populated by all-powerful deities and demons that one has grown up reading and hearing about. What was once dreadful becomes meaningful, as it is situated within a familiar territory.

To the Indian mind belief in psychic reality still belongs to a foreign framework even today. Psychic reality remains an unfamiliar, mystical terrain for the majority of Indians. Although it may be visited and revisited every now and then in dreams and fantasies, it is refracted through culture, placed against a background one is relatively familiar with. Indian traditional healing practices create a space where the possessed person can publicly express their rage or sexual desires in the presence of their family members, who are made to participate in their healing. Traditional healing also works because of the juxtaposition of this family-therapy-like-model with the establishment of the healer as a teacher-like figure in the internal world of the possessed person. While this teacher/guru may represent the cultural superego, s/he is sought for

> holding, the confirming presence of a benevolent, non threatening Other; an ambience of affective acceptance, without necessarily much interpretation of distress - all are akin to the kind of closeness to the good mother that the Indian child most yearns for. (Kumar, 2005)

Chapter 5

Psychoanalysis Under
the Banyan Tree

When the idea of this work was presented to Sudhir Kakar, he responded, "This is how psychoanalysis under a banyan tree would look like." Taking a cue from his comment, here I reflect on the nature of the conversations detailed in this book and the method that evolved from them. My struggle to converse with states of spirit possession would have become clearer by now. A language had to be conjured up by me, infused with the spirit of psychoanalysis but tailored to the psychic profile of the possessed person—a language that would allow me to interact with the possessed person at their precise psychic location.

The image of the banyan tree at the healing site is iconic. As I reflect on its significance, another associated image comes to mind, unbidden—baby Krishna lying on a banyan leaf and sucking on his toe while floating in the cosmic ocean after the apocalypse. Influenced by Ahuja's (2018) brief analysis of this image, I see it as a representation of the chaos I experienced as a researcher in the eerie terrain of spirit possession and exorcism. The participants and I—the two partners in the research process—wound our way through madness and playfulness, terror and meaning, as if caught in an interminable conversation. Being part of this research felt like an autoerotic activity—like sucking on one's toes while remaining aware of the possibility of drowning in the emotional flood that one is caught in.

THE GROUND BENEATH OUR FEET

How a researcher chooses the method of their inquiry is related to the philosophy of knowledge and how she understands human experience. The disciplines of philosophy and psychology have dealt extensively with the question of what it means to be a subject. In this connection, Freud posited that consciousness was anchored in the alterity or the otherness of the unconscious. Psychoanalysis has always engaged with this alterity, which is seen to elude the conscious mind. Various schools of psychoanalytic thought have engaged in different ways with the otherness in and of the self, with the broad understanding having emerged that what is "other" to the self crystallizes into a symptom. Inspired by Cartesian dualism, classical Freudian psychoanalysis regards the other or the foreigner within as a product of drives that originate in the body. Knowing the other person's mind is, accordingly, also a rational, intellectual exercise, distinct from knowing through sensuality or through the body. A framework that rests on such a strict dualism assumes, based on the mere presence of that body of the other person, that a mind exists in the body while also enforcing a split between the knower and the object of their inquiry. This model of "knowing" fails to consider the social, historical, and cultural embeddedness of the subject, imposing upon them a pre-existing set of notions before which their otherness dissolves. How does one recognize a person's otherness without making them an other?

In a set of essays published together under the title *Alterity and Transcendence*, French philosopher Emmanuel Levinas (2000) challenged the Cartesian bifurcation and established the importance of collaboration and one's relationship with the other in the birth of subjectivity. Levinas's ideas opened up for me new ways of imagining intersubjectivity, while Merleau-Ponty's (2013) ideas on phenomenology sharpened the focus on questions about how we experience ourselves and the world around us. Maurice Merleau-Ponty was a French phenomenologist whose thoughts on the lived body are particularly relevant to understanding possession states, in which the body plays a pivotal role. According to Merleau-Ponty (2013), having a mind is not the same as experiencing it. Advancing the conception of the lived body as a subject in itself or embodied subjectivity, he emphasized the body's centrality in our perception of the world and the immediacy of experience. Bodily perception of the world does not easily render itself to thought. Before the mind brings its thinking capacities to bear upon bodily perception, the experience born of perception enters the mind in a primordial pre-reflective state.

In its attempts to find answers to questions about how the mind makes somatic experience thinkable, psychoanalysis, especially with the emergence of the object relations school in the early 1940s, evolved from a one-person frame to what came to be known as two-person psychology. This school centralized the role of relationality in the evolution of a thinking apparatus. Leading the charge, Winnicott brought to the fore the encounters that comprise the dyadic relationship between the nursing mother and the infant, going so far as to note that "[t]here is no such thing as a baby . . . a baby alone doesn't exist" (1971). Through his theorization of the "transitional space" between the mother and the infant, a space where external reality and psychic reality merge in play, Winnicott paved the way for intersubjectivity to revolutionize psychoanalytic thought. However, it is in the works of Thomas Ogden that the idea of analytic intersubjectivity fully blossomed.

Building on Winnicott's reflections, Ogden (2018) wrote, "I believe that, in an analytic context, there is no such thing as an analysand apart from the relationship with the analyst, and no such thing as an analyst apart from the relationship with the analysand." Ogden (2018) sees the analyst–analysand unity as similar to that of the mother–infant dyad in that it coexists in dynamic tension with the separateness of both participants, a view that recognizes their distinct subjectivities and refuses to reduce their otherness to any pre-existing frameworks—the "analytic task involves an attempt to describe the specific nature of the experience of the unconscious interplay of individual subjectivity and intersubjectivity" (Ogden 2018). The separate subjectivities of the analyst and the analysand generate a unique dialectic, leading to what Ogden termed the intersubjective analytic third, "a subjectivity that seems to take on a life of its own in the interpersonal field, generated between analyst and analysand" (2018). Ogden's clinical cases demonstrate how an analyst's reverie helps in co-creating the analytic third along with the analysand. We learn, through an immersion in these cases, that the analyst's reverie carries their thoughts but also their pre-reflective somatic and sensuous experiences, and that this "third" space is not only co-created by the analyst and analysand but, being a space of mutual recognition, also shapes each participant as a subject.

Reading Ogden's clinical works and being under the close clinical supervision of Michael Eigen taught me that a psychoanalyst must remain alive to the different events and processes that unfold between them and the analysand from moment to moment during the clinical hour, a subject position that recalls Merleau-Ponty's phenomenology and Levinas's radical take on subjectivity. Levinas claimed that the other's alterity summons an ethical responsibility to welcome the other with care and establish a discourse through conversations. In his essay "Totality and Infinity: An Essay on Exteriority," Levinas (2012) wrote:

> To approach the Other in conversation is to welcome his expression, in which at each instant he overflows the idea a thought would carry away from it. It is therefore to receive from the Other beyond the capacity of the I, which means exactly: to have the idea of infinity. But this also means: to be taught. The relation with the Other, or Conversation, is a non-allergic relation, an ethical relation; but inasmuch as it is welcomed this conversation is a teaching. Teaching is not reducible to maieutics; it comes from the exterior and brings me more than I contain.

Psychoanalytic conversations, then, are spaces in which one is taught while one's unconscious wisdom opens up at the same time; they are spaces of knowing and being known. Both the parties involved in a psychoanalytic conversation are subjects and objects of introspective and empathic exploration—"interactively linked with the values of the investigator, inevitably influencing the inquiry in its process of arriving at some formulation and observations" (Guba and Lincoln, 1994). What were the values that were guiding me in my inquiry?

Even before I found meaning in the ideas of Levinas, Merleau-Ponty, Ogden, and Eigen, I approached the research field with some caution. My own subjective position had a bearing on how a method was evolved in this research. I grew up as a member of a minority religious community (Christianity) in a predominantly Hindu country. This status shaped my being in a certain way. Two sharp prejudices that I encountered in my growing years were the equation of anything "Western" with being Christian and the persistent allegation that Christians were persuading Hindus to convert to Christianity. These prejudices caused me distress and led to many unhealthy arguments with my friends and peers in school. When I approached my research field, I was very conscious of the need to not come across as someone who was there to convert the worldviews of my participants to fit them into psychoanalytic frameworks of knowledge originating from the West. Even before I came upon the thinkers mentioned above, my own subjective position informed my conduct in the conversations I carried out. On occasion, I failed to allow myself to be taught by my interviewees, and my eagerness on these occasions to dissolve all differences between us by finding answers that suited my psychoanalytic leanings led to my being shut out by my interviewees. As an analogy for this struggle, and also for the method of this research, let me refer here once again to the opening image of this book:

My daughter was nearly six months old. The night I am thinking of was much like other nights: I was carrying her in my arms as I generally did, gently rocking her, pacing up and down in the room, humming a lullaby. She looked extremely tired but was still curious and wide awake. She wanted to stay awake and continue exploring the buffet of sounds, sights and textures that the world around her offered. I tried to quieten her curiosity and usher her into the world of sleep/dreams. Occasionally, we exchanged glances and smiles; she stroked my face with her tiny fingers and sometimes tried to catch a lock of hair that had fallen loose from my bun. Gradually, she shut her eyes.

I could sense that she was not asleep yet but was trying really hard. Hours passed. She continued to try, even joining me in humming the lullaby, syncing her melody with mine, humming her own version of it. But, periodically, she would fidget, open her eyes and look around excitedly, even though her body was exhausted and her eyes red and sore. My own exhaustion began to mount, and with it my anger.

Unbridled, my mind went to its repository of countless eerie songs from old Indian horror films, songs that also had a lullaby-like quality, a lure, a deep yearning. They would generally be sung by a woman in vapory white attire; the same eerie melody, repeatedly, just like a lullaby. For the engrossed viewer, this melody served as a signal that something horrific was about to happen in the film. She, the ghost, always stood at the threshold of a door, singing, luring, summoning.

My reverie was interrupted by the awareness that my daughter had opened her big beautiful eyes and was staring into mine. She looked confused. Perhaps she had sensed a shift in the tone of the lullaby I was humming. Realizing that my anger had leaked into the lullaby, I paused. I had been grunting the lullaby instead of humming it; it had, unsurprisingly, turned eerie.

Wide awake now, my daughter was alerting me to this eeriness. I apologized to her. We revived the warmth that we were accustomed to in the space between us. I went back to feeling love for her and humming the lullaby as before. Soon enough, she fell asleep, and I tucked her in.

Perhaps there is a model for a method nestled in this anecdote. Perhaps I was trying too hard to make my daughter accommodate my own needs for rest and recreation. Just as, initially, in my pilot study, I had tried too hard to get my interviewees to accommodate my need for a confirmation of the psychoanalytic theory I was being schooled in. I was fortunate enough to be guided by Ashok Nagpal, my supervisor, whose psychoanalytic spirit is inspired by the works of Bion and Ogden. Nagpal would gently dare me to tolerate my doubts and uncertainties; in other words, he facilitated the emergence of a "negative capability" in me. Side by side, my immersion in the works of Eigen taught me the value of listening to the other while remaining in a state of "pure resonant passivity expressively waiting" (Eigen, 2018).

FOLLOWING THE GHOST: LANDING
UPON A METHOD

The conversations I had afforded me glimpses of emotional lives that were unfortunately marred by absences and terrors, by environmental facilitation that was incongruent with the needs of selves yet to develop a sense of an "inside" and an "outside." I intuited this lack and it set off frantic attempts by me to extend facilitation to, and organize it for, the possessed persons I came to know closely. Such attempts left me somewhat disoriented and confused, too.

It seemed reasonable that emotional lives marked by such early experiences of terror were characterized going forward by a persistent and all-pervasive sense of anxiety. Psychoanalysis orients us to view how primitive defenses are organized around such anxiety. These primitive defenses contain those experiences that are "known but not yet thought" (Bollas, 1987). Terror does not lend itself to thinking or words. Living with terror is best expressed through behavioral patterns. Unaware of these underlying patterns, I desperately sought order in the narratives I came across. I looked for content related to repressed sexuality or hostility. My eagerness led me to frantically grope for details my informants were holding close to their hearts, partly as secrets and partly as irrepresentable panic. And the more I groped, the more I was shut out, the more frustrated I got and the more my research suffered.

With time, I realized I had to give up on this frantic search for meaning that made sense only to me. I had to learn to welcome whatever form of communication I encountered. My experiences during the pilot study taught me that conversations enable movement from "'knowing' an experience' to 'thinking' it through." The various ways in which I came to relate to and converse with the grotesque spirits were conceived out of this movement, and this process of conceiving relationalities and generating communicable "preconceptions" (Bion, 1962b) is what I have come to understand as my method. To locate beauty in grotesquely broken states, I was required to give up the lens I had hitherto used and have faith in the eventual emergence of the hidden potential of the minds I ventured to know. My exposure to such states in others had left me with the sense that I stood on a cliff overlooking vast stretches of experience that this research entailed exploring.

I must admit the prospect made me somewhat uneasy. I was acutely aware that any uninterrogated attempt to gather this vastness into myself could induce instantaneous vertigo in me. The axiom guiding the evolution of my method was simply my faith in the inevitability of illumination, and the practices derived from this method were arboresque—entwined branches of feelings, thoughts, and positions that occasionally blossomed with leaves and flowers, producing in me child-like wonder. Bion's mantra—to abandon all memory, desire, understanding and expectation—or Kakar's explanation at a conference that his technique during research has been to simply listen served only to reinforce my sense that disoriented states, emerging from a reliance on enactments to express the unthinkable, could not be understood through a structured paradigm.

I was often confronted with the dilemma I had anticipated before embarking on this research—what language to speak? When I "spoke" psychoanalysis, I was met with resistance. Only gradually did I learn to speak the ghost's language—a language that was psychoanalytically sensitive and culturally nuanced enough to enable conversation with states of spirit possession. This idea of shifting from one language to another suggests Jean Laplanche's (1992) work on translation and de-translation. Through his discussion of the transmission of unconscious messages from mother to infant, Laplanche (1992) asked the psychoanalyst to consider the message underlying the spoken words of the patient and how to listen to and make sense of it. Extending Laplanche's wisdom to my research meant paying close attention to what was being said *through* the ghosts, to the messages the ghosts carried from the unconscious, while keeping psychoanalytic interpretations at bay and sustaining the fictional quality of the conversations, which was necessary to avoid overwhelming the possessed person.

I found that disowned parts, constituents of the "true" selves of the possessed, were encapsulated in the ghosts. The person who hid behind familial expectations and fantasies was found by the ghosts that possessed them—or the ghosts they possessed. The terror unlocked for me to experience belonged to that stage of life in which one communicated only by projecting one's own difficult states into the (m)other. Bion (1967) considered projective identification as a form of communication. According to him, psychopathology can result in how in infancy one's projective identifications were received or rejected.

Following in Bion's footsteps, Jeff Eaton (2005), in his article "The Obstructive Object," explored intense mental pain and self-attacks perpetrated by internal objects. He reflected on chronic self-attacks, "attacks on linking," obstructions to the growth of personal agency, and an incapacity to receive help and allow one's own internal transformation, focusing on patients who "give evidence of living with an internal object that is ego-destructive and that operates as a *projective identification rejecting object.*" Bion termed this ego-destructive internal object an obstructive object. Eaton proposed that "progress in working with the obstructive object scenario involves the analyst's capacity to become *a projective identification welcoming object* that the patient can use interpersonally and ultimately identify with."

I was required to welcome the projective communications of my participants while remaining curious about how these projections interacted with the residents of my own internal world, creating "dramatic dialogue" (Atlas & Aron, 2017) with them. Against this backdrop of psychoanalytic conversations, all kinds of rhythms assumed special significance—words, silences, pauses, sighs, gazes, shifts in posture, slight touches, laughs or giggles, vocal quivers, and so on. On many occasions, I felt forced to receive self-parts through unconscious communication, to touch a hallucinatory level of thinking so as to come as close as possible to that experience of the participant which was struggling to be heard. This is very reminiscent of the ideas of

Chefetz and Bromberg (2004) who note that dissociative processes forcefully disallow any links to develop with parts of self that encapsulate uncontainable areas of experience. "The dissociated part of the patient's self holding the unsymbolised experience is not in relationship with the therapist, and until the therapist feels its impact as an experience linked to a part of himself that has been dissociated, it stays lost and its existence remains enacted" (2004). As a result, the dreams, states of reverie and bodily responses stirred in me were also reflected upon, not only to expand my understanding about disavowed parts of *my* self but also to extend this understanding to imagining the experience of the research participant—how it felt to be possessed, to be captivated in a household with punitive males, to be forbidden and, most importantly, to live the terror owing to the fact that one's capacity to weave a web of intelligibility around it was crippled. The imagination of the other precipitated by states of dreaming, by nightmares and reveries and intervention intended to usher the possessed person toward transformation which was facilitated through a relational communication grounded in culture, led to corresponding changes in the formulation of the scene-as-fiction-an "as-if" quality in conversations that made it possible to dream the experience.

The affective states evoked in me during this work also include a particular experience of loneliness—loneliness in terms of the ideas and frameworks that can enable the processing of these states. One is left deriving patterns, perched within this very loneliness, with all its insecurities and uncertainties. I trusted that I would come across supportive literature, in whatever rarefied nutrients it could nourish my curiosities. A flexible stance was required, to move between terror and thinking, and while this stance was partly derived by me from the theories of Kakar, Winnicott, Bion, Ogden, and Eigen, the method itself evolved in each session—I had to remain permeable, guided by faith in whatever "new" would emerge from the meeting of two unconsciouses.

At the heart of any research lies a burning question. The mind is taunted (or haunted?) and sent into a frenzy by ideas that coil around it like snakes. In my case, this frenzy manifested in the difficulties around writing this work. A crucial role was played by the child in me that wondered how it could be that healing took place in an instantaneous manner when my grandfather (and other healers I observed in churches) laid his hands on a possessed person. Such was the impact of intensity of those countless experiences of healing I witnessed as a child that I do not even fully distinguish between what my eyes were seeing and what the rest of my body was playing about, what my hands were trying to slip away from and what was clasping me, what I thought was my voice in the scream and what I came to recover as things I still had to integrate in myself. The question of how healing transpired in these rituals not only haunted my nightmares but also served as a starting point for the psychoanalytic exploration I undertook in my research.

The matter of generating key questions also reminds me of a postulate of ego psychology—one that can be found expressed in the object-relational writing of Winnicott as well—which states that alliances, facilitation, and the metabolizing of the mother's ego are prerequisites to standing outside the terror and saying, "I am witnessing it in a bid to represent it." In the context of this work, the mothering was provided by my mentor, Ashok Nagpal who demonstrated for me a peculiar mode of functioning that Stephano Bolognini (2010) has termed "interpsychic":

> The interpsychic is a mode of functioning that connects two individuals internally in a healthy, livable, and cost-effective way. It is a functional level of high permeability shared between two psychic apparatuses, but it is not a general and stable structured condition; in a sense, it is describable as an event. The interpsychic is the psychic equivalent of the healthy and necessary fusional conditions and processes that in nature enable vital exchanges (nurturing and regulatory ones) between human beings in the early stages of life and growth. Think, for example, of the natural cooperation between mouth and nipple that allows mother and baby to work together.

In an interpsychic mode of functioning, the permeability between psychic apparatuses does not threaten their internal cohesiveness:

> When an individual functions interpsychically, there is no requirement of a continuous, obsessive reflection of the type: "I am me and I am not he or she, who are other than me" (which amounts to mentalization of separateness) . . . The ability of a human being to conjoin with someone else and effectively exchange internal elements can be exercised even without systematic monitoring and conscious control by the central ego.

On many occasions in this work, I think I operated on this level of mental functioning, although in some moments I did feel terror due to the permeability of my mind.

Containment was also sourced by me from thinkers like who, in their writings, have kept alive the spirit of witnessing aspect undaunted by the terror. Their writings persevered in the wake of terror, helping me to organize and chart the complex processes of psychic evolution in myself and my participants. It is to this facilitation that the method owes itself.

An appreciation of the beauty in brokenness is inherent to and facilitated by psychoanalysis, which conceives of the psyche as enveloped by the body and fueled by energy that flows between the interpsychic and intrapsychic dimensions. Biologically determined instincts form the psyche-soma in conjunction with our intersubjective experiences, originating in the psyches of the parents—their fantasies and expectations and their facilitation of a creative "potential space" (Winnicott, 1991) between the child and the mother. Under the weight of these external constellations, the psyche organizes its patterns and ways of experiencing and relating inside with outside. The psyche is formed by an imaginative elaboration of somatic experiences. The questions that guided me toward the possible origins of the ghosts, their purpose and the various psychological transformations that they enable in the person who is possessed by them emerged from my own personal life experiences and my discovery of allies in thinkers and pilot ventures.

The ghost manifests as that subjective object which is, as if, "grimacing through the corner of the self's eyes." The subjective object is the first signal of an inside forming. This ghost communicates with the external by evoking terror. One wonders if in this evocation of terror, in the one who witnesses the ghost, lies a ghost's cry to be rescued. As the ghost extends out into the world giving something external the color of the self, the self begins to evolve or form. Here lies the transitional space, where external and internal meet. In the field of traditional healing, when one is confronted by terror, god, and hymns take on the role of object that can be used.

> The creative nucleus, following Winnicott (1965), I assume is emanating from the true self zone at one end of the continuum of the person and needs to conclude its productions in the form of hymns, dance, prayers, etc. in the court of God at the other end of the continuum. In between, lay the seriously strange phenomenon of dreaming and reveries. Ghost, as a deformed form of true self, cries out to God to be preserved in its incommunicado. It is engaging with God to divest it further of its false-self longings that it feels incapable of de-cocooning itself from. (A, Nagpal, personal communication, September 2009)

Listening to that part of the self which wishes to remain incommunicado must be guided by being tuned in to moment-to-moment occurrences in conversations; I had to be an embodied listener. Christopher Bollas had a profound impact on how I listened to stories and organized them. In *The Infinite Question* (2009), he provides moment-to-moment accounts of sessions to demonstrate Freud's theory of the logic of sequence and offered a tribute to the human impulse to question, the interrogative drive. He illustrated how Freud's free associative method facilitated an ongoing birth of further questions and illuminated a more nuanced unconscious logic.

After having gained some understanding of my own life experiences (through personal psychoanalysis and supervision) and those of others (through supervised psychoanalytic clinical work), I arrived at a conviction in psychoanalysis as a discipline that fosters the development of an eye with which to see and an "I" with which to appreciate the beauty in the complexities that make each one of us human. When the pull toward identification with the other was overpowering me during my research, analysis pulled me back and helped me look at my experiences from a neutral point of view. The intention throughout this work has been to expand rather than to reduce our understanding of possession and to do so as 'humanly' as possible, by looking for the roots of individuals' present distresses amidst their past experiences and listening to that which was unspoken, the haunting parts that had lingered on and taken recourse to lived and embodied expression. The spirit driving this work is clinical because it draws from the participants' history, "the history of the illness, the history of the treatment, the comprehension of the relations between the past and the present, and the application of psychoanalytic concepts . . . seen from the angle of the specificity of the transference" (Green, 2005).

During my research, I often found a very particular fear playing itself out in my mind. Will a method arise and ensure the transformations of persons from being possessed to being aware? It was by relying on my ego processes and on cultural material to offer up creative linkages that would sustain my faith that the terrors of my participants were gradually organized as they appeared in the theatre of possession and were engaged with devotionally in the temple.

The main difficulty I faced was my informants' distance from their own states. To them, the prospect of talking about their distress in a deep and emotionally meaningful way was terrifying, and after some time I was pushed away—in some instances, the informants chose to break off all correspondence with me. Due to the lack of a reflective self or an observing ego in my research participants, I had to primarily rely on my own mental apparatus for psychic work. The participants used a variety of defensive mechanisms against emotional experience—dissociation, splitting, projective identification, etc.—making it necessary for me to scrutinize what those defenses provoked in me. Research, supervision, and my personal analytic work together provided me with the tools and bandwidth I needed to give up frantic meaning-making and look closely at these fraught interactions.

As a child, I received a legacy of faith from my father. He taught me to have faith in things unseen. Later in life, I was encouraged by my mentors to assume the affective attitude of faith when meeting the unseen unconscious. Psychoanalytic work succeeds in incarnating the inchoate and the ineffable so that something choate and effable emerges. Ghosts thrive in secret places of the mind. Psychoanalysis orients us that listening to the secrets of someone's private life involves "the somatic, emotional, imaginal, and intellectual stirrings of the self from moment to moment, from session to session, in a kind of dance, a movement to and fro, between what is known and what wants to be known" (Greenberg, 2015).

Only gradually did it dawn on me that a large part of what I was feeling was emanating from my own counter-transferential responses, evoked by projective identification. With some pain and reluctance, I came to appreciate that I was being borrowed or, perhaps, possessed. I realized that an expansion and openness toward plurality of experience on my part was called for, which would allow me to experience a range of emotions my participants could not bring themselves to feel. I experienced horror, enchantment, awe, bliss, pain, turbulence, chaos, comfort, discomfort, confusion, clarity, doubt, and a lot more.

I had to constantly negotiate the boundary between self and other. One approach to research that acknowledges this difficulty and yet creates from within it the opportunity to build greater knowledge and understanding is that of ethnography. Ethnography not only provides one access to the authentic nature of cultural phenomena but also, in doing so, illuminates the standpoints of those who create the primary meanings of those phenomena. By allowing one to interpret a phenomenon from within the context in which it appears, the ethnographic method opens windows into lived experiences—everyday struggles, rituals, practices, and shared beliefs—that shape the psyches, values and aspirations of individuals and communities, thus enhancing the researcher's sensitivity to the reciprocity between and mutual embeddedness of culture and psyche. By emphasizing the significance of the researcher's subjectivity, history, and social position to the construction of those under study, the ethnographic approach frames understanding as emerging from a co-creation of experiences.

Recently, I found in a work by Joshua Holmes on the "reverie research method," the expression of a position that resonated with my own. Holmes (2018) draws on intersubjective psychoanalytic theory, which upholds the importance of a mutual two-person interaction in a meaning-making process. He views reverie as a relational phenomenon and proposes that "[in response to] research interviews, the researcher's emotions, imagination and meaning-making capacities are activated" (Holmes, 2018). This receptive state gives rise to reveries in the researchers, which can then be linked to data and facilitate a deeper understanding of the participant.

The design of this research took shape around conversations with possessed persons. I wondered—how could I converse with someone who was absent to themselves? Ogden (2002b) tells us that conversing requires relentless efforts to tame and to free oneself (one's own human nature) "by transforming raw experience into words and gestures to communicate with others." Conversing, then, is the reverse of the tendency we encounter in possession states, which is to choose expression through actions rather than to allow for the transformation of raw emotional experience into words. The question, then, was how could I converse with someone who knew only to speak through enactments? The research method I evolved was an attempt to address this question.

An idea that was foundational to the development of my research method was coined by Wilhelm Dilthey, the main proponent of idealism. Dithey (1991) proposed the notion of "Verstehen" or "interpretive understanding." Verstehen suggests that "world is seen not as a collection of objects but as what is meaningful in human life." Therefore, the basis of inquiry is description and interpretation. In clinical encounters, Verstehen will correspond to the stance of empathy because it entails investigating the other's emotional world through recreation of their experience, which becomes internalized in the "therapist-as-researcher." This process works in two directions—it enables an understanding of the self through an understanding of the other and an understanding of the other through an understanding of the self. We gain an understanding of the other's actions by looking at meanings associated with those actions. These meanings are derived from the context in which the other is situated and are to be understood only within that context. This sensitivity to context leads the researcher to question their own context. Thus, research also becomes a "me-search" (Atlas, 2022). The researcher's own prior knowledge, interests, values, emotions, and cultural affiliations come under scrutiny in interactions with the research participants, as I have shared above.

From the recognition of multiple contexts arises a realization that there is no one single truth. Multiple meanings, versions and interpretations of the same experience can arise out of multiple contexts. A tolerance for contradictions and paradoxes is needed. I had to allow myself to be challenged and affected by the cultural meanings that informed my participants' experience of the world but were likely to be very different from my own meanings. I had to, in other words, adopt the stance of a student, rather than an expert, of the unconscious and make room for directionless-ness, be comfortable with not knowing where the conversations would lead. I knew I had to be an active participant, rather than a passive onlooker. Thus, I employed a combination of participation, non-participatory observation, and extensive unstructured interviewing.

With unstructured conversations came acute anxiety in me. I frequently found myself on the verge of either blurring the boundaries between myself and my research participant or highlighting the differences between us. My interactions with research participants were marked by directionless-ness at first and then by negotiations with terror, finally arriving at moments of calm as I watched each person heal in the ways that worked for them, the ways their contexts allowed them to heal.

According to Freud (1913), psychoanalysis is both a method of research and a clinical model. It provides hope that suffering can be diminished through love and insight resulting from an awareness and understanding of the ways in which the analyst and patient re-enact with each other their own early relationships. Hope lies in the discovery of meaning. In this sense, suffering—and, hence, the symptom—becomes meaningful through the coming together of two subjectivities. The thoughts of both Ogden and Freud, I think, bear kinship with a core postulate of postmodernism, i.e., "knowledge is not 'out there' to be discovered but is created or (to use a fashionable post-modernist term) 'socially constructed'" (Kakar, 1991). The "psychical" is seen, through this lens, as being born of the relational and the "social."

As I immersed myself in spaces of co-creation of meaning, I was thrown into the kinds of terrain from which emerged questions, remarks, comments and responses that, in hindsight, surprised me—I found myself asking, "How and why did I say that?!" What gave me solace at the time was Freud's note of caution against analysts who say they know what they are doing in a session. Not knowing why one said something and subsequently being gifted with moments of surprise as newer meanings are co-created with the patient is indicative of the functioning of an alliance with, and immersion in, the process that allows the therapist to grasp what is being unconsciously communicated. It is in these spontaneous renderings that one retrospectively appreciates the extent to which unconscious empathy was established during a session or exchange. The nature of my research caused some inevitable errors, particularly early on, but it is also important to note that closeness with the research participants and their internal processes and the method implicit in arriving at this closeness could only have been accomplished through the errors I made. It is the understanding that emerged from these errors that went on to constitute the data for this research.

The idea was to become a thinking couple or a couple-in-understanding. Dreaming the research participant's emotional experience or undertaking psychological work on their behalf thus evolved as an essential part of the method, allowing the emergence of data pertaining to deeper layers of the self and, in the process, facilitating its healing. This tremulous tip-toeing movement was undertaken while remaining anchored within my own internal nucleus of health, facilitating the forming of this thinking-couple. Eigen reminded me that "the horrific has its own beauty, its own ecstasy, and we ought not walk around it as if it were not there, no more than we should become one with it" (2004a). Research findings emerged in the garb of patterns, observations, and understandings.

Data gathered through interviews was organized in the form of case studies or, as I prefer to call them, "case stories." The case stories in this work have highlighted transformations. Writing them allowed me to survive transformation by encouraging me to go beyond merely gathering information about the life histories of the participants to intelligently evolving links between events, experiences and behaviors that could be shared with others. It was precisely to evolve these links that I chose to explore the material from the interviewees' narratives, conduct in-depth analyses of the same and turn them into case stories, arriving in the process at a deeper clinical understanding of the causes of and the restoration enabled through spirit possession and religious cures. The method that emerged gave me hope that, going forward, others involved in clinical work with primitive states might take cues from this research and contribute to expanding the existing knowledge base. Stories of transformations help instill faith that belonged to others in the healing profession that thinking around most broken states is plausible.

As would be clear by now, the initial phase of research was dedicated to the development of an in-depth understanding of the lives of individuals who experience possession states. Through life narratives gathered using interviews and observations; a deeper sense of the circumstances of each individual in the sample was sought. The possessed, their caretakers, healers, and other pilgrims at the healing sites were interviewed to get a clearer picture of how psychic distress is socially constructed under the label of spirit possession. I participated in many rituals and healing ceremonies and paid close attention to the utterances and actions of the possessed, the music and paraphernalia used during the rituals and the differences between different rituals and the practices of the priests and traditional healers or diagnosticians at different healing centers.

Subsequently, I shared my observations and ideas with my mentor, Ashok Nagpal, and also with other experts in the field—namely Eigen and Kakar, whose works are situated in the space between psychoanalysis and spirituality and whose writings have steadfastly given the mystical experience its due— for feedback. My exchanges with them helped me look at the lives of the possessed through a clinical lens, keeping in mind their cultural embeddedness. An enhanced understanding of this aspect, the cultural embeddedness of spirit possession, was brought about by an analysis of Satyajit Ray's film, *Devi*. While the individual stories helped me understand the intrapsychic as steered by relational dynamics, *Devi* helped me comprehend the interplay of intrapsychic and the interpersonal in possession, as alternately understood by the artistic mind of a filmmaker whose film was his dream work.

The main site of my inquiry was the temple of Balaji in Rajasthan, famous for exorcism rituals, where my interactions with pilgrims, possessed persons, their families, healers, priests, shop vendors and the workers in the *dharamshala* (guest house) I stayed at helped me gain a foothold on the cultural rock face of possession as it is comprehended within the Hindu tradition. Each person I came across, even if the encounter was only a brief one, contributed to familiarizing me with the notions of *samkat* (ghosts and spirits) and *samkat mochan* (exorcism). In subtle and at times stark ways, each person refined my understanding of the possession phenomenon and the healing process. In their own ways, the visiting healers who pursued and stalked me, offering to exorcise, in exchange for monetary and sexual gains, the ghosts they were convinced haunted me, brought me closer to imagining the dangers that surround a possessed person, even at a place as sacred as the temple of Lord Balaji himself.

Another research site emerged when, through a common friend, I met Shubha—a student who was interested in making sense of her own experience of possession.

As far as the Christian healing tradition goes, my own home offered itself as a seemingly convenient research site, given my family's engagement with the church and with possession and healing. I began interviewing possessed persons there, but, sensing profound hesitation in my participants that I did not have a chance to fully understand, I soon stopped. I visited many churches in Delhi looking for those who had experienced spirit possession and were willing to share their life-historical details with me. In this space I was met with suspicion—as if I were using psychology to question the existence of a god. Some of these experiences have been described in Chapter 2 of this book. Finally, though, it was at a church where my uncle was a priest that I met a possessed person who was willing to relate to me and, in the process, to her own self.

Although researchers generally choose their research participants, it seems to me in hindsight that it would be more apt to say my participants chose me, by alliances with my exploration. However, before the participants could choose me, I had to arrive at a certain ease with respect to the research field and its ethos. As emphasized already, although the Balaji temple and the churches made available to me the other's self as a research site, the demands that were placed upon me by the psychic constellations of my participants also opened up my own self as a research site. From the self-as-site, I was required to retrieve grotesque and ghostly parts of myself that also resonated with the ghosts that haunted my participants.

The research participants came with a certain readiness to talk, to express their emotions with or without the use of the possessing spirit. In the process of this research, I engaged with three women who had experienced possession and two men, both of whom were *bhagats*, or healers, but had arrived there through different routes: one of them became a healer soon after he was cured of his possession and the other became one after a lengthy spell of madness, faint residues of which still lingered in him. This neat division indicates that my process of selection, guided by my intuiting complex unconscious processes—wherein lay anxieties, fears, sexuality, seduction, primitive needs, envy, and so on—produced a peculiarly representative sample. In the battle against these "paranormal" forces, men were healers and the large majority of those who sought healing were women. This is reflective, rather implicitly, of the burdens placed on women and the responsibilities placed on men in my culture. These women, with their burdens, were blocked and blank, while the men, playing the roles of healers, took upon themselves the responsibility of recovering the women from these states of overwhelming blockage using authority, manipulation, seduction and sometimes even force.

Implicit in the choice of researcher by the participants is their perception of the researcher's usefulness to them. Both parties enable each other, every now and then, to achieve such surges of feelings as to erase thought and yet return to thinking playfully as though the erasure had never occurred. Difficult secrets of the lives of my participants could be deposited in me, in ways that kept their motives unconscious, while they relied on me to pull them out of the emotional dangers of acute panic and violent guilt.

At first, the interview process was characterized by anxiety and tentativeness from both sides. Only through faith, persistence and precariousness did it become possible to establish familiarity, ease, and rapport and to evolve a language together. This language was different for each research dyad, bearing in each case the mark of our unique idiom. With the development of ease, more space could be created for the forbidden to be relished in the world of words; secrets were shared, the disowned was gradually and painstakingly owned, what had hitherto remained unthinkable found thought, what had been the unspeakable found a tongue and a psychoanalytic ear that remained eager to listen. In their book titled "The Work of Psychic Figurability," Botella and Botella (2005) explore the negative in the psyche—parts of the psyche that are not represented and so remain unfigurable and unthinkable, felt only in somatic symptoms and inexplicable dread. While to some degree these unfigurable states found cultural representation in the image of the ghost, they became relatively figurable in conversations with me. The Botellas reflect on the role of analyst as a double for a patient who brings mental states with no representation. Being a double to a patient means relating in "that area of the psyche of which the subject was hitherto unaware and strives to find its way into consciousness." The analyst as a double validates experience, opens the psyche to fresh possibilities in the relationship between the self and the other. This double is like an echo chamber which receives the unfigurable parts of self. "From the terror of the nightmare to the marvelous world of the fairytale, the fundamental distress of *non-representation* is demolished."

From the initial sense of things being scattered and my desperately groping for firm ground beneath my feet, there began to emerge some structure as life details were shared, allowing me to evolve links and pose questions accordingly. The deepening of the relationship between me and my participants facilitated this emergence in a big way. Clarity was reached and themes explored through a nonjudgmental stance that allowed for permutations and circumambulations. With the development of a trusting relationship between me and my participants, the mist that surrounded their ghosts began to settle. The ghosts spoke, and, gradually, the human hiding behind the ghosts began to surface. The themes of early abandonment, abuse, violence, forbiddance, and so on, emerged in ways that imparted a clearer shape to the ghosts within. I noticed that, as the interviews deepened and more layers of self and other unfolded, the intensity of the symptom began to diminish, and this change also had an impact on or was impacted by the relationship between me and the participant. The conversations with each participant became peculiar. With Shubha, for instance, there were many moments when, unbeknownst to me, I spoke to her in the first person, echoing her as her double or perhaps as a way of "intuiting the (unconscious) psychic reality of the present moment by becoming at one with it" (Ogden, 2015).

My interactions with Riya shed light on the myth-like language that got co-created with her (and, in similar fashion, with other possessed individuals) to converse with the internal and external ghosts. During my undergraduate years, I was a member of the theatre group in my college, and I remember our instructor making all of us assemble to swear or hurl abuses at no one in particular. The idea was for actors to bring themselves to feel uninhibited by living the *vibhatsa rasa* or the emotion of disgust fully, and we had to do it in our native language, Hindi. Swearing in English was considered "polished." To me, with my suburban, pious Christian upbringing, swearing in Hindi felt obscene and scandalous. It was with great difficulty that I participated in this activity, but my inhibitions did not stop me from marveling at how creatively everyone else in the group invented terms that pivoted around human genitals and orifices. After a few days of being exposed to this exercise, I felt something loosen in my body—it felt bolder, less inhibited, and it unapologetically occupied more space where it sat or stood. I revisited this memory when I stood, mesmerized by the mass frenzy of the possessed individuals at the Balaji temple. In the possessed state, these individuals would direct the choicest of abuses at their family members and at Lord Balaji himself. I recall looking closely at their faces—eyes wide, nostrils flared, mouth dripping with saliva as they spat out the abuses—and wondering whether swearing could be pleasurable enough to make one salivate? Abusive slang conveys aggression soaked in sexual juices, as intimate male and female organs are imagined, entered and perhaps even symbolically devoured. I wonder if one would fragment under the weight of one's own aggression were these verbal abuses to be stripped of their sexual tone, the eros that serves to bind the self or keep it from fragmenting. Although uttered in anger most of the time, these special words bring the aggressor and the aggressed closer in intimate moments. Bodies are not actually touched, not until swearing is part of physical combat or becomes a way of enhancing arousal during a sexual act. Where bodies do not touch, swear words are words that not only touch but molest the body, thrusting into it with the affective charge they carry. Does this aggression ease the shame around sexuality? It is perhaps because swear words allow one to talk about sex without feeling ashamed that they are assigned a special role in the language employed by healers to interact with possessed individuals.

I frequently witnessed Riya, after she had entered the state of possession, hurl abuses at Balaji, the priests at the temple and her family members, especially her father, whom she addressed as "motherfucker," "sisterfucker," "asshole," "issue of a rotten vagina," and "possessor of a little-finger-sized penis." Interestingly enough, at home she tended to enter the state of possession when her entire family sat down to eat. In addition to my noticing such patterns in her, it was through her swearing and my internalization of her expressions through it that a language was built between us. This language incorporated the fears, affects, life-historical details and changing realities of the relationship between us to help me to become someone she could relate to and grow with, but only because I also grew with her.

MEETING BETWEEN THE LIVING AND THE DEAD

In India, one always finds banyan trees outside cremation grounds—a point of waiting, of arrivals and departures eternally going on between the living and the departed. The banyan tree bears witness to tears shed in longing, over unfulfilled desires, undreamt dreams, and unlived lives. Being in the presence of individuals who carried a part that wished to remain incommunicado felt like sitting with a scared child under a banyan tree at a cremation ground, waiting. The researcher in me was required to bear witness to the ghosts and allow myself to be noticed by them long enough for them to creep out and greet me. For Riya, her own sexuality was terrorizing her. Our conversations were shaped by this terror. As Dimen (1999) writes,

> Sexuality and sex evoke many feelings . . . Some get excited, some get over-excited, some get so excited that they can only feel anxious, guilty, or out of control . . . and as we know, it is very shameful to talk about shame, and in different ways, in all cultures, there is much shame around sexuality. (as quoted by Atlas, 2016)

How could I converse with a terrified person, hiding behind a veil, watching me with one eye while the other eye was kept focused on her ghosts? What kind of language was taking form between me and Riya?

I found refuge in Green's reflection (2013) on the kind of speech that is typical of psychoanalytic encounters:

The patient is not allowed to act but is asked to say everything which comes to his mind by means of language. This entails that analytic treatment necessarily leads to an "instinctualization of language." This results in language no longer being used for communication as in everyday life. Talking to the analyst involves entering into a very close relationship with him, which is both loving and destructive. There's no equivalent to this in everyday life. . . .

Green goes on to describe how the acquisition of language leads to what Hegel has termed "the murder of the thing." The relationship to the "thing" ceases to remain direct as language intervenes: "With the word, the thing is at the same time present and absent. . . . Naming something instead of touching it, smelling it, experiencing it through the senses creates some mourning of a previous relationship, which is based essentially on immediate contact." The psychoanalytic setting reactivates unmet longings, which spread even to verbalization. Analytic language is re-instinctualized.

It doesn't mean that words become instincts. It tries to account for the fact that the same sentence in a session and out of the session are quite different, because of the nature of the relationship-because of what you put in the relationship; because of all you expect from the relationship; because of what is prohibited by the relationship.

And thus, "analytic speech unmourns language." Now, extending Green's ideas to the peculiar nature of psychoanalytic conversations with states of spirit possession, I feel perhaps swearing is an example of the "instinctualization of language." Perhaps, in the realm of swearing, one can get in touch with the raw energy of instinctual juices.

The instinctual life is impacted by the culture as it uses the body as a scribe to lay down rules that bring both honor and humiliation. Our bodies carry notions of feminine beauty and virile masculinity, of what is forbidden, permitted, revered, and frowned upon. Any deviations from these ideal inscriptions leads to humiliation that is not just felt in one's body but goes through the skin to rattle the mind. Elsewhere (Masih, 2019) I have written about another young woman who, like Riya, was prone to feelings of humiliation and felt herself to be a nobody. She, too, sought recognition in her parents' eyes, but they preferred their son over her. Insofar as one adheres to the psychoanalytic adage—"anatomy is destiny," it helps us make sense of the sense of invisibility that a girl child carries in Indian culture. Alizade (1999) notes, "The anatomy begins to make fate. The phallus adheres anatomically to the penis, visible protrusion narcissistically overvalued. The vulva of the woman imagines a psychic space of 'not having.' In the Freudian frame, womanhood is seen woven around the spindle of 'lack' of the penis which the little girl hopes to find through the Oedipal father. Cultural preference for a male child consolidates the inscription of invisibility in a girl by her 'not having' a penis and 'not being' a boy" (Masih, 2019).

Riya's story demonstrated for me how her humiliation because of this inscription bred in her a contempt for the phallic order. I am reminded of Erikson's (1964) writing on "inner and outer space" and Alizade's (1999) on a "nothingic order." Both these thinkers propose an order other than a phallic one and weave a story of womanhood around the potential to give birth. Alizade (1999) considered "nothingness" as a site of possibilities and fertility:

> It is nothingness that insists and finds the subject, evoking the archaic, the uncanny and the demonic, leaving an invisible and mute trail . . . [I]t symbolizes enigmatic ignorance and the inevitability of human limitations, and is established through the "not-being" exemplified by fluidity.

The internal feminine somatopsychic universe is marked precisely by this "'not-being' exemplified by fluidity." As a woman when one embraces the thought that—one is nothing—it can open up a new vertex in the mind, a fresh perspective, that assigns relevance to a familiarity with finitude and paves a way away from the idealization of the phallus.

What becomes of the male child? How does he become a victim of reverence? When mothers, sisters and daughters are penetrated by their sons, brothers, and fathers in the realm of swearing, this instantly resonates with forbidden incestuous desires buried deep in the unconscious. When, through these expletives, phalluses are symbolically devoured or made impotent, it resonates with that unconscious fear of its loss which is sensed but never fully processed. I witnessed male healers dealing with this fear. During exorcism rituals I saw healers relishing the sight of possessed women suffering, falling repeatedly on the ground, as if being punished by their god. These men would abuse the ghosts with delight as they watched the women writhe in pain and would use sexually tantalizing language while talking to the women. I, too, was spoken to by them in this manner.

According to Benjamin (1991), female objectification results from an incomplete separation of men from their mothers. In a patriarchal family, the boy will be pushed to repudiate his needs for dependency and maternal identification to assume the power of the phallus. Perhaps affectively charged verbal images of the woman's body, as captured in swear words, also carry men's longing for a time in their experience before culture, with its emphasis on acquisition of language, intervened between their body and the maternal body, between senses and language. As discussed above, the advent of language makes the sensual experience twice removed. However, while using instinctualized swear words one does not have to *mind one's language*. When a man is at the receiving end of a fit of swearing, like Riya's father was on multiple occasions, it is conceivable that the experience will stir the deeper part that yearns for the lost touch with the maternal body—a longing the man was made to renounce. In my encounters with the states of possession, I made space for the instinctual language with all its affective charge. This language did not seem to me verbal abuse, but words dipped in the juices of instincts. It allowed us to talk about sexuality as if we were talking about dreams.

Chapter 6

Ghosts as Messengers

The spirit of this work can best be captured in words of Persian poet, Jalaluddin Rumi (2004), "A joy, a depression, a meanness. Some momentary awareness comes as an unexpected visitor. Welcome and entertain them all! Even if they're a crowd of sorrows, who violently sweep your house. Empty of its furniture. Still, treat each guest honorably. He may be clearing you out for some new delight."

This work has explored ways in which the ghost can be understood as a guest from beyond made familiar by culture. Culture makes available a language populated by supernatural entities. Some of these go on to become companions, like a child's imaginary friends, to help us undertake internal transformative journeys. They float in our collective consciousness, waiting for us to use them, to be inhabited by them. Through us, they utter prophecies, heal the sick, offer solutions to the distressed, demand obedience and sometimes personify destruction in its crudest form.

Winnicott made us aware that, to use these available "objects" that belong neither entirely to the outside world nor ultimately to the inside world, a child's imagination is called for. In *Devi*, Khokha represented, quite literally, this childish quality. Khokha's death, the death of the child's aliveness, caused the goddess to fall from the heights of adulation into the abyss of insanity. Daya disappeared, as a demoness, in the mist. As we journey through this book, we follow *Devi*, and are unknowingly ushered closer to the terror of coming across ghosts, ghouls, demons, and other ghastly beings, floating around in this mist. With terror, trepidation, curiosity, and faith, I took journeys from person to person, moment to moment, ghost to ghost, only to arrive at the end of the tunnel to find our ghosts slightly altered, serving an essential purpose for us.

Having given accounts of possession states, I shall now draw links between them and relevant theoretical concepts to arrive at an aesthetic resonance with the phenomenon of possession. As stated previously, I have grappled with nightmares and the fear of ghosts. Even today, they pay me unwelcome visits in my dreams, and it is only with unease that I could evolve a dialogue with them, to find them less scary with each visit. As a child, I often wondered how others who had been possessed and haunted by ghosts found a cure while I continued to be haunted by my fears.

I entered the research field with residual fear and curiosity and met Bishamber, Shubha, Ravi, and Riya. Colored by my own terror, my perception made me see the parts that haunted them as scary. My understanding had to evolve through the intrapsychic, intersubjective, and psychosocial dimensions. It is to my identification with the healers in my family—my father and grandfather—and my grandmother that I owe the capacity, mediated by my own curiosity, to look at the subjectivity in terror. To use Kohut's expression, my relationship with research participants was usually "experience-near"—marked by directionless-ness at first, and then involving a negotiation of terrors to reach moments of calm as I watched each person heal in subtle and profound ways. Now I position myself in an 'experience-distant' position to establish links between nuances I came across and theoretical concepts I have become familiar with, thus rendering all of it somewhat comprehensible.

My vision has been to paint a humanized portrait of the seemingly demonic individual. In the interest of rendering possession as a human experience, I present here my understanding of the journey from trance to transformation that I have witnessed in the lives I engaged with and analyzed in *Devi*.

TRANCE-FORMATION

American novelist, Anne Lamott (2020), reflecting on the quality of being conscious in the act of writing, notes that "to participate requires self-discipline and trust and courage, because this business of becoming conscious . . . is ultimately about asking yourself . . . 'How alive am I willing to be?'" My conversations with the possessed persons posed a similar challenge for me—how to remain alive when I and the other were both struggling with dread.

The presence of an apparition has an unmistakable quality that evokes revulsion and dread. Life experiences, too, expose us to this state, one in which our thinking reaches an impasse. In later, calmer states, what is remembered and recounted? A pounding heart, a trembling body, sweat, and chills running down the spine. We are consumed by fear. Winnicott's pursuit of the "baby self" in us showed us us that the self evolves out of a scatter. This evolution is facilitated by the mother magically or intuitively sensing the baby's wants thereby giving coherence to the internal processes of the child. This requires a safe home base "from which a child learns to explore and experience the world fully" (Winnicott, 1990).

Without this secure base, an infant's experiences take place in a psycho-social void marring their psychic development. It is in this void that dread develops, germinating from a failure in gathering: mis-links, mis-alliances, or mis-recognition of the infant's state on the part of the maternal environment. Reflecting specifically on alliances between mother and daughter, Kakar (2012) noted that the Indian mother is only too conscious of her daughter's fate—that one day the daughter will have to leave her family home for her marital home. As a result, the mother re-experiences the emotional conflicts her own separation from her mother aroused in the past. This unconscious identification leads her to indulge her daughter, contrary to expectations derived from social and cultural prescriptions. Kakar (2012) also observed that the enhancement in status granted to an Indian woman by her mother-hood adds a distinctive emotional quality to the nurturance she offers her infant, physical closeness between her and her baby amplifies sensuous gratifications. However, the experiences of my research participants reveal a different picture. The young women I had the chance to get to know did not experience their mothers as sufficiently invested in them. I suspect the terrors my research participants were grappling with set in after the fusion (between them and their respective primary caretakers), when the external world intervened in the fusion and brutally severed it. Reality intervened at a time when the nascent ego was still not sufficiently equipped to "recognize the externality of the object" (Benjamin, 1991) and acknowledge the lack of one's omnipotence. The mother often falters, perhaps assuming that, because the child has an inside, she also has a sense of an outside. In possession, the terror of the post-fusion phase is taken to God, who is counted on to contain it so that fusion can be restored.

Here it helps to draw from Kristeva's (1982) notion of the "abject," a state in which the distinctions between the subject and object are lost and, subse-quently, adhesive identifications emerge. According to Mitrani (2001), after an object is violently separated from the self with which it had been fused before, it retains a quality of being distinct from the subject. Such an object is formed out of a severed omnipotence. As a result, the self collapses. The jet-tisoned object and subject are caught in a tangle—there are no links of desire or hate between them, only a void toward which they experience a dreadful pull. The terror caused by the forcible coming apart of the subject and the object is equivalent to the terror of a nightmare.

When the subject also loses its distinction, we have a psychic state Matte Blanco (1988) has termed "symmetrical frenzy." This state is marked by the destruction of all "asymmetrical relations" between psychic contents. Asymmetry produces nuance and complexity in thought and the conscious-ness by which a locus can be created, including the choice or ability of the subject, to recognize the externality of the object and to relate to the other.

One example of the terrors and the arrival of the "abject" appeared in my nightmares where all distinction between myself and the other as well as between waking and dreaming was lost, as discussed in Chapter 3.

The fact that the ego is still evolving when it encounters the object causes the problems observed in possessed persons—confusion between self and other and difficulties in thinking through experiences and with mourning. It is inherent in the permeability of self and common in Indian culture for a child's internal space to be invaded with a sense of entitlement that is similar to the sentiment with which the abode of gods is claimed by those who seek his divine intervention in their lives. This invasion is performed to appropriate some aspects of the child's personality and align them with societal norms, making the child's self palatable to others around. Maternal abandonment, coupled with insistent control and impingement from the environment, only enhance the sense of derealization.

Bollas (2000) observed that an object turned bad if, instead of containing distress, it transformed contentment to discontent, utilizing the child as a container for its evacuative projective expectations. The child experiences this as possession. Implicit in the forbiddance of the child's explorations of sexuality and hostility is the idea that those around project their own notions of sexuality and hostility into the child, who is seen as a receptacle. These projections of others, or what Bollas (2000) has called "interjects," "interrupt and momentarily disorient the self, which can proceed only insofar as it accepts the interjection." Invasion from "outside" leads to interruptions "inside." The dissociative state testifies to the self's experience of being interrupted when the evolving self was subjected to overpowering projective evacuations by the objects. When the self manages to break through this subjugation, it is thrown into a state of disorientation, just as it had been during the invasion itself. In other words, when internal psychic contents threaten to break out, it is uncannily similar to and experienced as the invasion known from the past but not fully processed. The projections deposited by others and one's instinctual intensities are experienced alike as foreign entities invading one's being.

Among the possessed persons I spoke to, persistent control over their lives by family members and parents—who often wrongly or unfairly found fault with them—and extreme physical abuse were standard experiences. When a father leaves his child tied to a water tank on a terrace, his parental consciousness only imagines that the fear thereby driven home will result in an inculcation of discipline. However, this experience also opens the floodgates of the child's inner world. Psychoanalysis informs us that, when the self is under threat of fragmentation, the erotic part of the mind emerges with its binding function. One possible outcome of eros performing this binding function is the exacerbation of the child's tendency to comply with the wishes of punishing parents. In such cases, there will subsequently be attempts to play the role of the ideal child, the ideal sibling.

Riya was unable to achieve a successful binding when faced with the fear of being alone; her clinging to her mother indicates a groping, not knowing what it is that threatens and calls for binding, as if, when she was left alone, she could not even think of her mother as someone who offered containment. Her fear of the invisible presence was so powerful that she believed it could even take away her mother if she (Riya) did not hold on tight. In other words, her mother was not an internal presence. Her internal world had been corroded by destructive envy and hostility, and, thus, nothing nourishing could be retained in it.

What also contributed to Riya's inability to bind her terror was the relationship between her parents, marked as it was by strain, violence, humiliation, torture, and the invisibilization of the mother. To put it simply, there was also no love between the parental couple.

All the participants experienced household relational climates that led to a stifling of their internal processes, worsened by a stringent religiosity that thwarted the emergence of an ownership of thoughts, feelings, and actions. Kakar (2012) observed that the Indian child is not pressured to "give up non-logical modes of thinking and communication" and that there is often a

> lack of interest or effort on the part of the mother and family to make a child understand that objects and events have their own meaning and consequences independent of his feelings or wishes, contribute to the protracted survival of primary-process modes well into the childhood years . . . Compared with western children, an Indian child is encouraged to continue to live in a mythical, magical world for a long time. In this world, objects, events and other persons do not have an existence of their own, but are intimately related to the Self and its mysterious moods . . . [H]is own feelings are projected onto the external world and give it form and meaning . . . [O]bjective realities loom/disappear, are good/bad, threatening/rewarding, etc. depending on one's affective states . . . [A]nimistic and magical thinking persists . . . [T]he projection of one's own emotions onto others, the tendency to see natural and human objects predominantly as extensions of oneself, the belief in spirits animating the world outside and the shuttling back and forth between secondary and primary modes are common features of daily intercourse.

This peculiar relational matrix reinforces the use of defenses that keep the self and awareness of an object's externality at a distance. Pre-reality principle processes facilitate the immediate discharge and gratification of instinctual impulses. Impulsive actions replace thinking and articulation. In all the cases that I engaged with, the righteous and socially compliant role was part of the falsely constituted self. At the same time, the repressed rage and sexuality were preserved in the authentic self, which manifested in the possession state. The unprocessed states remain unthinkable, unspeakable, meaningless, causing frustration and evacuated via projection, splitting, and projective identification into the body or into the external world through action. Demands to process emotional experiences bring about a state of collapse. It is as if they carry pain without suffering it.

One form the possessing ghost takes is that of an alien entity that is kept at a distance—it is unfigurable and thus too grotesque and quickly evacuated like the filthy part of Riya's *samkat* that she believed would be consumed by Kali. An individual possessed by such a *samkat* is inclined to evacuate frustration through actions but also prone to inappropriate regulation of affect and conversationally bombarding anyone who will listen to them with casual factual descriptions of events, thus saturating the space between them and preventing the interlocutor from accessing a state of dreaming. I have discussed previously how, in possession, the parts of the self that emerge, grimacing and invading the territory of dreams, are the parts that were formed when the underdeveloped capacities to deal with certain emotional states caused the self and other to split into good and evil. These split-off, swept-under parts run amok, disrupting psychic processes, generating nightmares in response to life's anxious turns. The struggle is to weave a pattern of perspectives around the dread that informs the nightmares. In mapping the shift from dread to splitting, one kind of splitting emerges in images such as those of a filthy child; the primal scene; naked men and women. In the case of the healers the splitting takes the form of a tremendous fascination with women (Ravi) or a tremendous hostility toward them (Bishamber). The male split off part in its excess is a reckless doer, divorced from its relationship with the female split off part. This reckless male part evokes extreme thrill that cannot be inhabited by the body, thus plunging the body into a deep sea of fear. As I learnt in my conversations with Riya, it is this male element that the possessed person often seeks to dilute.

With the healers, there was a mistranslation of eros as depicted in the scenario where the healer spoke obscenely to Riya: here his needs were expressed through the exercise of power over Riya, resulting in the emergence of perverse dynamics. This split-off sexual component forecloses all chances for a relatively more complete imagination of a relationship, one in which the perception of absence left over from the past was not simply to be compensated for by another body, another aperture, another organ.

Cultural categories acknowledge such ambivalences at the level of feeling—perversion is judged harshly, but as a *samkat*, not as a part of oneself. The *samkat* is seen as an entity that has come to visit and will be dealt with; one does not have to put one's mind to it. The images of filth are not to be engaged with; they are important only insofar as they highlight the need to exorcise it. In other words, the split between what is beautiful and filthy inside is mediated by culture. This understanding guided me in my attempts to make the splits I encountered increasingly intelligible. I used or addressed the partly submerged, partly floating parts actively, particularly the male and female elements. Experiences of the prohibition of intimacy, of closeness, of playing, of exploration, and of opening oneself sensually to the world fuel the world of fantasies. The actual lives of possessed persons are marked by only a partial compliance with the prohibitions imposed on them. The consistent evocation of the fantasies that manifest in images the ghost makes one see, the dreams attributed to the work of the ghost, what the ghost utters—all of this produced an awareness in me of what each person desired but also feared. As a result of the conflict between desire and fear, the images are produced as though erotic, but they are in fact auto-erotic—the persistence of the images is a way of saying, "I am not going to have all that I fantasize about, even if these things lead me to a desired place." But the real erotic binding happens with the images, which begin to recur.

Significantly, when these recurrent images and the fantasies latent in them were being worked out in dialogue with me, I too was concurrently experiencing the unraveling—in fact, I would go so far as to say that the unbinding first occurred in me, facilitating communications through the unconscious-to-unconscious link that I have previously referred to.

Eigen (2011) wrote, "Our ability to produce states is way ahead of our ability to process them." Witnessing the frenzy of possession states evoked powerful surges of emotions in me. The images and sounds of possessed persons wailing and somersaulting, their ear-splitting screams and sinister laughs, of them beating themselves and others, pulling their own hair, twisting their bodies into shapes that left them beyond recognition, evoked fear along with an impulse to ease their pain somehow. The implausibility of this impulse is what led to the tension in me that had to be metabolized. How could I understand such intensity of affect when it threatened my capacities to think and tempted me to slide into enactments myself?

This tension even took somatic form, manifesting in headaches and chest pains that I could only relieve through weeping. Of course, a major part of this tension stealthily slid into nightmares. It is through dream work that the psyche attempts to process psychic content. However, "when that task is no longer possible, the psyche breaks off its natural activity; it pulls all the plugs, like the circuit breaker that saves a system from irreparable damage" (Zoja, 2011). A nightmare then signals that the dream work has failed. The startled waking of a dreamer is akin to fainting in waking life when faced with demands to process emotional content (Shubha). If the ego is equipped with a transformative function, the unintegrated, unthinkable part becomes integrated, a part of the self. Where the ego is ill-equipped, the unintegrated part haunts like an apparition. Dare I say the haunting part longs to belong to the haunted.

The body, too, is seemingly abandoned (or evacuated into) and taken over by this other. "One feels not only possessed and damned but also demoralized and dehumanized" (Grotstein, 1984). It is in these moments that it becomes particularly difficult to imagine what the horrors being experienced by the possessed entail. One way of thinking about it is to compare the mind to a body; then, the experience is like a tightening of the sphincters of conscious-ness. All paths toward representation and awareness are tightly shut. There is no sleeping and no dreaming because it would take one again to a place where the terrifying monster from the unconscious lives, the one that cannot be befriended.

Simply put, this is how fear and a sense of annihilation are dealt with, but what gets erased in the process is the hope of enhancing and expanding the self. Botella and Botella (2005) contend that

> non-representation is experienced by the ego as an excess of excitation; and if the mind does not arrive, by virtue of a transformation, at an experience of intel-ligibility accessible to the system of representations, the ego will experience it as traumatic.

Apart from discharge in actions and nightmares, the psychic tension is dis-charged in the form of hallucinations in the waking state. Faced with one's unthinkable and nonrepresented parts, one falls back or regresses from the pole of representation and consciousness to a motor (behavior) and hallucina-tory pole. Ogden (2005b) informs us that nightmares are in a space that one enters after having given up the desire to learn from experience. The self is unable to perform unconscious psychological work until this desire to learn from experience is reinstated. The night terrors that my research participants experienced were marked by a sense of a force or entity sitting on them as they slept, or following them, or standing next to their bed or at the thresh-old of their bedroom, and it was this sense, this terror, that caused them to wake up. Some degree of unconscious psychological work was done in these night terrors, and in nightmares of drowning, falling, being strangled by an unknown force—we may regard these as ways of putting one in touch with feelings of helplessness and vulnerability. Ogden (2005b) would say, "the patient awaking from a nightmare has reached the limits of his capacity for dreaming on his own." Nightmares, then, are a plea for another mind to dream the unbearable psychic content with.

My mind was called upon to shoulder this task, and I, too, found myself trapped at times in the confusing space between perception and hallucina-tion. My nightmares (mentioned in Riya's case in chapter 3) taught me that this crippling fear of the unthinkable dwelled in this in-between space, a no man's land that does not belong to the world of dreams, where unconscious psychological work is possible, or to reality, where conscious work is. Appropriately enough, religion views ghosts as inhabiting the space between two worlds—they live in limbo. With this nightmare, not knowing if I was inhabiting reality or a dream, I too became a ghost stuck in limbo and felt terrified, perhaps just like the departed might feel. Ghosts, stuck in limbo, do not have an address—they are, in a sense, homeless.

The fear of ghosts is indeed the fear of the unknown, the not-represented, the unintelligible and psychically unmetabolized—that is what evokes horror. For most of my informants, this unthinkable was also the sexual. My ability to welcome the haunting parts of my participants facilitated in them a loosening around sexuality. In general, however, what we see as the forms of these haunting parts is that which comes out as filthy, foul, evil, and so on. The beautiful is disconnected from the shit—it is inside but unseen, felt and experienced as taking shape in the innards and expressing its overtures to the outside through the leaping and contortions through the energetic waveforms of the flailing limbs.

In order to see this unseen beauty in what is left after the evacuation of the filth, Botella and Botella (2005) inspired me to consider the psyche's inherent predisposition toward figurability, which is based on the principle of convergence–coherence, i.e., making "all the data of the moment, internal and external stimuli, converge into a single intelligible unity aimed at binding all the heterogeneous elements" in order to take it increasingly closer to becoming coherent. In the context of possession, I would like to propose that convergence–coherence becomes convergence–evacuation–coherence. The tightening of the sphincters of the consciousness is an instance of convergence, the somatic evocations and nightmares in me are evidence of evacuation, and my ability to make sense of these evocations as unprocessed parts of myself and my informants, for which my mind was rented momentarily, produced the examples of coherence.

TRANSFORMATION

This work has been about the aesthetic appreciation of psychic capacities and/or reparative tendencies bound up with the primitive states we witness in possession. It is an appreciation and possibly an articulation of tendencies bound up with horrifying states that can help us design ways of healing. The possessed individuals I came to know seemed at first to be wandering, as if lost in the mist of insanity like the fallen "Devi," Daya. It has been established that ghosts served in each of the cases as containers for split-off, projected, unassimilated parts of personalities born out of peculiar psychosocial matrices. While a more time-consuming way out of the terror caused by these ghosts is via thinking, culture has revealed another route that begins with ghost's screams—cries to God for help?

Although the fear of being consumed is considered basal in psychoanalysis (Winnicott, 1965), it nonetheless comes with a hope of thinkability and figurability (Botella and Botella, 2005). When looking at terrifying states, we are trying to make use of the anxieties that drip from terror but do not completely erase a retroactive question—*What* is the force that is plaguing the person? I rely on dreams, reverie, transference, and countertransference to make sense of that which is not articulated but is communicated through evocations in the listener. The dread, like all symptomatic constellations, has both a pathological aspect and a somewhat hidden healthy one. In Riya's case, the part drawn toward Kali was the pathological one. Meanwhile, the part that was coming toward me found echoes in my own nightmares. Through dreaming, I had freed myself from the dread of the unthinkable. I was able to perform psychological work affected by the dread that produced congruence with Riya's affective states and tangible narratives as available in dreams and images.

In a sense, this work also traced the journey from dread to eros. It also involved looking at ghosts as images emerging from the state of dread, thinkable but not easily processable. These ghosts are brought to the feet of God, where they can be heard. In other words, God appears where there are ghosts, or ghosts take the person they haunt closer to God. A ghost, then, can be thought of as a "transitional phenomenon" (Winnicott, 1953) because it emerges by establishing a link with God. However, in most cases the repulsive filthy parts persist despite the establishment of this link with divinity.

The healers work on consolidating this link by looking for the beauty in the virtuous self that is sensed entering into a dialogue with the possessed person, as was attempted by the supreme priest who passed away—or by Ravi, whose efforts made Riya feel held. My approach was different—I tried to get close to the horror, which required me to shed my inhibitions, to resist being crippled and infected by dread. This stance of benevolent curiosity coaxed out a more evolved part of the beauty, as the dread trapped in various bodily symptoms gradually eased in the course of our conversations. I tried to encourage in my participants a positive imagination of the relationships in their lives and the extension of this imagination to those they envied, that they were scared of. In this attempt, there were images of love relationships (Riya), of lovemaking (Shubha) and of dependence (Ravi), images through which most intimate details were shared. My nonjudgmental stance in all these conversations was very close, I feel, to a solemn understanding conveyed by God that all is acceptable as long as one can be self-aware. The ethics of godliness lies in seeing the beauty in brokenness. "Man's fate is not one of pathos, but of transcendence. Only that which is broken can become whole" (Rosenbaum, 2009). My own Christian upbringing also instilled in me the image of Christ as being born in this world only for broken and downtrodden beings.

Instances of aesthetic resonance also emerged palpably when Shubha and Riya were able to express their desires and the moments of insight in their journeys toward self-awareness, which were felt by them as deeply meaningful summarized understandings of parts of them. Such moments of understanding ushered them toward a better relationship with their bodies and led to the emergence of psychic structures, the translation of those structures into relationships that became significant and intimate, the translation of those relationships into the strengthening of an identification with work, a respect for that work, and the increased involvement of close friends and family members in these areas.

Two of the case stories—those of Shubha and Riya—could be explored in depth because the concerned participants had in some senses subscribed to modern Western perspectives: Riya through her work as a beautician, which entailed enhancing physical beauty and evoked strong anxieties within the framework of a middle-class worldview that was susceptible to fears of rape, and Shubha through her inclination to internalize an evanescent subject like psychology. In both these cases, the participants' work provided them with a sense of differentiation, recognition, and autonomy. It was in large part through their work that these young women sought autonomy and respect. Accordingly, in possession this life-historical turbulence was picked up to stage an encounter with it in a religious context, and an aspiration for complete integration through this encounter was either shared with or intuited by me.

The healers' search does not go deep. Their eros was mis-translated, producing a process of narcissistic mirroring. Ravi's turning to me for help with Riya indicated the limitations of his own healing. The split-off part of the self is often bedazzled, the way one is when faced with God's beauty and appearance. The fact that Riya was possessed by a boy alerts us, meanwhile, to a very specific social fact. In Indian lower-middle-class families, there is a distinct preference for male offspring, and the expression of this wish by members of one's family can precipitate in one a potential self that remains split-off, with the result that, when children want to enact the wishes emanating from those split-off parts, they end up confused by the injunctions against such enactments. Is it likely that being haunted by images or ghosts of boys could be, in part, a playing out of a simple wish to receive all the love that would have been forthcoming if one had been born a boy? These ghost-boys are invested with all the traits and attributes on the basis of which one could say to one's family, "You want a boy? Here you go! This is the kind of boy I would have become!" The dream I had in which I ate the boy was a dream of Riya's oral greed and my own. The boy also symbolized the threat that I would be shooed out of the village—an expression of how my internal mother and sister kept me from being enlightened (conducting research in the dream), a role similar to that of the ghost-woman in white who thwarts all thought at the threshold of dreaming. Consumed, the boy became divested of his dangers and toxins and went to Riya through an unconscious-to-unconscious communication between us.

Each psychic state impinges upon us demands for conjuring ways and means of surviving it. Indian culture offers myriad ways of expressing and surviving the states we produce in the form of symbols like ghosts (*bhuta/samkat*) or rituals and in myth and folklore. There are ghosts for every psychic reason, creating spaces in which one can live the unlived parts of the self. Kakar demonstrated in his case studies that the ghosts possessing his informants were reifications of repressed, forbidden sexual and aggressive impulses incompatible with the values and strivings of the conscious. Possession states and exorcism techniques provide a space for abreaction, where the intensity of affects that tag along with repressed content is neutralized. Ghosts are *atripta* entities or unsatisfied desires that haunt. Indian culture offers up a buffet of such ghosts—*masan, jaljogini, churel, pichalpairi, preta, bhutna, sirkata, djinn*, and so on. Psychologically, each type of ghost can represent impulses and anxieties specific to those who avail of it. For instance, in his analysis, Kakar relates the horrific vision of *jaljogini* to "the Indian male child's dread of the mother's 'demonic' eroticism so that later for many who fall ill and suffer from acute anxiety—become possessed by the jaljogini" (1991). In the case of one particular woman's possession by a *masan*—embryo-eater—Kakar draws on her personal history to source the possession to an unconscious pregnancy fantasy. This overtly sexualized and ruthlessly destructive ghost represents a symbiosis of destructive and sexual wishes, just as Riya's *samkat* did.

Obeyesekere saw in possession an indirect expression of individuals' painful experiences. The public symbol of a ghost is invested with personal meaning and becomes meaningful to the person as well as ther group. The experience may be ego-alien but does not remain culture-alien because, in possession, it has been objectified as a part of cultural reality, thus saving one from a sense of estrangement. Any form of ghost can be unconsciously chosen according to the impulses and parts of one's self that are disowned and that haunt. Once a ghost is thus chosen, these disavowed haunting parts are externalized, deposited in the ghost, and lived out in possession. Riya's ghost was of unconscious envy, greed, forbidden sexual desires, and murderous rage and was finally lived out in raw vitality through the traits characteristic of the ghost possessing her. The guilt evoked was dealt with by subjecting the self/ghost to repeated punishments at Balaji's hands and throwing the self/

ghost into the gutter and forcing it to consume the filthy water, a punishment believed to be reserved by Balaji only for overtly seductive, aggressive, and especially stubborn ghosts. The unconscious choice to align her acting-out with the culture's expectation of a *masan* is itself suggestive of creativity—she unconsciously manipulated the symbol of possession in service of the objectification of her difficult states. This reminds me of the words of the physicist Paul Langevin: "Concrete is the abstract rendered familiar" (as quoted by Rosenbaum, 2009). The methods adopted by Riya allowed her guilt to escape processing and be, as part of the language of the larger community, understood as Balaji's wrath. The idea that somebody else caused the possession through the use of black magic facilitated the projection of her own unconscious envy into an image of an envious person while at the same time embellishing one's own self by propping up a narcissistic idea—"I arouse envy. I have something the other desires."

Obeyesekere (1981) held that behavior of a possessed person is intelligible to her/his society because that society has ideal models in its cultural system of and for behavior. He referred to these models as "myth models," and it is these models that constitute cultural conceptions of demons and deities. A possessed person's symptoms become intelligible if they fall in line with this prevalent model, which in turn feeds and is fed by these very symptoms and the psychological conflicts shaping them.

Myths, like fairy tales, function as transitional spaces where the inside and outside come together without arousing anxieties. We know how Riya made use of the myths prevalent in her culture to give voice to her emotional pain, without having to undergo the pain that comes from processing this pain, which would be the ideal response in psychoanalytic terms. Hymns formed a central part of Riya's myth-based toolkit. The Hanuman Chalisa is a popular hymn used in the Hindu tradition to ward off evil spirits. When it is recited, the possessed enter the frenzied state of *peshi* in accordance with popular belief and begin to sway, scream, and wail violently. The texture of the hymn is such that it evokes a strong need for empathic response from the mother of infancy and a burning desire for a "transformational object" (Bollas, 1987). It is infused with adoration, reverence, and a sense of submission to the all-mighty omniscient deity Hanuman, also known as Balaji, from whom is sought strength and wisdom.

Riya was able to facilitate, in herself, the formation of a parental couple through the worship of both Balaji and Durga. Balaji made available to her a space in which to live out her impulses (in the state of *peshi*), but when she was haunted by repulsive sexual images, it was another chant, the Durga Saptashati, which helped contain her anxieties. I have found Achreja's (2013) reflections on the Durga Saptashati very helpful in revealing the proximity of Bion's thinking with Indian philosophical notions concerning distress and its

nivaaran (resolution). Achreja (2013) looks at "the psychic delusional identifications of demons that Devi slays in the Durga Saptashati." This hymn,
comprising seven hundred verses, praises the mother who removes all difficulties. Interestingly, it begins with descriptions of a king and a merchant who
have both been abandoned by their respective families and kinsmen. Lost
are the luxuries they once enjoyed in their homes and kingdom. Both find
it difficult to understand why their hearts bear deep affection for those who
have driven them out. Together, they approach a sage to understand why their
minds are afflicted with sorrow. The sage enlightens them with the explanation that men are often thrown into pits of delusion.

The Durga Saptashati is a tribute to that part of the maternal which facilitates the evacuation of unthinkable states, of "she who tears apart thought."

> In this text of 13 chapters, Devi slays numerous asuras or demons . . . Swami
> Satyananda Sara Shubha of Devi Mandir in his acclaimed translation of Chandi
> Patha has recognized asuras as "thoughts"—thoughts that occlude sentient
> beings from perception and realization of their own inherent divinity. Truly,
> such psychic demons are enemies of our realization of godhead and, hence,
> they are enemies of devas. In a similar vein, devas may be understood as forces
> that combat thought-demons, that is, forces of clear perception. (Achreja, 2013)

Achreja then zooms in on the characterization of demons and gods in each
chapter in terms of delusions and capacities respectively. Demons represent
deprivation, greed, arrogance, pride, lust, rage, and so on, while gods represent creative capacities, serving to remove confusion and grant wisdom,
emancipation, omnipotence, equilibrium, all-pervading consciousness, bliss
of being, etc. Kali is perceived as the remover of darkness. As Vaishnavi,
Devi is the energy of the all-pervading consciousness; As Varahi, she is the
energy of the desire for union. As Chamundeshwari, she is the slayer of passion and anger. As Chandika, she tears apart all thoughts. And as Durga, she
is the destroyer of troubles and afflictions. This Durga chant charts out a
divine path through the removal of all thought-demons that obstruct clarity of
perception, diminish creative energies, and distort empathy. The devotee can
perceive and realize their own inherent divinity.

It is understandable that, in cultural thought, the evacuation of unthinkable
and unpleasant states is preferred to the narrower and tougher route through
emotional thinking. Nonetheless, the state to which one is transported during
the recitation of this chant is akin to that of a child who is yet to develop a
transformative alpha function and can only proceed inasmuch as they are
allowed to evacuate their states. In the story of Durga Saptashati, the previously mentioned depressed king and merchant are told about the glory of Devi
and take to worshipping her with great passion—they make an idol of her,

pray to it, abstain from food, offer blood sacrifices. Chandika grows pleased and grants the king power over his kingdom and the merchant supreme knowledge for self-realization. Like the king and the merchant, perhaps Riya and other possessed persons also find in Durga Saptashati a promise that pleasing the Supreme Mother or allying with her will restore a connection to a lost kingdom—the original erotic field where one relished the mother's eternal love. Perhaps Durga Saptashati also ignites the hope that one will finally attain wisdom from the mother goddess and be able to liberate oneself from the pain inherent in attachments, the grief associated with the unending cycle of life (resurrection) and death (destruction) in the internal object world and reach a capacity to forgive. In the permeable state of *peshi*, as the words of these hymns and chants are absorbed through the senses and echo inside, one is transported to the time before objects turned into ghosts, a time when experience was transformed by the comforting yet elusive spirit-like presence of the object one did not know that one depended on. The ghosts, reminders of the object's absence, are kept at bay with the mere mention of the deity's name and faith in or dependence on it, just as the first years of life are etched on the mind but rarely accessible to consciousness.

Like the mother of infancy, the deity is in sync with the one making the appeal, adapting perfectly to their needs, making all tasks easy, fulfilling desires, granting happiness, freeing them from ill-fated contingencies associated with rebirth (the rhythm of separation and union and the pain that accompanies it) in the world. Closeness with God frees one from the sense of death or the loss of the object. All this can be achieved because God becomes available to the subject, for whatever purpose is deemed necessary or desirable by them. The firm and ubiquitous presence of God is sought both inside and outside, and the transformational function of the divine object is integral to the belief in the deity's actual potential to transform the total environment.

This hymn is a declaration of absolute dependence on God. It instantly puts the faithful devotee in touch with their vulnerable self and its need to be held and lifted up from the pestering doom of loneliness. In my experience, hymns sung in our church that appealed most to those seeking cures of some sort shared a textual quality—they summoned the devotee to merge with the primary object that aided them in transforming all discomfort and restored a state of calm and tranquility in their internal world.

From different fantasies and fantasy systems emerge multiple self-representations that, fused together, make up an individual's identity. Under conditions of conflict, this composite identity may begin to disintegrate. One or another self-representation comes to the foreground of the consciousness, mediated by an unconscious fantasy in which the self-representation is expressed concretely, and if these happen to be communally held religious fantasies, they may appear as possession or trance. Thus, belief in spirit possession, just like belief in the Holy Spirit, is a communally held representational fantasy that precludes asking the holder of the fantasy-transitional object (for such fantasies are cultural transitional objects), "Did you conceive of this or was it presented to you from without?"

When the ways and means provided by culture for the conversion of unconscious content into content that is acceptable to the psyche are mediated by priests and healers who have devoted time and thought to arrive at their wisdom, a shift toward greater ego enrichment and evolution can be affected. Such healers or learned priests can blend the wisdom they have gathered about the human condition and their service to community, sense deeper longings for love and recognition and devise interventions accordingly.

As children, my sibling and I were taught by our mother to say a prayer before we slept at night. The words of the prayer centered on being kept safe from bad dreams and granted sound sleep. Just like a lullaby, the prayer gently enveloped us like a safety net. Knowing that her children had prayed made my mother feel relaxed; it meant she did not have to be physically present for us to feel safe. Belief in the power of prayer indicates the intensity of one's wish to be close to a protecting, warm figure. It is said that God created mothers because "He" could not be everywhere. I propose that, where the mother cannot be, God is. Where God is, a battle with terrorizing demons can be staged. Sometimes these battles are not won but lead to nightmares. Although, after the terror of a nightmare, one might repeatedly say that one doesn't want to go back to sleep, one might also feel a paradoxical wish to go back to the same state, to lose consciousness so that dream work can happen.

Ordinarily, we do not know how to move closer to the terror. Botella and Botella (2005) show how, in trying to meet the nightmarish terror of their clients, they inadvertently and involuntarily created playful enactments that had nothing to do with their better judgment as therapists. They note that an attempt to wake up from a nightmare requires, paradoxically, that we manage to go back to sleep, to rest, even as we are terrified. In the state brought on by a nightmare, we recall what feel like fortunate experiences of having had another person witness the babble, the fragmented voices, the sounds that are emitted when the nightmare is happening—this witness almost manages to piece together a narrative or at least to produce a limited image of what might be scaring the sleeper, and if the witness is a close companion, they then manage to link this image with other narratives from waking life. This is the sense in which the analytic listener manages to produce a remembering of fragmented images and events that may have happened; in other words, "remembering is dreaming . . . the past cannot become memory without a dream-work furnished by the analyst" (Botella and Botella, 2005). Herein lies the beauty of psychoanalytic conversations.

During my research, I, too, found myself on the edge of terrifying psychic states, in positions from which, through a few spontaneous interventions, I was able to "listen" to the way the body squirmed in a nightmare, in *peshi*, but also in conversations with me. This led to some fragments being recapitulated and produced tentative remembering, subject to confirmation by the participants of how it made sense to them, thereby enabling a healing of the terror into rest or sleeping.

Obeyesekere (1981) theorized that societies with no notions of ghosts were likely to feature higher concentrations of mentally ill persons. Ghosts provide hope and opportunity; a society of ghosts is a society in which the unthinkable is represented as the culturally thinkable and addressable. It performs the social correlate of the function of the psyche, in terms of facilitating figurability in culture, and the function of the analyst (as the analysand's double) in that it provides weapons of representation (ghosts as shields) against the distress of nonrepresentation. Psychic work is solicited (albeit not to the degree aimed at in clinical work) while the "right not to communicate" (Winnicott, 1963) is preserved. Something like a proto-dream state is brought about through ghosts. This state in my participants was elaborated into a dream state through conversations with me, as I could facilitate a remembering of life-historical details while appreciating the "right not to communicate."

My belief, stemming from my having been socialized into practices of praying and worshipping in the family unit, is that the meditative state of praying can, in the face of fear or terror, mobilize memory and even perceptual traces of that phase of life when the mother's benevolent presence caused all ghosts to disappear. It does not matter much whether these monsters are internal or external. What matters is the profound sense of feeling safe and secure. It rekindles those traces in memory and perception, which are laden with healing potential and are only gradually, after many years of clinical work, evoked through analysis.

There is a link here between tertiary processes, positivization, and possession. In worship, as one surrenders to the divine in utter obedience, asking for benevolent grace, one automatically assumes the status of an imperfect, deficient being. Psychoanalytically speaking, attributing unpleasant and pleasant psychic states to externalized sources of agency like ghosts and deities exemplifies the use of primary process thinking. However, Green (1986) wrote that, although primary process thinking obeys the pleasure–displeasure principle, it does not take negation into account or tolerate delay/expectation and, while it permits the realization of unconscious desires in certain forms, its value lies in the fact that, despite censorship, the repressed wish succeeds in finding satisfaction and ensuring the victory of the pleasure principle, thereby securing the continuity of the self.

In psychodynamic work, psychic evolution consists in working with the patient's preconscious to bring to consciousness the derivatives from the unconscious. The aim is to foster a transition from primary to secondary thinking. Green (2005) introduced the concept of "tertiary processes" that help in establishing links, thus facilitating a back-and-forth movement. Eigen refers to this capacity to move back and forth as our plasticity, a part of our nature (Eigen, 2011). Now, the confessional nature of prayer is a lot like free association in psychodynamic therapy. A priest I know once described how he had realized, while in the act of prayer, how unforgiving he was. The prayer itself was a common one and a daily ritual of his: "Lord, forgive my sins as I forgive those who have sinned against me." This time, however, he stopped after uttering these words because they did not seem to correspond to his self's experience. A thought process had been stirred in him that led him to the realization that he had been saying this prayer for a long time without realizing what he was asking for. The priest in question was going through a rough patch at this time in his life, and he had presented himself to God hoping to receive His mercy. But the line of prayer he had uttered had made him reckon instead with the fact that he had not forgiven anyone. It was actually very hard for him to forgive and forget those who had wronged him. He held on to past experiences of people betraying or hurting him. He realized how difficult it was to forgive, to be like Christ. He realized he was being a hypocrite. He wanted God to see him as flawed, as an imperfect human, but he could not see others as flawed. The meditative and confessional nature of prayer mobilized thoughts in him and facilitated a transition of unprocessed feelings from the unconscious to consciousness.

In psychoanalysis, there is a force that drives the analysand to internalize the analyst as a function. Similarly, running in the background of the process that was ignited in the priest was his need to be increasingly like his ideal object—to be like Christ in both deed and image. As a result, he gradually began to see himself and others in a new light. In this instance, the above prayer took on the role of the tertiary processes, linking primary with secondary thinking and initiating internal processes without being intrusive. The cultural process of prayer offered a gentler working-through of the preconscious, which is largely constituted by one's culture (Kakar, 2008), thus creating the possibility of positivization.

The negative, the unthinkable, can be named, articulated, thought about and thus turned into something positive, a representation. Green understood the space thus created by tertiary processes as a projection toward the outside in the mother–child relationship that accounts for what Winnicott has called the transitional space. Prayers, as culture's tertiary processes, open transitional spaces for positive and negative to come together, providing ways by which primary thinking can gradually move to secondary thinking. In

Bionian terms, prayers (if framed appropriately), myths, hymns, and sermons can serve alpha functions, transforming unmetabolized beta elements into thinkable alpha elements.

Rituals incorporate ceremonies patterned according to myth models, ceremonies that involve making offerings, praying, singing hymns, and listening to priests' or healers' interpretations of scripture. Like Rorschach ink blots, myths, too, remain ambiguous, opening up the imagination and making available a canvas onto which colors from inner worlds can be projected. In culture's clinic, each individual myth is projected into the collective myth and thus made intelligible. The gap between private and public is made narrow, the disturbing experience of alienation is bypassed. The unthinkable and unsayable psychic content is like "a quantum fish which only materializes once it has been caught" (Botella & Botella, 2005). By containing unconscious secrets in the form of shadows, spirits or ghosts, culture as mother performs its alpha function through the myths it offers as maternal reveries—capturing the unthinkable and unsayable elements of the self, making them intelligible at least to the culture one dwells in and thereby making one feel more connected to the world around them. The abstract substance of the unconscious is rendered familiar as one enters the known world visited in daily rituals and populated by all-powerful deities and demons. Terror becomes intelligible because it is now seen as belonging to a familiar territory.

In Winnicott's framework, the "interplay between originality and the acceptance of tradition," between separateness and union, that is available in the cultural field, is the basis for creativity. The opening that gets created for a potential space between inside and outside, subjective object and object-objectively-perceived, me-extensions and not-me, nothing-but-me and objects-and-phenomena-outside-omnipotent-control, baby and mother, child, and family, individual and the world, makes cultural experiences akin to or contiguous with play. This space is also the "area of faith" (Eigen, 2018)—myths, rituals, hymns, and prayers, much like a child's play, open an intermediate space that assumes sanctity, where symbolizing experience is possible and so is the experience of creative living.

The psychoanalytic stance of faith is then a space where one can play with one's whole mind and body. I found it interesting that, in my growing years, others would refer to the state of possession as *khelna* or playing. The language of the body of my participants, the rhythmic swaying movements of possessed persons during *peshi*, the repetitive narrative that Riya brought, the stiffness I noticed in Shubha and the metaphor that emerged from me— "tightening of the sphincters of consciousness"—all seem to point to Joan Symington's (1985) ideas on the survival function of primitive omnipotence. Drawing on Esther Bick's (1968) concept of the "second skin," Symington (1985) reflected on the primitive fear of unintegration and the first line of defense against it. Through examples, Symington demonstrated that one of the ways in which the infant makes use of this defense is by fixing their focus on an object, for example, fixing the gaze on a light bulb or focusing on the point where their skin touches their bed. This constitutes an attempt to gain mastery over the environment. As these defenses are sustained, an armor-plating of "second skin" develops around the personality. The fragility and the early experience of precariousness hides underneath muscular and mental toughness, becoming inaccessible.

In adults, the defense against the fear of unintegration or collapse manifests in various efforts to hold oneself together in the face of extreme stress. These infantile defenses and their derivatives manifest in the clinic as

> refusing to speak, holding back from expressing feelings, [which] can all be seen as variants of clenching the muscles tight to keep the baby self from spilling out, to avoid playing. Similarly, the stone-walling of other defensive attitudes, for example, the triumph or contempt of the manic defense, the stubbornness in the obsessional, have a primitive basis in muscular tightening. . . . Constant talk, flitting from one subject to another in a superficial non-stop manner, being busy all the time, can be seen as related to the primitive defense of constant movement. In a similar way, clinging to old ways of behaving and thinking, using stereotyped phrases and clichés, producing old stale material that got a response from the analyst on a previous occasion, are all ways of attempting to create a continuous unchanging psychic skin without any holes or gaps through which the self could spill. (Symington, 1985)

In possession then, the self is held together, in a twisted way, by the belief that the body is being held against its will. The self has an inside and a shell around this inside. The door opens to the most elementary level of experiencing—through the body. It is this body and its desires that lead us toward forbidden terrains. This body, when in rage, acquires the capacities for destruction beyond repair and, in seduction, leads one to dangers not known, only poorly anticipated. Owing to this awareness, the potential rebellion of bodily satisfaction must be subordinated by institutional controls to preserve the norms of society.

For Freud, civilization requires discontent. It is bought at the cost of instinctual satisfaction by the imposition of the demands of the superego over the id through the internal mechanism of guilt and conscience and the external mechanisms of social control. The body and its impulses are to be kept under rational control through the institutions of celibacy, monogamy, and discipline in service of labor and capitalism. The desires of the flesh are to be tamed or enclosed by religious ceremonies, rituals, and taboos in order to protect the social order.

Yet, at the same time, the divine body is sacred. The charisma of holy individuals typically flows through their body, as for instance in the laying on of hands and in the consumption of the holy water in which their feet have been washed. Human sinfulness has been located, by Christianity, in the conflict between the flesh and the soul, which finds its resolution in healing performed under the institutionalized control of the church. The bread of communion is symbolic of Christ's body, which is consumed with a belief that doing so will integrate Christ with the self. His blood will wash all sins away. His flesh will nourish the soul. A sin-breeding body is countered by the incorporation of the life-giving body of Christ.

In Hinduism, as I witnessed at the Balaji temple, holy water and food offerings blessed by Lord Balaji are invested with the belief that they are infused with the essence of Balaji himself and thereby with transformative powers that can exorcise the soul of its evil. As soon as this divine body is consumed, the evil is forced to reveal itself. The possessed body, being antagonistic to Balaji's pious body, is instantly thrown into a state of frenzy commonly understood in Hinduism as *peshi*. In such religious practices, the pull toward a primitive form of experiencing through the body is countered with a primitive form of incorporation—consuming food invested with a belief that it is the essence of God himself.

The ferocious, frenzied body of a possessed person can easily grip anyone who bears witness to it, leaving them mesmerized. From experience, I can say that it seems as if thought spirals and becomes suspended as the charged climate of the ritual mobilizes the dawn of a dream-like state in the audience as well. What generally comes across in the literature can be classified broadly into two categories: either vivid graphical descriptions of such bodily states or, at most, a link with a lack of inhibition. Kakar (1991) saw repressed fantasies in the bodies of possessed persons. A possessed person is, perhaps, merely a passionate lover, erotically invested in the body and its desires. The desire afflicts and seduces her while she endlessly engages with it, somewhat perversely.

Usually, at healing sites, possessed bodies buzzing with energy are chained, and these chains have locks. Each lock is for an affliction and is to be opened once the affliction is expelled. Locks are meant to keep things safe inside—by preventing any environmental impingement from entering. While the bad can be lived until it has been exhausted, the policy toward the unwanted intrusion from culture that once (b)locked body life is to lock it out. The possessed person's body in frenzy evokes horror tinged with awe in the audience, creating ample space for the enhancement of self-feeling by the narcissistic feed received by the body-ego through the uninhibited exhibition of emotions. As the paranoid haunted possessed person transforms into an exhibitionist in the state of *peshi*—the glaring gaze of the ghost is replaced by awe-filled looks from the audience marveling at power and audacity of the possessed person.

Once the knotted body finds expression in body-level omnipotence, a space is created for the person to begin to really notice their objects as they really are, with gratitude, and, gradually, there surfaces a drive for reparation toward the objects. It is only after this groundwork has been done that the scope for insight will open up. Eigen (2018) also suggested that the demon within diminishes after we begin to value what lies invisibilized in us. By giving the frozen part a space in which to unfreeze, either in a violent ritual of possession or in the space of therapy, a draining of destruction in frenzy or a taming of impulses occurs. Eigen considers psychopathic ideals and experiments in realizing them attempts to reclaim what has been left out of one's development. When a possessed person verbally abuses deities and abuses family members both verbally and physically, lacks remorse or concern and displays other destructive tendencies, they can be understood as attempting to break out of familial existence while remaining within the cultural realm. Breaking out and connecting coexist within the same behavioral paradigm. Beauty lies in this cooperation. It is in this space that the "ego extends its effective horizons and goes beyond itself by meeting and transforming psychic constellations previously alien to it, for example, representative of the id or shadow" (Eigen, 2018).

Just as Symington (1985) emphasizes the importance of interpreting the survival function of primitive omnipotence, Eigen, considers it a therapeutic error to interpret asocial acts committed during psychopathic episodes in terms of their supposed social meanings—for e.g., the responses they try to elicit from others. He wrote, "What for [the person in the grips of the episode] had constituted a momentary sense of exaltation in his self-experience is passed over in favor of emphasizing his underlying dependency and need to get something from others, that is, his weakness" (Eigen, 2018). The therapeutic error lies in attributing the need for power derived from such acts of violence to frustration or a feeling of impotence. One soon becomes deflated and succumbs to a psychology of need. What is required, Eigen suggests, is a mirroring of the patient's narcissism. Possession achieves this aim by evoking awe in the audience; through rituals and their emphasis on a fuller bodily experience, culture joins in celebrating the exhilarating sense of power that a possessed person exhibits. The fearful and awed audience is required to side with feelings of strength, not with the fear of weakness. Mirroring the sense of power makes it possible for the assimilation of the capacities and tendencies embodied in the pathology.

In Balaji, a fuller, more powerful bodily experience of the possessed is encouraged—a fuller and more forceful, frenzied *peshi*. The self is obliterated as the body twists and turns beyond recognition, until, through sufficient mirroring experiences, it can be embodied again. The host inhabits the ghost. Viewing *peshi* as a punishment by the deity is a denial of the wish to lose consciousness and further the dream. To an extent, our interviews offered Riya the space to relish the affect that accompanied her raw bodily performance in possession states. She could verbalize her hostility toward her family members, express her joy in destroying them and share in a tickled tone her imagination of the right man for her. The deviant part in Riya sought embodiment through the mirroring it hoped to receive in possession or in conversations with her healer and me. Through interviews, the body entered the world of words for the first time with all its aliveness; the mind–body dissociation was beginning to shatter.[5] It was evident that the self was striving for a closer mind–body connection, through living-out in possession and through conversations. Phases of psychopathic acting-out were in the service of repairing chronic narcissistic injury or the sense of injury. Such acts, attributed to the ghost, actually helped the damaged and constricted ego to enter and experience embodied life more fully.

The persistent attacks by the possessed persons on their family members, both verbal and physical, almost forcing them to address their needs and demands and actively participate in various healing rituals, and their awestruck descriptions of their own physical power during such vibrant states both hint at the fact that the reparative drive was at work. We get a glimpse of the reparative drive of the self in the seemingly deviant manifestations of the possessed person. Reparation is "the environment meeting the infant's experience of omnipotence; allowing itself to be created by the infant as in the area of transitional object and phenomenon, and allowing the infant to make his own contribution toward his caretaking environment" (Khan, 2018). Additionally, Atlas notes that, "reparation is an impulse of Eros, of life" (2022).

The research participants grappled with their own frightening erotic and aggressive emotions. However, from fear to relishing and living out the impulses in possession, they traversed a great expanse of psychic territory.

In the frenzy of possession, the body performs unusual feats. Eigen's theory of the alpha and the beta body is helpful in understanding this, as he notes

> that a ball player can make a great catch one moment and drop the ball the next. One moment, alpha body, the next a beta moment, one moment flowing, the next blocked, paralyzed. Likewise dancing. One moment you move fluidly and freely, dancing is wonderful; the next you are all left feet and stumble over yourself or your partner. Alpha movement one moment, beta another . . . Alpha one moment, loss of alpha another. (2011)

He went on to contend that what is required for this transition is "spirit" or "affective attitude":

> Affective attitudes mould the body and vice versa. This is the matter of spirit, some say intention or, I've sometimes called it, affective attitudes. There are affective attitudes that act as feasible frames of reference and modes of approach to experience, which enrich the human spirit and life, mediate the creation and digestion of experience. (2011)

Possession is one such mode of approaching experience, a mode that pushes the body into forms not possible otherwise. A healing site for possession, with all its paraphernalia should include music. Eigen noted that "[m]usic creates experience but also plays a role in processing experience . . . Dance creates experience and catalyses body processing of it at the same time" (2011). Additionally, this fuller bodily experience of living one's mess is made possible by the implicit requirement that one surrender to a higher power, for God sanctions the living out of impulses in their raw vitality. The stage is thus set for an alpha body experience, as the beta body, possessed with unthinkable and unlived elements of self, is given space to live out the unmetabolized impulses. To put it in more starkly Eigenian terms, in possession, the impulsive spirit conjured out of the affective attitude of faith in the presence of a non-judgmental God transforms the constricted beta body into an uninhibited alpha body.

After having witnessed such a frenzy, I noticed a change in my own body. It loosened up. There was a swing in my arms and a skip in my step. Such was the sense of omnipotence and power that seeped into me that I responded to a car being absent-mindedly reversed into me by waiting until it had almost hit me before slapping its rear window. The loud noise alerted the driver to my presence, and he stopped to give way.

It is as if the alpha body of a person in the frenzy of possession opens the knots in the body-self and makes possible a plurality of experiences. These knots are also "nots" or prohibitions that originate both outside and within the psyche. The movement from knots in the body being undone to openings appearing in thought is a gradual one. Bion (1990) began at one point to wonder if the body might play a role in creating the groundwork for thought. To him, the body appeared to be a storehouse carrying potential for thoughts that had never been thought before. Taking his idea of the bodily evacuation of incoherent beta elements further, he mused, "The poet Donne has written 'the blood spoke in her cheek . . . as if her body thought.'" This expresses exactly that intervening stage which, in Bion's grid, is portrayed on paper as a line separating beta elements from alpha elements. Bion cautioned that "[t]he practicing analyst has to be sensitive while the conversation is taking place to what is taking place . . . [A] situation of change from something which is not thought at all to something which is thought" (1990).

Much later, Armando Ferrari (2004, as quoted by Lombardi, 2008) and Lombardi (2008) took Bion's intuition further and attributed a centrality to the body that was largely missing in psychoanalytic thinking. The result was a systematic approach that focused on mind–body dialogue as a way of dealing analytically with disintegrated states. According to these thinkers, the maternal reverie (Bion, 1962b) and analyst's reverie in session serve to mediate between mind and body and lead to the representation of internal phenomena that previously lacked representation. The analyst must be the midwife for a thought that is struggling to be born. Drawing from Bion and Ferrari, Lombardi (2011) devised interventions in his clinical work with states like the bodily explosions of a possessed person. He proposed that providing a voice to such states and a tone to the affect accompanying them could help open/ create space for a better mind–body relationship and thereby an integration of crucial aspects of the self (Lombardi, 2011).

Psychodynamic work emphasizes the importance of ushering the analysand toward an articulation of their feelings—in effect, the importance of listening for the universalized part of the self's experience and facilitating its verbalization. Bion demonstrated the usefulness of listening for the potential to form links, even if the links were weak. Listening for this potential to form links can make the expression of the patient appear more meaningful to both the therapist and the patient and enable the latter to get in touch with the potential for psychic evolution. We fail to adopt this stance of listening because of our emphasis on the verbalization of psychic distress. Reflecting on wordless states, Eigen wrote:

> Some struggle to get into or out of words. The idea of putting feelings into words is an odd locution. How does one do that? Can you picture it? Sometimes I think of drawing feelings from a well and pouring them, a little at a time, into buckets of words. Often we do the reverse. We try to fill the well with words. Instead of drawing from a deep and bottomless well, we pour words into it. We lower word buckets down, hoping to catch something, often coming up with more words. Some of these words are juicy enough, some dry. But we fear that what we pull up is what we put in, missing living water. Winnicott calls attention to difficulties wordless people have in a world of words, Some babies specialize in thinking, and reach out for words; others specialize in auditory, visual, or other sensuous experience, and in memories and creative imagination of a hallucinatory kind, and these latter may not reach out for words. There is no question of the one being normal and the other abnormal. Misunderstandings may occur in debate through the fact that one person talking belongs to the thinking and verbalizing kind, while another belongs to the kind that hallucinates in the visual and auditory field instead of experiencing the self in words. Somehow

the word people tend to claim sanity, and those who see visions do not know how to defend their positions when accused of insanity. Logical argument really belongs to the verbaliser. Feeling or a feeling of certainty or truth or real belong to the other." (2011)

Possession involves experiencing at the level of the body; in a sense, its circumvention of adulteration using words makes it the purest form of experience, the one closest to an experience of self. Among my research participants, Shubha was the most articulate, owing to her association with the discipline of psychology. Possession helped her touch deeper layers of self than she otherwise could, and she was able thereby to learn more about her desires and struggles. To her, it was like a child's make-believe world, with the only difference being that she was playing with her family's beliefs. She came closer to her father and extracted warmth from her mother and from others, and perhaps even reached the neighborhood of the source of these desires—her body. The rage she felt toward the younger sister she envied was expressed through her body in all its force. Possession allowed her bodily closeness with her father, who was perceived by her as having become another mother—as if the father's body had developed breasts. Further, in contrast to the intrusive environment at home, possession allowed her body to move uninhibitedly.

In all these moments and through all these movements, Shubha was able to embody the haunting parts of her psyche. The beauty of her possession experience lay in the space that it created for passions of the body, for the aggressive to be voiced and the seductress to gain aliveness. Possession created a much-needed space for the establishment of a link between the dissociated body and mind. Psychology became an integral part of her preconscious and was employed to bring content from the unconscious to consciousness, where it could be further processed. Similarly, another possessed person would use the discipline of culture, with its myths and beliefs, to make her experience intelligible to herself. I refrained from commenting on Shubha's need to intellectualize emotional experience because I understood her intellectualization as a way of making unconscious contents psychically soluble until she had achieved enough psychic metabolism to be able to experience the experience rather than explain it away in terms of theories.

Later on, Shubha danced, touched herself while fantasizing about her lover's touch, urinated and perhaps experienced an orgasm. This sequence is very reminiscent of a thought by Bataille (1957) and later echoed by Alizade (1999), suggesting that eros was effectively a license to be alive until death. In bodily living-out, Shubha could touch her sexual desires until a peak was achieved that culminated in the orgasmic sensations experienced while urinating and the dawn of the realization that she was now a woman.

By repeatedly living out the need for an uninhibited free flow of impulses in the arena of possession created by culture, she was able to touch the guilt surrounding her destructive impulses, and this is what led to the recognition in her of her status as an incomplete being. Most importantly, this stage brought the (m)other's absence to the forefront of her psyche. From absence is born thought—her attempts to reflect upon and understand her experience—while the cost she had to pay was the death of her omnipotent, insatiable baby self. Contrary to the implications of Lombardi's work, in which the mutual dialogue between body and mind is brought about by the analyst's interpretations being designed to usher the body into analysis, here the possessing spirit brought together the body and mind through the chances it created for impulses to be lived out.

In her experience of possession, Shubha could mourn the loss of love objects. In possession, she could let the erotic enter the realm of her body, where it was lived in its concrete form. She was not entirely conscious in her use of the possession state; rather, she experienced it as a divided reality. On one side of the divide, she enjoyed the freedom that came through possession, and on the other, she felt trapped and engulfed. She was initially loved; her needs were gratified but not sufficiently for her to form the capacity to symbolize the breast in its absence. She was required to invest her subjective experience with cultural beliefs to render her possession valid. Her bizarre symptoms led to the strengthening of her belief in possession, and, in return, her erotic and hostile impulses came to be embodied. Possession gave body to both culture and the person. It balanced the weights of individual and culture. It provided the conditions for a variety of experiences, allowing Shubha to luxuriate in her hate on the way to rediscovering the love on which the hate was based.

In some cases, body parts were reconstituted. In others, parents originally constructed as tyrants were transformed into a couple in healing, with each member of the couple performing its function. The shift in Riya's *samkat*, which went from inhabiting her stomach to stimulating her vagina and appearing in the form of a penis, indicated that the child-part in her, capable of growth and aliveness, was maturing, developing sexual desires. This shift was facilitated by my being able to receive her communications—as mild as a sense of being cursed and as forceful as her wish to come alive through the sensuous bodily experience—nonjudgmentally, a stance that enabled a certain ease in our relationship but also between various parts of herself and, consequently, a loosening of the split-off tendencies. A dependence was thus created that led to secrets being shared and contained and the development of a sense of having been understood, a sense conveyed more palpably by Shubha.

In the larger context, this work has the responsibility of sharing that perhaps distress of the kind that has damage to body, mind, and relationships at its core, can be listened to not only in terms of conversations or speech that changes the concreteness of body but also in terms of the confidence and trust with which the patient begins relating. The researcher's role in the healing emanates from this stance—receiving the other nonjudgmentally, letting this other seep deep into one's unconscious, with an empathy that allows the other to be carried by the researcher, who then, through their apparatus, engages in psychic work with the deposited parts of the other, only to chew and return them in a detoxified form. In *Devi*, Khokha is the male self of Daya but also a male incarnation of the researcher. He witnesses dramatic rituals at home and takes up the empowering part of the rituals when he turns into a ghost to scare the Devi, without which his own terror, of not being invested in by his own mother, cannot be visited. I visited similar terrors in my participants. Although I watched Devi after gathering the stories of my participants, it retroactively gave me the sense that it is culture that first introduces us to spirits; only later do those spirits inhabit individuals who have been grappling with terrors.

In Indian culture, the healing potential is recognized and promoted in healing traditions and practices like yoga. Taoist monks in China use specific breathing and movement patterns to promote mental clarity and physical strength and undergird their techniques of meditation. Psychodynamically understood, impulse is the missing link that connects body and mind; this impulse is culturally understood as spirit. Therefore, the beauty of the possession experience lies in the potential of the possessing spirit to bring body and mind together, such that the performer and the audience are synchronous.

In keeping with Lombardi's approach, psychological growth has come to be known as an expression of those resources for containment that the mind can tap into when faced with the sensory emotional emanations of the body. I would like to believe that the mind's recourse to tapping into the resources available in culture in the form of spirits when confronted with unthinkable evocations arising from the body is a sign of some degree of psychological growth. It is in this possessed body that impulses and desires are embodied and made "alpha," thereby effecting an expansion of self.

THE WOUNDED HEALER

In the previous chapter, I mentioned Kakar's (2001) concept of "maternal enthrallment," which he presents as a condition that plagues the Indian male psyche. The Indian male infant enjoys a brief period of jouissance while discovering his own and his mother's sexuality. The father's arrival in this blissful haven introduces an interruption. However, the wish to return to the original erotic field and taste the luminous feelings associated with it lingers on. The result is an unconscious fantasy of perfect eternal sexual excitement tied to the mother's bodily and psychic presence.

However, the prospect of sexual intimacy with a woman evokes anxiety, as it resonates with deep incestuous desires and threatens to break the pleasurable unity with the mother in the fantasy world. According to Kakar, the Indian male in the state of maternal enthrallment resembles an infant seeking the woman sensually but splitting off the dreadful adult female sexuality, a dread that Nagpal (2000) observed is warded off by drawing strength from spiritual gurus and family patriarchs in a relationship of lifelong dependence upon them. This need for dependence was seen in both Ravi and Bishamber.

In both of them, it seemed as if the splitting in eros resulted in a failure to tame impulses that were yet to reach a conclusion. It was here that the mistranslation of eros happened. With Riya and Shubha, the *samkat* remained until the impulses had been adequately tamed, integrated sufficiently for them to move toward the life of work. Equipped with the *samkat* as a shield against God or expectations of good conduct, these women were able to experience a vicarious sense of other parts of themselves which were better understood by recourse to split-off psychic structures.

Bishamber was like a *duta* or a messenger of Balaji. With a mix of warmth, firmness, and selflessness, he brought possessed persons to the holy feet of Balaji, knowing that it was in doing so that his job was accomplished, that he could only do this much—leave the possessed person in the benevolence of Balaji. Having found an ideal parent, sibling and employer in Balaji, Bishamber did not feel upset about past losses. He came across as someone who had made peace with his past to a considerable extent. As I have mentioned, at a time during my research trip when I was especially scared of the sexual dangers abounding in the field, he protected me.

Ravi triumphed over his difficulties with determination and wisdom after traversing much grief and sadness. His zeal for helping other troubled, possessed persons and their families was admirable. The way Bishamber, Ravi, and Sanjeev catered to possessed persons was completely devoid of any conscious intention to satisfy materialistic needs. Even though my encounters have been with such compassionate healers, it is not to be denied that, in general, there is a lot of suspicion around the work a *bhagat* or healer does, which is seen by many as a way for them to take advantage of young women for sexual and monetary gains. The healers that I met had made attempts to evacuate the filthy parts of their respective ghosts, instead of promoting the integration of the ghosts with their personalities the way a contemporary healer or psychotherapist would. The techniques employed for this evacuation included seducing the ghost, exploiting it, resorting to physical violence to punish it, coercing it to apologize, recommending ceremonies, rituals, and prohibitions to discipline it, and also unwittingly facilitating a reconfiguration of relational dynamics in the family of the possessed person.

My curiosity was inclined toward understanding how people's patient-hood impacted the healer or, in their language, how the ghost would engage in battle with the healer. I was particularly drawn to the vulnerabilities in the healers. In Ravi's case, the vulnerability was in the sexual domain. In Bishamber's case, the vulnerability was in the narcissistic domain; it was more intense and involuntary. In a crucial moment, when he was expressing his dependence on me and experiencing fragility, I turned my gaze away. Before this happened, he was talking about his anger but in the mode of denial. He was bringing me closer to the anger that lay frozen inside him. Owing to the limits of my containing function in that moment, and perhaps to deepen that state, I turned to look at a wailing possessed woman, causing the narcissistically fragile part in him to come to the forefront and him to enter what is best described as a deep sulk. The omnipotence of Balaji had created a compliant and devoted part in him, but not a creative part. Just when he was about to express something intimate, I unconsciously received a slightly deeper layer of it—rage and hostility.

My experience with Bishamber made me aware of my limitations, and it was with this awareness that, two years later, I met Ravi, whom I now think of as a younger version of Bishamber. In Ravi, I encountered a certain incompleteness because the process of binding assisted by eros had thrown up a pattern that presented itself as wanderlust, which he admitted was a chal-lenge and expected me to be able to help him with. In a rather prescriptive stance I told him to focus on his relationship with his wife. As Ravi was able to let it become explicit to me that he was in a way managing to deal with his perverse tendencies, the tendencies did not have him fully in their grip. Further, the fact that he did not see the tendencies as the work of ghost tells us that he had managed to carve out a sphere of sexuality and eros away from the domain of religion. Ravi is a healer who had partly managed to evolve processes of sexual fantasy at a distance from his religious approach to heal-ing, and he had drawn closer as a result to the psychotherapeutic, dyadic approach to healing.

And then there was Sanjeev, whose dream of tearing the beautiful woman apart gripped me. The dread of the feminine was at play in a relatively starker way in Sanjeev. His nightmare was his attempt to cope with this dread. His having shared the dream put me in the same position as Botella and Botella (2005) when they had worked with a severely autistic child. By referring to the fantasy of tearing the woman apart, Sanjeev affected my listening. Later, when he called me, panting, there was a crescendo in his excitement suggest-ing that he was masturbating; he was enacting an intriguing play that I could not process and could only withdraw from. Today, emboldened by the work of Botella and Botella (2005), I ask—what happened to me, and if it were to happen today, how would I see meaning in it? Today, I might invite him to see the infant behind his perverse adult part. Back then, perhaps, he sensed that I was as afraid as he was. Had this encounter occurred in person, there is a good chance I might have assumed that he was attacking me, trying to tear *me* apart.

The episode played itself out over the telephone at an odd hour of the night, a time at which things are often naturally construed as sexual. Two features of his "method" stand out—firstly, that he was letting me know he wanted to enter me; secondly, that he chose to approach me through a phone call because of his dread of women. If I had met him and personally conveyed to him that fantasies about others were not uncommon but that it was important to only be so affected by them as to secretly masturbate, is to suggest immense blockage and an unthinkable terror that says—"I feel this urge, I feel too small here, I get daunted by the big cavity that a woman represents, the best that I can do is to reduce it."

CLINCHING THE IMAGES OF HEALING

Devi demonstrated that terrors can be wished away by cultivating a God within the space of the home, where God, or a goddess, can appear and take possession of a person to communicate with people's woes and suffering. This was my first glimpse of culture organizing narratives to indicate that gods can appear in all kinds of forms. Humans can speak through the gods rather than having to necessarily start at the lowly order of goblins and ghosts. *Devi* offered a narrative that enabled curiosity in me. *How do gods come closer to us?*

The baby-self in my research participants was constantly wandering. This baby-self sought God through the recognition of its aliveness and acceptance of its instinctual intensities and agonies. This baby-self, encapsulated in the ghost, feared abandonment and found solace in the omnipresent God. The mythical solution of the ghost lies in rituals meant to evacuate it. In the cases of Riya and Shubha, however, this solution did not work. They were far too well located in their bodies for them to unambivalently want it to be eaten up by the Devi or taken away in a ritual. Cultural processes provided opportunities to either instantly vanquish the ghost or tame it as a *duta*—but it was eventually left at the feet of God, who would then set the ghost on its path toward *moksha* or salvation.

The most important part of the ritual of exorcism is the space it allows for the baby-self to come out in bodily aliveness. Over the course of multiple, recurring opportunities to do this, the un-lived is somewhat lived or tamed. Not only do the mind and body come together, but another duality, which was brought to my notice by Kakar (2008) is also encountered in the trance of possession. Kakar thought of a truly alive ritual as involving a paternal, conservative component that protected against perceived dangers and closed the psyche and a maternal transformative component that augmented personal identity by opening up the psyche to new experiences. Atlas's (2016) thoughts on the enigmatic and pragmatic parts of the mother–infant encounter are very relevant here. According to her, the "pragmatic" includes the practical provisions that the mother offers through her care and nursing of the infant, while the "enigmatic" includes the mysterious communication unconsciously shared between the mother and infant. It is as if, through various rituals and ceremonies, culture-as-mother enables the "pragmatic" while the more ambiguous transformative messages that underlie these rituals constitute the "enigmatic" parts of the encounter between person and culture-as-mother.

In retrospect now, the use of prayer and its effect on Riya are seen by me to have clearly incorporated the element of the transformative mother, allowing Riya to open herself up to the good object, and the protective father element, protecting her identity by being distant and non-intrusive and nonthreatening. Kakar observes about possession rituals that

> Such rituals with embodied deities or spirits from another world can produce a mild state of altered consciousness in even the most skeptical of onlookers. The dramatic aspect of these healing and worship rituals is certainly one reason why they can shake an onlooker's habitual way of experiencing the world, give ordinary reality a significance it did not have earlier, even when he knows that what he is witnessing is just a "drama," a performance. (Kakar, 2008)

In possession, evacuation serves the purpose of protecting one from the dangers posed by an aspect of oneself or by others. The disavowed parts of oneself are deposited in the image of the ghost and identified with in possession while one remains protected from the dangers posed by one's destructive and sexual impulses. The angry and desirous part is not lost but rather preserved. The dual function of a ritualistic belief lies in the mother/ transformative part creating an opening for new experience, allowing for the experiencing of primitive longings through the ghosts that haunt, while the father/protective function guards one's sense of identity as a person who is free from evil.

This groundwork is partially achieved in Balaji when the possessed persons are encouraged to enter a fuller trance state. The visiting healers and the wise priests of the Balaji temple refer to this state as "*khul ke peshi,*" which roughly translates to "a fuller manifestation of the ghost." Musical instruments are beaten and played vigorously as a crowd surrounds the possessed person, loudly singing, chanting, and clapping. The rhythmic music, chanting, and clapping infuses one's being and fosters transportation into a different world—a world where the body is twisted beyond recognition, going back to the state in which it was only becoming, not-yet-embodied. The lack of the alpha function implies that emergent sensations in the body evoke terror, and the body is not experienced as one's own. This state is best described in Freud's (1938) words: "Psyche is extended; knows nothing about it." As the stage for exorcism is set, all bodily inhibitions are lifted and one is free, encouraged to dance, to move the way one likes.

This reminds me again of one of the Botellas' (2005) autistic patients, with whom the analysts' spontaneous use of the language of fairy tales only served to advance "preconscious formations susceptible of attracting, one day, other representations, of serving as manifest content." The hope that, in time, other representations (closer to consciousness) would emerge and serve as manifest content seems to guide the use of myths, their elaborations in sermons, hymns, and rituals and my interventions through prayer with the aim of gently nudging the person toward some form. When faced with such states, which are commonly seen in possessed persons, a psychotherapist may benefit from using myths, legends and the creative aspects of ghosts and gods as resources residing in the patient's preconscious.

In the psychoanalytic work undertaken by me during my research, my being able to open a space in which the participants felt heard was a maternal act, while my phrasing prayers and sharing my understanding with them, compelling them to pause and reflect on their experiences, were paternal acts. The aspect that promoted thinking and reflection was, in a sense, saying, "This is something you have not thought of. Why not think about this now? Let's see where we reach." Looking back now, I realize that this paternal act separates the other and encourages them to think, values the thinking that is accomplished, and does not dismiss the destination to which the thinking leads.

Another paternal aspect of our conversations was their fictional element or the as-if quality. It was this fictional element that took the edge off the harsh internal and external realities. The fictional quality made it possible for us to dream. The researcher in me created a bridge by dint of my need to understand the mess, causing the participant's need for evacuation to be postponed and replaced by an implicit demand made on them to help me extract, within the limits of each person's capacities, the healing potential from seemingly bizarre states, until a state was reached in which one could part with one's ghosts. In this process of mutual healing, the researcher in me was left with the sense that, although I had awakened to parts of myself, my research participants had not been—but my hope was that they would be.

Today, my participants can *live* in relationships. Shubha is happily married and the mother of a beautiful boy. Riya, too, is happily married to a man she described (in a tongue-in-cheek way) as nothing like her father. He is very supportive of her career. Ravi has expanded his business and continues to serve the possessed. My hope is that Bishamber, too, is continuing to provide his service with warmth and compassion. Just as Khokha represented emotional aliveness for Daya, my nephews and my daughter represented the same for me during my periods of research and writing, respectively, allowing the researcher in me to become more child-like and thus creative, facilitating the emergence of child-like awe, curiosity, and innocence and the ability to express dependence and to trust that the dependence would be met with favorably. The researcher in this work is not only learning and orienting herself to thought-provoking texts, but is also, in her becoming, encountering the child-parts in her.

Insofar as spirits possess the body, they are also attempts to create new relationships between that inside which is lost and that outside which seemed hostile in the past. The possession experience also cultivates faith in the outside's conduciveness to the generation of newer forms by which the loss of the inside can be compensated for. In culture's clinic, ghosts are also imagined as entities that need to be allowed to fulfill their unfulfilled desires. They are seen as awaiting their fate, in limbo. They are deposited in the clinic with the hope that they will transform into the *duta*. As a *duta*, the ghost is not banished; it finds a home. Possession, then, brings with it the possibility of a *duta* emerging, a part that will serve others with kindness and compassion. Perhaps this is the conception of beauty that Indian culture associates with terrifying states—the conception that ghosts can potentially, eventually transform into messengers or even ancestral spirits. As *duta*, the ghost receives the love of God.

How did this *duta* part appear in four case stories? We find that in all the stories, the last shots show the protagonists returning to their families. In Riya's case, that family was reconstituted, but in terms of functions that were relevant to her modern, futuristic self. In Shubha's case, it was her active, excited imagination of dancing, of an active relationship with the desire to have a companion, a lover, a family. In Ravi, it was his desire to share difficulties, not for the purpose of acting on them but to have them received. In Bishamber's case, it was the act of awakening me to guilt when I was drawn away from his somewhat grandiose self to someone writhing in pain. My guilt stems from the belief that at a different stage of life I could have given him more. This remains the unfulfilled ghost in me (my *atripta bhut*)—guilt arising from the perception that I failed to be the container he needed.

I believe love brings us closer to other peoples' entirely native images of where they want to be, while simultaneously making us aware of ways in which we are yet to complete ourselves. In that sense, we begin to see ourselves as *dutas*, messengers of love. The provision by culture of a receptacle in which something disavowed can be seen as originating outside is an offshoot of an understanding of love that takes the form of deep fantasies enabling us to not only visualize but very deeply imagine, wish, desire that both parties experience an exclusive, mutual claim over each other. It is the kind of love in which one may say, "This other can go inside me, inside my life, traverse me and find beauty everywhere, just as I have an identical right to do the same to/with it/him/her/them." Possessing each other in this manner is the backbone of the imagination of love that I am referring to.

Perhaps the ghosts that haunt are the parts of us that long for such freeing love, parts that long to belong to the haunted. A ghost story, then, is also a love story. Possession states are feeble, misdirected nightmarish attempts to connect with the emptiness in place of which the possession serves a partial function. If possessing forces can be brought in contact with benevolent processes, a transformation of those forces into something akin to love can be accomplished. This is where beauty in brokenness appears. In retrospect, I realize, this work has been facilitated by the spirit of psychoanalysis that is guided by Freud's conviction that it is essentially through love that healing happens.

In the Bionian sense, this work awakened me so I could incorporate dreaming and break myself off from the vicious circle of sleeping-waking-sleeping. The awakened one has the capacity to understand the dream and its relationship with reality and to mull over early losses and the terrors emanating from them. Set on a path toward evolution, I could creatively bridge gaps between my own early losses and early deprivations, the sources of terror.

Now that we are at the end of this journey, let me share with you one last clinical vignette to give you a sense of how my research shaped me as a psychotherapist. I began this book by describing an encounter between me and my little daughter, whom I was trying to usher toward sleeping/dreaming. At the end of this book, I think it only fitting that I describe an encounter between me and a girl who found it extremely difficult to dream.

Years after I had completed the research that produced this book, I sat in my clinic waiting for Alice. Alice suffered from psychosis. I remember the first time I saw her—a short, fragile-looking young girl making every attempt to hide between the folds of her oversized clothes, her face hidden behind disheveled hair. At the very first sight of her, I wondered whether something in her wished to remain anonymous, to not be found.

I was told by her mother that Alice experienced vaginal discharge every time she heard any loud noises. There was nothing medically wrong with her. Sometimes, Alice felt that she was a man. She also hallucinated that her body grew taller sometimes, while at other times it shrank. Perhaps this is why I thought of Alice from *Alice in Wonderland* when I had to choose a pseudonym for her.

Alice was the youngest of three children. It was revealed to me that her father was a scary figure for both Alice and her mother. The mother held herself responsible for Alice's condition, linking it to her preference for a male child when she was expecting Alice.

A strange stench emanated from Alice's body, which made me feel disgusted but also made me aware that she remained oblivious to her own body and its needs. Our work began. Vaginal discharge coincided with emotional discharge in sessions. The vaginal discharge also occurred at home, whenever she heard the voice of her father. Each time the topic of her father came up in our work, it was followed by silence and an intense urge to defecate or urinate. I wondered what had to be excreted—Fear? Rage? Fear of rage? Erotic feelings and fear of them? I did not know. One thing was clear—her body became a medium for the evacuation of whatever feelings were difficult for her mind to process. I sometimes experienced confusion and panic in my work with her, not knowing how to resolve the many questions that she stirred in me, But I recalled Ashok Nagpal telling me during my research (as my mentor) that the beauty in our work lay in persistent exploration in the face of all kinds of terror.

My sessions with Alice felt alive. However, one day we reached a dead end. She walked into the session just like she always did—like an old lady with a hunched back, dragging her feet. At some point during the session, she heard a car honking outside the clinic and suddenly started screaming.

A: Now I am becoming tall! Just now! There was a noise! I am becoming tall. It's the cars. They are doing it. I am growing tall . . . I am growing tall . . .

Her body grew tense and her eyes went wide as she continued to scream.

A: It is not stopping! Tell me?! Tell me?! What's happening to me? What's happening to me?! Tell me!

Tell her what? What was there to tell? What was I to say? I felt her panic seeping into me. Even my questions abandoned my mind. Pure bodily sense kicked in. In response to her persistent screaming—"Tell me! Tell me!"—I felt my breathing constricting and goose pimples rising on my skin. Was I also abandoning my body?

She grew taller, and my mind shrank. I had no instant answer to offer to ease her pain. I did not know what to say. Yet something in me refused to collude with her tallness. Against the backdrop of her insistent pleas, which were almost commands, I was touching panic.

Me: I don't know. I am small.

A: (calmer) I just shrank back.

With her having shrunk in size, perhaps we had reached a certain sameness. I found my thinking being unlocked and a link with psychic reality being reinstated. An image sprang into my mind out of nowhere, of the puffer fish, which inflates itself in the face of any danger in its environment, giving predators the illusion that it, the potential prey, is larger in size than imagined. This is witnessed quite commonly in the animal kingdom. I decided to use this gift that had emerged from the meeting of our minds.

Me: Loud noises can seem threatening. Perhaps growing in size is your way of defending yourself against some threat?

A: See!? Now the discharge has come out! Just now! I liked what you said and the discharge just came out. See! This is how my brain works!

To be understood was pleasurable. To feel understood was to feel real.

She felt touched. Perhaps we were not just emotionally in sync, but also physically. Conversations with possessed persons brought about in me an ease with the admission of my ignorance and shaped me into an embodied listener. Perhaps, through my listening, Alice received a sense of embodiment and a surface that she could hold on to as "real." My attunement to Alice's sense of her body was made evident through the emergence of the puffer fish. Her bodily sensations acquired new meaning.

The mutual impact of my research participants on me and of me on them awakened the dreamer in me. This was only possible because I surrendered "the desire to learn from experience" (Ogden, 2005), much like how one surrenders to sleep and awaits dreams. It is this waiting for the dream that Nagpal alludes to when he notes that "the psychoanalytic method lies in loving 'I don't know' (not knowing)" (2023). In this state of love, the other is welcomed in one's internal space, both spark something in each other and get past potential alienation and begin to experience psychic growth.

My conversations, detailed in this book, taught me how psychoanalysis is essentially a "talking cure" facilitated by love for even the most alien, othered, ghostly parts of us.

References

Achreja, Vikram. 2013. *"Who Are The Demons That Devi Slays?"* In *Times of India: The Speaking Tree*, October 10, 2013.

Ahuja, Naman. P. 2018. "The Dead, Dying, and Post-death: Visual Exemplars and Iconographic Devices." In *Imaginations of Death and the Beyond in India and Europe*, edited by Gunter Blamberger & Sudhir Kakar, 85–100. Springer Nature Singapore Pte. Ltd. 2018.

Alizade, Alcira Mariam, and R. Horacio Etchegoyen. *Feminine Sensuality.* London: Karnac Books, 1999.

Atlas, Galit. *The Enigma of Desire: Sex, Longing, and Belonging in Psychoanalysis.* Routledge, New York. 2015.

———. *Emotional Inheritance: a therapist, her patients, and the legacy of trauma.* (First edition.). Little Brown Spark, 2022.

Atlas, Galit, and Aron, Lewis. *Dramatic Dialogue: Contemporary Clinical Practice*. United Kingdom: Taylor & Francis, 2017.

Bataille, Georges. *"El erotismo."* Buenos Aires: Sur, 1957. Page 103.

Benjamin, Jessica. "Father and Daughter: Identification with Difference: A Contribution to Gender Heterodoxy*."* *Psychoanalytic Dialogues*, 1 (1991): 277–300.

———. "Beyond doer and done to: An intersubjective view of thirdness." *Psychoanalytic Quarterly*, 73 (2004): 5–46.

Benjamin, Jessica and Atlas, Galit. "The 'too muchness' of excitement: Sexuality in light of excess, attachment and affect regulation." *International Journal of Psychoanalysis*, 96 (2015): 39–63.

Bick, Esther. "The experience of the skin in early object-relations." *The International journal of Psychoanalysis* 49 (2) (1968): 484–46.

Bilu, Yoram. "Dybbuk Possession and Mechanisms of Internalization and Externalization: A Case Study." In *Projection, Identification and Projective Identification*, edited by Joseph Sandler, 163–78. Karnac, London. 1989.

Bion, Wilfred. "On Hallucination." *International Journal of Psychoanalysis. Sept.– Oct.*; 39 (5) (1958): 341–49.

———. "Attacks on linking" In *Second Thoughts*. London: William Heinemann, 1967, pp. 93–109, First published in *Int. J. Psychoanal.* 40 (1959).

———. "Learning From Experience." London: Karnac, 1962a. 1984.

———. "A Theory of Thinking." *International Journal of Psychoanalysis*, 43 (1962b): 306–10.

———. *Elements of Psychoanalysis*. London: Karnac, 1963.

———. "Catastrophic Change," unpublished paper, 1966.

———. "On arrogance." *International Journal of Psychoanalysis*, 39 (1958): 144–46. Reprinted in Bion (1967). Second Thoughts. New York: Jason Aronson; pp. 86–92.

———. "Notes on Memory and Desire." In *Cogitations*. 1967a. London: Karnac, 1992.

———. "Emotional turbulence." In *Clinical Seminars and Four Papers*. Abingdon: Fleetwood Press. 1976.

———. *Brazilian Lectures*. London: Karnac Books. 1990.

———. *Cogitations*. London: Karnac Books. 1992.

Boddy, Janice. "Spirit Possession Revisted: Beyond Instrumentality." *Annual Review of Anthropology* 23 (1994): 407–34.

Bollas, Christopher. "Extractive Introjection." In *The Shadow of the Object: Psychoanalysis of the Unthought Known*. New York: Columbia University Press. 1987.

———. *Hysteria.* London & New York: Routledge, Taylor & Francis Group. 2000.

———. The Infinite Question. Routledge/Taylor & Francis Group. 2009.

———. *Forces of Destiny: Psychoanalysis and Human Idiom*. (1st ed.). United Kingdom: Routledge. 2018.

Bolognini, Stefano. *Secret Passages: The Theory and Technique of Interpsychic Relations*. United Kingdom: Taylor & Francis, 2010.

Botella, Cesar, and Botella, Sara. *The Work of Psychic Figurability: Mental States without Representation. Brunner-Routledge*. Taylor and Francis Group: Hove and New York. 2005.

Britton, Ronald. *Belief and imagination: Explorations in Psychoanalysis*. London and New York: Routledge. 2003.

Bromberg, Philip. M. *"Standing in the spaces: The multiplicity of self and the psychoanalytic relationship."* *Contemporary Psychoanalysis*, 32(4) (1996): 509–35.

———. Standing in the spaces: Essays on clinical process, trauma, and dissociation. Hillsdale, NJ: Analytic Press. 1999.

———. *"The gorilla did it: Some thoughts on dissociation, the real, and the really real."* Psychoanalytic Dialogues, 11 (3) (2001): 385–404.

———. *"One need not be a house to be haunted."* Psychoanalytic Dialogues, 13 (2003): 689–709.

Carlson, Elizabeth A., Yates, Tuppett M., and Sroufe, L. Alan. "Development of Dissociation and Development of the Self." In *Dissociation and the Dissociative Disorders*. edited by Paul F. Dell and John A. O'Neil, 39–52. New York: Routledge. 2010.

Civitarese, Giuseppe. *"Truth and the Unconscious in Psychoanalysis."* New York: Routledge, 2016.

———. "The concept of time in Bion's 'A Theory of Thinking." *The International journal of psycho-analysis*, 100 (2) (2019): 182–205.

Chefetz, Richard A., and Bromberg, Philip, M. "Talking with 'me' and 'not-me': A dialogue." *Contemporary Psychoanalysis*, 40(3) (2004): 409–64.

Crapanzano Vincent, and Garrison Vivian. *Case Studies in Spirit Possession.* New York: Wiley, 1977.

———. *Tuhami—Portrait of a Moroccan.* Chicago and London: The University of Chicago Press, 1980.

Dilthey, Wilhelm. *Introduction to the Human Sciences.* Princeton: Princeton University Press, 1991.

Dwyer, D. G., Dwyer, G. (2003). The Divine and the Demonic: Supernatural Affliction and Its Treatment in North India. United Kingdom: Taylor & Francis.

Eaton, Jeffrey L. "The obstructive object." *Psychoanalytic Review*, 92 (3) (2005): 355–72.

Eigen, Michael. "On Demonized Aspects of the Self" In *The Electrified Tightrope.* Routledge. 2018.

———. "The Area of Faith in Winnicott, Lacan, and Bion." In *The Electrified Tightrope.* Routledge. 2018.

———. "Psychopathy and Individuation." In *The Electrified Tightrope.* Routledge. 2018.

———. The Psychotic Core. Routledge. 2019.

———. Contact with the Depths. London: Routledge. 2011.

Erikson, E. "Inner Space and Outer Space: Reflections on Womanhood." In *Daedalus, Vol. 93, No. 2, The Woman in America* (Spring 1964): 582–606.

Fairbairn, William, R. D. "Schizoid factors in the personality." In *Psychoanalytic Studies of the Personality,* Boston: Routledge, 1940. 3–27.

Ferrari, Armando B. *From the Eclipse of the Body to the Dawn of Thought.* London: Free Association Books, 2004.

Fonagy, Peter, and Target, Mary. "Dissociation and trauma." In *Current Opinion in Psychiatry,* 8 (1995): 161–66.

Freed, Stanley A., and Freed, Ruth S. "Spirit Possession as Illness in a North Indian Village." *Ethnology*, 3 (1964): 152–71.

Freud, Sigmund. and Breuer, Josef. "On the psychical mechanism of hysterical phenomena: preliminary communication." *Standard Edition*, 2 (1893): 1–17.

Freud, Sigmund. *The Standard Edition of the Complete Psychological Works of Sigmund Freud,* 7 (1905): 255–68.

———. Totem and Taboo. In *Standard Edition,* 13 (1913): 1–161.

———. On narcissism: an introduction. In *Standard Edition,* 14 (1914): 30–59.

———. Instincts and their Vicissitudes. In *Standard Edition,* 14 (1915): 111–40.

———. Mourning and melancholia. In *Standard Edition,* 14 (1917): 239–58.

———. Seventeenth Century Demonological Neurosis. In *Standard Edition,* 19 (1923): 69–105.

———. Findings, Ideas, Problems. In *Standard Edition,* 23 (1938): 299–300.

———. An Outline of Psychoanalysis. Wiltshire: Redwood Press Ltd. 1940.

———. Studies on Hysteria. New York: Basic Books Preliminary Communication, 1957. 3–19.

Gellner, David N. "Priests, Healers, Mediums and Witches: The Context of Possession in the Kathmandu Valley, Nepal." In *Man,* New Series, 29(1) (1994): 27–48.

Green, Andre. "The dead mother." In *On Private Madness.* London: The Hogarth Press Ltd, 1986.

―――. "Andre Green." In *The Inward Eye: Psychoanalysts reflect on Their Lives and Work*. Edited by Raymond, Laurie W., and Rosbrow-Reich, Susan. New Jersey: The Analytic Press, Inc., 2013. 77–105.

―――. *The Work of the Negative*. London: Free Association Books. 1999.

―――. *Psychoanalysis: A Paradigm for Clinical Thinking*. London: Free Association Books. 2005.

Greenberg, Robin E. "Transformative secrets and the privacy of analysis." In *Jung Journal: Culture and Psyche*, 9 (2015): 80–81.

Grotstein, James S. "Forgery of the Soul: Psychogenesis of Evil." In *Evil: Self and Culture*. Edited by Marie Coleman Nelson & Michael Eigen. Vol. IV, Self-in-Process Series. New York: Human Sciences Press, 1984. 203–26.

Guba, Egon G., & Lincoln, Yvonna S. "Competing paradigms in qualitative research." In *Handbook of qualitative research*. Edited by Norman K Denzin and Yvonna S Lincoln, Thousand Oaks, CA: Sage. 1994. 105–17.

Harper, Edward. B. "Spirit Possession and Social Structure." In *Anthropology on the March: Recent Studies of Indian Beliefs, Attitudes and Social Institutions*. Edited by Bala Ratnam, L. K., and L. Krishna Anantha Krishna Iyer. Madras: Book Centre, 1963. 165–97.

Holl, Adolf, & Kakar, Sudhir. On the Indian view of things. Published September 16, 2006. Original in German, Translated by Simon Garnett First published by Wespennest 144 (2006) (German version).

Holmes, Joshua. *A practical psychoanalytic guide to reflexive research: The reverie research method*. Abingdon & New York: Routledge, 2018.

Hopkins, Brooke. "Jesus and Object-Use: A Winnicottian Account of the Resurrection Myth." PSYART: http://psyartjournal.com/article/show/hopkins_phd-jesus_and_object_use_a_winnicottian_acco. July 22, 2021. In Transitional objects and potential spaces: Literary uses of D. W. Winnicott. Edited by Peter L. Rudnytsky, 1993. 249–60. Columbia University Press. (Reprinted from "International Review of Psycho-Analysis," 16, 1989)

Huskinson, Lucy. "Analytical Psychology and Spirit Possession: Towards a Non-Pathological Diagnosis of Spirit Possession" In *Spirit Possession and Trance: New Interdisciplinary Perspectives*. Edited by Bettina E. Schmidt and Lucy Huskinson. London: Continuum International Publishing Group, 2010.

Jadhav, S. "The ghostbusters of psychiatry." In *The Lancet*. 345(8953) (1995): 808–10.

James, William. *The Varieties of Religious Experience*. Edited by Matthew Bradley. Oxford World's Classics. London, England: Oxford University Press, 2012.

Janet, Pierre. *Psychological Automatism: An Experimental Psychology Essay on the Lower Forms of Human Activity*. Alcan. 1889.

―――. *The mental state of hystericals: A study of mental stigmata and mental accidents*. Translated by Caroline Rollin Corson. New York-London: G. P. Putnam's Sons; The Knickerbocker Press, 1901.

Kakar, Sudhir. *Shamans, mystics, and doctors: A psychological inquiry into India and its healing traditions*. Chicago, IL: University of Chicago Press, 1991.

―――. *The Essential Writings of Sudhir Kakar*. New York: Oxford University Press, 2001.

————. *Culture and Psyche: Selected Essays*. New York: Oxford University Press, 2008.

————. *Mad and Divine*. India: Penguin Books India, 2008.

————. *The Inner World: A Psychoanalytic Study of Childhood and Society in India*. Fourth Edition. New York: Oxford University Press, 2012.

Kakar, Sudhir, and Sarin, Madhu. "A Conversation with Sudhir Kakar." In *India International Centre Quarterly*, 35 (2) (2008): pp. 168–82. India International Centre, Delhi, India.

Kapferer, Bruce. *A Celebration of Demons: Exorcism and the Aesthetics of Healing in Sri Lanka*. Washington: Berg Smithsonian Institution Press, 1991.

Khan, Masud. The Evil Contest: From Cumulative Trauma to Ego Mastery. In *Evil, Self, and Culture*. M. C. Nelson and M. Eigen, Eds. New York: Human Sciences. (1984).

Klein, Melanie. "The development of a child." In *International Journal of Psycho-Analysis*, 4 (1923): 419–74.

————. "Infant Analysis." In *International Journal of Psychoanalysis*, 7 (1926): 31–63.

————. "Early Stages of the Oedipus Conflict." In *International Journal of Psychoanalysis*. 9 (1928): 167–80; reprinted in Klein (1975), vol. 1, pp. 186–98.

————. "The importance of symbol-formation in the development of the ego." In *The International Journal of Psychoanalysis*, 11 (1930): 24–39.

————. "A contribution to the psychogenesis of manic-depressive states." In International Journal of Psycho-Analysis, 16 (1935): 145–74.

————. "Mourning and its relation to manic-depressive states." In The International Journal of Psychoanalysis, 21 (1940): 125–53.

Kohut, Heinz and Goldberg, Arnold. *How does Analysis Cure?* Chicago, IL: University of Chicago Press, 2013.

————. *The Analysis of the Self: A Systematic Approach to the Psychoanalytic treatment of Narcissistic Personality Disorders*. Chicago, IL: University of Chicago Press, 2009.

Kristeva, Julia. *Powers of Horror: An Essay on Abjection*. New York: Columbia University Press, 1982.

Kumar, Mansi. "In a bid to restate the culture-psyche problematic: Revisiting the essential writings of Sudhir Kakar." In *Psychoanalytic Quarterly*, LXXIV (2005): 561–87.

Kumar, Mansi, Dhar Anup & Mishra, Anurag. *Psychoanalysis from the Indian Terroir: Emerging Themes in Culture, Family, and Childhood*. New York: Lexington Books, 2018.

Lamott, Anne. Bird by Bird: Instructions on Writing and Life. United Kingdom: Canongate Books, 2020.

Laplanche, Jean. "Psychoanalysis, time and translation." In *Jean Laplanche: Seduction, translation, drives*. Edited by John Fletcher & Martin Stanton. London, UK: Institute of Contemporary Arts, 1992. pp. 161–77.

Levinas, Emmanuel. 2000. *Alterity and Transcendence*. Translated by Michael B. Smith. New York: Columbia University Press.

References

————. *Totality and Infinity: An Essay on Exteriority*. Netherlands: Springer Netherlands, 2012.

Lewis, Ioan M. "Spirit Possession and Deprivation Cults." In *Man*, 1(3) (1966): 307–29.

————. *Ecstatic Religion: An Anthropological Study of Spirit Possession and Shamanism*. Harmondsworth: Penguin Books, 1978.

————. *Religion in Context: Cults and Charisma*. United Kingdom: Cambridge University Press, New York. 1996.

Lombardi, Riccardo. "The body in the analytic session: Focusing on the body-mind link." In *International Journal of Psychoanalysis*, 89 (2008): 89–110.

————. "The body, feelings, and the Unheard Music of the Senses." In *Contemporary Psychoanalysis*, 47(1) (2011).

Masih, Shalini. "Devil! Sing me the Blues: Story of a Life Struggling to be Born in Being and Work" In *Rethinking the Relation between Women and Psychoanalysis: Loss, Mourning, and the Feminine*. Edited by Hada Soria Escalante. New York: Lexington Books, 2019. 55–74.

Matte-Blanco, Ignacio. *Thinking, feeling and being: Clinical Reflections on the fundamental antimony of human beings and world*. London, New York, NY: Routledge, 1988.

Meltzer, Donald, and Williams, Meg H. *The apprehension of beauty: The role of aesthetic conflict in development, art and violence*. Karnac, London: The Harris Meltzer Trust, 2008.

Merleau-Ponty, Maurice. *Phenomenology of Perception*. N.p.: Taylor & Francis, 2013.

McWilliams, Nancy. *Psychoanalytic Diagnosis: Understanding Personality Structure in the Clinical Process*. New York: Guilford Press, 2011.

Mitchell, Juliet. *Mad Men and Medusas: Reclaiming Hysteria and the Effect of Sibling Relationships on the Human Condition*. London: Penguin, 2000.

Mitrani, Judith. *Ordinary People and Extraordinary Protections*. London: Brunner-Routledge, 2001.

Nabokov, Isabelle. *Religion Against the Self: An Ethnography of Tamil Rituals*. Oxford: Oxford University Press, 2000.

Nagpal, Ashok. "Cultural continuity and change in Kakar's works: some reflections." In *International Journal of Group Tensions*, 29 (2000): 285–321.

Neumann, Erich. *Depth psychology and a new ethnic*. New York: Harper Torchbooks. 1973.

Obeyesekere, Gananath. *Medusa's Hair: An Essay on Personal Symbols and Religious Experience*. Chicago, IL: University of Chicago Press, 1981.

Ogden, Thomas. *The Primitive Edge of Experience*. 1st ed. London and New York: Routledge. 1992.

————. "A new reading of the origins of object-relations theory." In *International Journal of Psychoanalysis*. 83 (2002a): 767–82.

————. *Conversations at the Frontier of Dreaming*. London: Karnac (Books) Ltd, 2002b.

————. "On psychoanalytic writing" In *The International journal of psycho-analysis*, 86 (2005a): 15–29.

————. *This Art of Psychoanalysis—Dreaming Undreamt Dreams and Interrupted Cries*. East Sussex: Routledge, 2005.

————. "Intuiting the Truth of What's Happening: on Bion's Notes on Memory and Desire," In *The Psychoanalytic Quarterly*, 84:2, (2015): 285–306.

————. "How I talk with my patients." In *The Psychoanalytic Quarterly*, 87 (2018): 399–413.

————. *Subjects of Analysis*. United Kingdom: Taylor & Francis, 2018.

Opler Morris E. "Spirit Possession in a Rural Area of Northern India." In *Reader in Comparative Religion: An Anthropological Approach*. Edited by William A. Lessa and Evon Z. Vogt, Pearson, 1997. 104–17.

Ortner, Sherry B. "Spirit Possession in the Nepal Himalayas." Edited by John T. Hitchcock and Rex L. Jones. Warminster, England: Aris and Phillips, 1976. Xxviii, 401 Pp. *The Journal of Asian Studies* 38, no. 2 (1979): 413–15.

————. *Alienation in Perversions*. New York: Routledge, 2018.

Pollak, Tamar. "The 'body-container': A new perspective on the 'body-ego'" In *International Journal of Psychoanalysis*, 90 (2009): 487–506.

Ranganathan, Shubha, Tanmay Bhattacharya, D. Parthasarathy, & Meenakshi Gupta. "Spirit possession in a healing centre: View from within." In *Psychological Studies*, 53 (3–4) (2008): 219–25.

Ray Satyajit. *Devi (The Goddess)*. Satyajit Ray Production. 1960.

Rosenbaum, Michael S. *Dare to be Human: A Contemporary Psychoanalytic Journey*. New York: Routledge, 2009.

Rilke, Rainer M. *The Selected Poetry of Rainer Maria Rilke*. Edited and Translated by Stephen Mitchell. New York: Vintage International, 1989.

Rumi, Jalaluddin. Rumi: Selected Poems, trans. Coleman Barks with John Moynce, A. J. Arberry, Reynold Nicholson. London: Penguin Books, 2004.

Siegel Allen, M. *Heinz Kohut and the Psychology of the Self*. London: Routledge, 2008.

Spillius, E. B. "Some developments from the work of Melanie Klein." In *The International Journal of Psychoanalysis*, 64(3) (1983): 321–32.

Symington, Joan. "The survival function of primitive omnipotence." In *The International Journal of Psychoanalysis*, 66(4) (1985): 481–87.

Symington Joan and Symington Neville. *The Clinical Thinking of Wilfred Bion*. London: Routledge, 1996.

Winnicott. Donald W. "Transitional objects and transitional phenomena." In *International Journal of Psycho-Analysis*, 34, (1953): 89–97; and in Collected papers, through paediatrics to psychoanalysis (pp. 229–42). London: Tavistock, 1958. Additional material was added to the paper in his Playing and reality. (pp. 1–30) London: Tavistock, 1971.

————. Winnicott, Donald W. "Communicating and Not Communicating Leading to a Study of Certain Opposites." In The Collected Works of D. W. Winnicott: Volume 6, 1960–1963, edited by Lesley Caldwell, and Helen Taylor Robinson. (New York, 2016; online edn, Oxford Academic, 1 Dec. 2016).

————. *The Maturational Processes and The Facilitating Environment*. London: Hogarth Press Ltd. 1965.

————. "The use of an object" In *International Journal of Psychoanalysis*, 50 (1969): 711–16.

————. "Fear of breakdown." In *International Review of Psycho-Analysis,* 1 (1–2) (1974): 103–7.

————. "Primary maternal preoccupation." In *Through Paediatrics to Psychoanalysis: Collected Papers.* Edited by Donald W. Winnicott. London: Karnac, 1984 (1956). 300–305.

————. *Home is where we start from.* Nw York: W.W. Norton and Company, 1990.

————. *Playing and Reality.* London: Tavistock Publications; reprinted London Routledge. 1991.

Zoja, Luigi. "Nightmare and the Invention of the Other." In *On Dreams and Dreaming.* Edited by Sudhir Kakar. India: Penguin Books Limited, 2011. 68–85.

Index

abject state, 221–22

absence: fathers, 9, 45, 59, 60, 61, 62, 75–76, 118, 159; with inability to process emotion, 14, 76; with infants, mothers and mirroring, 190–91; mothers, 12, 14, 67, 95, 158, 190, 245; of reliable support and self-efficacy, 8; self and, 208; of stimulus with hallucinations, 14

absent meanings, xii

abuse: child, 7, 41–42, 71, 72–74, 76, 83, 86, 94, 222; physical violence and, 23, 102, 166, 170, 176; sex, 30, 65, 83, 86, 90, 168, 229; spousal, 73, 110; threat of, 132–33, 163; verbal, 146, 214–15, 216, 217

Achreja, Vikram, 231–32

adultery, 26, 129

aesthetic conflict, 192–93

aesthetic vertex, xi

Ahuja, Naman. P., 197

Alizade, Alcira Mariam, 217, 244

alpha body, 241, 242, 246

alpha elements, 14, 162, 163, 191, 237, 242–43

alpha function, 13–14, 162, 163, 191, 232, 237, 251

Alterity and Transcendence (Levinas), 198

analytic experience, transformed into fiction, xix

analytic third, xxiii, 199

ancestral spirit, 28, 90, 252

anger, 23, 67, 73, 87, 131, 133, 139, 175; in dreams, 25, 26; in families, 40, 44; healers with, 27, 248; hostility, 63–65, 120–21, 123, 125, 136, 145, 146, 148, 151, 157, 159–60, 170, 222, 223; sadness and, 40, 65; sexuality and, 135, 140, 145, 167. *See also* rage

Anna O., 1–2

annihilation, fear of, 4, 226

annual pilgrimage (*kavar yatra*), 78, 188n3

appetites, of entities, xxiv, 38, 138, 142, 151

astrology, 111

Atlas, Galit, xx, 18, 19–20, 189, 241, 250

atriptaicchayein (unfulfilled yearnings), xxv

attachment, 17, 19, 121, 233

Aulagnier, P., xi

baby, Krishna as, 197

baby self, 49, 220, 238, 245, 249–50. *See also* infants

music, 84, 99, 242, 251
mystical experiences, x, xxiv,
88, 195, 211
mystical moments, xii
myths, 22, 90, 131, 194–95, 251; Hindu,
103; models, 231, 237

Nabokov, Isabelle, 4
Nagpal, Ashok, 195, 201, 205, 211,
247, 254, 255
nameless dread, 61, 191–92, 193
narcissism, 34, 41, 44, 152, 240; *Devi*
and, 51, 56, 57; Freud and, 56;
mirroring, 229; object-love, 13, 121;
object-tie, 12–13, 120
narcissistic development, 13, 121
negative capability, 193, 201
negative thoughts, 103, 106, 107, 116
Neumann, Erich, 122
New Delhi, India, 11, 21, 22
nightmares, xxiii, 15, 23, 153–54, 204,
222, 228; night terrors, 226–27;
waking state and, 22, 25, 225, 226,
234. *See also* dreams
not-me states, 12, 17–19, 52, 237

Obeyesekere, Gananath, 4, 5–7, 20n3,
20nn2–3, 21, 230–31, 235
object: relationship, 13, 44, 120, 121,
163, 190, 198, 205; self and, 221,
223; usage, 44
objectification, 5–6, 217, 231
object-love, 13, 121
object-relating, 8, 43–44, 190, 205
object-tie, 12–13, 120
obsessive-compulsive disorder, 15
"The Obstructive Object" (Eaton), 203
Oedipus complex, 9, 52, 55, 100–
101, 118, 217
Ogden, Thomas, 12, 13, 16, 100, 120,
200, 204, 226; on analytic experience
and fiction, xix; analytic third and,
xxiii, 199; on conversing, 208;
postmodernism and, 210

"oneness," in mystical and psychotic
experience, x
oppression, of women, 3
orgasm, 37, 244, 245
other: knowing, 198, 199; self and,
11–12, 20n2, 193, 208, 213,
214, 222, 224; thought with
absence of, 191

pain, 31, 83, 98, 104, 247; bodies
in, 22–24, 35, 36, 39, 47, 84, 87,
95, 137, 141; of depression, 2,
61; emotional, 13, 35, 63–64, 74,
76–77, 86, 87, 96, 231; of loss,
xxvi, 13, 107, 120, 121; possession
and, 230; sorrow and, 107; symbol
formation and, 5
panic attacks, 15
panicking, 148, 151–52, 202,
213, 254–55
Paramatma (Divine), 108
parasitic relationships, 192
parathas (Indian flat bread), 188n8
parents, xii; children with sexuality
of, 18–19, 61, 65; healing and,
160, 178–79; Rama and Sita as
ideal couple, 67, 158. *See also*
fathers; mothers
partridges, 104
paternal love, loss of, 119
patriarchy, 90, 195, 217, 247
Pemavati, Black Prince and, 6–7
penis (phallus), 155, 168, 217;
contained, 173; with experiences of
empowerment, 177–78; father with
"finger-sized," 215; fear of, 147, 173,
174; image of, 166; incorporation
of, 170, 171, 172; possession of,
146, 169–70; procreative function
of, 186; *samkat* as, 148, 150, 156,
163, 172–73, 245; splitting of phallic
self-representation, 195
"personal idiom," spirit
possession and, 195

About the Author

Dr. Shalini Masih is a Psychoanalytic Psychotherapist registered with the United Kingdom Council for Psychotherapy. She has taught psychoanalysis in institutions like Ambedkar University Delhi, India, and Birkbeck College, University of London, UK. Her interest lies in experiences of displacement, Dissociation, Psychosis, Dreams and Nightmares, Sexuality & Intimacy, impact of motherhood on the clinician, cultural processes and reflecting on rethinking psychoanalytic theory and technique making it increasingly feasible to changing contexts. She is especially interested in reflecting and writing on the subjectivity of the psychotherapist.

She has received the prestigious Scholar Award from Division 39, APA in 2020.

Her clinical thinking and psychoanalytic writing have received a lot of appreciation which also includes one of her papers which was nominated for Gradiva Awards 2020 under the Best Article Category.

Currently, Dr. Shalini Masih is practicing as a psychoanalytic psychotherapist in United Kingdom.